PARIS

AND THE ILE DE FRANCE

DUMONT GUIDE

PARIS

AND THE ILE DE FRANCE

by
KLAUS BUSSMANN

translated by
RUSSELL STOCKMAN

STEWART, TABORI & CHANG
PUBLISHERS, NEW YORK

FRONT COVER:
Notre Dame (© Lionel Isy/The Image Bank)
BACK COVER:
Versailles (© Gerard Champlong/The Image Bank)
FRONTISPIECE:
Ile de la Cité, in the eighteenth century (Plan Turgot)

Library of Congress Cataloging in Publication Data
Bussmann, Klaus.
DuMont guide to Paris and the Ile de France.
(DuMont guides)
Translation of: Paris und die Ile de France.
Includes index.
1.   Art, French—France—Paris. 2.   Art—France—
Paris. 3.   Art, French—France—Ile-de-France (Region)
4.   Art, France—Ile-de-France (Region) 5.   Paris (France)
—Antiquities. 6.   Ile-de-France (France: Region)—
Antiquities. I.   Title. II.   Title: Paris and the Ile de
France.
N6850.B8713   1984   914.4'3404838   83-15546
ISBN 0-941434-39-7

Published in 1984 by Stewart, Tabori & Chang, Publishers, Inc.,
under exclusive world-wide English language license
from DuMont Buchverlag GmbH & Co.
All rights for all countries are held by DuMont
Buchverlag GmbH & Co., Limited, Cologne, West Germany.
The title of the original German edition was
Paris und die Ile de France by Klaus Bussmann.

The Practical Travel Suggestions were prepared by John Sturman.

Second Printing, 1985

Distributed in the United States by
Workman Publishing, 1 West 39 Street,
New York, N.Y. 10018

Printed in Spain

C O N T E N T S

FROM ANCIENT LUTETIA
TO THE
MODERN METROPOLIS

P   A   R   I   S

CHURCHES, MONASTERIES, PALACES, STREETS, AND SQUARES

ILE DE FRANCE

THE GREAT CATHEDRALS

MEDIEVAL CASTLES AND MONASTERIES

RENAISSANCE CHÂTEAUX

PALACES FROM THE CLASSICAL PERIOD

OTHER POINTS OF INTEREST IN THE ILE DE FRANCE

PRACTICAL TRAVEL SUGGESTIONS

INTRODUCTION TO FRANCE

PARIS AND THE ILE DE FRANCE

FROM
ANCIENT LUTETIA
TO THE
MODERN
METROPOLIS

THE GALLIC AND GALLO-
ROMAN BEGINNINGS

Little is known about the prehistory and early history of Paris. Pre-Celtic settlers appear to have already established themselves in the area by the third millennium B.C., and it is from them that the Celtic Anavisii, who occupied the country in the third century B.C., took over the settlement's name, Lucotesia, or Lutetia. The Parisii, a race of sailors, hunters, and fishermen who supplanted the Anavisii, built their huts on the Ile de la Cité, probably not before 250 B.C., and enriched themselves by collecting tolls at this important crossroad of northern Gaul.

The density of the population was apparently already rather high, for the Parisii sent 8,000 men to support Vercingetorix in his struggle against the Romans before the inhabitants abandoned the city in 52 B.C., burning their homes and bridges behind them to hinder the advance of the Roman troops.

Lutetia then became, in 51 B.C., a Roman colonial city of moderate importance for more than 300 years, its predominantly Celtic population never exceeding 10,000 people. Although situated in the center of fertile farmland and grown rich through the commerce of its boatmen—who, in the Middle Ages, would control the exchange of goods between Champagne (Troyes) and the sea (Rouen)—it never attained the political significance of Lyons or even of Reims.

The Romans respected the old core of the city, the Ile de la Cité, erecting there a temple, possibly a forum, but, most important, an administrative building. On the site of the later Palais de la Cité (see pages 137–140), this structure housed the center of power for the state, and through it Lutetia first entered into world history in A.D. 360: it was here that the Roman general Julian the Apostate had himself proclaimed em-

11

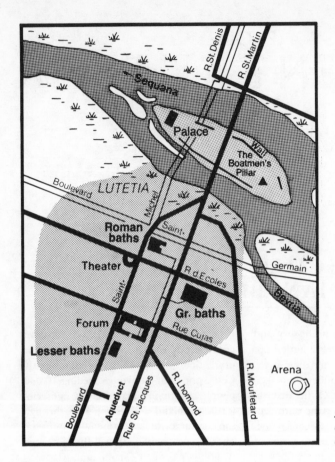

Street grid of the Roman city of Lutetia and its major buildings.

peror by his troops. In this period, Lutetia assumed the name Paris.

There are no visible monuments from the Gallo-Roman period in present-day Paris except for the remains of the baths (Palais des Thermes; see page 105) and the amphitheater (Arènes de Lutèce; see pages 105–106). However, the Roman plan of the city, together with the Seine, determined the entire course of later development and is still apparent in the routes of specific streets. As in most Roman settlements, this plan was characterized by the cross axis of the *cardo* (main street) and the *decumanus* (cross street), each of which was accompanied by parallel secondary axes. The *cardo* of Roman Lutetia was a road coming from Orléans in the southwest, crossing the island roughly in its center, and then leading northeastward between the Montmartre hills and Belleville toward Senlis. This main axis is preserved today in the Rue St-Jacques on the Left Bank and the Rue St-Martin on the Right, along with a secondary *cardo* in the course of the

Rue St-Michel, Rue de la Harpe, and Rue St-Denis. The *decumanus maximus* was most probably located along the course of the present-day Rue Cujas and Rue de Vaugirard and led in a westward direction toward Dreux, while a second *decumanus* on the Right Bank, leading in the direction of Melun, can still be discerned in the route of the Rue St-Antoine.

The swampy Right Bank was scarcely settled in Roman times, although the temples of Mercury and Mars were built on the heights of Montmartre. And only very little is known about settlement of the Ile de la Cité. The Roman city proper evolved on the Left Bank, on the slopes of Mont Ste-Geneviève. Its forum, consisting of temples, a basilica, and rows of shops, lay along the Rue Cujas between the Boulevard St-Michel and the Rue St-Jacques. Its baths, on the northern slope, faced the Seine, next to the Hôtel de Cluny and beneath the Collège de France; its amphitheater was built on the eastern slope, Rue Monge; and large villas stood on the western side, on the grounds of the Jardin du Luxembourg. An aqueduct roughly nine miles long brought water from the vicinity of Rungis; remains of it may be seen near Arcueil.

The extraordinary diversity of readily available building materials—gypsum on the Right Bank, limestone, sandstone, and sand on the Left—promoted the construction of monumental buildings. Limestone was extracted from under Mont Ste-Geneviève; until modern times, the foundation of Paris would continue to be a gigantic quarry.

Construction of the Roman city ended in about A.D. 250. Germanic tribes were pressing in upon Gaul with increasing frequency, and, in 275, the Franks and the Alemanni crossed the Rhine and advanced deep into Roman territory without meeting any resistance. The Roman colonial cities surrounded themselves with defense girdles, and Paris was no exception. It became a fortress with a ring wall, which protected only the structures of the Ile de la Cité.

This same period yields the first evidence of Christian congregations. According to Gregory of Tours, St. Dionysius (St. Denis) and seven comrades were dispatched to missionize Gaul in about 250. His cathedral possibly even stood on the Ile de la Cité. Legend has it that he was beheaded in about 280 at the foot of Montmartre and interred in St. Denis, later the necropolis of the French kings.

PARIS: CAPITAL OF THE MEROVINGIAN EMPIRE

In the struggles between the Roman Empire and the Germanic invaders, Paris became a fortification of increasingly great strategic importance; even after the collapse of the empire, it kept the region free of Frankish dominion until 486. Under the leadership of its bishop, St. Marcel, and St. Genovefa (Ste. Geneviève), it escaped occupation by Attila and his armies of Huns in 451. Only with the victory of Clovis over the Roman leader Syagrius at Soissons in 486 did Paris and its environs fall to the Franks, and they actually settled the area only after 700 (Latin remained the language of the Parisians).

Clovis's defeats of the West Goths and acquisition of southwestern France led him to transfer his residence from Soissons to Paris in 508. It then became the capital of the Frankish empire—and remained so until the death of Dagobert I in 639.

Clovis's conversion to Christianity in 496 paved the way for total Christianization of the country, and under the Merovingian kings, Paris would become a center of ecclesiastical life, even though its bishops remained under the supervision of the archbishops of Sens until 1622. After Clovis's death in 511, his son Childebert commissioned a great cathedral, to be built on the Ile de la Cité, consecrated to St. Stephen, with five aisles, a west tower, and a vestibule. Its foundations have been excavated in the square in front of Notre-Dame, which did not replace it until the twelfth century (see pages 112–132). Large monasteries with extensive land holdings were founded, and they came to play a decisive role in the further development of the city. On the Left Bank, Ste. Croix–St. Vincent became the burial place of the bishop St. Germain of Paris in the eighth century and assumed the name St. Germain-des-Prés (see pages 106–110) because it was situated outside the old settlement. On the hill to the east of the Roman forum was the cloister of St. Pierre-et-Paul; the body of Ste. Geneviève was entombed in its church in 512, and it soon became the goal of great streams of pilgrims. In the southeast, the church of St. Marcel stood in the middle of an extensive cemetery.

On the Right Bank, the monastery of St. Martin-des-Champs (see pages 110–112) was built on the old Roman *cardo*, the present-day Rue St-Martin, which led to the north via St. Denis (see pages 281–288), where, as early as 475, a church had been erected over the tomb of the first bishop of Paris. Dagobert I had this church replaced with a new structure that had cloisters and lodgings for pilgrims, and St. Denis became the patron saint of the French kings, his church the resting place of the rulers of France until the Revolution. Between Paris and St. Denis, there developed a market, the Lendit, that became the meeting place for farmers and merchants of the whole region and posed serious competition for the international markets of Champagne in the Middle Ages.

The economic ascent of Paris continued, even when the political center of the Frankish empire moved elsewhere—primarily to Aix-la-Chapelle (Aachen), although some rulers preferred Laon and St. Denis in the Ile de France. In about 800, Paris had between 20,000 and 30,000 inhabitants, and its boatmen controlled the Seine all the way to Rouen and provided the city with foodstuffs and wine. Syrian and Jewish merchants had settled in Paris, and the Cité became a dense network of streets, buildings, and churches. The city's wealth attracted the Vikings, and its easy river access to the sea proved to be its undoing. In a series of raids, in 845, 856, and 861, Normans plundered the city, ravaged the settlements on the Left Bank, and burned the monasteries to the ground. Only in 885 and 886 was the rapidly fortified Cité capable of withstanding a long siege. The defender of the city, Eudes, Comte de Paris, was elected the first non-Carolingian French king at Compiègne in 888—a prelude to the ultimate downfall of the Carolingians and the ascent of the Parisian Capetians after 987. The Vikings settled in Normandy and made no further attempts to sack Paris.

THE DUKES OF FRANCIA
BECOME KINGS OF FRANCE

Hugues Capet, Comte de Paris and Duc de Francia, was elected French king at Senlis in 987, and this event once and for all tied the fate of Paris to that of the monarchy. Through the long period of consolidation of royal power and expansion of the Crown's domains, the importance of the city grew considerably. Although Hugues and his successors ruled primarily from Orléans, the kings, beginning with Philippe I in the middle of the eleventh century, came to spend more time in the palace on the Ile de la Cité. The defeat of rebellious vassals by Louis VI and the conquest of Angevin lands by Philippe Auguste were the most important early steps toward the centralization of power under the king. The end of the Albigensian Wars in 1229, under Louis IX (St. Louis), marked the victory of Frankish influence (characterized by the langue d'oïl dialect), whose unquestioned center was Paris, over the Romanic southwest (characterized by langue d'oc). The king established Parlement as the highest court and gave it a permanent place in his capital, making Paris the last court of appeal for all French justice. But the title *capitale du royaume* began to appear in documents only in 1415,

Royal palace on the Ile de la Cité, from the west.

shortly before the Anglo-Burgundian occupation and, paradoxically, at the time when the French kings were building their residences primarily in the Loire Valley, where they were to remain until the return of François I to Paris in 1528. The royal courts and administrative offices never left Paris, however, and by about 1300, the city had confirmed its role as the capital. Under Philippe IV le Bel (Philip the Fair), the palace on the Ile de la Cité was rebuilt to house the central administration, and the University of Paris became the most respected school in Europe, serving not only as the stronghold of theology, but also, along with the school at Orléans, as a center for jurisprudence. It trained the jurists who gave legal support to the king's expansion of his territory to include Valenciennes, Toul, Verdun, Lyons, and Viviers. The network of roads surviving from antiquity, which concentrated on Lyons, was gradually replaced by one with Paris as its center—a development that has continued, often in grotesque ways, up to the present. Even though the exact number of its inhabitants is contested, it appears that Paris in about 1300 was, along with Venice and Milan, one of the most populous cities in Europe, with almost 80,000 inhabitants (as compared with 56,000 in Ghent, 40,000 in London, and 30,000 in Cologne). Certainly the city's population density, even that of the entire Ile de France, was the highest in the whole Western world.

CONFLICT BETWEEN THE MONARCHY AND CIVIL SELF-RULE

Unlike the municipal republics of Italy or the rich merchant cities of Flanders and in spite of the wealth of its merchants, Paris never developed the typical image of a middle-class city with marketplace, city hall, and proud patrician houses. And although the presence of the king provided the city with privileges and protected it from the encroachments of power-hungry barons, it prevented the development of a middle-class, municipal entity with its own charter. The inhabitants of the city were *bourgeois du roi*, not governed by a mayor but by a royal administrator, the *prévôt royal*, who resided in the Châtelet, on the Right Bank opposite the palace on the Ile de la Cité. Not only was he responsible for public order, but he also controlled commerce and the trades.

Not until about the middle of the thirteenth century did anything like a municipal administration develop, created by the most influential guild of the city, that of the boatmen. The spokesman of this guild, the *prévôt des marchands de l'eau*, became the director of this rudimentary city government, and he was assisted by four jurors. The seal of the guild, a ship with the inscription *Fluctuat nec mergitur*—"It tosses, but it does not sink"—became the city's coat of arms. From 1296 on, there was a city council of twenty-four councilmen, which was in charge of maintaining the streets, city walls, quays, harbors, wells, and drainage canals. These municipal representatives originally met in the Parloir aux Bourgeois next to the Châtelet, until in 1357, Étienne

Marcel, the most famous of the *prévôts des marchands*, purchased a building in the Place de Grève, on the site of the present-day city hall.

The fate of Étienne Marcel illustrates the tense relationship between the king and the Paris citizenry. A wealthy cloth merchant who was elected to the post of *prévôt des marchands* and an influential agent for Paris in the Estates General, Marcel demanded from the dauphin Charles (the viceroy of Jean II le Bon [John the Good], who was being held prisoner by the English) far-reaching autonomy for the city and more supervisory rights for the Estates. When the dauphin refused, Marcel had two members of the court, the marshals of Champagne and Normandy, killed before the prince's eyes and then organized a revolt of the citizens of Paris, who forced the dauphin to flee to Compiègne. Marcel became the ruler of the city, entering into an alliance with the rebellious farmers of the Beauvais, the so-called Jacques. The dauphin laid siege to Paris, and Marcel sought support from the troops of English-allied Navarre, thereby arousing the anger of his fellow citizens. The crown prince won back the city after having Étienne Marcel murdered by a trusted lackey. The citizens' revolt, which had been preceded by others early in the century and would be followed in 1382, after taxes were once again raised, by the riot of the Maillotins (named after the leaden hammers that the citizenry took up to battle the royal soldiers), led the king to give up his residence on the Ile de la Cité in favor of the fortified Louvre (see pages 151–156) and a palace near the Bastille, the Hôtel St-Paul. And now, for the first time, the Crown thought to move the residence out of Paris completely: for times of trouble, Charles V had the palace of Vincennes (see pages 141–142) expanded into a fortress bristling with towers, which he could easily reach by way of the Faubourg St-Antoine.

The Maillotins' revolt of 1382 led to the suspension of the municipal constitution. In 1411, the *prévôt* and his jurors were reinstated, shortly before the tradesmen—in a new rebellion by the guilds in 1413, under the leadership of the butcher Simon Caboche—massacred the followers of the royal party, the Armagnacs, and thereby attained new privileges from the Burgundians, who were engaged in a civil war with the royalists and were occupying the city.

In the disorders of this civil war, Paris never stood on the side of the king. After the slaughter of the Armagnacs in 1418, Charles VI was forced to leave the city, and he henceforth lived in Troyes, while his son, the sixteen-year-old dauphin (who became Charles VII) continued the war against the English and the Burgundians and headed the Armagnac party from Bourges. In 1429, an unsuccessful attempt to conquer the city was made by Jeanne d'Arc (Joan of Arc), who was wounded at Porte St-Honoré.

It was not until 1528 that François I decided to move his residence back to Paris. The absence of the court (though not the administration) for more than a hundred years had not only political and social consequences but distinct economic ones for the citizens of the capital. In the fourteenth century, for example, up to one-third of the meat consumed in Paris was bought by the court, and a large percentage of the city's craftsmen were occupied with the production of luxury goods for the court's upper stratum. In the court's absence, therefore, business suffered.

THE CITY OF
THREE PERSONALITIES

Beginning in the middle of the eleventh century, the inhabitants once again tended to move out of the crowded Ile de la Cité and settle on the two banks of the river, which had been largely uninhabited since the Norman raids but used as pastures, fields, and vineyards. In contrast to the situation in Roman times, it was not the Left Bank, but rather the Right, surrounded by swamps and often flooded, that became the focus of this new expansion: only here could ships be moored, and here began the direct road to Flanders, whose growing cities were steadily becoming the most important trading partners of the Parisian merchants. A first harbor developed at the Place de Grève, for which Louis VII granted the concession to the citizens in 1141. Royal privileges gave the boatmen a monopoly on the transport of all wares on the Seine in and out of Paris. The powerful guild of butchers settled across the Grand Pont, the large bridge connecting the palace on the Ile de la Cité with the Châtelet on the Right Bank. Densely built up, like all medieval bridges, the Grand Pont was the center for goldsmiths and money-changers. In 1142, Louis VII prohibited all exchange of monies except on this bridge —hence its new name, Pont au Change. Italian moneylenders came to settle in the Rue des Lombards. The street names in the early period quite often designated the profession that was primarily practiced in them: Rue de la Vannerie (basketmaking), de la Poterie (pottery), de la Verrerie (glassmaking), de la Ferronnerie (ironmongery), and so on. By the middle of the twelfth century, economic activity had progressed to the point

that, in 1136, Louis VI had the market moved from the Place de Grève to fields outside the newly developed *bourg*—the middle-class city, possibly already surrounded by a wall. The grounds of the new market, called *champeaux* (little fields), were still unprotected and without solid structures, but as early as 1183, Philippe Auguste had the first pavilions constructed to shelter the dealers, after having also moved the market of St. Lazare here two years before. The Halles du Roi were then continually expanded, developing into the core of a new quarter, which (like the butchers' quarter, with its church of St. Jacques-la-Boucherie) was provided with a new parish church, that of the Innocents (guiltless children).

Settlement of the Left Bank was slower and resulted from entirely different motives. Small communities had developed around the rebuilt Merovingian monastery of St. Germain-des-Prés and around the church of St. Marcel; the settlement near St. Marcel was even protected by a wall. And a number of dealers from the Cité had moved across the Petit Pont (along the axis of the old Roman *cardo*) to the Left Bank, where, toward the end of the eleventh century, the old Merovingian churches of St. Julien-le-Pauvre (see pages 132–133) and St. Séverin (see pages 142–143) became parish churches. But the Left Bank owed its rise to another group of inhabitants of the Cité who sought to escape its constriction: professors and students of the Cathedral School of Notre-Dame, who lived, together with the canons, in the buildings around the cloisters of the cathedral, where classes we.e held. The first to leave the Cité was the school's most famous philosopher, Guillaume de Champeaux, who settled in a hermitage on the Left Bank in 1108, near a chapel consecrated to St. Victor. A few years later, in 1113, Louis VI founded here the abbey of St. Victor, providing it with rich lands and a splendid library. Under Guillaume de Champeaux and Hugh of St. Victor, its school came to rival the Cathedral School and maintained relations with the most important theologians of the time, such as Bernard of Clairvaux and Thomas of Canterbury. Its most famous pupil, Pierre Abélard (1079–1142), became a teacher and came to attract several thousand students.

Next to St. Victor, the old abbey of Ste. Geneviève (see pages 246–248) developed into a third center of intellectual studies; its lectures were held initially in the cloisters of the monastery and later in the streets of the developing quarter. Vineyards between Ste. Geneviève and the Seine gradually gave way to a quarter dedicated exclusively to scholarship: dormitories for impoverished students, dwellings for their teachers, and convents for the new mendicant orders that had established themselves in Paris in the early thirteenth century and opened their own schools—the Dominicans (called Jacobins after their chapel in the Rue St-Jacques) and the Franciscans (known as Cordeliers because of the twine that held their cowls together). The teachers of these mendicant orders, the German Albertus Magnus, his pupil Thomas Aquinas, and St.

The city of three personalities: Ville, Cité, Université.

Cemetery of the Innocents, with charnel houses and the church of the Innocents.

Bonaventure, made Paris the stronghold of scholastic theology.

One of the reasons for the emigration from the Ile de la Cité had been the bishop's claim to authority over the schools and his demand of large fees for teaching licenses. In the conflict between the bishop and the schools, both the pope and the king took the side of the latter. Philippe Auguste withdrew teachers and schools from the juristic grip of the bishop, and Pope Honorius III, in about 1219, acknowledged the teachers and students—the *universitas*—as a separate corporate entity that was given the right to elect its own representatives to the curia, to keep its own seal, and to administer its own affairs. In about 1220, this academic body organized itself into four faculties —theology, liberal arts, medicine, and jurisprudence—and its students came from everywhere, primarily from northern Europe. The founding of a college for impoverished students in 1257 by the royal chaplain Robert de Sorbon, whose name was later transferred to the whole university, occasioned a number of endowments toward the end of the century, so that at times the number of students in Paris exceeded 10,000.

In the middle of the thirteenth century, then, Paris developed a threefold personality that to a certain extent continues today:

1. The *Cité*, with the seats of the king and the bishop
2. The *Ville*, on the Right Bank, a city of merchants and the middle class
3. The *Université*—the *civitas philosophorum*—which today, as the Quartier Latin on the Left Bank, from the Faculté des Sciences on the grounds of the former abbey of St. Victor past the Sorbonne to the Faculté de Médecine, carries on the medieval tradition.

PARIS: THE GREATEST FORTRESS OF THE KINGDOM

Up to the reign of Philippe Auguste, the city's expansion had both followed the lines of streets existing since antiquity and conformed to preexisting topographic features. The monks of the cloisters outside the city, especially those of St. Opportune, to whom most of the swampy arm of the Seine belonged, aided development by draining and cultivating the area.

For the further growth of the city, though, the land policies of the church became a decisive factor. Until the Revolution, two-thirds of the land of the city of Paris belonged to the bishop, the parish churches, and the monasteries, and the exploitation of new property and speculation on real estate constituted the chief sources of income for the church.

A first attempt to determine the growth of a city that was expanding in all directions was undertaken by Philippe Auguste, who, in 1190, decreed that the northern section of the city be surrounded by a wall. About twenty years later, this wall was extended to ring the city. Almost 5,800 yards long, roughly 30 feet high and 10 feet thick at the foundations, with 6 gates on either side of the river and towers every 20 feet, the wall enclosed nearly a square mile, divided roughly equally between the two banks. Toward the end of the Middle Ages, the northern portion of the wall would become twice as large as the southern one. Parts of the original wall have survived to the present, the largest segment lying behind the Lycée Charlemagne, next to the choir of the church of St. Paul–St. Louis. It appears that the citizens of the Right Bank had to pay for their wall themselves, while the king, who desired that the Left Bank be more densely settled, assumed the cost of the southern portion.

Beginning in 1200, the defensive ring was strengthened by means of a projecting fortress in the west, the Louvre, to which a simple tower on the other side of the Seine, later called the Tour de Nesle, corresponded. Fortifications on the two bridges across the Seine, the Grand and Petit Châtelets, were rebuilt. The ring wall enclosed all of the *bourgs* of the city, but it included neither the large monasteries of St. Germain-des-Prés, St. Victor, and St. Martin-des-Champs, which had their own fortifications, nor the

small settlements around St. Marcel and St. Médard. Lying less than forty miles from the nearest English base, at Gisors, Paris had become the strongest fortress in the kingdom as a result of this defensive building.

About 150 years later, Charles V ordered construction of a new, taller city wall, with deep outer trenches, on the Right Bank; this wall enclosed the cloister of St. Martin-des-Champs and its village, the area surrounding the Temple—the old establishment of the Order of Templars—and the royal residences to the east of the city, which were protected by a mighty bastion, the Bastille. Begun shortly after the accession of Charles V in 1364, the new wall started on the west at the Seine, near the present-day Guichets du Carrousel, and ran toward the Porte St-Denis across today's Place du Théâtre-Français, Jardin du Palais-Royal, Place des Victoires, and Rue d'Aboukir. From the Porte St-Denis, its course corresponded as far as the Bastille to the modern Grands Boulevards, which replaced it during the reign of Louis XIV. From the Bastille, the wall swung westward, rejoining the Seine at the Quai des Célestins. The Seine itself could be closed to shipping by means of a

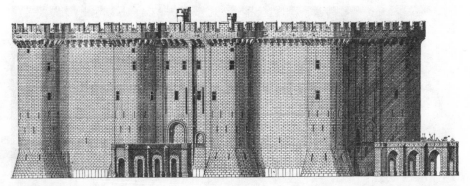

The Bastille: bulwark along Charles V's wall as protection for the royal residences in the Marais.

23

Medieval Paris from the south, with the wall of Philippe Auguste.

chain stretching across the Ile St-Louis. The new city gates were constructed beginning in 1370: the Portes St-Antoine (next to the Bastille), du Temple, St-Martin, St-Denis, Montmartre, and St-Honoré, where, in 1429, Joan of Arc vainly sought to break into the city.

The city had thereby grown to more than 1.5 square miles. But shortly afterward, during the disorders of the Hundred Years' War, the kings transferred their residences to the Loire Valley. Paris was forced to endure repeated occupations, and urban growth came to a standstill for almost a century.

THE BEGINNING OF THE RENAISSANCE UNDER FRANÇOIS I

The city's resurgence following a series of horrors—the Hundred Years' War, the Civil War, epidemics of plague, and famines —started slowly after the beginning of the fifteenth century. It was prompted primarily because the large landowners of the Ile de France, chief among them the cathedral chapter of Notre-Dame, were able to increase profits from agriculture after the withdrawal of troops. Paris won back its position as a central market, where grain and wine from the Ile de France were traded for fish, salt, eggs, and vegetables from Normandy. And the first rudiments of local industry were established: along the bank of the Bièvre, cloth-dying factories were set up after 1443 by the Italian Canaglia and the Fleming Jean Gobelin. The Parisian bourgeoisie invested in the sea trade of Toulouse, Marseille, and Rouen. A stratum of society that lived from the profits of capital developed. It was Parisian money that ransomed François I from Spanish imprisonment in 1526 after his defeat in the Battle of Pavia.

Two years after his return from Madrid, François I wrote to the city of Paris: "It is our intention in future to spend the greater part of our time in our good city of Paris

and its surroundings rather than in other parts of the kingdom...." Thus ended the long period in which the kings had ruled from their castles in the Loire Valley. Nevertheless, François I had the châteaux of Chambord and Blois constructed and expanded, invited Leonardo da Vinci and other Italian Renaissance artists to work on them, and thereby laid the foundations for a first form of the French Renaissance. The king's decision not only reestablished the political center of the country in the Ile de France, but also led to the development of Paris and its environs as the artistic center of the country.

As early as 1528, work began in Fontainebleau, and soon the Renaissance châteaux of St. Germain-en-Laye and Madrid were constructed (the latter, no longer existing, at the edge of the Bois de Bologne). Paris began to be surrounded by a wreath of royal or princely residences and hunting lodges: Anet (see pages 363–367), for the mistress of Henri II, Diane de Poitiers; the châteaux of the Montmorency, Écouen (see pages 361–362) and Chantilly (see pages 358–361); Versailles (see pages 391–412), the most important; and Compiègne (see pages

26

419–420). These edifices, along with their parks and forests, profoundly affected the local landscape.

When in Paris, François I resided in the Hôtel de Tournelles and in the Louvre, which had remained essentially unchanged since the time of Charles V. In 1528, the king commanded that the route connecting the Pont au Change, which led to the palace on the Ile de la Cité, and the Louvre be expanded into a broad quay along the Seine; this is the present-day Quai de la Mégisserie, which was constructed between 1530 and 1539. Next, the king had sections of the old Louvre torn down so that the construction of a modern palace could begin. Pierre Lescot and Jean Goujon began this renovation in 1546, and François I died in the following year. In 1559, following the unfortunate death of Henri II, at a tournament at the Hôtel de Tournelles, Henri's widow, Catherine de Médicis, finally abandoned the east of the city to move into the Louvre, at that time still a construction site.

In 1563, Catherine de Médicis requested that Philibert de l'Orme build her a palace outside the city walls, some 550 yards to the west of the Louvre, the Tuileries (see pages 156–158), thereby laying the groundwork for a construction problem that would occupy almost every French ruler up to Napoleon III: how to connect the Louvre with the Tuileries. For Catherine's was an initial step in a direction that would prove decisive for the city's further development; it established a commanding axis radiating westward from the palace, one for which André Le Nôtre, roughly a hundred years later, would submit the first artistic conception (fig., page 156). The first step toward connecting the two palaces was the construction of the Petite Galerie, but only in

1610, under Henri IV, was the two-story connecting corridor, the Grande Galerie along the Seine, completed. The presence of the Tuileries led to the rise of a new quarter to the north of it, the Faubourg St-Honoré—for which the chapel of St. Roch (see pages 236–238) was erected in 1578—and thus to the expansion of the city to the west. But it also highlighted the critical problem of the city in the sixteenth century—its expansion beyond the medieval city walls.

A royal edict of 1548 had forbidden any further expansion of the *faubourgs*, a prohibition dictated not only by military considerations—for in the event of war, it would be impossible to defend this part of the city —but also by concern for the rights of the guilds and for the economy; the citizens of the *faubourgs* were not subject to the city's tax laws, and their craftsmen were not regulated by its guilds. But only two years later, at the urging of the *prévôt des marchands*, who thought it better to protect the *faubourgs* than to destroy them, Henri II decided to have a new wall drawn about the enlarged area of the city, which—especially on the Left Bank, where the ring wall had not been expanded since the time of Philippe Auguste—spread well beyond the fortifications.

In spite of long negotiations between the king and the city, virtually no construction was undertaken except in the west on the Right Bank: at the insistence of Catherine de Médicis, a "Porte Neuve" was constructed at the end of the Jardin des Tuileries, from which fortified trenches were dug in a large arc around the new Faubourg St-Honoré to the Porte St-Denis. Louis XIII had a new wall constructed along these trenches, on the course of the western portion of the later Grands Boulevards.

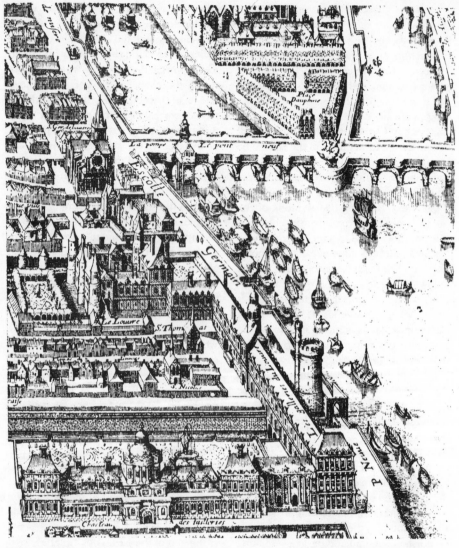

The new residence: the Louvre and the Palais des Tuileries connected by the Grande Galerie.

The only additional fortification, by Charles IX, son of Henri II and Catherine de Médicis, merely involved some bulwarks and bastions on the Right Bank at the Arsenal and at the Porte St-Antoine. On the Left Bank, work was abandoned for lack of funds.

The city thus had to expand within the narrow circuit of the medieval walls, and, increasingly, the remaining fields, vineyards, pastures, and gardens had to be sacrificed to new construction. It is estimated that between 1500 and 1610, the close of Henri IV's reign, the population doubled—from roughly 200,000 to roughly 400,000 inhabitants. In 1539, the Crown began to issue various edicts to make the purchase of building sites easier, and Henri IV even commanded, in 1609, that properties be auctioned if the owners were unable to commence reconstruction or new building within six months. But in spite of these measures, by the middle of the sixteenth century, a housing shortage began to be felt—and it would only grow more intense during the course of the succeeding centuries.

As early as 1550, it was no longer possible for citizens with small incomes to rent an entire house, and buildings began to be broken up for multiple renters or owners. The population density led to troubles with the water supply and a worsening of hygienic conditions. The kings sought to deal with these problems by building new wells (Fontaine des Innocents; see pages 159–160) and pumps on the bridges over the Seine (La Samaritaine, on the Pont Neuf, was built under Henri IV), digging drainage canals (the first covered one, égout de Ponceau, was constructed in 1605), paving the streets, and making proclamations about their cleanliness and illumination. After 1599, along with the *prévôts*, a *grand voyer de France* supervised the streets and squares in the public interest. The state's ability to dispose of property to accommodate new streets was drastically expanded: thus François Miron, who was both *prévôt royal* and *prévôt des marchands* under Henri IV, was

able to have three property owners who had resisted the laying out of the Rue du Ponceau hanged with a single rope, and Henri IV himself threatened the Augustinian monks who, in 1606, refused to sell a portion of their grounds for the extension of the Rue Dauphine: he warned that if their garden walls were not demolished within a day, he would have them blasted down with cannon fire.

The kings themselves made new construction sites available. In 1543, François I arranged that a row of *hôtels* that belonged to the royal family but were not inhabited, chiefly the Hôtel St-Paul, be sold and the properties divided into smaller parcels. A few years later, the prior of the neighboring church of Ste. Catherine was given permission to sell some of its land as building lots. Thus the cultivated fields of the Couture Ste-Catherine, which had once been swampland, made way for a new quarter, the Marais, which became a favored residential area for the nobility because it was still largely open.

After Henri II was killed in the tournament at the Hôtel de Tournelles, Catherine de Médicis put this *hôtel* up for sale, without immediate success. It would be left to Henri IV to have a row of uniform *hôtels* built here around a newly created square, the Place Royale (Place des Vosges; see pages 178–179), the first planned square in Paris.

The sale of royal *hôtels* and church lands not only created new building sites and was not only designed to beautify the city; for the parties involved, the sales were a welcome source of income, as François I openly admitted. Thus, in the 1550s, despite his own prohibition of settlement outside the walls, Henri II sold the royal vineyards along the Rue St-Jacques—*clos du roi*—for construction sites, after the Jacobins had already sold theirs in 1546. This gave rise to the

Faubourg St-Jacques. A bit farther to the east, along the road to Fontainebleau, dense new building along the Rue Mouffetard and the Rue St-Médard filled the open spaces between the city and the Bourg St-Marcel, on the Bièvre. Among those who settled here was the banker Scipion Sardini, from Lucca; legend had it that he had come to France as thin as a sardine and was now as fat as a whale. His highly ornamented *hôtel* is still partially preserved at 13 Rue Scipion.

The Faubourg St-Germain, on the Left Bank, was connected to the city in 1539 by opening the Porte de Buci. Several new streets were laid out here in the sixteenth century. In 1606, Marguerite de Valois (La Reine Margot), divorced from Henri IV, settled on the Pré-aux-Clercs and had a large garden, which she opened to the public, laid out along the Seine. Only after Marguerite's death did the Pré-aux-Clercs become a favorite place for the Parisian upper class to build because a new bridge, the Pont Rouge (Pont Royal), had been built in 1632 to connect this part of the Left Bank with the Tuileries and the quarter ennobled by the presence of the Palais du Luxembourg (see pages 181–184), the widow's seat of Henri IV's second wife, Marie de Médicis. For a long time to come, however, the Left Bank would not be as densely populated as the Right. In 1588, when names for the various quarters of the city were newly fixed, there were thirteen quarters on the Right Bank and only two on the Left.

HENRI IV: THE FIRST CITY PLANNER OF PARIS

Only under Henri IV did the Left Bank begin to catch up with the Right. On his entry into Paris in 1594, the king encountered a ruined city. His energetic policies, a reorganization of administration and finances by his minister Sully, and, above all, his advanced economic policies led to a rapid rebuilding and an economic flowering that lasted until the death of his son, Louis XIII. Henri IV took up again the grand building projects of the court that had been interrupted by the religious wars: the expansion of the Louvre; its connection, along the Seine, to the Palais des Tuileries (fig., page 156); and the completion of the Pont Neuf, which had been begun by Henri III in 1578. This was the longest bridge in Paris and the first without buildings on it. Paris still did not have a general plan for development like the one that Amsterdam adopted in 1607, yet the period of systematic city planning began with Henri IV: straight street lines, proclamations regulating the paving and cleanliness of the streets, ordinances regulating the maintenance of the line of the street, prohibition of projecting gables, and layout of regular squares in geometric forms with uniform building around their borders. All these directives tended to place zones of order (as symbols of the ordered state) in the midst of medieval chaos, and—as in the case of the Place Dauphine, the Pont Neuf, and the newly laid out Rue Dauphine, or the Place de France, which was never completed due to the assassination of the king—were to become the points of departure for an all-encompassing ordered plan for the city. The lines of streets radiating from the semicircular Place de France represented the first approach toward a star-shaped square that structures an entire quarter—a concept that was based on the three-rayed square, or "trident," of the Piazza del Popolo in Rome. Jules Hardouin-Mansart would return to this form when planning the Place des Victoires in the seventeenth century (see pages 230–232), and the Place de l'Etoile made the trident the very symbol of nineteenth-century city planning.

The uniform design of façades—*l'ordonnance*—which became a leitmotif of Parisian architecture beginning with Henri IV, had an early precursor in the rows of houses on the Pont Notre-Dame, developed by the Italian Fra Giocondo and built between 1500 and 1512. Fra Giocondo, who had been a member of the architect Donato Bramante's circle, here used some concepts that Bramante had developed in his plan for the uniform building of the city of Vigevano.

The strict rationality of plan that characterizes these architects' designs also defines the single great building project that Henri

IV was able to initiate before his death and that illustrates the social components of his policies: the Hôpital St-Louis (see pages 177–178), outside the city walls, the first new hospital since the Middle Ages.

The systematic planning that came into being in the time of Henri IV was a result of a development that, although already begun under the Valois, would now touch all of France and its political, social, and economic systems: the emergence of a nation-state with a centralized, bureaucratic administration whose entire strength was concentrated in the person of the king. The symbol of this nation-state became its chief metropolis, whose rearrangement and beautification (*"embellissement"* was the slogan in the seventeenth and eighteenth centuries) mirrored the progressiveness of the state.

With the Place Royale, in the middle of which stood a monument to the king, France created a type of imposing city design that Italy did not know (although the conception of an imposing forecourt to set off a splendid building was never properly developed in France). And the continuation of the royal axis extending from the Louvre would occupy the nation even after the demise of the monarchy. The state's love of self-display would influence urban planning from now on—it is not coincidental that

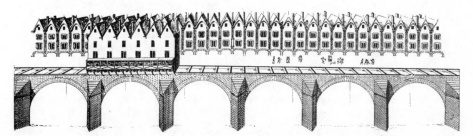

Pont Notre-Dame, after plans by Fra Giocondo.

City planning under Henri IV: Place de France, according to the plan by Claude Chastillon.

the *prévôt des marchands* had by now also become a royal official who was provided with a *grand voyer de France* to supervise architecture (under Henri IV, this position was filled by the minister Sully) and, beginning in 1666, a *lieutenant de police*.

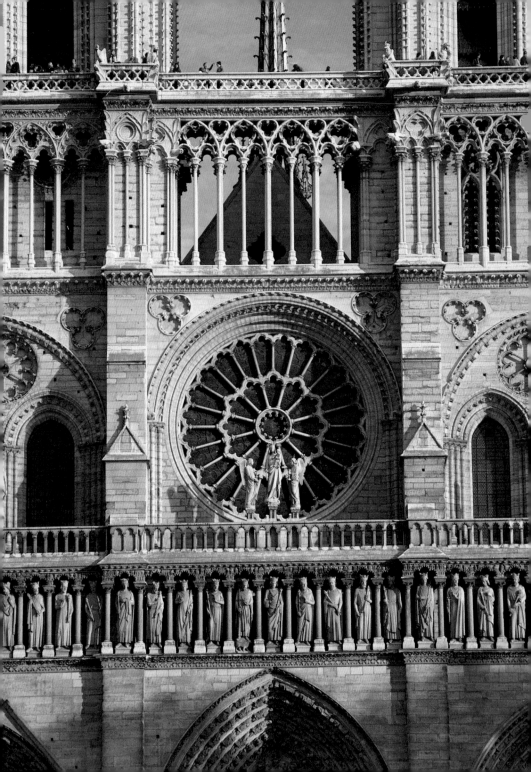

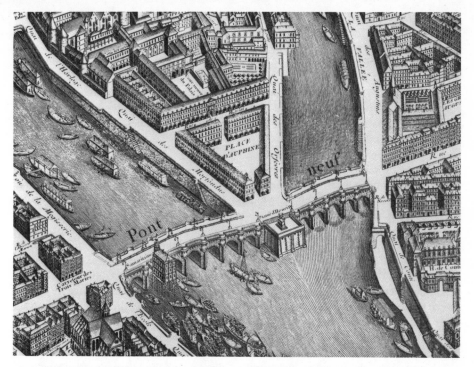

Tip of the Ile de la Cité: Place Dauphine and the Pont Neuf (Plan Turgot).

THE CITY OF THE NOBILITY: THE MARAIS AND THE ILE ST-LOUIS

In addition to court-sponsored construction —of public buildings, streets and squares, city gates and bridges—ecclesiastical and private building, initiated primarily by nobles and citizens in the service of the king, contributed to the conscious transformation of the city into a capital. The history of the creation of the Place Royale is an illustration. Henri IV originally planned to erect a silk factory on the north side of this square, with dwellings for its workers on the remaining sides. However, Sully insisted—and he got his way—on surrounding the entire square with aristocratic mansions (purchased for the most part by his colleagues) as a suitable setting for the equestrian statue of the king that was finally put in place in 1639. Sully envisioned the square as the germ of an entire quarter designated for the aristocracy, the Marais, which today, as the result of recent restoration to repair its disfigurement in the nineteenth century, belongs among the most impressive seventeenth-century ensembles in Europe.

The Marais had been favored by the aristocracy since the time of Charles V, and in the sixteenth century it was here, with the Hôtel Carnavalet (see pages 158–159) and the Hôtel Lamoignon (see pages 160–177), that the prototypal Parisian city dwelling for the nobility was developed: a *corps de logis*, (main residential part of a house) between courtyard and garden, with low wings embracing the courtyard, which is generally closed off from the street by a high wall with a *porte-cochère* (carriage gateway) (the Late Gothic Hôtel de Cluny [see pages 145–146] and Hôtel de Sens [see page 145] represent precursors of the form). This style would become, from the reign of Louis XIII, when truly intensive building began in the Marais, the model of the appropriate sort of city dwelling for the aristocracy and the elite bourgeoisie—the financiers, jurists, and prominent artists who for almost eighty years made the Marais the center of social life in the capital. In contrast to the less expensive combination of brick (or roughcast quarry stone) and hewn stone that was still common under Henri IV, more and more light-colored Parisian limestone was used as a building material; it could be cut with great precision, and it permitted an exceptional degree of façade relief. The exuberance of ornament in sixteenth-century court façades increasingly gave way to a more rigid sobriety coupled with extremely carefully calculated proportions. Unlike Italian or central European Baroque palaces, the Parisian *hôtel* does not flaunt its owner's status on the street, but rather concentrates the wealth of its ornamentation on the garden side and especially in the interior. Rational distribution of interior spaces, as well as their design as appropriate to one's rank, and increasing refinement in decorative style are the main themes of French architecture of the seventeenth and eighteenth centuries. One can trace the process of refinement from the early Hôtel de Mayenne (see page 185) through the Hôtels de Sully (see pages 184–185), de Châlons-Luxembourg, d'Aumont (see page 202–203), de Guénégaud (see page 203), Salé ((see page 201), and Amelot de Bisseuil (see page 201) up to the late Hôtels de Soubise (see pages 235–236) and de Rohan (see page 236), which belong to the eighteenth century and brilliantly end the series—excluding such latecomers as the Hôtel d'Hallwyll, an early work by Claude-Nicolas Ledoux. An exception to the type is the Hôtel de Beauvais (see pages 201–202), whose uncommon ground plan places its main façade—once richly decorated—toward the street and aligns it with the adjacent rows of buildings.

Despite the great influx of the upper class to the Marais, it continued to display the social mixture that characterized more or less all of Paris until the nineteenth century. In addition to the mansions, middle-class row houses were built, as were rental dwellings for the craftsmen who worked in the district and establishments for the monastic orders, which had played a major role in this vicinity since the Middle Ages. Only after the Revolution, when the noble householder went into exile or to the gallows, did the social structure of the quarter change fundamentally: craftsmen and small businesses moved into the palaces, and additions and partitions, as well as poor maintenance, altered the structures past recognition.

Another quarter that was established on

Ile St-Louis (Plan Turgot).

initiatives of Henri IV and that to an extent serves as a continuation of the Marais has survived virtually unchanged: the Ile St-Louis. Consisting of two islands, the Ile aux Vaches and Ile de Notre-Dame, that belonged to the cathedral chapter and were undeveloped until the early seventeenth century, the area was turned over to a contractor in 1614 by the royal bridge-building administration—against the protests of the cathedral chapter, whose suit to block the action dragged on until 1642. This contractor was charged with the jobs of tying the islands together with a masonry embankment, constructing a bridge to each bank of the Seine, and adhering to a pre-scribed building scheme that divided the space by means of a simple grid: one long axis down the middle of the island and one cross axis connecting the two bridges, with two secondary cross streets parallel to it. The contractor, Christophe Marie, immediately began to construct the bridge (named after him) across to the Marais in 1614. It was completed by 1635, with a double row of tall, narrow buildings on it; these were demolished in part in 1658 and totally removed in 1769. The island began to be built up with houses for craftsmen and merchants in 1618. The nobility began to construct their mansions along the embankments only in 1638, when an end to the

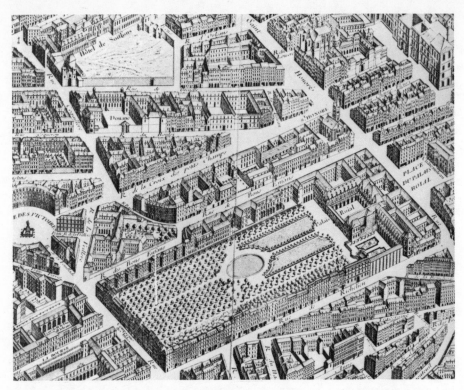

The Palais-Royal with the Hôtel de Soissons and the Place des Victoires (Plan Turgot).

legal battle with the cathedral chapter was in sight. The architect Louis Le Vau constructed some of the most prominent *hôtels* on the Ile St-Louis, such as the Hôtel Lambert (see pages 198–200) and the Hôtel de Lauzun (see pages 200–201), and erected an imposing residence for his own use at 3 Quai d'Anjou. At his own expense he also built additional structures, which he was then able to sell at a considerable profit.

The architect as contractor is a common figure in the history of Paris (Jules Hardouin-Mansart, for example). However, the role of contractors and even of speculators began

to be a decisive factor in the development of whole districts only after the reign of Louis XIII. As a case in point, the expansion of residential building to the west is attributable to the enterprising spirit of a certain Le Barbier. In 1622, he and a number of partners purchased the Domaine des Pré-aux-Clercs, a tract along the Seine more than half a mile long and between 80 and 220 yards wide that had belonged to Marguerite de Valois, the first wife of Henri IV, who had died in 1615. Le Barbier divided its length by two parallel streets, the Rue de Bourbon (Rue de Lille) and the Rue de

Verneuil, and opened up six cross streets between the Rue Bonaparte and the Rue de Bellechasse, tying the whole to the Right Bank and the Palais des Tuileries with a bridge, the Pont Royal, first constructed of wood but rebuilt in stone in 1684. For land on the Right Bank, Le Barbier struck an advantageous deal with Richelieu. He promised to add walls and bastions to the Fossés Jaunes, the city boundary, begun in the sixteenth century, which ran westward from the end of the Jardin des Tuileries. In exchange, he was given the grounds of the old fortification that had been built under Charles V. Richelieu reserved one parcel of this land for himself, and here he built the Palais Cardinal (see page 250), which led a whole series of high-placed personages to settle in the new Quartier Richelieu.

Among the new buildings between the Rue de la Croix-des Petits-Champs, and the Rue de Richelieu were the Hôtel Tubeuf (see page 185), later bought by Mazarin and expanded to princely proportions, the Hôtel de la Vrillière (Banque de France), and the new parish church, Notre-Dame-des-Victoires (see page 188). A short time later, Jules Hardouin-Mansart's Place des Victoires would connect this quarter with old Paris.

Starting in 1667, the district was extended westward by twelve new streets that were built by contractor Michel Villedo, with Louis Le Vau as architect. The musician Jean-Baptiste Lully built his residence here in 1671, based on plans by Daniel Gittard. Just as the opening of the former Pré-aux-Clercs to construction triggered the development of the Faubourg St-Germain, which attracted the aristocracy after 1700, so this expansion on the Right Bank established the core of the Faubourg St-Honoré, conveniently close to the Louvre, where various important ministers, among them Colbert and François Louvois, would follow the example of Richelieu and Mazarin and set up residence.

The court was no less active in its building than were its ministers and high officials. Henri IV had completed the Grande Galerie of the Louvre, and he wanted to complement it with a wing on the north and to demolish the chaos of structures between the Louvre and the Tuileries. After his death, his widow, Marie de Médicis, abandoned the palace and built a new one on the southern boundary of the city. Because of her family connection, this palace, called the Luxembourg after the former owner of the property, has often been compared with the Palazzo Pitti of the Medici in Florence. However, if one ignores its rusticated stonework, it is nonetheless a typically French product, an adaptation of the Parisian *hôtel* to palatial proportions, with parallels not only in the works of its architect, Salomon de Brosse, but also in country seats in the Ile de France, especially the château at Vermeuil, designed by Jacques Androuet Du Cerceau the Elder. The size of the site permitted the design of an aristocratic garden of luxurious dimensions.

In 1624, after his accession to power and his appointment of Richelieu as prime minister, Louis XIII immediately applied himself to further construction on the Louvre. He decided to quadruple the Pierre Lescot structure into a "Cour Carrée" and the remains of the medieval Louvre were to disappear for good. Jacques Lemercier added the Pavillon de l'Horloge to the west wing and one duplicate of the Lescot wing, while it was left to his successor Louis Le Vau to complete the Cour Carrée in 1664, at least its two lower stories, and to deal with the problem of the exterior façade.

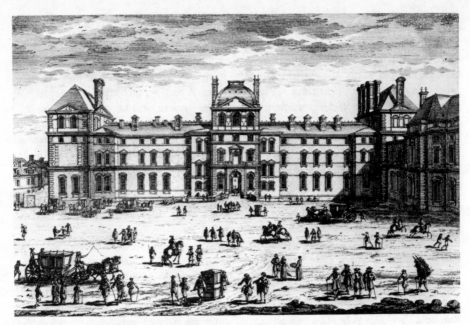
West façade of the Louvre during the reign of Louis XIV (Perelle).

THE "SECOND ROME": CENTER OF THE COUNTER REFORMATION

Almost even more spectacular than the construction by both the court and private individuals was the transformation of Paris into a "second Rome" by the Catholic church. Even during the chaos of the religious wars of the sixteenth century, most Parisians had held fanatically to Catholicism. Ignatius of Loyola founded his order of Jesuits on Montmartre, and the languishing Sorbonne revived in the battle against the heretics. The first Protestants were executed as early as 1523, and lynching murders of Protestants took place through the rest of the sixteenth century, culminating in the St. Bartholomew's Day massacre in 1572. Even after Henri IV issued the Edict of Nantes in 1598, Protestant services were not tolerated in the city. The Protestant "temple" was first located in Grogny and later in Charenton. In 1623, construction began on a new temple, designed by Protestant Salomon de Brosse, who therewith created a model imitated not only by many Protestant churches but by Jewish synagogues as well. In 1685, after the revocation of the Edict of Nantes, this church was leveled. It was the same de Brosse whose design for the façade of St. Gervais–St. Protais (see pages 146–148) in 1616 gave classical formulation to the unique French type, as opposed to Roman Baroque façades. Resistance to Roman models—above all, the pervasive ground plan of the Jesuits' mother church, Il Gesù (a Latin cross with a hall-like nave and side chapels between the retracted pilasters, emphasizing the crossing by means of cupola atop a drum)—characterized church architecture of the Counter Reformation in Paris.

Between 1600 and 1638, some sixty new convents were established in Paris, and by 1640, twenty new churches had been built here. The Jesuits, Carmelites, Ursulines, and Oratorians settled in the city, and François de Sales here founded the new order of Visitandines. Paris became a center of missionary activity for the world; seminaries like St. Sulpice were founded to improve the preparation of priests. St. Vincent-de-Paul founded his charitable order; Mother Angélique Arnaud turned the Port-Royal (see pages 206–207) into the center of Jansenist reform. In 1622, Paris was made an archbishopric and thereby ceased to be dependent on Sens. It also served as a refuge for many persecuted English Catholics.

Very few of the new convents and churches survived the Revolution, and yet those that remain define the silhouette of Paris to a great degree. The church of St. Joseph-des-Carmes (today the chapel of the Institut Catholique), built in 1613, was the first church in Paris to take the Roman form with a cupola above the crossing. Yet with the Jesuit church of St. Paul–St. Louis (see pages 185–186), which followed the scheme of Il Gesù, the Baroque church in Paris began to assert itself as something unique because the design of its façade followed that of St. Gervais–St. Protais. The church of Ste. Ursule-de-la-Sorbonne (see pages 186–188), financed by Richelieu, translated the Roman façade scheme into something characteristically and elegantly French; its north façade was a combination of a Pantheon portico and a towering cupola, which would have been unthinkable in Rome.

The unification of cupola and lower structure into a single effective façade occupied French architects from François Mansart, in his Chapelle de la Visitation (Temple de la Visitation Ste-Marie; see pages 188–189) and no-longer-existing church of the Minimes, through Charles Errard's much-criticized Notre-Dame-de-l'Assomption (see pages 207–208), and on up to Jules Hardouin-Mansart's inspired Dôme des Invalides (see pages 225–226). The problem was taken up again in the eighteenth century in Jacques-Germain Soufflot's Ste. Geneviève (Panthéon; see pages 246–248) and finds its vulgar apotheosis in the cupola of Sacré-Cœur (see page 263–264). These cupolas of Paris are quite striking: they either dominate an entire quarter from a hilltop, like the Panthéon or Sacré-Cœur (illus. 58, page 128), or serve as a focal point at the end of the visual axis of a newly cut street, like the Sorbonne, the Panthéon, des Invalides, Val-de-Grâce, and the nineteenth-century St. Augustin. Val-de-Grâce (see pages 189–194), though actually begun after the death of Louis XIII, marks both the close and the triumph of the brisk period of church construction during his reign. It combines a ground plan strongly influenced by Roman models with a splendid façade and a palace-like cloister complex reminiscent of the Escorial in Spain. The Spanish style would be referred to frequently in the grand structures of the new king, Louis XIV, the Sun King.

The period of the new king's minority, during which the Val-de-Grâce was constructed, was one of economic decline and inner tensions despite French gains in the Peace of Westphalia. Cardinal Mazarin ruled for Louis XIV; he was an Italian who expanded and solidified the strength of monarchical absolutism as had no other statesman, thereby provoking the higher ranks of French nobility and the Parlement to rebelliousness. The young king's humiliating experiences during the Fronde and his ignominious flight from Paris were to deeply influence his attitude toward his capital. The expansion of Vincennes by adding the Pavillon du Roi and Pavillon de la Reine, commissioned by Mazarin, was a prelude to the final transfer of the court to Versailles.

The palace of Vincennes with Louis Le Vau's additions (Perelle).

THE SELF-DISPLAY OF
THE ABSOLUTIST STATE

The Collège des Quatre-Nations (see pages 196–198) was built in accordance with the will of Mazarin, who bequeathed to the city of Paris money for the establishment of a college. Like the expansion of Vincennes, this was the work of his protégé Louis Le Vau. The structure, an uncommonly Baroque one by Parisian standards, is oriented toward the south façade of the Louvre and was the first in a series of monumental buildings along the Left Bank. The magnificence of this gift cannot disguise the fact, however, that when the cardinal died and the king took over the government, the city was in desolate condition. The populace was largely impoverished, even the middle classes. Out of a population of roughly 450,000, there were almost 50,000 beggars. Food had become expensive and scarce, hygienic conditions were atrocious, and medical care was limited. There was an increasing shortage of housing, and buildings—for the most part surviving from the Middle Ages —were overcrowded. These were by no means new problems, but they had become more acute, and even the vigorous policies of the king's new minister, Colbert, could not solve them.

Still, a few specific measures improved the situation: the *lieutenant de police*, La Reynie, who had been appointed in 1667, attempted to control the city's gangs and swindlers, ordered that all buildings be equipped with latrines and cesspools, and tried to accelerate paving and illumination of the streets. With the creation of the Hôpital Général de Paris and the Salpêtrière

(see pages 204–205), almost 10,000 beggars, swindlers, and prostitutes were interned and put to work. The Hôtel des Invalides brought relief for ailing and elderly soldiers. New pumps on the Pont Notre-Dame and fifteen new wells were installed in an attempt to end the city's chronic water shortage. State-owned factories, such as the Gobelins and the Savonnerie, and private ones that were granted royal privileges and set up to produce luxury goods—glass, gold articles, mirrors, tapestries—created thousands of jobs, and Paris soon replaced Venice as the center of the luxury industry. The king himself turned over a portion of the Louvre to be used as workshops for highly qualified craftsmen; the famous cabinet-maker Charles André Boulle was one of these.

Voltaire and Saint-Simon (Claude Henri de Rouvroy) accused Louis XIV of taking no interest in Paris. And, in fact, since the Fronde, the king did have a certain antipathy to the city. In 1680, he transferred the country's seat of government to Versailles —the first step taken by the revolutionaries in 1789 was to force the king to reside in Paris once again—and between 1700 and 1715, the year of his death, he was in the city only four times. Nevertheless, no ruler put his stamp on the city as decisively as the Sun King, thanks largely to pressure from Colbert. The minister insisted that the greatness of the monarchy had to manifest itself in the grandeur and beauty of the capital, but he saw to it that the representation of greatness, *le grand style*, went hand in hand

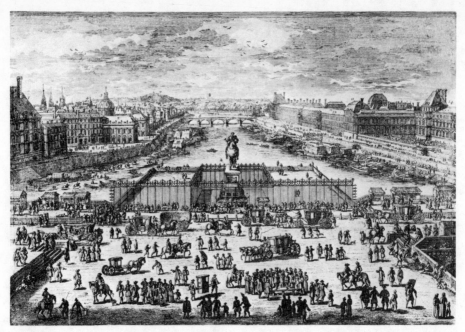

The monument to Henri IV on the Pont Neuf, with the Louvre and the Collège des Quatre-Nations (Perelle).

with utility. For the first time, something like a master plan for the reorganization of the city was developed. On August 5, 1676, the king wrote:

> In the desire that future construction undertaken in the city be regulated by a specific plan ... we have commanded that a precise map of this city be prepared, indicating not only the projects that have been accomplished at our command but also those that we wish to continue and bring to completion.

And by 1715, a total of 132 streets had been newly laid out, and the area of the city was enlarged from about 3 square miles in 1652 to nearly 4.5.

To accomplish these goals, the royal building administration was highly organized. From 1664 on, Colbert, as prime minister, was not only responsible for finances, but he was also placed in charge of the "buildings, arts, and manufacturing of France." Answering to him were a whole troop of "art officers," notably the *premier architecte du roi* (Louis Le Vau, 1654–1670; Jules Hardouin-Mansart, 1685–1708), the *premier peintre du roi* (Charles Le Brun), and the *premier jardinier du roi* (André Le Nôtre).

Corresponding to such strict organization of building was a rigorous uniformity in the development and teaching of aesthetic theory. In 1660, Colbert founded the Académie de France in Rome for the study of

Porte St-Bernard, with Notre-Dame and the Ile St-Louis toward the end of the seventeenth century (Perelle).

the art of the "ancients," and in 1671, the Académie d'Architecture was established in Paris. Under its dogmatic director François Blondel, this institution developed the doctrine of classical art that would liberate France from its artistic dependence on Italy and solidify the predominance of French taste throughout Europe.

Debate about the construction of the east front of the Louvre (see page 154) was ended by Colbert with a political decision in favor of this classical doctrine. A monumental style was created, one in which the ideals of magnitude (*grandeur*) and beauty (*beauté*), grounded in the aesthetics of antiquity, combined with the demands of functionalism (*utilité*) and appropriateness (*convenance*). The *grand style* under Louis

XIV was an expression of the absolute power of the monarch, and it transformed even the simplest utilitarian structures. To stress the completeness of royal authority, showy building became the exclusive privilege of the king. In 1660, all private construction was made subject to a special license from the king, so that the houses of the financiers would not be more splendid than his. Thus until the end of the reign, scarcely any extravagant *hôtels* were constructed; the king's intimate circle among the nobility was bound to the court at Versailles, and only a few close confidants of the king were able to afford splendid houses in the city. Among these were a number of artists' residences (for example, those of Jules Hardouin-Mansart, Rue de Tournelles [see page 203];

of Libéral Bruant, Rue de la Perle [see page 203]; of Jean-Baptiste Lully, Rue Ste-Anne; and of Charles Le Brun, Rue du Cardinal-Lemoine [see page 234]).

Almost all of the king's building projects were undertaken during the first part of his reign. In 1661, immediately after taking over the government, he commissioned Le Brun to redesign the second floor of the Petite Galerie of the Louvre, which had been destroyed by fire. The result was the Galerie d'Apollon, a first hymn to the Sun King. Louis Le Vau constructed the south façade of the Louvre, facing the Seine (replaced not long afterward by Claude Perrault's new building), and began to build the east façade, facing the city. But Colbert dismissed Le Vau in 1664 because of his many speculations, accusing him of having induced the king to spend inordinate amounts of money. To find a replacement for Le Vau, Colbert set up a competition in which a number of Italian architects participated, among them Pietro da Cortona and Gian Lorenzo Bernini. Bernini's first design for the east façade, a magnificent Baroque structure with an oval-shaped central pavilion from which two concave wings led outward to rectangular pavilions at the corners, was dismissed by Colbert as being impractical and unsuitable for the site. (Le Vau's concept for the Collège des Quatre-Nations may possibly represent a reflection of this plan, however.) In 1665, Bernini came to Paris and was given a princely reception. His second design was accepted and a cornerstone laid, but after his departure nothing further was done. In 1667, Colbert sent him a dismissal.

A commission composed of French artists —Le Vau, Le Brun, Perrault, and François d'Orbay—was charged with working up a new design. The result was the Louvre Colonnades (see page 154), a triumph of French classicism as the expression of royal dignity. In 1680, construction was halted—the ornamental statues, vases, and trophies missing, not to mention the roofs. Only in the eighteenth century, under Louis XV, was the structure completed.

At the opposite end of the mammoth complex of royal palaces, André Le Nôtre, in 1664, began to lay out the broad perspectives of the Jardin des Tuileries, extending the gardens westward in the form of a new avenue, the Champs-Élysées, leading toward St. Germain-en-Laye. This project was meant to express man's absolute mastery over nature. In 1670, the avenue was opened to coach traffic as far as the Rond-Point; Marie de Médicis had introduced coaching to Paris with the completion of the Cours-la-Reine after 1610.

After 1670, Louis XIV opened up the city in a spectacular manner. Following the conquest of Artois and Flanders and the securing of the country's borders with Sebastien Vauban's fortifications, the king had the city walls torn down and a semicircle of tree-lined *allées*, the Boulevards, laid out along the walls' former course on the Right Bank. For a century and a half, Paris became an open city—an act of self-assurance, and a deliberate slap at France's archenemies, the Hapsburgs, whose capital, Vienna, was threatened by the Turks. Triumphal gates glorifying the king greeted travelers approaching the city from the north and east (see pages 229–230).

On the Left Bank, where the old city walls had been buried by later building, the construction of boulevards never really started. Yet it was here that the three building projects that best capture the monumental impulse of the age of Louis XIV were under-

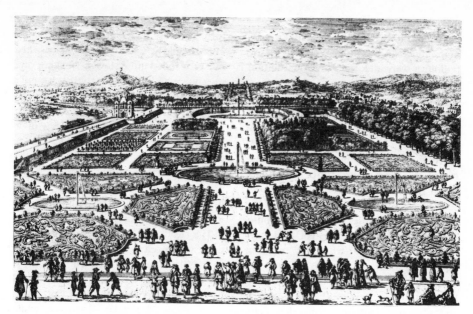

The Jardin des Tuileries, according to plans by André Le Nôtre, with a view of the heights of Chaillot (Perelle).

taken: the Hôpital de la Salpêtrière, the Hôtel des Invalides, and the Observatoire (see pages 205–206).

The vanity of the cult of the king is especially evident in the two royal squares that were built on the Right Bank under Louis XIV. Jules Hardouin-Mansart began to plan one of these, the Place des Victoires, in 1685 as a setting for a monument by Martin Desjardin that showed the king in his coronation regalia, crowned by Immortality and trampling three-headed Cerberus (symbolic of the Triple Alliance). Placed atop a high pedestal ornamented with reliefs and figures of slaves, the monument was to be a kind of sanctuary; four memorial flames on tall columns surrounding the monument were to be kept burning day and night. In form and architecture, the square was intended to accentuate the monument. Laid out on the grounds of the former Hôtel de la Ferté-Senneterre, the Place des Victoires was to be a circle, something new for Paris, but one that was cut across on its east side by the straight fronts of two large *hôtels*, between which the Rue de Fossés-Montmartre would lead from the square. The remaining arc was divided into three roughly equal segments by two additional streets. With a diameter of 126 feet, the square's width was roughly three times the height of the monument. The façades— with blind arcades on the ground floor, two stories of unequal height above, Colossal pilasters, and a roof interrupted by dormer windows—enhanced the uniformity and regal status of the square. Later times showed little respect for the Place des Victoires, however. As early as the eighteenth century, a new street was cut from it to the Hôtel de la Vrillière; and in the nineteenth century, a number of the buildings were deformed by the addition of new stories.

Unlike the almost cultic enclosure of the Place des Victoires, the Place Vendôme was originally planned as a sort of public royal forum (see pages 232–234). In 1685, Louvois, the former minister of war who replaced Colbert as director of royal building in 1683, suggested to the king the construction of a "Place des Conquêtes" on the grounds of the earlier Hôtel de Vendôme. This was to be a "manifestation of [the king's] military and political triumphs," with an equestrian statue of Louis XIV, by François Girardon, surrounded by the chancellery, the Mint, the academies, the royal library, and other state buildings. A first design, by Hardouin-Mansart, proposed a rectangular square —open to the south and leading on the north, by way of a triumphal arch, to the portal of the new Capuchin church. The buildings were to have open arcades on the ground floor, supporting two stories proportioned like those at the Place des Victoires, with a large entablature concealing a flat roof.

But by this time, the king's interest in public buildings for Paris had declined, while his need for funds was undiminished. He decided that the properties behind the uniform façades, which had been begun in 1686, should be sold to private citizens; their sale proceeded quite slowly. The king gave the square and its façades to the city and a contractor, and in exchange, the city was required to build a barracks for his musketeers in Charonne. The new property owners were granted the right to build whatever they chose behind Hardouin-Mansart's façades, using the architects of their choice. The new occupants began to arrive in 1700, primarily *nouveaux riches*, landlords, and military suppliers.

The façades of the octagonal Place Vendôme were even more decorative than those of the Place des Victoires. The centers of the long sides and the angled corners had projecting entryways with full Corinthian columns and triangular pediments, while grand pilasters ornamented the remaining structures. Corresponding to what was now a more private use, the ground floor was closed with round-arch, blind arcades. In the center of the square stood the equestrian statue of the king. Toppled in the Revolution, this was replaced by Napoleon with the tall victory column (Colonne d'Austerlitz) in imitation of a Roman original. The column destroyed the relationship between the center of the square and the buildings around it.

THE RETURN OF PRIVATE BUILDING

Construction of the Place Vendôme, finally completed in 1717 by the Scottish financier John Law, was the prelude to a boom in private building that turned the Faubourg

OPPOSITE: Equestrian monument to Louis XIV in the Place Vendôme (Mariette).

63

St-Honoré into the stronghold of the French moneyed aristocracy in the early eighteenth century. At the same time, the *noblesse de cour*, the dukes and peers of France, liberated from residence in Versailles toward the end of the reign of Louis XIV and under the regency, settled in the elegant Faubourg St-Germain. Here, in the first half of the eighteenth century, especially along the Rue de Varenne and the Rue de Grenelle, more than forty mansions for the nobility were constructed by the best architects of the time (see pages 238–242).

The relaxation of courtly etiquette promoted the flowering of a cultural life in Paris, and in the salons of the *hôtels particuliers*, the leading lights of the period—the philosophers of the Enlightenment, poets, and artists—were received by the social elite of the country. In the eighteenth century, Paris experienced an extraordinary economic upswing. Its population, which had stagnated during the reign of Louis XIV, rose to roughly 650,000 by 1789. The luxury industry brought many workers into the city, especially into the *faubourgs*. And with the establishment of the stock exchange in 1724 and the Caisse d'Escompte in 1776, Paris became an important financial center, attracting investments from other cities in France, so that notables from all over the country came to settle in the capital.

A remarkable amount of building was done in the first half of the century, and it was financed almost exclusively by the private sector. The king, the city, and the state built almost nothing—except for the lovely but poorly situated fountain in the Rue de Grenelle by Edme Bouchardon in 1739, contemptuously described by Voltaire as "much stone for little water" (fig., page 238).

THE RETURN TO CLASSICISM

On the death of the Sun King, the finances of the state were devastated, debt running almost twenty times as high as annual income. Only after 1750, during the second half of his long reign, was Louis XV in a position to resume building in Paris. A number of public buildings were then constructed in rapid succession. The École Militaire (see page 242) was begun in 1752; the palaces of Place Louis XV (Place de la Concorde; see pages 244–245), in 1757; the Mint (see pages 243–244), in 1768; the École de Droit, in 1770; and the École de Médecine (see pages 249–250), in 1779, under Louis XVI.

This resurgence of public building after a period of only private construction—most notably the *hôtels particuliers* with their Rococo interiors—was greeted with enthusiasm by contemporary art critics. The return to the classical tradition, the *grand style* of the age of Louis XIV, is most clearly manifest in the work of Jacques-Ange Gabriel, who imitated and reinterpreted Claude Perrault's Louvre Colonnades in the Place Louis XV and whose École Militaire echoed the classical art of the seventeenth century in its overall plan and its details. Gabriel's revival of classicism had been foreshadowed in 1732: instead of the exuberant Baroque

1. View of the Quartier Latin from the tower of ▷ Notre-Dame: the church of St. Julien-le-Pauvre and, behind it, the Sorbonne.

2. Boulevard St-Germain and the tower of St. Germain-des-Prés.

3. St. Martin-des-Champs: the former refectory, now a reading room.

4. Nave of Notre-Dame with a view of the choir.

5. Place du Parvis-Notre-Dame and the west façade of the cathedral. ▷

6. The Ile de la Cité and the Pont Neuf, from the Seine.

7. Hôtel de Sens: entrance portal.

8. Donjon of the palace of Vincennes.

9. The west façade of St. Germain-l'Auxerrois, opposite the Louvre.

10. The chapel in the Hôtel de Cluny.

11. Exterior of the choir of St. Gervais–St. Protais.

12. View of St. Merri from the Centre Beaubourg. In background on left are Notre-Dame and the Panthéon.

13. St. Eustache: view into the nave from the side aisle. ▷

14. St. Eustache across "le trou des Halles."

15. St. Étienne-du-Mont: interior with the rood screen by Philibert de l'Orme.

16. Hôtel Carnavalet: main courtyard.

17. Fontaine des Innocents.

18. The oldest section of the Louvre: the façade by Pierre Lescot.

19. Entrance pavilion of the Palais du Luxembourg, seat of the French Senate.

20. Façade of St. Paul–St. Louis in the Rue St-Antoine.

21. Fontaine Médicis in the Jardin du Luxembourg.

22. Courtyard side of the Hôtel de Sully.

23. St. Gervais–St. Protais: the façade by Salomon de Brosse.

24. Val-de-Grâce: interior of the church.

25. Val-de-Grâce: façade and crossing cupola.

of Meissonnier's design for the façade of St. Sulpice, it was Giovanni Niccolò Servandoni's severe double portico (see pages 194–196) that was chosen—and freely imitated some twenty years later in the façade for St. Eustache (see pages 148–149).

The classicism that emerged during the later years of the reign of Louis XV was not merely oriented toward the nation's own tradition, but it also drew on more precise archeological knowledge of the architecture of antiquity and even its historical derivatives. Jacques-Germain Soufflot's Ste. Geneviève became a symbol of this new movement, which manifested itself not so much in actual structures as in an almost frenetic production of architectural tracts and designs.

This return to antiquity was not content merely to reproduce ancient models with archeological authenticity (which was largely the extent of the second phase of classicism at the beginning of the nineteenth century), but it attempted to gain fundamental insights into the universal essence of architecture. Its most radical expressions were the architectural fantasies of Étienne-Louis Boullée or even the tollhouses attached to the new Parisian customs wall that Claude-Nicolas Ledoux began building in 1784 (see pages 254–256). Although these have taken their place in art history as Revolutionary architecture, they characterize in fact the last phase of the *ancien régime*. The severe grandeur typical of these public buildings also carried over into the private realm after 1760. Small country houses outside the city, called *folies*, were erected after Palladian models (Folie Favart in Ménilmontant, Bagatelle, and so on), and the *hôtels* in town took on a strict arrangement of pilasters and tended to imitate public structures (for example, the Hôtel de Salm, today, the Palais de la Légion d'Honneur; see pages 241–242).

The leading architects of the time, Jacques-Germain Soufflot and Pierre Patte, developed far-reaching schemes for modernizing and restructuring the city with new squares and streets, anticipating much that would ultimately be realized under Napoleon III and Haussmann. However, the greatest city-planning achievement of the period was the design of the Place Louis XV (Place de la Concorde), which was preceded by a competition. Many of the suggestions contributed to the final form of the square. The overall concept departs from that of the enclosed square, which was familiar in Paris. Lying at the end of the Jardin des Tuileries, its open structure created a tie between city and country and a link in the royal axis created by the Louvre, Tuileries, and Champs-Élysées. A new street, the Rue Royale, led northward from the square to the Madeleine (see page 256), and a bridge, designed by Perronnet in 1771, connected it to the Left Bank. Under Napoleon, the square's surroundings were made more dramatic by the construction of the temple façade of the Palais-Bourbon across the river and the reconstruction of the Madeleine. The character of the square was further highlighted by surrounding it with an octagonal depression, delineated by balustrades and sentry boxes, so that the equestrian statue of the king by Edme Bouchardon rose up as though placed in the middle of an island.

The redesigning of the square during the July Monarchy (the reign of Louis-Philippe, so-called after the month of its birth in 1830) replaced these details with monumental fountains, rich candelabra, and an obelisk in place of the statue, which had been toppled during the Revolution. The trenches were filled in in 1853, under Napoleon III. Jacques-Ange Gabriel's plan had called for three streets to radiate westward from the square; the Avenue des Champs-Élysées in the center, the already-existing Cours-la-Reine along the Seine, and toward the northwest a new avenue through the Faubourg St-Honoré to the Chaussée d'Antin, to a quarter that was one of the centers of building activity in the late eighteenth century. This avenue, however, was never built.

It was under Louis XVI that the first great renovations in medieval Paris were begun. In 1783, the old structures surrounding the Louvre began to be demolished, and the buildings on the bridges were dismantled beginning in 1786. The palace on the Ile de la Cité was almost entirely rebuilt after the fire of 1776, and the Cour de Mai was added, just as the Palais-Royal had been reconstructed after the fire of 1764. Victor Louis built here, on the site of the former gardens, a center of municipal activity (see page 252). New squares were laid out—for example, those in front of the Odéon, Ste. Geneviève, and St. Sulpice—or at least planned. Among the latter were one to be constructed in front of St. Eustache and another to replace the Bastille, which was scheduled to be torn down.

A 1783 decree required that new streets be at least 33 feet wide and that buildings not exceed 65 feet in height. The first sidewalks appeared in 1782 in the Rue de l'Odéon. Flat nameplates for all streets had been in place since 1729, and the numbering of all buildings was completed later in the century. In 1757, oil street lamps were introduced, and beginning in 1765, trade signs had to be mounted flush against façades to reduce blockage of sunlight.

Considerable improvements were also made in regard to hygiene. The drainage canal in the north of the city was channeled and covered over, which hastened urban expansion. Cemeteries, especially the mass cemetery at the church of the Innocents, had always posed the threat of pestilence. These graveyards were removed, and the bones were deposited in abandoned subterranean quarries, dating from the time of the Romans, now called the Catacombes. Cemeteries in the south (Montparnasse), the north (Montmartre), and the east (Père-Lachaise) were proposed, and these plans were largely carried out in the nineteenth century.

In 1774, Verniquet, the *commissaire général voyer*, commissioned a large-scale topographical map of the city. This map was to be used by a planning committee to which, beginning in 1783, all building and design proposals had to be submitted.

REVOLUTION AND EMPIRE: THE TRIUMPHAL BUILDING OF NAPOLEON

The Revolution drastically altered the French political system and assigned to architecture and the arts a new role—one of responsibility to society and the nation. However,

Public life in the garden of the Palais-Royal at the time of Louis XVI.

it contributed very little to the overall development of the city. It took no advantage
of the extraordinary opportunity it had—
due to the nationalization of properties belonging to the church and to aristocrats and
others who had fled the country—to make
fundamental improvements in the city's
streets, in housing for the poor, in hygienic
conditions, or in the expansion of parks and
public gardens.

On the contrary, general living conditions
grew worse. Under the *ancien régime*, the
king's gardens and those of the monasteries had been open to the public. Now these
precious open spaces were broken up into

tiny parcels and sold to speculators and the
highest bidders; the few notable new street
layouts of the 1790s originated in just this
way. Care of the sick and the poor, for which
the church had devoted a quarter of its income, totally collapsed. And the chaotic situation of the country seriously endangered
the supply of foodstuffs to the city.

The work of setting up a new political
system, as well as the struggle against outside threats, prevented the new Republic
from immortalizing itself in stone. Étienne-
Louis Boullée's plans for a "Palais National"
never got beyond paper. However, the *Plan
des Artistes*, prepared between 1793 and

83

1797, incorporated all the projects for the redesign of the city that had been discussed in the preceding decades and became, to a large degree, the basis for nineteenth-century city planning.

The beginning of the new century—and the advent of Napoleon—brought a complete loss of municipal independence to Paris. Beginning in 1800, a *préfet de la Seine* and a *préfet de police* administered the city on behalf of the government. And Napoleon's vision of Paris as the "most beautiful city imaginable" and the capital of Europe stands in sharp contrast to what was actually accomplished during the First Empire. His architect Pierre Fontaine proposed a spacious residence for the emperor on the heights of Chaillot—on the site of the later Trocadéro—opposite the Champ-de-Mars, from which a new administrative center would unfold down to the Esplanade des Invalides, with palaces housing the university, the archives, the newly founded École Normale, and so on. Of this entire scheme, only the Pont d'Iéna was completed. Of the sixty fountains that Napoleon envisioned, only fifteen were constructed. One, the Fontaine du Fellah, next to the Rue de Sèvres, was built in the Egyptian style that had become fashionable following Napoleon's Egyptian campaign (as were the Rue du Caire and the classical Fontaine de Mars, Rue St-Dominique).

What was realized, or at least begun, were the monuments to Napoleon's victories: the Arc de Triomphe du Carrousel (illus. 52, page 124) in front of the Palais des Tuileries, in imitation of the Arch of Septimius Severus in Rome; and the Arc de Triomphe (illus. 53 and 54, pages 125–126) in the star-shaped square (the Etoile) at the end of the Avenue des Champs-Elysées. For the marriage of Napoleon and Marie-Louise in 1810, a temporary facsimile of the arch provided the impression of imperial grandeur; the actual monument was dedicated under Louis-Philippe. It was Napoleon III and his prefect Haussmann who gave the Etoile its final form by commissioning its uniform buildings, by Jacob Hittorf, and its twelve radiating *allées*.

Another Napoleonic structure intended to rival a Roman model was the Colonne d'Austerlitz, which was placed in the Place Vendôme where a statue of Louis XIV had stood. The 425 bronze reliefs of this column depicted the campaign of 1805 in the manner of Trajan's Column. The three "temples" built by the emperor were also inspired by Roman originals. One of these, in his soldiers' honor, was constructed on the site of the scarcely begun Madeleine. Across the Seine was the second, the Temple of Law. And on the grounds of a former monastery, the third, the Temple of Money, or La Bourse (see page 258), was built; this initially had been intended to stand behind the Madeleine.

Napoleon, like his royal predecessors, lived in the Palais des Tuileries, which he had modernized. In accordance with a Revolutionary directive, the Louvre was converted into a museum. The upper floors of the north and east wings of the Cour Carrée were finished, and new stairwells were installed behind the Colonnades. The Grande Galerie was redesigned, and an old project was resumed: the connection between the Tuileries and the Louvre on the north side. A first section of this, in imitation of the Grande Galerie on the south side by Jacques Androuet Du Cerceau the Younger, was built between the Palais des Tuileries and the Pavillon de Rohan.

The most important city-planning achievement of the Empire was begun in 1802: the layout of the Rue de Rivoli on the north side of the Jardin des Tuileries. Such a street had long been needed to extend eastward from the Place de la Concorde. Following plans by Charles Percier and Pierre Fontaine, the street was perfectly straight. It led across the grounds of the monastery of the Feuillants and boasted open arcades on the ground floor and uniform façades in hewn stone that were tied together by the balcony railing running along its entirety. Builders along this street not only had to accept the façades, but they also were faced with a number of limitations regarding potential uses. All crafts were prohibited whose smells or noise might be disruptive—butchers, bakers, confectioners, and blacksmiths, for example. Furthermore, no shop sign could be placed on a façade. These restrictions kept away a large number of interested parties, so that as late as 1813, in spite of offers of tax reliefs for builders, only a few buildings rose up above the arcades constructed by the government.

To the east, the Rue de Rivoli ended at the Place des Pyramides; only later was it continued. And it was connected to the Boulevards by the Rue de Castiglione—to which François Mansart's façade of the church of the Feuillants was sacrificed—a street that continued as the Rue de la Paix on the north side of the Place Vendôme.

Napoleon always trusted engineers more than architects, whose ideology he tended to suspect. Thus his chief contributions to the city were in the realm of technical improvements. For the first time, the problem of the water supply was attacked on a large scale. A canal was built to lead the water of the Ourq, in the northwest of the Ile de France, into the center of the city. This canal, expanding into a large reservoir at the Porte de la Villette and running underground below the Place de Bastille, was also intended to revive the neglected east side of Paris by means of accompanying *allées* and new boat traffic. A splendid new street leading from the Louvre to Vincennes was to serve the same purpose, but it was never constructed.

After a devastating flood in 1802, work was begun on new stone quays around the Ile de la Cité, and many of the surviving ones were renovated. Four new bridges were built to improve access between the two halves of the city: the Pont de la Cité in 1803 between the two islands; the Pont des Arts in 1805 between the Louvre and the Collège des Quatre-Nations, the first iron bridge in France; the Pont d'Austerlitz in 1806; and the Pont d'Iéna in 1812. More than six miles of new drainage canals were installed.

A reorganization of the city's markets served to improve the distribution of produce. The grain market (Halle aux Bleds) was rebuilt, beginning in 1807, as a circular structure with an iron and glass dome designed by François Bélanger. And it was decided to construct the great Halles as a central market that would extend from the Marché des Innocents to the Halle aux Bleds—an anticipation of Napoleon III's concept. This central market was supplemented by district markets—Marché St-Martin, Marché des Carmes, and others (of which the Marché St-Germain has partially survived)—a flower market on the Quai Desaix, and a new Halle au Vin on the grounds of the former monastery of St. Victor.

Rue de Rivoli in the early nineteenth century.

THE EXPANSION OF THE CITY
DURING THE RESTORATION

Despite a rising standard of living, relatively little private residential building was accomplished under the Empire. The new nobility settled into the mansions surviving from the eighteenth century. The most spectacular example of an Empire interior is the Hôtel de Beauharnais, which was renovated by Germain Boffrand. Only under the Restoration (the resumption of power by the Bourbons following the exile of Napoleon) would whole new quarters spring up as well-funded societies of contractors were given a free hand in erecting vast new residential sections—the Quartier François I, the

Quartier Europe, the Quartier Poissonnière. These districts consisted of blocks of apartments with severely elegant façades; they attracted a well-to-do middle class that was migrating in increasing numbers to the so-called *beaux quartiers* in the west of the city.

Contrary to the emphasis on state display in the Empire, the Restoration was extremely reserved in its public building. But it was left to Louis-Philippe to continue the ambitious building projects of the Empire —the Arc de Triomphe and the Madeleine— and even of the *ancien régime*—the redesign of the Place de la Concorde beginning in the 1836, the expansion of the Palais du Luxembourg beginning in 1836, and the enlargement of the Hôtel de Ville beginning in 1837.

The Catholic church, however, was extremely busy building. The churches were returned to it in 1801, but many were in very poor condition and others had been torn down—often sacrificed, as in the case of St. Jacques-la-Boucherie and Ste. Geneviève, to new streets. But in the new quarters, a number of remarkable new churches were built in a very cool and academic classical style. As early as 1815, the Chapelle Expiatoire was begun in the mode of an ancient necropolis (see pages 258–259); it was followed in 1823 by Notre-Dame-de-Lorette, with its Corinthian portico, and in 1824 by St. Vincent-de-Paul (see pages 259–260), in the form of a Roman basilica with an interesting combination of twin towers and a portico.

This late classicism was followed under the July Monarchy by a movement that sought its models—not without some impetus from German Romanticism—in Gothic architecture of the thirteenth century. Re-discovery of the Middle Ages led to the first systematic study of Gothic architecture, which would culminate in the Second Empire in the work of Eugène Viollet-le-Duc. The most important architects of the epoch combined Gothic structural principles with a rationalistic functionalism to create— thanks to the logical use of modern materials, primarily iron and glass—such extremely progressive designs as Henri Labrouste's Bibliothèque Ste-Geneviève (and later his reading room of the Bibliothèque Nationale), the *passages* (see pages 260–261), Victor Baltard's Halles (fig., page 95), Jacob Hittorf's Gare du Nord, and Duquesney's Gare de l'Est.

However, from the standpoint of Parisian history, the Restoration is remarkable primarily because it was the setting for the transformation of the ancient capital into a modern metropolis. The bourgeoisie had profited from the Revolution because it had taken over the property of the church and of the nobility. And it was this class, which was responsible for the Industrial Revolution, that now began to determine the development of the city. Factories and workshops sprang up around the periphery; in 1837, the first railway was begun—from Paris toward St. Germain-en-Laye as far as Pacq—and in 1842, legislation was enacted to provide for six railways that would lead out of Paris toward the major cities of France. The first railway stations were built. Banks, insurance companies, and financial corporations mushroomed, and wholesale and retail commerce set the tone of new quarters in the north of the city.

Armies of workers were attracted to Paris, and—since the bourgeoisie almost wholly occupied the more desirable residential sections—the newcomers crowded into the already-bursting old districts. Some 350,000 migrants swarmed into the city under Louis-Philippe alone. By 1846, Paris had more than 1 million inhabitants.

The housing crisis and miserable living standard of the lower classes—in 1848, some 65 percent of the population of Paris paid no taxes because they were too poor—led to uprisings and high suicide rates. Appalling hygienic conditions in the old slums led to an outbreak of cholera in 1832, the first in 200 years, in which 20,000 people died. The prefect Rambuteau, who administered the city from 1833 until the end of the July Monarchy, attempted to improve the supply and quality of the water by constructing the Fontaine Molière, the Fontaine des Quatre-Évêques, and more than 2,000 street fountains. A first step toward clearing the thicket of the medieval quarters was the rather narrow Rue Rambuteau, leading from St. Eustache to the Marais. But the political system was basically not prepared to solve the most pressing problems of a city suffering from overly rapid development.

Instead, it was decided, in 1841, to construct a very costly girdle of fortifications that would include a number of suburbs: Auteuil, Passy, Les Batignolles, Montmartre, La Chapelle, La Villette, Belleville, Charenton, Bercy, Vaugirard, and Grenelle. The 22-mile wall, with 94 bastions and trenches over 16 yards wide, was completed in 1845. It was surrounded by a strip of open ground 275 yards wide. Paris had found its ultimate shape; the present-day Boulevards des Maréchaux and Boulevard Périphérique follow this former fortification line.

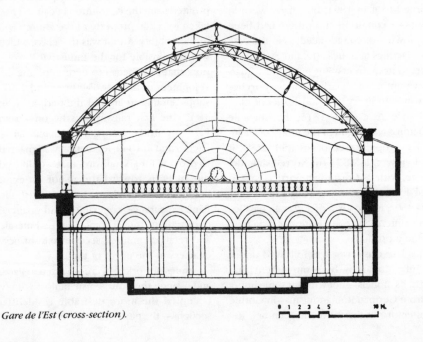

Gare de l'Est (cross-section).

THE SECOND EMPIRE: THE MODERNIZATION OF PARIS UNDER HAUSSMANN

The transformation of Paris into a modern, cosmopolitan city was completed during the Second Empire. Present-day Paris, except for the most recent changes since de Gaulle, is essentially the Paris that Napoleon III's prefect, Baron Georges-Eugène Haussmann —and, following in his footsteps, the Third Republic—created.

Under no government was the city so drastically restructured as under Napoleon III and Haussmann. A new network of streets tore into the old structures and opened up the medieval core; 20,000 buildings were torn down and 40,000 new ones erected. A ring of railroads almost nineteen miles long and with twenty-seven stations connected the outer sections of the city. New railway stations were built and linked to one another by broad boulevards.

Beginning in 1854, the Compagnie Générale des Omnibus provided public passenger service along 30 routes, with 500 coaches. More than 30,000 buildings were equipped with direct water connections,

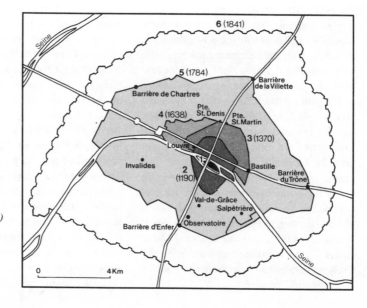

The city walls of Paris (1190–1841): (1) Gallo-Roman wall; (2) wall of Philippe Auguste; (3) wall of Charles V; (4) wall of Louis XIII; (5) tollhouse wall; (6) wall of Adolphe Thiers.

and the most modern sewer system in the world, totaling over 310 miles of drains, was created after plans by the engineer Belgrand.

In 1860, the suburbs lying within the new ring of fortifications were incorporated into the city. Between 1852 and 1870, the population climbed from roughly 1 million to almost 2 million. More than 100,000 of these new residents were foreign workers. The state invested more than 2.5 billion gold francs to remodel the city, a commitment made possible by a general upswing in the country's economy.

Haussmann's modernizations have been called brutal by some because they demolished not only the old slums but also many artistically and historically valuable structures. Baudelaire lamented in 1860: "Le vieux Paris n'est plus (la forme d'une ville change plus vite, hélas! que le cœur d'un mortel)" ["Old Paris is no more (the form of a city changes faster, alas! than the heart of a mortal)"]. The renovations were also accused of having been motivated by military strategy, so that troops could control rebellious districts more easily (although, in fact, during the Commune uprising, the army *avoided* the wide boulevards for fear of being fired upon by the insurgents). More to the point is the charge that they drove "the people" out of the city; the process of social segregation—the banishment of the lower classes to the edge of the city and into the *banlieue* (suburbs) and the distinction among the upper-class "Paris de luxe," the bourgeois Paris, and the Paris of the common people—was now made once and for all. But, in Haussmann's defense, it is difficult to think how the city could have survived and continued to function relatively well, even today, without the reforms of the Second Empire.

It was not Haussmann alone, but also Napoleon III, who had quite precise ideas about necessary renovations. During his exile, Louis Bonaparte had been able to study how England was successfully battling its slums, how important green stretches were to its cities, and how it was meeting the demands of modern traffic. He thus supported Haussmann without reservation. Haussmann himself felt he was following in the tradition of Colbert and Marigny, and in his city planning he hoped to surpass the pragmatic English by applying the aesthetic ideals of French classicism: monumental perspectives—Haussmann always tried to have his new streets end in dramatic focal points—straight axes, uniform façades, star-shaped squares, and a deliberate sense of proportion between the width of a street and the height of the structures along it.

Beginning in 1855, Haussmann launched his great campaigns. Medieval buildings on the Ile de la Cité disappeared almost totally, except for a few remnants to the north of Notre-Dame. The Place Dauphine was preserved. A broad square was created in front of Notre-Dame, with the Hôtel-Dieu to the north of it (it had been located across the Seine). West of this square came first a barracks (Préfecture de Police), then the flower market and the Tribunal de Commerce, and finally new structures for the Palais de Justice, built around the heavily restored remnants of the old palace and stretching as far as the Place Dauphine. This "reclaimed" core was connected with the Left and Right banks by the new north–south axis of the Boulevard du Centre, which extended from the Gare de l'Est in the north to the Observatoire in the south (today's Boulevards de Strasbourg, de Sébastopol, and St-Michel).

On the Right Bank, this new boulevard

ran between the Rue St-Denis and the Rue St-Martin. Its construction not only was less costly than widening one of these two streets would have been, but also served to clear one of the city's densest slum areas. At the point where the boulevard reached the Seine, Haussmann had the square on the site of the former Grand Châtelet enlarged and redesigned with the addition of two matching theaters. As a focal point for this axis, the Tribunal de Commerce was provided with a Baroque cupola. And on the south side of the Ile de la Cité, a monumental fountain by Gabriel Davioud marked the starting point for the southern segment of the axis. The Rue de Rivoli was extended as far as the Hôtel de Ville, where it met the Rue St-Antoine— the first new crossing of perpendicular axes in the center of the city since antiquity. The existing Boulevards were expanded by extensions toward the west as far as the Place de l'Etoile (Avenue de Friedland and Boulevard Haussmann, the latter of which was not fully completed until 1929) and toward the east, where they radiated from a new, elongated, star-shaped square, the Place du Château d'Eau (Place de la République). From here, another boulevard (Boulevard Richard-Lenoir) was built over the canal to the Place de la Bastille, with another branch extending in a straight line to the new Place du Trône (Place de la Nation). This square was also connected to Les Halles by the Rue de Turbigo and to the two new railway stations, the Gare de l'Est and Gare du Nord, by the Boulevard de Magenta.

Haussmann loved the symmetry of diagonal intersections, and he was especially partial to those with a notable piece of architecture in the center. Therefore the Boulevard de Malesherbes was created to meet the Boulevard de la Madeleine, with the church of St. Augustin serving as the focal point. And out of the same impulse he developed the diamond-shaped square on which the Paris Opéra was to be built. The buildings on this square were given uniform façades by their architect, Hubert Rohault de Fleury, who was also expected to design the Opéra. However, the planned unity of this structure and its setting was destroyed when, as a result of a competition in 1861, Charles Garnier's much more Baroque design for the Opéra was selected (see pages 261–262). As a tie between this "cathedral of the bourgeoisie" and the city center, the Avenue de l'Opéra, leading toward the Louvre, was begun, but it was not completed under Haussmann. The Louvre itself was finally given its northern connection with the Palais des Tuileries in a heavy, overburdened style by Hector Lefuel after plans by Louis Visconti. The same style would characterize the structures of the inner courtyard west of the Cour Carrée. Buildings still standing between the Louvre and the Tuileries were at last demolished to make room for formal gardens.

Haussmann's main achievement on the Right Bank was the design of the large Place de l'Etoile surrounding the Arc de Triomphe. This round square boasted a diameter of 980 feet, 12 radiating *allées* (illus. 56 and 57, page 127), and uniform surrounding buildings designed by Jacob Hittorf. The entries to these buildings face away from the square; access is provided by surrounding ring streets (Rue de Presbourg and Rue de Tilsitt). Haussmann did not like Hittorf's façades and sought to conceal them as much as possible by planting rows of trees in front of them.

The showpiece of the Etoile plan was its connection to the Bois de Boulogne, the Avenue de l'Impératrice (Avenue Foch). Four hundred feet wide, it was lined with *contre-allées* (access roads), flower beds, and luxury-class residences. The districts opened up by the Etoile, especially the Sixteenth Arrondissement to the south, became favored by the upper middle class, and the former villages of Passy and Auteuil, adjacent to the Bois de Boulogne, became *beaux quartiers*.

Corresponding to the Place de l'Etoile in the east of the city was the Place de la Nation, which had played an important role in the *ancien régime* as the point of entry for travelers coming from the east. The social discrepancy that had meanwhile developed between the west and the east of Paris was noticeable in the lesser degree of attention that development of this square received.

On the Left Bank, the creation of a new thoroughfare designed to extend the Grands Boulevards into a ring road devastated the priceless architecture of the Faubourg St-Germain. The new Boulevard St-Germain was laid out as a flat curve from the Pont de la Concorde to the tip of the Ile St-Louis. Only under the Third Republic would it continue via the Pont de Sully to the Boulevard Henri IV and thereby connect with the Place de la Bastille. A second, outer ring of boulevards between the Hôtel des Invalides and the Salpêtrière was completed with the creation of the new Boulevard de Port-Royal and Boulevard St-Marcel. A tie between the Gare Montparnasse and the city center posed something of a problem. Haussmann contented himself with creating a direct connection between the outer and inner rings, the Rue de Rennes, ending at the church of St. Germain-des-Prés; to have continued it on to the Seine would have meant the sacrifice of the Collège des Quatre-Nations. Haussmann attacked the problem of linking the Left and Right banks by building new bridges and, where necessary, access streets for them; the Pont de l'Alma, with the Boulevard de l'Alma and the Avenue Bosquet, is an example.

The network of Haussmann's wide streets essentially carries inner-city traffic today. And the creation of these streets involved the construction of the type of row house that characterizes present-day Paris. The Rue de Rivoli became the model for stretches of buildings with five stories tied together by Corinthian pilasters and, above them, a sixth or even a seventh floor set back under the roof. These comfortable structures could be afforded only by the upper middle class, and they were for the most part constructed by private building societies—often with funds gained through dispossession procedures. (The *ancien régime* had not needed to compensate displaced residents in this way, since the land belonged to the king; the individual had only usage rights that the king could withdraw, although such withdrawal was extremely infrequent.) The style of the residences built under Haussmann continued, with only minor variations, to be prevalent in Paris until the early twentieth century. (Toward the end of the nineteenth century, it was embellished by bay windows and extensive ornamentation.) This strict adherence to *l'ordonnance*, the uniform design of façades that Haussmann imposed on residential building (under strong criticism from the liberal opposition), kept classicism alive.

However, *l'ordonnance* had no parallels in public and ecclesiastical building. And

Haussmann's new streets are cut through: construction of the Rue de Rennes near St. Germain-des-Prés.

with the exception of the Opéra, with which Garnier hoped to create, as he himself claimed, the Napoleon III style, there are few remarkable or original achievements in these sectors; rather, there are signs of a decline in quality that has persisted into the present. Hittorf, although not highly valued by Haussmann, was one of the best architects of the Second Empire, as proved by his Gare du Nord, his town hall of the First Arrondissement, and, above all, his Cirque d'Hiver. Théodore Ballu, on the contrary, who worked in almost all possible styles—the Romanesque (St. Ambroise), the Gothic (the bell tower of St. Germain-l'Auxerrois), the Renaissance (La Trinité),

and the Baroque (Tribunal de Commerce) —and Joseph-Louis Duc, who designed the west façade of the Palais de Justice, clung nervously to established historical traditions. This insecurity would extend, with the exception of the Art Nouveau architects, into the twentieth century.

The most interesting buildings of the time were utilitarian structures in which new materials were used to achieve excellence in terms of both engineering and aesthetics: Victor Baltard's Halles, constructed at Haussmann's insistence on a site that was no longer appropriate even then; the same architect's slaughterhouse of La Villette; Henri Labrouste's magnificent, domed im-

Boulevard Haussmann in the nineteenth century: l'ordonnance et l'alignement—*Haussmann's ideals.*

perial library (Bibliothèque Nationale); and the many local market halls, almost all of which have been sacrificed to modernization in recent years. Likewise vanished are the evidences of the first world's fair in 1855, which exerted quite a prominent influence over the city during the second half of the century.

Since his exile, Napoleon III had been an admirer of English parks. His dream was a Hyde Park for Paris. The densely built-up city scarcely offered any room for such extensive green spaces, and therefore English-style landscaped gardens were planned outside the city's boundaries.

Haussmann's associate, Alphand, devised a comprehensive program to create green stretches for the capital: two parks of con-

siderable size to the west and east of the city, the Bois de Boulogne and the Bois de Vincennes, respectively, each comprising what had been royal hunting grounds; and two smaller parks, Alphand's masterpiece of a Romantic garden, Buttes-Chaumont, on the site of some abandoned quarries in the north, and the park of Montsouris on an empty tract in the south. In addition, twenty-four expensively designed small, local parks based on English examples were laid out.

The Franco-Prussian War of 1870 to 1871, which brought about the fall of Napoleon III and the siege of Paris, abruptly ended Haussmann's lavish modernization plans. In the uprising of the Commune that followed the siege, Parisian craftsmen and workers, supported by progressive intellectuals, sought

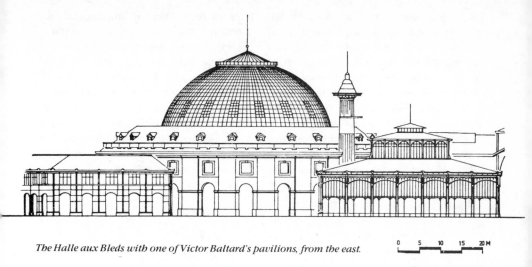

The Halle aux Bleds with one of Victor Baltard's pavilions, from the east.

0   5   10   15   20 M

to defend their rights against the new, bourgeois Third Republic. Still surrounded by the Prussians, Paris experienced perhaps the most dreadful weeks of its history—the civil war between the Commune and the Republican army. The destruction resulting from these battles was greater than that caused by the Prussians' siege and onslaughts. Some of the most important public buildings went up in flames: the Palais des Tuileries, whose outer walls survived and were not torn down until 1882; the Hôtel de Ville, together with all of the municipal archives and civil registers; the Ministry of Finance on the Rue de Rivoli; the accounting office and Senate, on the site of the present-day Gare d'Orsay; the Palais-Royal; the Préfecture and Palais de Justice; the Palais de la Légion d'Honneur; and countless others. And whole stretches of streets were demolished, including portions of the Rue de Rivoli, the Rue du Bac, and the Rue Royale.

The government's revenge against the rebels was cruel. Roughly 4,000 Communards had fallen during the fighting, and once the city was reconquered, almost 20,000 were put to death and almost 9,000 were deported. Paris required about fifteen years to recover from the war and the Commune, but the reconstruction of demolished buildings continued until the turn of the century. Little new planning was accomplished during this period, although some of Haussmann's projects, such as the Avenue de l'Opéra, were completed. Domestic policies under the Third Republic were set by the provinces, often with a strong bias against Paris; until 1879, the government remained in Versailles.

The city council was now determined by open elections, and it quickly set about rebuilding the Hôtel de Ville (see pages 262–263). The Catholic church concentrated on the construction of a church of reconciliation, Sacré-Cœur, on Montmartre. The state, however, refrained from any such symbolic building, making great efforts instead to improve medical care, education, and scientific research. A great number of hospitals, schools, and institutes came into being. These were constructed in historical styles and were of uniformly mediocre architectural quality. They included the new Sorbonne; the Lycées Louis-le-Grand, St-Louis, Montaigne, and Buffon; and the Hôpitaux de la Pitié, Laënnec, and St-Antoine.

The bourgeois government turned over large building projects to industry and private interests. There sprang up, generally along the Boulevards, large department stores such as Lafayette, Samaritaine, and Printemps, banks like the Société Générale —until World War I, Paris was the most important banking center in the world—palatial offices of insurance companies, luxury hotels, and the richly decorated, tall sandstone façades of residential blocks for the upper middle class. The *beaux quartiers* had assumed their present form.

The world's fairs of 1889 (for which the

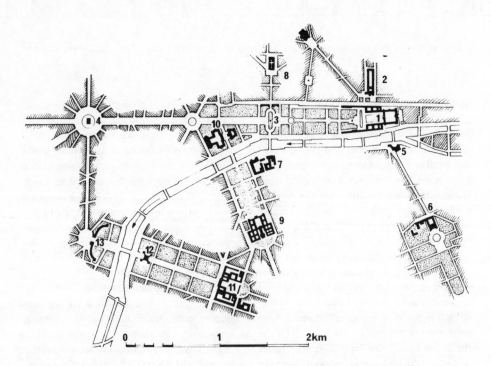

Major building projects since the Louvre as they relate to one another, the Seine, the royal axis, and its perpendicular axes:
(1) Louvre; (2) Palais-Royal; (3) Place de la Concorde; (4) Place de l'Etoile and Arc de Triomphe;
(5) Institut de France; (6) Palais du Luxembourg; (7) Palais-Bourbon; (8) Madeleine;
(9) Hôtel des Invalides; (10) Grand and Petit Palais; (11) École Militaire; (12) Tour Eiffel;
(13) Palais de Chaillot.

Tour Eiffel was built) and 1900, which sought to repeat the tremendous success of the exposition of 1855, were testaments to the liberal, capitalist world's unclouded optimism and faith in progress. To the foreigner, and even to the visitor from the provinces, Paris—with its brightly lit boulevards, its bustling cafés, cabarets, and restaurants, its luxury shops, and its elegant populace—appeared to symbolize the very best that life had to offer.

In the realm of literature and the fine arts, Paris became—thanks to Émile Zola and Victor Hugo, to Gustave Courbet, to the Impressionists, and to Auguste Rodin—the unchallenged capital of the world, casting thousands of artists under its spell. Much of the history of modern art would be made here. And from the opening of its first cinema in 1895, Paris would become a film center equaled by few cities in the world.

INDUSTRIALIZATION OF THE BANLIEUE AND STAGNATION IN THE THIRD AND FOURTH REPUBLICS

Beneath the brilliant veneer of the Belle Epoque, fundamental economic and social changes were paving the way for the Paris of today. The most important change was the relationship between the city and its surroundings. Heavy industry began to settle in the *banlieue* in the 1890s, and the landscape became dotted with metalworking concerns, automobile factories, chemical plants, paper mills, food-processing plants, and so on. France's largest industrial area grew up around Paris, one in which more than 1.2 million workers were employed by 1933. In the early twentieth century, the population of the *banlieue* grew at a rate more than seven times faster than the city's, so that in 1930, Paris's population was 2.8 million and the *banlieue*'s, 6 million. For decades, the resulting housing and traffic problems were completely ignored. Investment in profitable residential construction for the upper classes was not matched by

any commitment to housing for the less fortunate. Only in 1912 was a law passed to create the framework for a residential building policy favoring the low-income classes, but not until the 1920s was it applied—and hesitantly even then. A 1914 rent strike posed the gravest threats to the owners of ancient buildings, who were scarcely in a position to modernize their properties. In the overcrowded, decaying slums of the central city—which even Haussmann could not eradicate completely—four times as many people died of tuberculosis as in the Sixteenth Arrondissement. In 1923, seventeen housing complexes were condemned as unhealthful, but after years of proceedings only two were torn down. There was much talk of the establishment of parks, but nothing was done to create them. Paris had gained almost 1,200 acres of parkland with the incorporation of the already-existing Bois de Boulogne and Bois de Vincennes.

But it passed up the chance for a girdle of green when, in 1920, demolition of the wall and fortifications circling the city began. Except for a few athletic fields and the Cité Universitaire in the south, this land was given over to traffic and intensive building.

Development in the *banlieue*, an area shared by more than 250 municipalities, was absolutely chaotic. With no overall regional plan and little coordination among individual communities, the land became increasingly choked with factories, workshops, apartment complexes, and—most of all—the *pavillon de banlieue*. This was the simple detached house, favored by the government, that was viewed as adequate consolation for the ordinary people who had been driven out of the city. The need to commute between home and work made traffic a problem as pressing as the housing shortage.

In spite of its expanding metropolitan area, and against the wishes of the government, the city of Paris pushed through the building of a subway system that was confined within the city limits, independent of the existing railway lines, and did not even connect the major railway stations. The first line of the Métro was put into operation between Porte Maillot and Vincennes for the 1900 world's fair. It was only in 1934 that the extension of the lines to the suburbs was begun.

In the city proper, the advent of the automobile brought new problems. In order to accommodate the city's increasing automobile traffic, a ring-highway system was laid out in 1920 along the route of the razed fortification girdle. Surrounding all of Paris, these Boulevards des Maréchaux were embellished, in the old tradition of the monarchy, with monuments and squares at important entrances to the city (Porte de St-Cloud,

Porte Dorée, Porte de la Muette, and Porte Maillot, for which a competition was held).

This revival of classical traditions noticeably characterized official architecture and city planning in the 1920s and 1930s in spite of the revolutionary modernism of Le Corbusier and Robert Mallet-Stevens that was challenging urban design to move in completely new directions (see pages 269–270). The work of Auguste Perret did represent a legitimate attempt to synthesize classicism with the modern use of reinforced concrete (see pages 268–269). But more typical of this mode were the 1937 world's fair buildings. The Palais de Chaillot, whose central terrace is a pathetic attempt to provide a view of the city, and the Palais de Tokio (Musée d'Art Moderne), with its barren colonnades, offer proof of a hollow classicism.

The depression of the 1930s, World War II (including the German occupation), and the postwar troubles of the Fourth Republic halted any major city planning for Paris. The problem of integrating the city with its surroundings began to be discussed in 1928 at the insistence of Raymond Poincaré, and in 1932, the *Région parisienne* was officially created. This resulted in a general plan for improving traffic and zoning the region. The plan called for linking Paris to a network of national express highways, but only one tiny portion of it was realized before the outbreak of the war—the tunnel under the park of St. Cloud, which served the Germans as a munitions depot for four years. Economic recovery only really began after the end of the Indochina war in 1954. This upswing was responsible for the one significant city-planning project that was initiated during the Fourth Republic: the transfer of a number of fiscal and administrative offices out of the city into the area around the Place de la Défense in Puteaux, to the west of Neuilly, in an extension of the triumphal east–west axis of royal times. It was here, in 1957, that the exhibition hall of the Centre National des Industries et Techniques was begun; this building was considered to be sensationally modern. But the final planning and realization of this Parisian Manhattan was reserved for the growth optimism in the 1960s and 1970s.

While attempts to unburden the city by moving certain functions out of it were under way, Paris took on new, international roles. It became the seat of NATO, which constructed a very conventional building in the spirit of the French academic tradition at the Porte Dauphine, and of UNESCO, whose building next to the École Militaire in the heart of old Paris sought to harmonize the aesthetic and structural ideals of international functionalism with French classical surroundings (see page 270). The state itself made only a single significant contribution toward French participation in international architectural development—the headquarters of the national radio network, ORTF, in the Sixteenth Arrondissement on the bank of the Seine. It is a circular, fortress-like structure with a central tower that was originally supposed to extend even higher, and architecturally it bears no relation to its surroundings.

THE TRANSFORMATION OF THE CITY SINCE DE GAULLE

These rather cautious measures were followed by dramatic changes to the city during the Fifth Republic. Even its first major gesture was spectacular, though purely cosmetic: the state ordered the cleaning of the façades of all the buildings in the city (applying a statute that had existed since 1852). This cleaning, the first stage of which was completed in 1972, completely changed the face of the city. Even though, given the level of air pollution, such newly won brilliance could be only short lived and continual repetition of the process would be necessary, the psychological effects of this cleansing were incalculable. Suddenly Parisians and tourists alike found new pleasure in the city and its architecture, and they took a greater interest in preservation and restoration. These concerns were bolstered in 1962 with the enactment of the "Malraux statute." Before passage of this statute, only individual structures of special historical value had been restored, and only inadequately. Now, though, the focus expanded to the preservation of whole ensembles, and a series of impassive restoration campaigns got under way. In the Marais, for example, work already had begun on the removal of all but the most significant old structures between the Hôtel de Sens and St. Gervais–St. Protais, replacing them with dismal low-income housing. However, a comprehensive plan was developed to provide for extensive preservation of this historic district over the long term.

Along with these positive efforts toward restoration and renovation and toward improved living conditions for whole quarters

—though benefiting primarily the upper-income groups—there has been destruction in the name of renovation to an extent unseen in Paris since the nineteenth century. Wholesale demolition destroyed venerable lower-middle-class districts where workshops, small businesses, and modest houses with small gardens were replaced with sterile, standardized apartment houses up to thirty stories high. In the Porte d'Italie section, some 10,000 apartments housing 21,000 people were replaced with 16,000 apartments for 49,000 inhabitants. In Belleville, which was completely robbed of its character, comparable figures apply. There, an estimated 80 percent of the original inhabitants could not afford the new rents and were forced to move to the *banlieue*. Thus the trend toward gentrification of the city continues, strengthened by a development that is less obvious than such large-scale demolition but that probably has attained even larger dimensions: real-estate speculation. The typical investor will replace a modest dwelling and its garden with high-rise that offers high return of profit.

In addition to the Quartier de la Défense, other office quarters along the Seine, including the so-called Front de Seine (illus. 81, page 174), have arisen. One of Georges Pompidou's plans even proposed the transformation of the entire Right Bank between the Boulevards des Maréchaux and the Rue de Rivoli into a separate "city" reserved for stock exchanges, banks, and insurance companies—a scheme intended to make Paris into the greatest international financial capital after New York. The 1973 energy crisis and the change of presidents halted both this project and another one for an international trade center on the grounds of Les Halles, but still the transformation of

living space into office space continued, especially in the area around the Champs-Élysées and in the Sixteenth Arrondissement.

It is obvious that these changes can only have aggravated the city's traffic problem. Today's traffic may take a heavy toll on the nerves of Parisians, but it seldom actually reduces the city to utter chaos. For this, thanks are due not only to Haussmann and to the Métro but also to certain important decisions made by the Fifth Republic:

1. A newly completed limited-access freeway running parallel to the Boulevards des Maréchaux and linking up with the national highway network. This Boulevard Périphérique runs along the former defense line, so no residential quarters had to be leveled to build it. Only in the Bois de Boulogne, where at great additional expense it was run underground beneath a lake and a new stadium, were some 5,000 trees sacrificed to it; and its link to the Autoroute de l'Ouest cut a painful swath through precious parkland. Although this ten-lane thoroughfare is often overcrowded, it does keep a great deal of through traffic out of the city.

2. An expressway along the Seine on the Right Bank. Although a number of picturesque quays were sacrificed, this road was placed out of sight, beneath the remaining quays, from the Place de la Concorde to the Hôtel de Ville. It therefore scarcely disrupts the views along the Seine, and it provides considerable relief for east–west traffic. A corresponding expressway planned for the Left Bank was abandoned in 1974 on instructions from Valéry Giscard-d'Estaing.

3. A comprehensive program for the creation of underground garages beneath

a number of squares and boulevards, which has created over 40,000 parking places. The entrances to these subterranean garages are remarkably discreet, as a rule. A number of planned garages that would have endangered old trees or venerable structures were not built because of public protests—in the Place des Vosges, for example.

4. The modernization of public transport, above all the Métro, whose service was made more attractive and efficient. Some quite imaginative new stations were designed, a new depot for subway cars was created, the network was expanded, and the traveling speed increased. Bus service was also improved; for instance, bus lanes were established. Planning for the new Quartier de la Défense precipitated the creation of an additional underground rapid rail system known as the R.E.R., the first section of which connected La Défense directly with the city center and whose lines will in time lead far out into the suburbs. The intersection of its main lines is the underground station at Châtelet–Les Halles, below the former market in the heart of the city (see page 271).

5. The transfer of Les Halles also definitely helped to relieve congestion in the inner city by cutting down the amount of wholesale traffic. Whether it was necessary and sensible to destroy the Halles of Victor Baltard is another question.

6. One project that may have contributed to the improvement of traffic, but that certainly most enraged Parisians and contributed to the destruction of the city's appearance, was the new Gare Montparnasse. Here, a typical, though modest, Parisian quarter was sacrificed to traffic.

On the grounds of the old railway station, the tallest office building in Europe was built, one that obtrudes disruptively into many formerly grand vistas (illus. 82, page 175). Today such a project would hardly find approval. Understanding of the threat to the city's identity has increased since 1961, when the Montparnasse renovation was begun, and world economic problems have enforced a greater degree of modesty. The Centre Beaubourg (illus. 83, page 176), the legacy of President Pompidou, appears for all its modernity almost as a fossil from a period that had faith in boundless growth and unlimited availability of sources of energy.

At the close of his *Histoire de l'urbanisme à Paris*, Pierre Lavedan poses this question:

What do we want Paris to be? From the point of view of function? A complete city. It is impossible to do away with the discrepancy between Paris and the French wilderness by cutting off the city and developing the province. Part of the true meaning of Paris is handwork: the clothing trades, the production of luxury articles, little mechanical inventions. The mechanic, the cabinetmaker from the Faubourg St-Antoine, and the small seamstress are just as much a part of the Parisian populace and just as legitimate a part as the office worker and the company director. Their offspring, the street children of Poulbot [a Montmartre artist] have a right to the Parisian pavements—it would be better still if they were given a garden. As a cityscape? We would like to see the cityscape of Paris continue to be Parisian, that it not merely become a replica of

Moscow or New York.... Is there a specific Parisian cityscape after all? Fortunately there are a number of them: Belleville (before the development of the Hauts-de-Belleville), Montmartre, the Faubourg St-Antoine, the Marais, the Seine with its *bouquinistes'* stalls and its fishermen, the two tips of the Ile de la Cité, the Ile St-Louis, but also the Avenue de l'Opéra, the Faubourg St-Honoré, the Boul' Mich, and the gardens (Palais-Royal, Tuileries, Luxembourg, Buttes-Chaumont). And many others. What do they have in common? First, they are varied; they shun tedium—most important—which cannot be said of what is often presented to us. For they are all of a scale, made for people, in scale with people. Finally history teaches us that they were not all created at one time. Paris was not built in a day. That means that the cityscape of Paris is not without movement. Things can be added, but under the condition that they continue to be Parisian, which is to say humane and not tedious.

For the future we refuse to see Paris re-created according to any fixed formulas. Even Haussmann did not work that way. He went into the streets in order to judge each individual case. Certain such schemes have been successful most recently on the banks of the Seine that have been familiar for half a century on other shores and often enough rejected, things like zoning or concentration. In the United States it is known that it is better not to fix any zones at all than to make bad distinctions. All too often "renovation" means "making money." Under the pretext that the space is being underused, one-family dwellings with gardens are forbidden. At the same time, we know the practical and financial disadvantages of high-rises. One high-rise here and there, so be it. But forty high-rises strung along next to each other are, aside from being monotonous, not merely an accent, but a roar.

Solutions for city-planning problems cannot be expected to come from formulas or from machines. You have to consult people, especially the Parisians themselves. The use of the referendum is permitted for major political decisions, why not for what affects us most, the framework of our daily lives. A number of times, especially following competition exhibits, the Parisians have been able to give their opinion; it was never the opinion of the technocrats, who then had to back down. Whenever there have been petitions, the results have been the same. The people of Paris—men and women—should decide what Paris is to look like.

PARIS

CHURCHES, MONASTERIES, PALACES, STREETS, AND SQUARES

Thermes de Cluny*

Corner of Boulevard St-Germain and Boulevard St-Michel; entrance through the Musée de Cluny, 24 Rue du Sommerard, V^e

This bathing establishment of impressive dimensions (325 by 210 feet) was constructed around A.D. 200. Its central hall, the *frigidarium* (cold bath), with its massive cross-groined vaulting, has been preserved—the largest vaulted space from the Roman period in France. The other rooms—including the *tepidarium* (warm bath), the *caldarium* (steam room), and two long rectangular rooms for exercise and repose—survive in part as ruins and in part as foundations visible from the Boulevards St-Michel and St-Germain. The baths were excavated during the Restoration and combined with the Hôtel de Cluny, whose owners had used the vaulting of the *frigidarium* as a roof garden, to form the Musée de Cluny.

The unique support for the vaulting in the *frigidarium*—depicting prows of ships laden with weapons—is thought to indicate that these baths (a second, smaller establishment once stood on the grounds of

the present-day Collège de France) were sponsored by the fraternity of Seine shippers, already powerful in antiquity. Their votive column, the Pilier des Nautes (Boatmen's Pillar), incorporating reliefs of Roman and Gallic deities, was discovered in 1711 under the choir of Notre-Dame and then set up in the *frigidarium*. Its inscription reveals that the column dates to the reign of the emperor Tiberius (A.D. 14–37). Remains of the aqueduct that brought water to the baths from Rungis have survived in Arceuil.

Les Arènes de Lutèce

Rue des Arènes, V^e

Second only to the baths, the arena, which was built toward the end of the first century A.D., is the most important evidence of the Roman epoch still visible in Paris. It was discovered in 1869, when the Rue Monge was being laid out, and promptly partially destroyed, over the protests of scholars, to make way for the new row of buildings. Restored and completed in 1917 and 1918, the layout reveals the combination, typical

*The most important attractions in chronological sequence—from the Roman baths to the "new towns."

105

in Gaul, of arena and theater. The oval of the arena, whose rows of seats were set into the slope of the Luticius hill, was tied to a proscenium at the bottom of the hill that originally had rich architectural ornamentation.

The structure, which could accommodate over 15,000 spectators, was imposing for the relatively small settlement of Lutetia. The arena was roughly 173 by 153 feet; the proscenium, 134 feet long; the total dimensions, 425 by 325 feet.

St. Germain-des-Prés

Place de St-Germain-des-Prés, VIe (illus. 2, page 66)

This is the oldest and most important of the great abbeys that surrounded Paris in the Middle Ages. It was founded by the Merovingian king Childebert I and consecrated to St. Vincent and the Holy Cross in 558 by Germanus, the bishop of Paris. It served as the burial place of the Merovingian kings until the reign of Dagobert and was reconsecrated to Germanus (St. Germain) after his canonization in 754. The abbey owned a great deal of land on the Left Bank, and, following the Norman raids, it was rebuilt under the abbot Morard. A market village, the Bourg St-Germain, grew up around the abbey and remained outside the boundaries of Paris even after the construction of the city wall under Philippe Auguste. Only in the seventeenth century did the Bourg St-Germain abandon its own ring walls as the village expanded westward to include the aristocratic Faubourg St-Germain. In the eighth century, St. Germain-des-Prés became a Benedictine cloister directly under the authority of the pope, and it experienced its fullest flowering in the High Middle Ages: in about 1150, a new monks' choir was erected; and a hundred years later, the cloisters, refectory, and Lady

St. Germain-des-Prés: nave and vestibule (cross-section).

Chapel were rebuilt by Paris's most notable architect of the time, Pierre de Montreuil. Later, in the seventeenth century, after the Benedictine order was reformed in 1631, its monks —such as Jean Mabillon, Bernard de Montfaucon, and Michel Félibien—laid the foundations of the modern science of history. Dissolved under the Revolution, the monastery suffered the massacre of more than 300 of its members in 1792. Over the next ten years, all of its buildings except the church and the abbot's residence were destroyed.

The surviving church structure is not uniform, and the various phases of its construction are readily discernible. Its massive, buttressed western gate tower and angular stair towers survive from the time of the abbot Morard, around the year 1000. The two eastern towers between the transept and the choir may also belong to this period; the upper portions of the choir were removed during restoration in 1821. The three-tower layout resembles that of the small church of Morienval (see page 431), which was built slightly later. The nave and transept were constructed in the middle of the eleventh century. The broad central nave was altered by the addition of vaulting be-

St. Germain-des-Prés: nave, crossing, and choir (longitudinal section).

ginning in 1644 (originally the church was either flat-roofed or furnished with an open wooden gable roof) and by bright-colored plastering in the nineteenth century. Tall three-quarter columns set against the walls and broad, round-arched arcades opening onto the side aisles, likewise supported by three-quarter columns, give a rhythmic definition to the space. High, round-arched clerestory windows above wide, closed wall surfaces complete a spatial organization of great simplicity and clarity, suggesting comparison with Norman and Rhenish structures of the period.

A full hundred years after the construction of the nave, the choir was begun; it was consecrated by Pope Alexander III in 1163. Its ground plan derives from the choir of Noyon Cathedral (see pages 307–309): three bays with semicircular end wall and surrounding aisle, onto which open four rectangular chapels and, on the curve, five semicircular ones (the central one enlarged in 1819). It is only three stories high, unlike Noyon. Above the arcades, which are still largely round-arched, there is a triforium whose arches were originally pointed, and in which small columns from the Merovingian basilica were reused.

Above this comes the clerestory, whose wide windows were extended down into the region of the triforium in the eighteenth century, causing the triforia to be closed off horizontally.

Compared with St. Denis, whose design, surprisingly, had no influence on the structure of the choir, St. Germain-des-Prés appears more primitive and is still completely Romanesque in the design of its wall arrangement (blind arcades in the chapels, round columns in the central nave, and so on), in the form of its vaulting, and in the independence of the choir chapels from their connecting aisle. Recent removal of disruptive colored plaster from the nineteenth century choir aisle and chapels has made even more apparent the extraordinary quality of this structure, the most significant building in Paris prior to Notre-Dame.

The capitals of St. Germain-des-Prés are extremely important. The original capitals from the eleventh century in the nave, re-

OVERLEAF: St. Germain-des-Prés: church, cloister, refectory, Palais Abbatial, and the other monastery buildings in the seventeenth century.

placed by copies during restoration by Victor Baltard in 1848, may be seen in the Musée de Cluny. The capitals of the choir with their acanthus motifs, four of them tightly packed with fabulous animals (eagles, lions, pelicans, and others), are original.

Concurrently with these choir capitals, a stepped portal was created in the western entryway with eight jamb figures (known only from engravings). Its design influenced portal designs from the west portal of Chartres (illus. 104, page 303) through St. Denis and up to the magnificent portals of the Gothic cathedrals. Only the lintel with its depiction of the Last Supper has survived in place, and it is badly damaged. The upper story of the west tower (renovated by Baltard and fitted with a pointed roof) was built at the same time as the choir, while the broad flying buttresses were added to the choir only around 1200.

St. Martin-des-Champs

292 Rue St-Martin, IIIe (illus. 3, page 67)

This abbey was founded by Henri I in 1060 in the fields to the north of Paris and was placed under the rule of Cluny in 1079. Under the prior Hugues I (1130–1142), the cloister precinct was fortified (this work was demolished in the nineteenth century, although fragments of the walls and two defensive towers survive in the Rue du Vertbois and Rue St-Martin and the Rue de Bailly), and work on a new church began. The choir was completed under Hugues I, but the single-aisle nave dates from the thirteenth century, during which the cloisters, refectory, dormitories, and chapter house were also rebuilt.

The abbey was rebuilt again between 1702 and 1742, except for the church and the refectory. The monastery was dissolved in 1790 and has since seen various uses; it

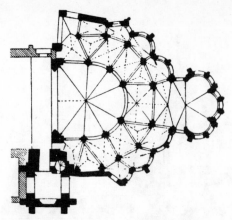

St. Martin-des-Champs: choir (ground plan).

now houses the Collège de Technologie et Industrie, for which instructional and research buildings were constructed in the late nineteenth century to replace the eighteenth-century structures. The surviving church and the refectory have been extensively restored. The former is now the Musée Nationale des Techniques (Conservatoire des Arts et Métiers; see page 482), affiliated with the school, and the latter now serves as the reading room of the college library.

The historical importance of St. Martin-des-Champs lies in the architecture of its choir, which uses, though uncertainly and experimentally, a fundamental structural concept of the Gothic style that was then being developed and that would be realized more confidently a short time later with St. Denis (see pages 282–283)—a double ambulatory around the choir with a wreath of chapels, with a spatial integration of these radial chapels and the aisle.

The irregularity of the ground plan—no bay resembles any other—is partly the result of adaptation to older structures (for example, the tower abutting the choir on the south, of which two stories survive, is a

Notre-Dame: west façade.

fragment of an earlier building). But it also expresses the architect's insecurity in the face of the new technological possibilities —such as cross-ribbed vaulting, which was first used in Paris in the high choir and the central chapel here. Moreover, this central chapel was to be in the shape of a trefoil and stand out considerably from the remaining ones—certainly an uncommon design at the time. The bays of the ambulatory still have cross-groin vaults, and the capitals, the other architectural ornaments, and the appearance of the exterior in general are still completely Romanesque. The exterior boasts an unusual, broad arcade that arches across the angles formed by the chapels, forms the base of a cornice surrounding the whole like a uniform wreath, and supports a broad, continuous roof. The high choir rises above the arcade. Even taller than the choir was the front end of the nave, which was designed in the early thirteenth century as a simple, rectangular hall and roofed over with a wooden barrel vault that was replaced in 1885.

The double-aisled refectory also dates from the early thirteenth century. Its delicate cross-ribbed vaulting is supported by slender, elegant round columns on high, polygonal bases. The large windows on its side walls—double lancet windows combined with round ones of a double quatrefoil design—are more primitive than those of the church and certainly more so than those of the Sainte-Chapelle, with whose architect, Pierre de Montreuil, the refectory was once associated. (It is more likely that its architect was someone commissioned by the Plantagenets.) The pulpit is particularly remarkable for its rich ornamentation of leaves, a motif also found on the columned portal that originally led to the cloisters. A combination of nearly Cistercian severity and extreme lightness makes this refectory one of the loveliest halls from the High Middle Ages surviving in France.

Notre-Dame

Place du Parvis-Notre-Dame, IVe (color plates, pages 38–39; illus.1, 4, and 5, pages 65, 68, and 69)

Construction of Paris's magnificent cathedral began in 1160 under Bishop Maurice de Sully. The choir was almost complete by 1177; the high altar was consecrated in 1182; the transept was roofed in 1198; and a short time later, the nave was completed and the cornerstone laid for the west façade, much of which was finished by 1225. The towers were completed in about 1245.

Notre-Dame was designed according to an ambitious, grandiose plan of great unity. Its basilica has five aisles and a transept that initially did not extend beyond the side aisles; these side aisles continue around the choir as a double ambulatory. Even before the original design was completed—its architect unknown—chapels were added between the buttresses, beginning in 1225, so that the exterior walls of the transept were recessed in relation to those of the chapels. Therefore, beginning in 1246, the transept was extended by the addition of one bay at either end, and new façades for it were built on the north and, starting in 1258, the south after plans by Jean de Chelles. The south façade was completed by Pierre de Montreuil. Construction of the choir chapels began only toward the end of the thirteenth century, and they were finally completed in 1330.

The interior (illus. 4) originally followed the four-story scheme of Early Gothic cathedrals in the Ile de France, of which Notre-Dame is the last and the largest. Above the arcade was an open gallery running around the entire structure; above this, instead of the customary triforium, was a rosette; at

26. St. Sulpice: the façade by Giovanni Niccolò Servandoni.▷

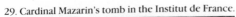

27. Hôpital de la Salpêtrière: the chapel by Libéral Bruant.

28. Collège des Quatre-Nations.

29. Cardinal Mazarin's tomb in the Institut de France.

30. Courtyard side of the Hôtel Salé: the future Picasso museum.

31. The Bureau des Marchands Drapiers in the garden of the Musée Carnavalet.

32. Place des Victoires with the equestrian statue of Louis XIV.

33. Hôtel des Invalides: view into the church of St. Louis-des-Invalides.

34. The Louvre Colonnades by Claude Perrault.

35. Expansion of the Louvre under Napoleon III, the wings by Louis Visconti and Hector Lefuel.

36. The Grande Galerie in the south wing of the Louvre.

37. The collection of antiquities in the Salle des Cariatides of the Louvre.

⊲ 38. At the edge of the Jardin des Tuileries: *Mercury Riding a Winged Horse*, by Antoine Coysevox.

39. A portion of the royal axis: the Jardin des Tuileries and the obelisk in the Place de la Concorde.

40. The great pond in the Jardin du Luxembourg.

◁ 41. The Dôme des Invalides by Jules Hardouin-Mansart.

42. View into the main courtyard of the Hôtel des Invalides.

43. Hôtel des Invalides: entrance portal by Libéral Bruant.

44. Garden side of the Hôtel de Rohan, part of the Archives Nationales.

45. Main courtyard of the Hôtel de Soubise, seat of the Archives Nationales.

46. Main courtyard of the Hôtel de Salm, the Palais de la Légion d'Honneur since 1802.

47. In the columned portico of the Panthéon.

48. Chapelle Expiatoire: the Restoration's church of atonement.

49. Rotonde de la Villette by Claude-Nicolas Ledoux.

50. Napoleon's sarcophagus in the Dôme des Invalides.

51. La Bourse: the stock exchange by Alexandre Brongniart.

52. Arc de Triomphe du Carrousel in the courtyard of the Louvre.

53. Arc de Triomphe de l'Etoile and the Champs-Élysées. ▷

54. Avenue des Champs-Élysées and the traffic of Paris.

55. Avenue des Champs-Élysées: headquarters of international firms.

56. Place Charles-de-Gaulle-Étoile and the Avenue des Champs-Élysées.

57. At the end of the royal axis: Avenue de la Grande-Armée with La Défense in the background. On the right, the tower of the Palais des Congrès at the Porte Maillot.

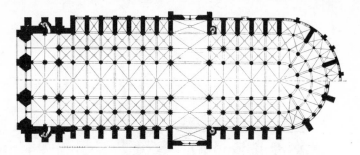

Notre-Dame (ground plan, lower half without chevet).

the highest level was a relatively small clerestory. Given the extraordinary height of the central nave, 115 feet, the amount of light admitted through these clerestory windows was clearly inadequate to illuminate the main space. As early as 1240, it was decided to enlarge them so that they would reach the tops of the gallery arches, thus doing away with the rosette and producing a three-story interior.

As a consequence of this change, the double flying buttresses on the exterior were replaced by single ones. And with the expansion of the choir chapels by the architects Pierre de Chelles and Jean Ravy, the upper part of the choir acquired the sweeping flying buttresses that distinguish the east view of the cathedral.

Extensive modernization in the choir was undertaken under Louis XIV by Robert de Côtte; the rood screen and portions of the choir rails by de Chelles and Ravy were sacrificed. In 1756, the medieval windows, except for the rose windows, were replaced with clear panes. During the Revolution, in 1793, the cathedral was transformed into a "Temple of Reason," and the sculptures in the Galerie des Rois and large sections of

◁ 58. The hill of Montmartre with Sacré-Cœur, as seen from the Arc de Triomphe.

the portals were destroyed. The building was returned to the faith in 1795. Beginning in 1845, comprehensive (and controversial) work by Eugène Viollet-le-Duc, who designed the tall flèche, gave the structure its present form and included the restoration of most of the ornamental sculpture.

The balance and compactness of the ground plan corresponds to the exterior of the cathedral (illus. 5), which appeared more blocklike before the redesign of the buttresses. With Notre-Dame, Early Gothic cathedral architecture attained perfection. And several aesthetic principles that characterized Parisian architecture through all its stylistic changes until the nineteenth century were first manifest here: a blend of mass and elegance, proportion and austerity, balance and aversion to excess—in short, a classical harmony.

Despite heavy restoration in the nineteenth century, the three west portals still provide a good idea of the thirteenth-century sculptural program. And recent cleaning has made it possible to distinguish more clearly between their original and restored components. Parts of the right-hand portal, the so-called Porte de Ste-Anne, apparently were commissioned when construction began in 1160. The tympanum portrays the Madonna accompanied by two angels and three other figures—possibly

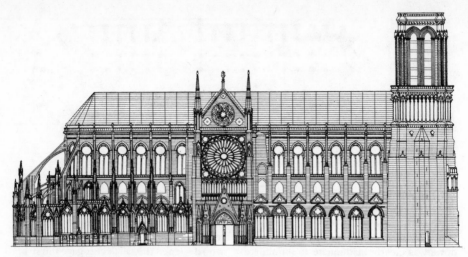

Notre-Dame: north façade.

Louis VII, Bishop Maurice de Sully, and the dean of the cathedral chapter, Barbedor, in commemoration of the royal donation for Notre-Dame. The upper band of the lintel depicts Mary's visit to the Temple, Isaiah, the Annunciation, the Visitation, the Nativity, the Annunciation to the Shepherds, Pharisees and scribes, Herod, and the Wise Men. These sculptures are closely related to early works in Chartres and St. Denis. In the thirteenth century, they were joined to the lower lintel, which illustrates the story of St. Anne and Joachim, and incorporated into a jambed portal, with a more pointed arch, whose archivolt figures are difficult to identify. The jamb figures were all replaced in the nineteenth century. Only the central one, showing Bishop Marcel of Paris, has survived; it now stands, badly damaged, in the cathedral's north tower chapel.

The central portal, which is slightly taller, is the Porte du Jugement. Christ sits enthroned between two angels who hold the instruments of the Passion. John the Baptist and Mary kneel on either side as inter-cessors. In contrast to its counterpárt, the south portal at Chartres, the accompanying figures do not surround the entire portal but are instead assigned to the six archivolts. They include two concentric rows of angels and seated figures of patriarchs and prophets, saints, martyrs, and the Wise and Foolish Virgins.

The Last Judgement is depicted in two lintels: the lower one (new; fragments of the original are in the Musée de Cluny) presents the awakening of the dead; the upper one, the segregation of the righteous from the damned (restored in the middle). Scenes of hell continue in the lower portions of the archivolts to the right. These include extremely graphic depictions of tortures, some of them taken directly from the Apocalypse. The Christ on the trumeau column was removed in 1771 during redesign of the doorway by Jacques-Germain Soufflot, and the jamb figures of the apostles were destroyed during the Revolution; thus, all the standing figures had to be re-created in the nineteenth century. Original, however

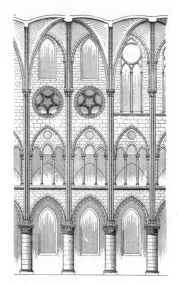

Notre-Dame: nave, with original rosette and new clerestory windows (cross-section, with gallery and buttressing).

—though carefully overhauled in the eighteenth century—are the remarkable reliefs appearing in two rows below the bases of these figures. In the upper row are allegories of the virtues; below, in medallions, are the vices.

The left-hand portal, known as the Porte de la Vierge, reveals an unusual iconography in a number of respects. The Tree of Knowledge on the base of the trumeau is related to Mary as the "Nova Eva." She is accompanied on the jambs by saints (new), whose identification is possible from the reliefs at the base (old), which illustrate typical scenes from the life of each. The tympanum depicts the coronation of Mary and, below this, an unusual scene showing both Mary's death and her exaltation by angels in the presence of apostles seated and standing around her sarcophagus. The lower lintel, with the Ark of the Covenant inside

the tabernacle and surrounded by patriarchs and Old Testament kings, points symbolically to the bodily assumption of Mary into heaven and also to Christ within Mary's womb. On the archivolts are angels and figures from the Old Testament. On the doors, flat reliefs present a complicated cosmological inventory including zodiacal signs, a calendar, the ages of man, and allegorical plants.

The comprehensive sculptural program of the façade, which includes the Galerie des Rois (completely restored; original fragments discovered in 1977, now in the Musée de Cluny) and statues of St. Stephen, Synagogue, Ecclesia, and St. Dionysius (St. Denis) in the buttress tabernacles (new), reveals influences of various sculpture workshops that hint at close connections to the cathedrals at both Laon and Chartres. Started about 1200, the last of these sculptures may have been completed in the 1220s.

The transept portals were created after 1250. Surviving from the original north façade are the trumeau, showing the Madonna, and the tympanum, the lower band of which presents scenes from the life of Mary. The two bands above this have scenes from the legend of Theophilus: Mary as the savior of the repentant sinner Theophilus, who had bound himself to the Devil.

The portal of the south transept, erected around 1260, portrays the life and martyrdom of St. Stephen and is the final link in the rich sculptural adornment of the cathedral's façades, this one doubtless already influenced by the workshops of Reims. The small portal on the third chapel to the east of the north transept, the so-called Porte Rouge, which depicts the coronation of Mary on its tympanum and the life of the canonized Bishop Marcel on its archivolts, was likely created at about the same time.

St. Julien-le-Pauvre

Rue St-Julien-le-Pauvre, V^e (illus. 1, page 65)

Since Merovingian times, a cloister and hospice have stood on this site, favorably situated near both the Seine and the old main road to Orléans, now the Rue St-Jacques. The church became a priory of the Cluniac monks of Longpont in the twelfth century and was a center of university life from the thirteenth through the sixteenth centuries.

The present church structure dates to around 1170, when the choir was begun; the whole was completed after 1250. It was restored in 1651, when the first two bays and the façade were removed. Since 1889, it has been the center for Paris's Greek Orthodox congregation. Together with the small Square René-Viviani and its pictur-

Notre-Dame: transept and north façade.

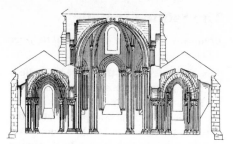

St. Julien-le-Pauvre: choir portion (cross-section).

esque false acacia trees planted by Jean Robin in 1680 and the recently restored houses in the Rue Galande and Rue St-Julien-le-Pauvre, some of them surviving from the Middle Ages, the church constitutes one of the few almost villagelike spots in which one still has a sense of medieval Paris.

The choir of the church is important because it was the first to be patterned after that of Notre-Dame, with a six-part vault, round columns supporting elegant pointed arcades, and two extremely fine capitals (the famous mythical birds on the north side). The nave, which originally possessed a triforium, was drastically altered during restoration in the seventeenth century and furnished with a barrel vault.

St. Pierre-de-Montmartre

2 Rue du Mont-Cenis, XVIIIe

This church stands on the hill known in hea-

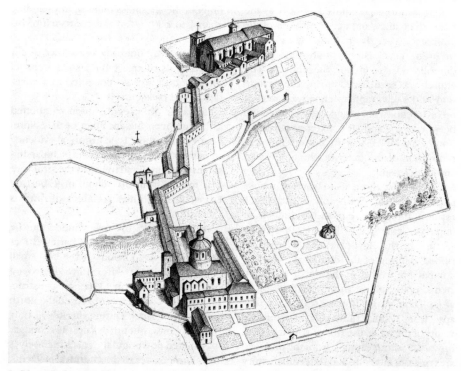

St. Pierre-de-Montmartre.

133

then times as Mons Mercore after the temple of Mercury standing on it. Nearby, according to legend, St. Dionysius (St. Denis) was martyred with his companions. In commemoration of this event, the hill was renamed Mons Martyrum, and thus Montmartre. There was a church here even in Merovingian times, columns from which have been incorporated in the present structure. A Benedictine monastery was founded here in 1134 by Louis VI le Gros (Louis the Fat) and his wife, Adelaide of Savoy, who was buried in the new church. The church was consecrated by Pope Eugenius III in 1147, when only one bay of the nave had been completed; the western ones were added a short time later. The choir apse was renovated as early as 1200.

Restoration was required as early as the fifteenth century, and major portions of the monastery were destroyed by fire in 1559. In 1686, the cloister was abandoned and demolished except for the church. The church was secularized during the Revolution, and a telegraph antenna was later set up on its choir roof to serve the connection between Paris and Lille. Extensive restoration began in 1834, with almost complete renovation of the exterior, the bell tower, and the crossing.

This modest, three-aisle structure, whose upper walls lean noticeably outward as a result of the pressure of the vaulting, is an important example of Early Gothic architecture in the Ile de France. The cross-ribbed vaulting of the choir bay, which is comparable to that in the tower hall of St. Denis, is the oldest in Paris. The capitals are still completely Romanesque. The choir apse, from 1200, is quite elegant, while the vaults of the nave, the ribs of which extend upward, without capitals, from the pilasters, are typical of fifteenth- and sixteenth-century Parisian parish churches.

The Sainte-Chapelle

Boulevard du Palais, Ier (color plate, page 223)

Next to Notre-Dame, the Sainte-Chapelle is the most important monument from medieval Paris. It owes its existence to Louis IX (St. Louis). The king was passionately devoted to relics, and in 1239, he succeeded in gaining possession of what he presumed to be Christ's Crown of Thorns by settling a debt of 135,000 pounds owed to Venetian merchants by the emperor of Byzantium, the French nobleman Baudouin. Two years later, Louis was able to buy further relics of the Passion from Byzantium—fragments of the True Cross, drops of Christ's blood, and so on. To house this wealth of devotional objects, he commissioned a freestanding chapel to be built in the courtyard of his palace on the Ile de la Cité. Consecrated in 1248, it served not only as a showcase for his precious reliquary but also as a chapel for the court; it was connected by a corridor to the palace itself.

Pierre de Montreuil is often mentioned as having been the architect of the Sainte-Chapelle, but there is no historical evidence to support this claim. Recent scholarship seems more inclined to credit the structure to a master from the school of Robert de Luzarches, the chief architect of Amiens Cathedral.

In about 1485, the rose window on the west side was renovated by Charles VIII, as were the upper portions of the two small towers flanking it. After a fire destroyed much of the palace in 1776, new construction almost completely obscured the north side of the chapel. During the Revolution, the chapel was put up for sale, the reliquary was melted down, and the relics themselves were turned over to the church at St. Denis. (Today, the Crown of Thorns and the frag-

The Sainte-Chapelle in the courtyard of the royal palace.

ment of the Cross are in the cathedral treasury of Notre-Dame.) In 1803, the Sainte-Chapelle was turned into a storeroom for archives, and the installation of bookcases damaged the lower portions of the glass windows. Restoration began in 1840 under Duban and Jean-Baptiste Antoine Lassus. The fresco paintings were restored and extended under the direction of Émile Boeswillwald, and the stained glass was painstakingly restored after drawings by Steinheil.

Today, the Sainte-Chapelle is surrounded by ugly nineteenth-century buildings of the Palais de Justice, but it originally stood apart in the palace courtyard—an exquisitely proportioned two-story structure resembling the high choir of a cathedral. Its exterior is characterized by narrow buttresses that grow slightly smaller toward the top and are crowned by finials. Between the buttresses, the tracery windows of the Chapelle Haute stretch upward for almost 50 feet, their gables extending well above the edge of the roof. The vertical thrust of the building is enhanced by the absence of flying buttresses, by the soaring flèche (restored in the nineteenth century), and by the two small towers from the end of the fifteenth century that flank the west façade. Projecting from the front of the façade is an open, two-story vestibule, above which blooms the great rose window, from around 1485, in the Flamboyant style of the period of Charles VIII. On the south side, there is a small oratory, dedicated to St. Louis, that dates from the end of the fourteenth century.

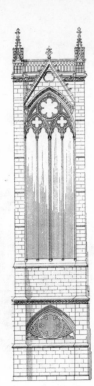

The Sainte-Chapelle (elevation of a single bay from inside and out; cross-section through the upper and lower chapels).

The Chapelle Basse served the members of the court. It is only 21 feet high and serves as the base for the Chapelle Haute, which was reserved for the royal family. The columns of the Chapelle Basse, unlike those of the Chapelle Haute, are set out into the room to keep the vaulting from being too deep. As a result, narrow side aisles are created, and graceful braces overhead connect the columns to the outside walls. The tops of the arches in these aisles are the full height of those of the broad central nave, giving the Chapelle Haute a level floor. Light falls into the Chapelle Basse through relatively small windows onto an elegant blind arcade that circles the entire space. The windows on the north side have been sealed over because of the proximity of the Palais de Justice, to which a thirteenth-century sacristy was also sacrificed. Along the long sides, unusual windows, in the shape of curved triangles, and their adjacent spandrels fill the entire space between the tops of the aisle arches and the blind arcade. The naturalistic capitals from the thirteenth century are extraordinarily varied. One's sense of space is distorted by the painting done in the nineteenth century, some of which bears little relation to the original work.

The Chapelle Haute is a single-nave hall

136

consisting of four rectangular bays and a choir. It is astonishingly tall (67 feet), delicate, and elegant—a glass house that totally dissolves into a space of pure color and light. Slender three-quarter columns support the cross-ribbed vaulting. Fifteen windows completely fill the space between the vaults and a low base of blind arcades; these windows are the oldest and most important stained glass in Paris. In 1,134 scenes, of which 720 are original, created between 1245 and 1248, the story of the Salvation is narrated. Deep, radiant colors are used, and the harmonious juxtaposition of red and blue is especially prominent. There is also a generous amount of outline drawing.

The scenes begin with the first window to the left of the entrance and end with the Apocalypse in the rose window on the west wall; they are to be followed in ascending order from bottom to top within each lancet. On the long sides are events from the Old Testament; in the choir apse, along with the central event of Christ's Passion, are the stories of John the Baptist and the Evangelists; the window to the right of the entrance details the story of the relics of the Passion. The splendor of the windows is further heightened by the polychrome painting of the chapel itself, which should be thought of as having been more radiant and less obtrusive than the nineteenth-century restoration now renders it.

Six of the highly important statues of the apostles that stand in front of the columns around the room are original (the fourth, fifth, and sixth on the left; the third, fourth, and fifth on the right); the rest have been copied from damaged originals now housed in the Musée Cluny. The reliquary rostrum in the choir is a nineteenth-century reconstruction that incorporates portions surviving from the original.

Palais de Justice

Between Boulevard du Palais, Quai de l'Horloge, Rue de Harlay, and Quai des Orfèvres, Ier

This large, interlocking structure from the eighteenth and nineteenth centuries encloses, in addition to the Sainte-Chapelle, the remains of the oldest residence of the French kings in Paris. Indeed, the western portion of the Ile de la Cité has constituted the center of power and jurisdiction since antiquity. This is where the Roman governor's palace stood—where Julian the Apostate had himself declared emperor in 360. And it was the residence of the Merovingian kings and later the counts of Paris, who became kings of France in 987. The oldest portions of the Palais de la Cité complex surviving today date from the time of St. Louis: the Sainte-Chapelle and the lower parts of the Tour Bonbec, the westernmost tower on the Quai de l'Horloge (whose crenelated upper story dates from the nineteenth century).

Extensive additions from the time of Philippe IV le Bel have been preserved in the Conciergerie (a world-famous prison): the Salle des Gens d'Armes from 1301 to 1313 and the Tour d'Argent and Tour de César. The Salle des Gardes, like the Tour de l'Horloge and the Cuisines de St-Louis, adjacent to this easternmost tower, dates from a later phase of expansion under Jean II le Bon (around 1353).

After the revolt led by Étienne Marcel in 1358, Charles V abandoned the palace as the royal residence in favor of the Hôtel St-Paul, across the Seine in the Marais. An administrator (*concierge*) remained in the palace, which was finally turned over to Parlement in 1431 by Charles VII. By 1400, the rooms on the ground floor had begun to serve as a prison.

Ile de la Cité, with the palace and Notre-Dame, in the eighteenth century (Plan Turgot).

The Première Chambre Civile, or Grande Chambre, above the Salle des Gardes was decorated in the style of the Italian Renaissance by Giovanni Giocondo of Verona in 1509. The Salle des Pas-Perdus above the Salle des Gens d'Armes was rebuilt as a double-nave hall by Salomon de Brosse after a fire in 1618. In 1776, the old royal residence burned, and the three-wing complex around the Cour du Mai (today part of the Palais de Justice) was constructed by Couture and Jacques Antoine.

During the Second Empire, the Palais de Justice was extended westward with the addition of the Vestibule Harlay and an imposing staircase, also the gallery structures along the Quai de l'Horloge around the Cour de Cassation (by Joseph-Louis Duc and Daumet, 1857–1868). Beginning a year after a fire during the Commune of 1871, the Salle des Pas-Perdus was rebuilt by Duc and Daumet. Additional expansion, especially on the Quai des Orfèvres, continued until 1914.

Even though the palace ceased to function as a royal residence, it has continued to serve as the seat of France's supreme court until the present. Parlement, the highest court of law in the monarchy, convened here until the Revolution. Indeed, this court helped to instigate the Revolution when it demanded that the Estates General convene; however, it lost many of its members to the excesses of the Revolution. The Revolutionary tribunal took over the Parlement buildings, and the prisons of the Conciergerie became waiting rooms for the guillotine. Between January 1793 and July 1794, more than 2,700 prisoners were taken from here to be executed at the Place de Grève, the Place de la Nation, or the Place de la Révolution (Place de la Concorde).

It is difficult to identify surviving portions of the old royal palace among the new buildings and reconstructions of the nineteenth century. The clock on the Tour de l'Horloge is an example. It was donated by Charles V in 1370 and was the first public timepiece in Paris. In 1585, under Henri III, it was set into a richly ornamental frame by Germain Pilon, and in the nineteenth century still another border was added. Substantial portions of the two gate towers and of the Tour Bonbec are also old. But these must be imagined as having been less squat, for originally they extended down to the level of the Seine. The Quai de l'Horloge was constructed only in 1611; therefore, the surviving rooms in the bases of these towers now lie some 23 feet below street level.

Most interesting to the art historian is the Salle des Gens d'Armes, which dates from the beginning of the fourteenth century. Originally a refectory and common room for court servants and directly connected to the Cuisines de St-Louis, this four-aisle hall, whose central row of columns had to be repeatedly strengthened, is one of the most impressive surviving examples of secular architecture from the Middle Ages. It is 225 feet long and almost 100 feet wide. The winding stair in its northeast corner, which led to the Salle des Pas-Perdus above, was originally cantilevered. The last bay on the west side, set off by a grille, connects the Salle des Gens d'Armes with the Galerie des Prisonniers and a small chapel, which evoke memories of the Revolution, and with the Salle des Gardes, a double-nave hall with cross-ribbed vaulting and richly decorated capitals from the mid-fourteenth century. The ground floor of the Cuisines de St-Louis, which was built at the same time, also has survived. Adjoining the Tour de l'Horloge on the west, this kitchen is a square room into which nine round pillars have been set. They support heavy cross-ribbed vaulting reminiscent of Cistercian structures. The four huge fireplaces in the corners are con-

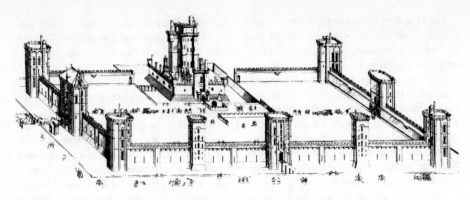

The palace of Vincennes before Louis Le Vau's reconstruction (Du Cerceau).

nected to the outer pillars by something like flying buttresses.

Of the remaining structures of the Palais de Justice, the only notable one is the quite severe façade along the Cour de Mai in the Louis XVI style. Its superb iron railing and portal by Thomas Bigonnet (1783) closes off the courtyard from the Boulevard du Palais.

Vincennes
(illus. 8, page 70)

On the site of a castle built by St. Louis in the forests east of Paris, Philippe VI began to construct a fortress with a donjon, or residential tower, in 1337. After the uprising of Étienne Marcel in 1358, Charles V chose the castle as an alternative to his city residence at the Hôtel St-Paul. He had it expanded into a fortification that resembled a whole town, to which his court could withdraw in times of stress. The donjon, with its own fortifications, was incorporated into the huge, rectangular girdle wall that boasted nine additional high towers. The plans for this fortification, the most modern in Europe at the time, were possibly prepared by Raymond Du Temple. The complex was completed in 1373. Six years later, the cornerstone for a court chapel modeled after the Sainte-Chapelle was laid, but the structure was not finished until 1552 by Philibert de l'Orme.

Marie de Médicis commissioned a modernization of the medieval layout. Beginning in 1654, Louis Le Vau constructed two elongated residential structures connected by galleries in the southern part of the fortress (the Pavillon du Roi and Pavillon de la Reine); these served as the first residence of Louis XIV after he moved from the Louvre. Napoleon set up an arsenal in the fortress and had all the towers, except the central one on the north side (the Tour du Village), reduced to the height of the walls. Louis-Philippe provided the ring wall with casemates as part of his fortification of Paris. Restoration was begun under Eugène Viollet-le-Duc and again under André Malraux, who also had Le Vau's colonnades refurbished.

Despite many changes, Vincennes is still the most impressive example of France's highly developed military architecture in the fourteenth century. It also represents a combination of fortification and residence typical of the time, although little of the original sculptural ornamentation of the king's apartment in the donjon has survived.

The chapel is a last product of the declining Flamboyant style, with a complete resolution of the solid wall into window, tracery, spandrels, and finials. Stained glass from the Renaissance has been preserved in the apse, showing scenes from the Apocalypse. The two rectangular and slightly monotonous pavilions by Le Vau and the colonnade, the center of which has been developed into a triumphal arch, are important examples of the severe style of French classicism as it developed after 1650.

St. Germain-l'Auxerrois

2 Place du Louvre, Ier (illus. 9, page 71)

Even in Merovingian times, there was a church on this site consecrated to St. Germain, bishop of Auxerre in Burgundy, who had died in 448. The church took on greater importance after it was incorporated into the city by Philippe Auguste and became the church for a parish that extended as far as Passy and Chaillot. Once the kings moved to the Louvre, it also became the parish church for the royal family, whose pew, created in 1682 by François Mercier after a design by Charles Le Brun, is preserved in the northern side aisle. St. Germain-l'Auxerrois is also the church where artists employed at the Louvre were buried—among

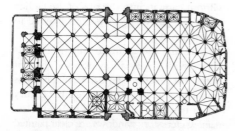

St. Germain-l'Auxerrois (ground plan).

others the architects Louis Le Vau, François d'Orbay, Jacques Lemercier, Robert de Cotte, Jacques-Ange Gabriel, and Jacques-Germaine Soufflot; the sculptors Antoine Coysevox, Nicolas Coustou, Guillaume Coustou, and Vassé; the painters Noël Coypel, Jean Restout, François Boucher, Jean Marc Nattier, and Jean-Baptiste Chardin; the engravers Isräel Silvestre and Charles Cochin; and the designer Berain. On the eve of St. Bartholomew's Day (August 24) in 1572, the bells in the tower of St. Germain-l'Auxerrois chimed the beginning of the attack on the Protestants, whose leader, Admiral Coligny, lived in the neighborhood and was the first of more than 3,000 Huguenots to be murdered that night.

Colbert proposed cutting a triumphal street between the Bastille and the Louvre, a scheme later entertained by Napoleon as well, which would have meant the demolition of this church. The project was finally abandoned under Haussmann; instead, the church was linked to the neo-Renaissance façade of the town hall of the First Arrondissement by a neo-Flamboyant bell tower.

The present church dates essentially from the fifteenth century. The lower floors of the tower between the south transept and the choir survive from a preceding Romanesque building, and the portal, the choir, and the Lady Chapel date from about 1220; but the remaining structure—the nave and side aisles—was built between 1420 and 1425. Between 1435 and 1439, the architect Jean Gaussel added a vestibule in the Burgundian fashion, a transept, and the side-aisle chapels on the north side. After 1500, the choir was given a second ambulatory and chapels. In the eighteenth century, the interior of the church was extensively modernized: Gothic stained glass was removed in 1728, as was Jean Goujon's Renaissance rood screen in 1754. During the same period, the pillars of the choir were transformed into fluted columns with garlanded capitals.

The exterior contrasts the horizontal, open vestibule—its five arcades growing wider and higher toward the center—and the towering, vertical nave, with its Late Gothic rose window and double flying buttresses whose pillars end in ornamental finials.

The interior is spacious though a trifle barren, like most fifteenth-century parish churches in Paris, with side aisles that continue around the choir. The central nave has two stories, broad windows that reach down almost to the tops of the arcades, and simple cross-vaults whose slender ribs continue down the walls as three-quarter columns without capitals. Important remnants of ornamental sculpture have survived in the Porte du Jugement, dating from 1230, and in the Lady Chapel, especially the figure of St. Germain, which came from the former central pillar of the main portal and was rediscovered in 1950. Highly original gargoyles from the fifteenth century surround the church.

St. Séverin

1 Rue des Prêtres-St-Séverin, V^e

On the site of a succession of preceding structures, this church was built about 1220 and was largely destroyed by fire at the beginning of the fifteenth century. The only portions to have survived are the tower on the northwest corner, the façade, the westernmost three bays of the nave, and the inner side aisle on the south side. The nave has simple round columns, a triforium (originally blind), and elegant pilasters. Reconstruction of the nave and the side aisles was completed by 1450; the choir, in 1495; and the chapels, by 1520. Jules Hardouin-

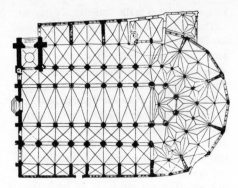

St. Séverin (ground plan).

Mansart added a communion hall in 1673 The old churchyard is on the south side, in a cloisterlike setting that consists of the galleries of the charnel houses; ten of their original twenty bays have been preserved.

St. Séverin is one of the most important examples of the Flamboyant style in Paris. The richly decorated south side, facing the cemetery, with the tracery-filled gables of the chapels, the pinnacles above the buttressing, and a wealth of gargoyles and sculptures, offers—along with the tower of St. Jacques-la-Boucherie—the best idea of the art of the very late Middle Ages in the city. The interior of the church is spacious and light; it has five aisles but no transept. Most remarkable is the vaulting of the side aisles and ambulatories, with slender, sharp-edged columns flowing upward without capitals into the ribs of the fanlike vaults that Joris-Karl Huysmans likened to a palm forest.

There are also fantastic and varied keystones with Christian symbols and plant motifs. The first three bays have stained glass from the end of the fourteenth century (taken from St. Germain-des-Prés); the remaining clerestory windows are clear painted glass from the late fifteenth century; the win-

St. Jacques-la-Boucherie: tower.

dows of the triforium are nineteenth century; those of the choir chapels are modern, created by Jean Bazaine in 1966. Fragments of a Baroque marble veneer from 1680 are in the choir. A remarkable Rococo organ from 1745 obscures the large west window from the late fifteenth century, which depicts the Tree of Jesse.

St. Nicolas-des-Champs

254 Rue St-Martin, IIIe

As early as 1184, a parish church was established for the community that had settled around the Cluniac abbey of St. Martin-des-

Champs. Its first chapel was replaced by a new structure in Late Gothic style between 1420 and 1480. The façade, bell tower, and first seven bays of the nave and inner side aisle date from this phase of building, as can be seen from the pointed arches of the arcades, the Flamboyant tracery of the west window, and the sharp outlines of the ribs that fan out without capitals from the pillars.

During a second period of building, in the second half of the sixteenth century, four additional bays were added to the nave, this time with round arches and Tuscan pillars (which were fluted during modernization in 1745) but preserving the same height in the vaulting. At the same time, the side aisles were doubled and provided with chapels. Finally, without any significant change of style, the choir and two additional bays of the nave were completed by 1615; the choir was now twice its original size and completely encircled by chapels. The result is an interior space almost 300 feet long, uninterrupted by transepts and of a uniform style despite the protracted period of construction. Unfortunately, the monumental marble high altar—incorporating two splendid 1629 paintings by Simon Vouet, *The Apostles at the Empty Tomb of Mary* and *The Assumption of Mary into Heaven*—blocks one's view into the elegant, spacious ambulatory.

The western façade reveals rich Flamboyant decoration on the portal and windows (the statues were restored in the nineteenth century). On the south side of the church, in addition to remains of the Late Gothic charnel houses, there is one of the most important Renaissance portals in Paris. It was created between 1576 and 1587, during the second phase of construction, and is quite similar to the choir portal of St. Germain-l'Auxerrois: four fluted pilasters frame two narrower entries, with niches, and a wide central one, whose round-arch arcade is filled by a priceless carved door in bas-relief dating from the first phase of construction. Documentary sources give Colo as the name of the artist who carved this masterpiece. Angels carrying palms, in the style of Germain Pilon, fill the spandrels, and a triangular gable embellished with angels playing trumpets above a richly decorated entablature completes the whole. This portal strongly resembles Philibert de l'Orme's design for a "Porte Corinthienne" for the Hôtel de Tournelles that was published in his *Architecture françoise*.

In the first bay stands an organ built between 1587 and 1613 and enlarged in 1633 and at several times in the eighteenth century. It is one of the most important Baroque organs in Paris. The side chapels boast a wealth of paintings from the sixteenth to eighteenth centuries, many of which show Flemish influences.

St. Leu–St. Gilles

92 Rue St-Denis, Ier

Squeezed between the narrow Rue St-Denis and the Boulevard de Sébastopol, the church of St. Leu–St. Gilles (after St. Loup, bishop of Sens, and St. Gilles-Aegidius, the hermit from Provence) is of interest less for its unimposing exterior than for its picturesque interior.

Only portions of the portal of the first church, built in about 1235, have survived on the Rue St-Denis. That structure had become too small, and beginning in 1319, it was replaced by a single-nave structure with six bays, to which transepts were added in the sixteenth century, followed by a choir with ambulatory and *chevet* (altar end of a French cathedral) in 1611. For the order of the Knights of the Holy Sepulcher, whose

chapel on the Rue St-Denis had been torn down, the architect Charles de Wailly created a remarkably classical crypt beneath the elevated choir in 1780. It was necessary to dismantle the choir chapels when the Boulevard de Sébastopol was laid out. The apse was closed off in 1860 with a simple neo-Renaissance structure by Victor Baltard, which conforms to the row of buildings lining the new boulevard.

The interior presents a contrast between the low nave, whose strengthened pillars accentuate the separate bays, and the tall choir, in an arid, belated Gothic. In the second chapel to the left, there is a marble statue of St. Anne with Mary, created by Jean Bullant for the palace at Écouen in 1510.

St. Médard

141 Rue Mouffetard, V^e

St. Médard counts among the "village churches" of Paris that lie somewhat off the beaten path and comprise a mixture of the Flamboyant style, Renaissance elements, and eighteenth-century modernization that is typical of many of the city's churches. It stands at the end of one of the most popular old streets of Paris, the Rue Mouffetard (illus. 67, page 166), which has retained much of its almost-provincial charm in spite of the fact that it has seen quite an influx of tourists in recent years. (In the Middle Ages, this street was the main thoroughfare of the rural Faubourg St-Marcel.) The present church was begun in about the mid-fifteenth century to replace a Romanesque structure on the site. To the completed nave and façade, a choir was added after 1560, and the whole structure was redesigned in the Greek style by Petit-Radel in 1773. At this time, the pillars were turned into fluted Doric columns, and the Lady Chapel was attached. After 1661, St. Médard became, along with St. Jacques-du-Haut-Pas, one of the shelter parishes of the Jansenist sect. In 1727, the tomb of the deacon Pâris, in St. Médard's cemetery, became the scene of ecstatic healings and was a shrine that attracted hordes of believers until Louis XV ordered an end to these pilgrimages in 1732.

Hôtel de Sens

1 Rue du Figuier, IVᵉ (illus. 7, page 70)

Aside from the tower of the Hôtel de Bourgogne (Tour de Jean-sans-Peur, 20 Rue Étienne-Marcel), only two of the countless medieval town houses of the great noble families, bishops, and abbots of France have survived. These are the mansions that belonged to the archbishops of Sens—to whose metropolitan see the diocese of Paris belonged until 1622—and to the abbots of the powerful Burgundian monastery of Cluny.

The palace that Archbishop Tristan Salazar commissioned for himself between 1475 and 1507 on the edge of the Marais, near the royal residence at the Hôtel St-Paul, serves as a fine example of the basic conservatism of Parisian architecture in the waning Middle Ages. It is a structure with five wings and an irregular ground plan. The exterior is almost fortresslike, with high walls and round, projecting corner towers near the entrance, whose portal has lost its tympanum. A massive stair tower in the inner courtyard commands the entire ensemble; the full impression was distorted by extensive and misleading restoration in the nineteenth century. The west wing, with its irregular window arrangement and its orientation toward the restored Renaissance garden, exhibits features reminiscent of the somewhat more modern Loire châteaux that

were being built at the same time. Almost none of the original interiors have survived. Today, the mansion houses the Bibliothèque Forney.

Hôtel de Cluny

24 Rue du Sommerard, Vᵉ (illus. 10, page 72)

Opposite the Hôtel de Sens is the city residence of the abbots of Cluny, which was constructed for Jacques d'Amboise, bishop of Clermont and abbot of Jumièges, between 1485 and 1510. It has a regular layout with three wings; its courtyard is closed off from the street by a crenelated wall. In spite of its Flamboyant decoration, it somehow appears more modern than the Hôtel de Sens. A double cornice surrounding the building separates the two stories, serving as part of a regular grid of horizontal and vertical lines that enlivens the façades with a balanced rhythm. The polygonal stair tower projecting into the courtyard is embellished with the shell of St. James, the patron saint of its builder. The roof, with a surrounding balustrade completely given over to tracery and richly decorated roof crests, softens the severity of the façade. The west façade is open on the ground floor as a pointed-arch arcade.

Inside, only the chapel has survived in its original form. Its apse projects beyond the blank wall of the structure as an oriel completely given over to glass. A single, sharp-edged pillar supports the palmlike network of vaulting, the fields of which are thickly set with fish-bladder ornamentation. In niches around the walls there are statues of members of the Amboise family beneath quintessentially Gothic baldachins. A similarly ornamental grille in the corner of the chapel leads to a winding stair to the ground floor of the palace.

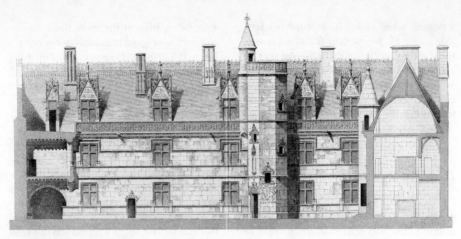

Hôtel de Cluny: courtyard side.

The *frigidarium* of the Roman baths (see page 105) directly abuts the *hôtel*; at one time its massive vaults supported a roof garden. The Musée Cluny, which has been set up in the Hôtel de Cluny, offers the best idea available today of the spiritual and secular culture of medieval Paris (see pages 476–477).

St. Gervais–St. Protais

Place St-Gervais, IVe (illus. 11 and 23, pages 72 and 78)

Standing behind the Hôtel de Ville, the church of St. Gervais–St. Protais shows how church architecture in Paris held to Late Gothic forms even into the sixteenth century. It was built on a slight elevation, on the site of an older church that stood between 1212 and 1420, of which portions remain in the tower on the north side. St. Gervais–St. Protais is one of the oldest parishes in Paris, one especially favored by the merchants of the Right Bank—above all, its wealthy wine dealers. Begun in 1494 after a plan that was possibly the work of Martin Chambiges, it was completed in the early

seventeenth century under Louis XIII. The Lady Chapel behind the choir was begun in 1517 and consecrated in 1540; the transept was completed in 1578; the nave was finished between 1600 and 1620. In 1616, the cornerstone of the façade was laid; the design of the façade was executed by Clément Métezeau the Younger, probably after plans by Salomon de Brosse.

The interior, with nave and side aisles, is quite vertical in proportion, in a Late Gothic style with high arcades, above which the tall clerestory windows rest on a slender cornice. The pillars continue upward without capitals into the ribs of the star-shaped vaulting. There is a wealth of stained glass, painting, and sculpture, as well as a carved set of choir stalls from the sixteenth century and a beautiful stone retable, depicting the death of Mary, in the third chapel on the left.

The façade (illus. 23) placed on this Late Gothic structure marks the beginning of

OPPOSITE: *St. Gervais–St. Protais: Salomon de Brosse's façade (Mariette).*

147

classicism in French church architecture. With its three stories—one Doric, one Ionic, and one Corinthian—it rightly counts as one of the most famous early-seventeenth-century works in Paris.

Around the church is one of Paris's most charming surviving old quarters, one that has recently been restored magnificently. On the north side is a severe, elongated structure from 1733, an important example of Parisian apartment-house architecture in the eighteenth century. Behind it are the remains of the old church cemetery with its galleries, chapels, and charnel houses. The buildings behind the choir, some of them from the Middle Ages, are dwarfed by the tall choir apse with its chapels and massive, wide buttresses, which extend almost to the edge of the roof as decorative, freestanding walls (illus. 11).

St. Gervais–St. Protais is one of the centers for church music in Paris. This tradition was founded by the Couperin family, which provided the church's organists from the seventeenth until the early nineteenth century.

St. Merri

78 Rue St-Martin, IVe (illus. 12, page 72)

Even more strongly tied to its old surroundings than other Parisian parish churches is St. Merri (or Merry, named for Medericus, the abbot of St. Martin in Autun). It is a typical example of the preference for the Late Gothic tradition by the wealthy Parisian bourgeoisie as late as the sixteenth century; the choir of the church, with its circular ambulatory, was still inspired by Notre-Dame. The nave was completed around 1520; the transept and façade, in 1526; the choir, in 1558. In 1743, a chapel of the sacrament was added by Germain Boffrand, and modernization of the choir

by the sculptor Michel-Ange Slodtz began in 1752. At that time, some of the stained-glass windows from the sixteenth century were removed; a planned renovation of the façade was abandoned for lack of funds. The Revolution destroyed all the statues of the portal, which were replaced by newly designed ones in 1842.

The façade is in the purest Flamboyant style, with tracery facing on the walls, pinnacles, and spandrels. Its rich, leafy frieze is comparable to the decoration of the nearby tower (fig., page 127) of the church of St. Jacques-la-Boucherie (constructed from 1519 to 1523 by Jean de Felin and razed after 1797).

The interior of St. Merri has a nave and side aisles, transept, ambulatory, and *chevet*. The nave is two stories high, with well-balanced proportions (91 feet high and 229 feet long), a leafy frieze set with figures above the arcades, and some complicated vaulting and extravagant keystones.

In the nave, transept, and choir, there are a number of remarkable tracery windows with Renaissance painted glass. The chapels contain several important paintings from the sixteenth through the eighteenth centuries. The marble facing in the choir and the altars in the transept are by Slodtz, whose brother, Paul-Ambroise, designed the palm-supported pulpit.

St. Eustache

Rue du Jour, Ier (illus. 13 and 14, pages 73–74)

This church offers the most impressive testimony to the persistence of medieval ideas in Renaissance Paris. It was begun in 1532 with a gift from François I and stands on the site of an older church that had mainly served the dealers at Les Halles. St. Eustache rivals Notre-Dame in its ground plan and its dimensions. It comprises five aisles, with a circular ambulatory and chapels, transept, and very tall inner aisles that have their own windows above the lower, outer ones. The church is 346 feet long, and its nave is 111 feet high. Despite its round arches and Renaissance details, St. Eustache is still completely Gothic in its light, vertical structure (illus. 13). The pillars reveal a totally unorthodox combination of motifs from antiquity and ornamentation from the northern Italian Renaissance, which here makes its first appearance in Paris. The network of vaulting, with pendant keystones, is uncommonly extravagant. In spite of the long time it took to complete the structure—the choir was completed in 1630, the nave in 1637, the façades of the transept in 1640—the original plan, whose architect is unknown, was strictly adhered to. The façade of 1754 (illus. 14), which was never completed, was designed by Jean Hardouin-Mansart-de-Jouy, who planned to incorporate it into a large new square on the pattern of the Place St-Sulpice.

This free and imaginative combination of medieval construction and Renaissance idiom led architecture critics of the nineteenth century, especially Eugène Viollet-le-Duc, to scorn the structure. But more recent scholars have come to recognize it as a transition experiment unique in France,

St. Eustache: façade of Jean Hardouin-Mansart de Jouy.

one that stands in refreshing contrast to the academic austerity of many of the French classical churches thanks to its wealth of spatial contrasts, its irrational light effects, and its decorative inventiveness.

As the parish church of a residential quarter inhabited not only by the merchants of Les Halles but also, being close to the Louvre, by the nobility, St. Eustache was richly endowed with sculptures and paintings. It was also the burial place for a number of famous people from Jean de La Fontaine and Jean-Philippe Rameau to Colbert, the prime minister to Louis XIV, for whom Charles Le Brun designed a monument in the seventh chapel along the north side. Executed by Antoine Coysevox and Jean-Baptiste Tuby, this tomb is one of the most significant works of seventeenth-century French sculpture. Since the nineteenth century, St. Eustache has served as a center for music: Berlioz premiered his *Te Deum* here in 1855, and in 1860, Liszt heard the

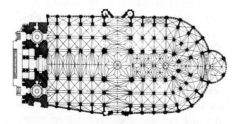

St. Eustache (ground plan).

first performance of his mammoth *Mass*.

St. Étienne-du-Mont

Place Ste-Geneviève, V (illus. 15, page 74)*

The history of St. Étienne-du-Mont is closely tied to that of the abbey of Ste. Geneviève. That foundation was established by Clovis and his wife, Clotilde, in the sixth century and came to house the tomb of Ste. Geneviève, the patroness of Paris who died around 500. From its hillside, it dominated the Left Bank for centuries. To the north of it, construction of a parish church to serve the local farmers and vintners began in 1222, and the patronage of St. Étienne was transferred there from the cathedral on the Ile de la Cité (which was demolished to make room for Notre-Dame). This church was then replaced, beginning in 1492, by the present one. By that time, the congregation had grown much larger, owing to the development of the University. The new structure ranks with St. Eustache as one of the most remarkable churches constructed during the transition between the Late Gothic period and the Renaissance. The choir, ambulatory, rood screen, and tower were completed in about 1540; the side aisles, by 1568; and the nave and transept, by 1585. In 1605, construction began on the "Charniers," a cloisterlike gallery with three wings that ran around the cemetery behind the choir. In 1610, the cornerstone of the façade was laid by Marguerite de Valois, and the façade was completed in 1622. In 1737, it was decided to remove the rood screen (as in most Parisian churches), but protests by the congregation prevented its destruction. In 1793, the sculptures of the façade were removed, and the neighboring monastery church of Ste. Geneviève was razed to make way for the Rue Clovis in 1802. Victor Baltard began restoration of the church in 1861. Blaise Pascal and Jean Racine are buried here.

The interior, whose ground plan was still influenced by that of Notre-Dame, gives the impression of an uncommonly wide and light basilica; the side aisles rise to nearly the height of the nave, so that the slender, round pillars stand freely in the central space. In the nave and choir, they are connected halfway up by an unusual gallery that is interrupted only by the transept and from which tapestries with scenes from the life of St. Stephen (after designs by Laurent de La Hire) once hung. The rood screen stretches in a broad arch between the first pair of choir pillars, with an elegant balustrade and angels in the spandrels that were executed by a follower of Jean Goujon. The design for this screen, which is enhanced by winding staircases around the pillars and portals to the side aisles, has traditionally been ascribed to Philibert de l'Orme, the architect of the château of Anet and the first Palais des Tuileries. The side portals, however, were added by Pierre Biard only in 1605. There is an immense web vault in the crossing, with a keystone that hangs down almost 18 feet. Painted glass from the sixteenth and seventeenth centuries has survived in the nave, choir, and galleries.

The façade of St. Étienne-du-Mont, constructed at almost the same time as that of St. Gervais–St. Protais, was designed by Claude Guérin. It combines the Gothic motif of the pointed gable with the rounded pediment characteristic of the Renaissance and a nearly Baroque portico above the entry. The statues and reliefs were created in the nineteenth century, but the rest of the architectural ornamentation is original and demonstrates by its elegance and freshness the extremely high quality that has distinguished Parisian architectural sculpture since the early Renaissance.

The Louvre

Place du Louvre, Ier (color plate, pages 40–41; illus. 18, 34–37, pages 75, 116–117)

The present-day Louvre, which houses one of the world's greatest museums (see pages 483–489), as well as France's Ministry of Finance and the Musée des Arts Décoratifs (see pages 474–475), appears at first glance to be mainly a gigantic assortment of nineteenth-century buildings. The extraordinarily complex history of this former royal residence is largely obscured in the existing structure and can be retraced only with the aid of old ground plans and reconstruction drawings. The origins of the Louvre, whose name is generally thought—by no means with certainty—to derive from the word *louveterie* (kennel for dogs kept for wolf hunting), go back to the Merovingian period.

Before setting off for the Third Crusade in 1190, Philippe Auguste commanded that a fortress be built here to protect his new city wall and to control access to Paris from the west and from across the Seine. The result was a nearly rectangular walled keep with semicircular corner towers and a round, 105-foot-high donjon in the center. The fortress was encircled by a moat and guarded by elaborate gate houses. The west side and the side facing the river were built twice as thick as the rest; and between the easternmost tower and the Tour de Nesle on the Left Bank, the final bastion in the wall circling the south of the city, it was possible to stretch chains across the Seine to stop the flow of river traffic.

The donjon soon came to be called the Tour de Paris, although in fact it stood outside the boundaries of the city. It became a symbol of royal might to both the vassals of the surrounding countryside and the citizens of Paris. It did not serve as the king's residence (this was still the palace on the Ile de la Cité), but it housed the royal

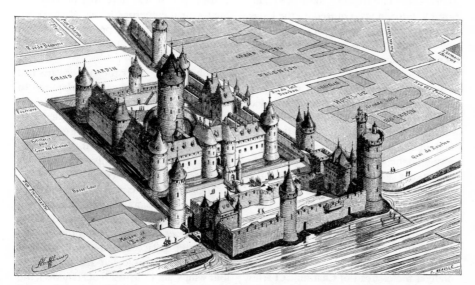

The Louvre in the Middle Ages.

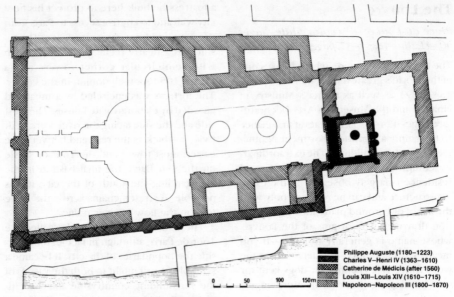

Philippe Auguste (1180–1223)
Charles V–Henri IV (1363–1610)
Catherine de Médicis (after 1560)
Louis XIII–Louis XIV (1610–1715)
Napoleon–Napoleon III (1800–1870)

0   50   100   150 m

The growth of the Louvre in its most important phases.

archives, the state treasury, the armory, and movable furnishings required by the kings in their continual tours about the country.

With the expansion of the city's boundaries under Charles V, the fortress lost its strategic significance. The king then commissioned Raymond Du Temple to convert it into a livable castle. Du Temple expanded the east and north wings of the old fortress until they nearly connected with the freestanding donjon, and he created large entryways on the west and south. It is possible to view this late medieval castle, bristling with battlements and pointed towers, in the background of a retable from the grand hall of the Parlement de Paris, which is now in the Louvre. It is also depicted on one of the pages of months in the *Très Riches Heures du Duc de Berri*, which is now in the Musée Condé at the château of Chantilly. Charles V had his famous library installed in the new Louvre, and it was here that he received the German emperor Charles IV. However, the kings still generally preferred to stay at the Hôtel St-Paul or at the Hôtel de Tournelles in the Marais.

Only in 1527, after the city of Paris had provided most of the ransom required to free François I after the Battle of Pavia, did that king resolve to move his residence to the Louvre. He had the structure restored and the old donjon demolished. Then shortly before his death, he commissioned plans for a completely new palace.

These new plans were completed by Pierre Lescot, canon of Notre-Dame, Seigneur de Clagny, and superintendent of the royal palaces. Assisting him in the decoration of the palace was the sculptor Jean Goujon. Lescot projected a vast layout of four wings; after the death of François I, the scope of the design was reduced by his successor, Henri II. A rectangular *corps de logis* was built in place of the old west wing (illus. 18). It was flanked on the Seine side by a corner tower, the Pavillon du Roi, which contained the king's apartments. Beginning in 1550, Goujon created a ceremonial hall (Salle des Cariatides) that filled the entire width of the *corps de logis* and included a musicians' gallery. A throne room (Salle du Tribunal) was fashioned next to it in 1556 to 1558.

Following the death of Henri II in 1559, a second *corps de logis* was begun along the Seine to the south. Following the same design as the west wing, this was to serve as the residence of the queen, Catherine de Médicis, who continued with its construction for her sons François II and Charles IX until the beginning of the civil and religious wars of the late sixteenth century.

Meanwhile, in 1564, Catherine had commissioned Philibert de l'Orme to build a palace for her retirement some 550 yards west of the Louvre on the site of an earlier tileworks (*tuilerie*). This land had been purchased by François I, who had intended to build a palace there for his mother, Adelaide of Savoy, and connect it to the Louvre by means of an enlarged quay along the Seine. But it was Catherine under whom construction of a link between the two palaces began. This first step was a new wing, the Petite Galerie, leading from the Pavillon du Roi toward the Seine, presumably after plans by Lescot. Then in 1595, under Henri IV, a rectangular pavilion, the Salle des Ambassadeurs (rebuilt by Louis Le Vau in the seventeenth century and now the Salon Carré), and a two-story structure, the Grande Galerie, were begun along the Seine. The eastern portion of the Grande Galerie followed plans by Louis Métezeau. Its western end, which reached the corner pavilion of the Palais des Tuileries, the Pavillon de

Flore, was completed only after 1600 by Jacques Androuet Du Cerceau the Younger. In 1595, Henri IV also commanded that work on the south wing of the Louvre be resumed.

In 1608, the king had the gallery's ground floor turned into shops, studios, and lodgings for sculptors, craftsmen, and painters (functions it served until 1806, under Napoleon); the upper story was furnished as a connection between the Louvre and the Tuileries. After the assassination of Henri IV, the only king to die in the Louvre, his widow, Marie de Médicis, continued to develop the interiors of the gallery. But after her son Louis XIII became betrothed to Anne of Austria in 1612, she, like Catherine, commissioned the construction of a new palace for her retirement—the Palais du Luxembourg (see pages 181–184). It was Louis XIII who then set out to enlarge the Louvre, which meanwhile had become too cramped. Beginning in 1624, the remaining Gothic wings from the time of Charles V, on

The Cour Carrée of the Louvre: Jacques Lemercier's Pavillon de l'Horloge.

153

the north and east, were razed. After plans by Jacques Lemercier, a tall pavilion was built on the north end of Lescot's structure, followed by a precise replica of that wing. Finally, as a counterpart to the Pavillon du Roi, there was built a final pavilion, the Pavillon de Beauvais. Lemercier, meanwhile, was also busy constructing the mansion for the chancellor, Cardinal Richelieu, north of the Louvre (see page 250). A further *corps de logis* was built to the east, off the Pavillon de Beauvais, forming a northern counterpart to the south wing and identical to it in height. In 1630, the Salle des Cariatides, which had had only a beamed ceiling, was fitted with arched vaulting.

After the death of Lemercier in 1654, Le Vau began to direct palace construction. Following a fire in the Petite Galerie, Le Vau widened that structure toward the west in 1661—the new western façade can be seen today from the Cour du Sphinx—by adding the Galerie des Rois (Galerie d'Apollon) on the upper floor. Charles Le Brun took charge of the decorations.

Lemercier's plan had called for expanding the existing U-shaped layout to produce a closed square, with an east wing with a central pavilion to correspond to the Pavillon d'Horloge on the west side. Le Vau retained this idea. First he extended the north wing by constructing a central pavilion and a replica of the existing *corps de logis*. Then he turned to the south wing, which was particularly important to him because he was simultaneously building the Collège des Quatre-Nations directly across the Seine (see pages 196–198) and had designed that new complex to complement the Louvre. Therefore, for the south wing, he suggested accenting the central pavilion more strongly by means of columns tying the first and second floors together, statues, triangular pediments, and a high cupola. Another

pavilion, corresponding to the Pavillon du Roi, would complete the wing on the east. In spite of widespread criticism, this project was carried out by Louis XIV. The king also approved the construction of the east wing, which would close off the Cour Carrée, and would be especially important because its façade would face the city.

In 1663, Le Vau began to tear down old buildings to create room for the new east wing, and the foundations were begun in 1664. Then Colbert intervened and brought construction to a halt. A public competition was announced for the design of the new wing, and it was won not by an architect but by the physician Claude Perrault, brother of the writer of fairy tales Charles Perrault. Since it was feared that French architects would be offended, it was decided to hold another competition, this time an international one, for which the Italians Pietro da Cortona, Francesco Borromini, Rinaldi, and Laudiani submitted designs. Louis XIV even invited the papal architect, Gian Lorenzo Bernini, to Paris in order to discuss the project. A battle of principle ensued: whether France should adopt the High Baroque style of Rome or develop a national, classical style of its own. In the end, Colbert succeeded in pushing Perrault's design past a building commission to which both Le Vau and Le Brun belonged. At the wish of Louis XIV, the design was enlarged so that the east wing would be taller than the existing portions of the palace. By 1670, the façade was completed: the famous Louvre Colonnades (illus. 34). Because of the extra height of the wing, another story had to be added on the courtyard side as well, one that simply repeated the arrangement of the ground floor. The new façade extended some 40 feet beyond the façade of the south wing. Therefore, a series of rooms was added in front of Le Vau's façade, and

The Louvre: the Cour Carrée in the eighteenth century (Plan Turgot).

a new façade—a somewhat reduced version of the Colonnades—was designed by Perrault.

Colbert had found it difficult to obtain Louis XIV's approval of building projects in Paris from the start. Then, in 1678, the king moved to Versailles, once and for all, leaving the new buildings unfinished and without roofs. Various academies moved into the royal apartments, artists and nobles settled in other vacated spaces, and dwellings were even improvised in the Cour Carrée. Only under Louis XV was it finally possible for the Marquis de Marigny, brother of Mme. de Pompadour and superintendent of the royal buildings, to see that the Colonnades were restored, beginning in 1775, and completed. He also managed to have the last of the old structures cleared from the square in front of the east façade.

There were attempts to turn the Grande Galerie into a museum as early as 1783, but it was the National Convention that decreed in 1793 that it become a "Musée Central des Arts" to house the collections from the various royal palaces except Versailles. Napoleon urged this transformation forward through his architects Charles Percier and Pierre Fontaine: all but the west wing of the Cour Carrée were provided with a third story (to which even Lescot's mezzanine in the south wing had to be sacrificed); a double staircase was installed behind the Colonnades; and the high roofs were removed from the pavilions (except the Pavillon de l'Horloge) in favor of flat roofs and triangular pediments. The emperor, who himself resided in the Palais des Tuileries, again took up the old scheme of a complete tie between the two palaces. He had a second gallery begun on the north side, along the Rue de Rivoli, whose inner façade copied Du Cerceau's Grande Galerie. Percier and Fontaine also redesigned the interior of the Grande Galerie as a single long corridor rhythmically punctuated by arches resting on double columns (illus. 36). The still-open north side of the two-palace layout was completely closed under Napoleon III. The architect Louis Visconti constructed two symmetrical groups of buildings to the west of the main block of the Louvre, each arranged around three courtyards. These linked up with the gallery begun by Napoleon along the Rue de Rivoli and masked the irregularity in the ground plan where the Louvre and the Tuileries joined. The decoration of these new structures was carried out after Visconti's death in 1853 by Hector Lefuel in a virtually Baroque and highly florid manner. This architect also had the Pavillon de Flore, on the south end of the Palais des Tuileries, torn down along with the adjacent portion of the Grande Galerie by Du Cerceau, only to rebuild them in a form consistent with the new structures.

The Palais des Tuileries was torched by the Commune, and the fire damaged the corner pavilions as well as the beginning of each of the structures leading to the Louvre. Also destroyed was the Louvre library in the northern part of Visconti's new structure, a space that has been occupied by the Ministry of Finance since 1873. The walls of the gutted Palais des Tuileries were finally razed beginning in 1882, so that the Louvre opened out onto the Jardin des Tuileries and the axis leading to the Place de la Concorde and the Arc de Triomphe in the Place de l'Etoile.

Jardin des Tuileries

(color plate, page 42; illus. 38 and 39, pages 118 and 119)

Beginning in 1649, even before developing the plan for Vaux-le-Vicomte (see pages 387–391), which would make him famous, André Le Nôtre worked on redesigning the Jardin des Tuileries. (In 1637, he had taken over from his father the post of gardener of the Tuileries.) His revision of this Renaissance garden triggered one of the crucial city-planning developments in Paris—the evolution of the great east–west axis that was finally exposed when the Palais des Tuileries was razed. This axis has contin-

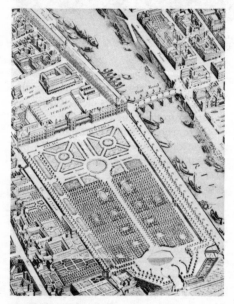

The Jardin des Tuileries and the Seine (Plan Turgot).

André Le Nôtre's double ramp at the end of the Jardin des Tuileries, with a view of the Champs-Élysées.

ued to play an essential role even in recent years, as in the planning of the skyscraper cluster at La Défense (see pages 273–275).

Le Nôtre placed a terrace in front of the Palais des Tuileries, from which a series of broad steps led down to a first level of planting. The focus of this level was a round basin with fountains; smaller pools were centered in squares on either side. A broad *allée* led westward from the central pavilion of the palace, and this served as the axis of the whole design. It cut across the first level, expanding into a circular walk around the main basin, then continued between plantings of trees to a second, octagonal basin and on to the garden's western gate. Nor did it end there: Le Nôtre charted it across the open fields of the Champs-Élysées as the Avenue des Tuileries clear up to the present-day Place de L'Etoile on the heights of Chaillot. Le Nôtre's plan provided for its extension as far west as St. Germain-en-Laye.

Within the gardens themselves, there is an elevated terrace that runs parallel to this central axis on either side of it. The terrace on the north side is a riding path; the one on the south is a tree-lined walk above the quay along the Seine. At the end of the garden these terraces turn toward each other and the central axis, from which semicircular ramps lead to them.

The completion of the park required several decades. Clearings for games and theatrical performances were laid out amid the plantings of trees. The first statues, of the four seasons, were placed around the octagonal basin in 1680, and in the early eighteenth century, a number of other sculptures were moved here from Marly, a château that had begun to fall into decay: the river gods by Corneille van Cleve and Guillaume Coustou and, in 1719, the equestrian statue of Mercury (illus, 38) and the goddess of fame by Antoine Coysevox. The sculpture of the horse-tamer by Coustou from Marly was placed at the entrance to the Champs-

Élysées in 1798. But most of the sculptures in the gardens date from the nineteenth century, when two buildings were constructed at the ends of the terraces: the Orangerie in 1853, and the Jeu de Paume in 1862 (the latter now houses the Impressionist collection of the Louvre; see pages 483–489). After the demolition of the ruins of the Palais des Tuileries in 1882, the gardens were extended between the wings of the Louvre. Here, at the urging of André Malraux, sculptures by Aristide Maillol were placed in the 1960s.

Hôtel Carnavalet

23 Rue de Sévigné, III (illus. 16 and 31, pages 75 and 115)*

In 1548, Jacques de Ligneris, the presiding justice of the Parlement de Paris, built himself a mansion on a plot that he had purchased from the congregation of the church of Ste. Catherine. It was a rectangular dwelling flanked by pavilions. A short time later, he constructed in front of it a gatehouse with a three-bay portal and two two-story pavilions on either side. The pavilions were connected to the main structure by means of one-story galleries that opened in great arcades onto the resulting courtyard. Above the gate was a story set back somewhat and connecting the two pavilions of the entryway. In the venerable French fashion, each separate structure had its own tall, gabled roof.

Yet the architectural idiom was extremely novel. The ground plan was severely symmetrical; there were pilasters in the galleries, dormers with balustrades in the gables, rusticated stonework on the gatehouse, and,

Hôtel Carnavalet: façade of the portal structure after François Mansart's remodeling (Mariette).

above all, a rich yet discreet use of ornamental bas-reliefs. The four bays of the residential wing, for example, are embellished on the second story with allegorical figures of the four seasons, each with a sign of the zodiac above it. Above the entrance to the stairwell on the left side are protective spirits with torches; the relief across from it is a nineteenth-century copy. On the gatehouse are allegories of abundance and authority above trophies and *putti* that support a coat of arms.

The design for this first private Renaissance *hôtel* has been attributed, without proof, to Pierre Lescot, who was the architect of the Louvre at the same time. The sculptural decoration must be assumed to be from a follower, if not the studios, of Jean Goujon. The mansion changed hands a number of times; one owner was the widow of the Breton nobleman François de Kernevenoch (or Kernevenoy), and the name of the house is a corruption of that name. In 1651, it came into the possession of the theatrical manager Claude Boislire, who commissioned François Mansart to make extensive changes. Although this work went on until 1661, the integrity of the existing structures was respected as much as possible. The gatehouse and galleries were provided with a noble, classical second story with pilasters and triangular pediments. Along the courtyard sides of the wings, reliefs of Flora, Diana, Hebe, Juno, and the four winds were added by Gerard van Obstal in imitation of the sculptural decoration of the main façade (illus. 16).

Mme. de Sévigné leased the house from 1677 until her death in 1696, and it was here that she wrote her witty observations of life in the court of Louis XIV and in Paris. It has belonged to the city of Paris since 1866; additional wings were built on the site of the former garden, and the *hôtel* is now the Musée Carnavalet (Musée Historique de la Ville de Paris; see pages 475–476). Three architectural fragments from now-vanished Parisian buildings were incorporated into the new wings: the Arc de Nazareth (illus. 31), an arched doorway from the sixteenth-century Palais de Justice that faced the Rue des Francs-Bourgeois and boasts sculptural ornamentation by a member of the circle around Goujon; the façade of the Bureau des Marchands Drapiers (fabric dealers) from 1660, whose sculptures have been restored; and the central pavilion of the Hôtel des Marêts (or de Choiseul) from 1710. The statue of Louis XIV by Antoine Coysevox, from the former Hôtel de Ville, has been set up in the old main courtyard; this is the only statue of the king in Paris that survived the Revolution.

Fontaine des Innocents

Square des Innocents, Ier (illus. 17, page 75)

In the middle of a small square marking the spot where the church of the Innocents and its cemetery stood until 1786 (fig., pages 36–37), there now rises above a high, stepped base one of the most important remnants from the early Renaissance in Paris. Today it is a square structure with a flat cupola, but it was originally an open sort of loggia that Henri II commissioned Pierre Lescot to build in 1547 on the corner of the Rue St-Denis and the Rue aux Fers. Completed in 1549, the fountain had three sides; the fourth backed onto a wall of one of the church buildings. It stood on a high foundation and consisted of double pilasters and semicircular arcades, above which were a frieze and low, triangular pediments. One arcade opened onto the Rue St-Denis and two onto the Rue aux Fers; their balustrades provided spots from which notables could watch the ceremonial en-

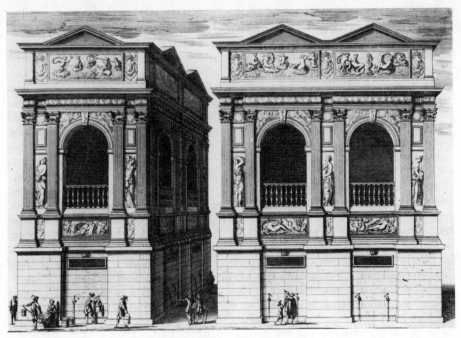

Fontaine des Innocents: original appearance (Mariette).

trances of the king into the city via the Rue St-Denis. At the base of each arcade were two spigots, from which the people of the Les Halles quarter could draw their water. Jean Goujon provided the sculptures for the structure: between the pilasters were elegant Naiads with water jars; on the frieze and in reliefs below the balustrades (the latter are now in the Louvre), the gods of the sea rode on sea monsters and shells.

After the church was razed, the art critic Quatremère de Quincy salvaged the fountain, and it was moved to the center of the former churchyard, which had become a marketplace. It was given the form of a square temple; its fourth side was created by Augustin Pajou, and the three missing Naiads were designed by Jean-Antoine Houdon, in imitation of Goujon. In 1865,

Gabriel Davioud replaced the vertical base with the present cascade arrangement, putting a cupola on top of the structure and a basin fountain inside it.

Hôtel Lamoignon

24 Rue Pavée, IVe

This *hôtel* was constructed as a city mansion for Diane de France, the legitimized daughter of Henri II and the Duchesse d'Angoulême. The design is attributed to Baptiste Du Cerceau, the son of Jacques Androuet Du Cerceau the Elder, who had planned the châteaux of Verneuil and Charleval. Planned in about 1585, the building

59. Fountaine St-Michel in the Place St-Michel. ▷

160

A LA MÉMOIRE
ES SOLDATS DES FORCES   AISES
L'INTÉRIEUR ET DES FRANC   EURS
APARTISANS.ELEMENTS O   E
TROUVÈRENT LA MORT

60. The church of St. Vincent-de-Paul by Jean Baptiste Lepère and Jacob Hittorf.

61. Hôtel de Ville: seat of the mayor of Paris.

62. Passage Véro-Dodat: charm of a vanished elegance. ▷

63. Galerie Vivienne.

64. Passage du Grand-Cerf.

65. A bistro in Montmartre.

66. Montmartre: a stairway off the Rue Foyatier. ▷

67. Delivering *baguettes* in the Rue Mouffetard.

68. "Le ventre de Paris": Les Halles before they were demolished.

69. The Bourse de Commerce at the edge of the former Halles.

70. Pont Alexandre III: showpiece of the Belle Epoque. ▷

72. Parisian Art Nouveau: an apartment house by Hector Guimard at 142 Avenue de Versailles.

73. Entrance to the residence at 29 Avenue Rapp, by Jules Lavirotte.

74. Entrance to the house at 142 Avenue de Versailles, by Hector Guimard.

75. Entrance to the Castel Béranger, 14 Rue La Fontaine, by Hector Guimard.

76. Métro station at the Place Dauphine.

77. Hector Guimard's own   78. Hôtel Mezzara, 60 Rue La Fontaine.
    house in the Avenue Mozart.

79. Cubist houses in the Rue Mallet-Stevens.

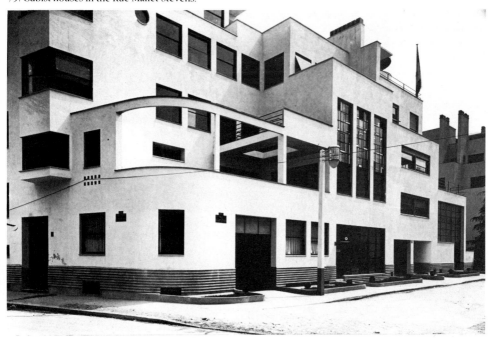

80. An Art Déco department store: the Samaritaine, next to the Pont Neuf.

81. The Front de Seine: new apartment and office center in the Fifteenth Arrondissement.

82. Tour Montparnasse: the tallest office tower in Europe. ▷

83. Centre Beaubourg: a magnet for 8 million visitors a year.

may not have been constructed until 1611. It was the first private Parisian mansion with pilasters in the Colossal order. The entablature is interrupted by inset dormers. There is a low, triangular pediment above the central axis, which is otherwise unstressed. The flanking projecting structures boast rounded pediments that are richly adorned with sculpture. Beginning in 1620, two additional wings were attached by Jean Thiriot for Charles de Valois, Duc d'Angoulême (one was removed in 1834); they had interesting, small projecting towers. Guillaume de Lamoignon, president of Parlement, bought it in 1658, and his son had a gatehouse built in 1708. The mansion has had a garden and other additions built on. Since 1969, it has housed the Bibliothèque Historique de la Ville de Paris. In the reading room, there are painted beams (showing Diana and the hunt) that date back to the time of construction.

St. Germain-des-Prés: Palais Abbatial

1 Rue de L'Abbaye, VIe

Aside from remnants of the Chapelle de Notre-Dame, on the Place Laurent-Prache, the only structure surviving from the extensive monastery buildings of St. Germain-des-Prés is the Palais Abbatial, erected in 1586 by Cardinal Charles de Bourbon, the uncle of Henri IV and the heir apparent appointed by the Catholic League. It was constructed with the picturesque combination of light-colored hewn stone and red brick, crowned with steep slate roofs, that would remain typical through the time of Henri IV (fig., pages 108–109).

The residential wing comprises nine bays and is set off by a taller corner pavilion with richly sculptured triangular pediments. Typical of the period is the interruption of the

cornice by dormers that appear to have slipped down along the roof area. The extraordinarily vertical proportions give the structure a monumental dignity, which is heightened further by the formal courtyard in front of it. Belonging to the recently restored palace is the complex of stables around the Place de Fürstemberg. These have been considerably altered and now serve as residences. In No. 6 is the former studio of Eugène Delacroix, now a museum (see page 477).

Hôpital St-Louis

40 Rue Bichat, X^e

This was the first hospital constructed after the medieval Hôtel-Dieu, which was next to Notre-Dame. The Hôpital St-Louis was primarily intended to accommodate and isolate victims of the plague; almost 70,000 people had died in a plague epidemic in 1562, and there were new outbreaks in 1605 and 1606.

Henri IV laid the cornerstone in 1607 outside the city, before the Porte du Temple. The hospital's original, very rational layout has survived as a core in spite of nineteenth- and twentieth-century additions and alterations. Four wings, each nearly 400 feet long, surround a square courtyard. These wings, which were reserved for patients, are only a single story on top of a high foundation floor, which takes the place of a cellar in this marshy spot. Taller pavilions mark the four corners and the center of the court. At a distance of 130 feet from this core structure were four two-story buildings, one at each corner, which housed the nursing staff and housekeeping personnel. The entire complex was surrounded by a ring of gardens, which in turn was encircled by a wall. The outside world could be reached only through the gatehouses and the chapel, which straddled the wall so that the local farmers could attend services. The symmetry of the design and the use of hewn stone and red brickwork with steep, tiled roofs call to mind the squares created under Henri IV at about the same time.

Place des Vosges

Under Henri IV a series of systematic and rational city-planning endeavors were undertaken; these would make Paris the model for many European cities from the early seventeenth century on. After the king resumed work on the Louvre, he had an architectural commission plan a uniform square on the site of the former Hôtel de Tournelles, which had not been lived in since the accidental death there of Henri II in 1559 and had been turned into a horse market. Among the architects involved were Louis Métezeau, Jacques Androuet Du Cerceau the Younger, and Claude Chastillon.

The original plans provided for the establishment of a royal silk factory on the north

Place des Vosges (Plan Turgot).

side of the square. The other three sides were to be lined with uniform private mansions. Beginning in June 1605, lots were sold to interested members of the nobility. The buyers agreed to quite rigid restrictions that not only ensured the construction of uniform façades but also forbade any later alterations.

The idea of placing a factory on the square was abandoned in 1608, and the north side was also parceled out for mansions. As early as 1612, the square was officially opened with a carrousel, or tournament, on the occasion of the double wedding of Louis XIII to Anne of Austria and of his sister Elisabeth to the future Philip IV of Spain.

The square was completely closed, and each of its sides measured 350 feet. Around it stood thirty-eight identical pavilions with two-story façades above open arcades. The façades were joined to produce picturesque walls of rhythmic uniformity, enlivened by the contrast between the light-colored stone and stucco that imitated brickwork. The centers of the north and south sides were accented by taller pavilions, one intended for the king and one for the queen but never in fact used by them. The square was accessible to the surrounding streets only by means of passageways beneath the two royal pavilions and the two houses on the northwest and northeast corners, which were torn down when the Rue des Francs-Bourgeois was cut through in 1822. It was both a place for spectacles and a park for its noble residents; it was the center of aristocratic social life in the seventeenth century.

In 1639, Richelieu set up an equestrian statue of Louis XIII in the center of the square, then known as the Place Royale. During the Revolution, the statue was destroyed and the square was renamed in honor of the first *département* to pay its taxes to the new government. The marble statue that

Place des Vosges in the late seventeenth century (Perelle).

now adorns the square dates from the nineteenth century, as does the design of the gardens, which recently have been reduced in size in the course of a restoration of the square and a number of its buildings.

The layout of this square was quite revolutionary in the scheme of French city planning and was immediately imitated in Charleville. These unpretentious residences, which introduced French doors with balcony railings in the *bel-étage* (main story of a building)—a leitmotif of French domes-

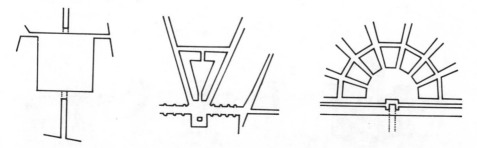

Schemes of the squares of Henri IV: Place des Vosges; Place Dauphine; Place de France.

179

tic architecture—would become a model for later private buildings, especially in the Marais.

Place Dauphine

Three major city-planning projects occupied the reign of Henri IV: the Place Royale; the Place de France (never realized), which was intended to be a ceremonial entrance into the city in the north, in the vicinity of the Temple, and the nexus for a new system of radial and transverse streets; and the Place Dauphine. This last complex has been more drastically altered than has the Place des Vosges, but it is still recognizable in its basic details. In 1578, Henri III laid the cornerstone for a bridge that would cut across the western tip of the Ile de la Cité and connect the Left and Right banks. Henri IV carried this project forward, and the Pont Neuf was completed by 1607, its two arms extending across twelve broad round arches (illus. 6, page 70). This was the first bridge in Paris without buildings on it; instead, there was a sidewalk for pedestrians and semicircular turrets that served as vendors' stalls. For the first time Parisians now had an opportunity to admire the new Louvre from the middle of the river. Henri IV also connected the new bridge to the Faubourg St-Germain on the Left Bank by several new streets. He had hoped that the Rue Dauphine, the new main thoroughfare leading to the Porte de Buci, would be built up as uniformly as the Place Royale, but this never happened. However, he did sell to Harlay, the president of Parlement, a site on the Ile de la Cité that had been a royal garden and was adjacent to the Pont Neuf on the west and the palace on the east. With the sale went the condition that construction on the site follow a precise, symmetrical plan.

Uniform rows of buildings were begun around this triangular square in 1607. Their façades were made of hewn stone and red brick, and they had two stories above a ground-floor row of arcades for shops. A continuous tile roof connected them, with tall dormers at regular intervals. The square could be reached by a central axis that cut through the row of buildings on the east and led to a square platform between the two arms of the bridge. Marie de Médicis, widow of Henri IV, placed a monument to her husband on this platform, the first statue to stand in an open square in Paris. Giovanni da Bologna, in Florence, received the commission to design it in 1604, but it was completed in Paris by Francesco Bordoni in 1618. In 1792, it was destroyed, then replaced by a copy in 1818 (fig., page 58).

Pont Neuf with the Samaritaine pump in the eighteenth century.

Front of the Place Dauphine, facing the Pont Neuf (Perelle).

The buildings surrounding the square were purchased mainly by merchants, bankers, and goldsmiths, who very soon enlarged and altered them, for the restrictions on building were not rigid as those that governed the Place des Vosges. The row of buildings along the east side of the square was razed in 1874 in order to open up the view of Joseph-Louis Duc's new façade for the Palais de Justice.

Palais du Luxembourg

15 Rue de Vaugirard, VIᵉ (illus. 19, 21, and 40, pages 76 and 119)

Shortly after Henri IV was assassinated in 1610, Marie de Médicis began buying up properties along the Chemin de Vaugirard, near a Carthusian monastery on the Left Bank, where she intended to build a widow's palace. In 1611, she dispatched Louis Métezeau to Florence to prepare a plan based on that of her family's residence, the Palazzo Pitti. The actual commission for the design of the palace went to Salomon de Brosse, who was then at work on the façade for St. Gervais–St. Protais. It was to be a mansion of regal dimensions, and it was the first palace in Paris to be surrounded by an extensive park.

Work began on the palace in 1615, and Marie de Médicis moved into it in 1625, although much was still unfinished. It was finally completed in 1631, and in that very year the queen was forced to leave Paris; she died alone in exile in Cologne in 1642. Her palace remained in the possession of the royal family, however, and in 1750, a public painting gallery—the first in France —was opened in its left wing. (Since 1818,

181

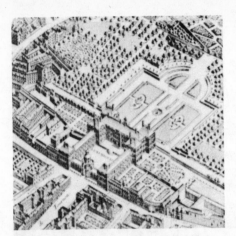

Palais du Luxembourg with its courtyard.

the painting gallery has shown only the very newest work; in 1885, it was moved to the Petit Luxembourg, an early-eighteenth-century mansion designed by Germain Boffrand to replace an earlier one that had belonged to Comte François de Luxembourg. This older *hôtel* gave its name to the entire complex once it was taken over by Marie de Médicis. Today, the Petit Luxembourg serves as the residence of the president of the Senate.)

After the Revolution, extensive alterations were undertaken by Jean-François Chalgrin to adapt the palace for the newly created Senate, which began to meet here in 1804. The structure was then enlarged between 1836 and 1841 by Alphonse de Gisors, who built a new central section with side pavilions facing the garden, strictly imitating the original style. Supplementary buildings have been built across the Rue de Vaugirard very recently, and they have been designed to conform to the style of French classicism.

In structure, the Palais du Luxembourg is not an Italian *palazzo*, despite similarities to Bartolommeo Ammanati's Palazzo Pitti, particularly in features such as the use of rustication and the highly sculptural modeling of columns and walls. Rather, it is an Ile de France château of the kind created by Jacques Androuet Du Cerceau the Elder at Verneuil and by de Brosse himself at Coulommiers. A long, narrow *corps de logis* is framed by large corner pavilions at either end. Two long wings connect these corner pavilions with the main structure to form a great forecourt, which is closed off from the street by a low wing with arcades that were originally blind. The center of this latter wing is marked by a separate pavilionlike structure of three stories: a gateway on the ground floor, a square salon above it, and a circular room beneath the crowning cupola (illus. 19). Narrower corner pavilions link this building with the side wings, which were designed to accommodate in their upper story long galleries with paintings glorifying Henri IV and Marie de Médicis. An ambitious cycle of works was painted for the right wing by Peter Paul Rubens between 1622 and 1625; these are now in the Louvre. A staircase by Chalgrin takes the place of the original gallery.

A blend of severe monumentality and diversity—the individual structural elements are distinct from one another yet not isolated—makes the Palais du Luxembourg the first masterpiece from a century that produced a rich array of palaces. Horizontal lines are maintained throughout in entablatures and cornices, broken only where the court façade joins with its frieze and in the corner pavilions with their fully developed third stories.

Despite changes to the roof lines, the view from the street and from the forecourt is essentially the same today as it was originally. Only the court directly in front of the *corps de logis* has been altered; it formerly was a raised marble terrace that extended

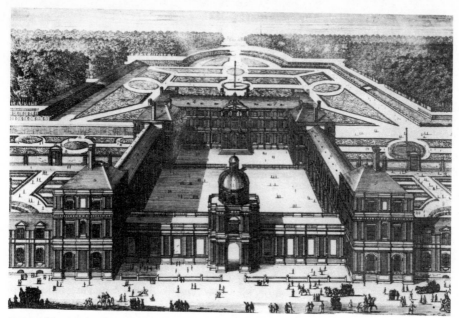

Palais du Luxembourg and Jardin de Luxembourg (Perelle).

as far as the corner pavilions, and a semicircular stair led up to it at the center. The garden side, however, is wholly a product of the nineteenth century, though a precise copy of the original façade by de Brosse. Originally, the façade of the upper floors of the *corps de logis* stood somewhat back from the ground-floor arcades, creating a terrace at the level of the *bel-étage*. The projecting central structure once housed a chapel for the queen, who established immediately adjacent to the palace a convent with its own chapel for the order of the Daughters of Calvary. Remnants of this chapel still stand at 19 Rue de Vaugirard.

The interiors were completely altered to suit the requirements of the Senate. Remains of the original ornamentation may be seen in the Salle du Livre d'Or. Notable among the nineteenth-century alterations is the reading room of the library in the south wing, with frescoes by Eugène Delacroix.

In its essentials, the park goes back to plans made by Boyceau in 1612, although it was considerably enlarged by Chalgrin toward the end of the eighteenth century. Demolition of the Carthusian monastery following the Revolution permitted expansion of the grounds to the southwest. In the nineteenth century, a city-planning scheme linked the palace with the Observatoire by the broad Avenue de l'Observatoire.

The broad expanse of well-tended gardens was originally set on the edge of the city and bordered on open countryside. Now it is the most important recreation area for the thickly settled Left Bank, providing a meeting place for students, housewives, maids, and grandmothers watching their grandchildren at play. The park is full of ornamental sculpture, including a series of statues of queens of France and another of famous nineteenth-century women. All that survives from the original stonework is the Nymphaeum of the Fontaine Médicis to the east of the palace (illus. 21), and even its statues date from the nineteenth century.

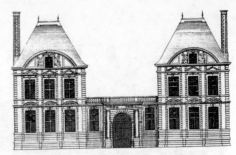

Hôtel de Sully: façade of the wings and portal (Marot).

Hôtel de Sully

62 Rue St-Antoine, IVᵉ (illus. 22, page 77)

Restoration of the Hôtel de Sully began in 1956, sparking the renovation of the entire Marais quarter that is still going on. The mansion was originally built for the inspector of finance Mesme Gallet, Sieur du Petit-Thouars. It was begun in 1624, presumably after plans by Jean Androuet Du Cerceau, and completed in 1630 by Roland de Neufbourg. It represents the most richly ornamented and most stylistically uniform private mansion from the time of Louis XIII in Paris. In 1634, it was bought by the Duc de Sully, one-time minister to Henri IV. His heirs added a garden wing that conformed to the existing architecture. The building is not large; it consists merely of a U-shaped structure around a forecourt, a *corps de logis* between the forecourt and garden, and a one-story gatehouse between corner pavilions with large curved gables. The portal itself is flanked by Doric columns.

The courtyard gives the appearance of being quite closed, since the side wings (the right one provided with arcades and serving as a coach house) are the same height as the main structure and are ornamented in the same way: rounded gables above the rusticated windows of the ground floor; tri-

angular gables with shells above the window lintels of the *bel-étage*, which are graced with draperies and female heads; and recessed dormers supported by volutes. The central bay of each wing is flanked in the *bel-étage* by niches containing relief sculptures. On the main structure, these represent autumn and winter; on the wings, reading from left to right, they symbolize the four elements: air, fire, earth, and water; allegories of spring and summer are found on the garden side. The whole decorative scheme is a later reminder of that of the Hôtel Carnavalet.

At the end of the garden is an elongated garden pavilion, the Petit Sully, which dates from 1628. Its ground floor, whose arcades were once open, served as an orangery, behind which was a long salon with a fireplace. Housekeeping rooms were in the upper story. The decoration of its façade corresponds to that of the main house.

The mansion is now the headquarters of the French preservation agency, Caisse des Monuments Historiques, which presents exhibits on French architectural history in the main building. A richly ornamented double staircase and painted beamed ceilings have survived in their original state.

The original concept provided for a structure of brick and hewn stone, in the traditional Henri IV style. A nearby structure that was actually built in this style has survived, although it was later altered and is in poor condition—the Hôtel de Mayenne, at 21 Rue St-Antoine. This *hôtel*, built between 1613 and 1617 by an Androuet Du Cerceau (possibly Jean) for Henri de Lorraine, Duc de Mayenne, was one of the first Parisian mansions to stand between forecourt and garden and to have side wings, corner pavilions, and a low gatehouse (this one was made higher at a later date).

Hôtel Tubeuf

8 Rue des Petits-Champs, IIe

Built by the architect Le Muet in 1635, this was one of the last Parisian mansions to use the combination of brick and hewn stone, possibly at the wish of the man who commissioned it, Duret de Chevry. By 1641, the building was in the possession of the inspector of finance Jacques Tubeuf, and Cardinal Mazarin began to live here in 1643. The cardinal commissioned François Mansart to build a two-story gallery into the garden in 1645.

The *hôtel* has a U-shaped layout and was originally closed off from the street by a simple wall with a portal. The building is two stories high with tall window bays (altered on the ground floor in the eighteenth century). The façade consists of alternating rusticated window frames and narrow strips of brick wall. The central ornamentation is slightly stressed by the addition of garlands of flowers and a rounded pediment similar to that of the Palais du Luxembourg.

The Galerie Mansart in the Rue Vivienne matches the Hôtel Tubeuf in its alternation of hewn stone and brick. Its interior still contains remnants of the decorations by Italian artists that were commissioned by Mazarin—most notably the ceiling frescoes by Giovanni Romanelli, a pupil of Pietro da Cortona, in the upper story (Galerie Mazarine). These can now be reached through the Bibliothèque Nationale.

Beginning in 1719, the Galerie Nueve was added for the Scottish banker John Law. This was then reworked in 1731, along with portions of the former Hôtel de Nevers, to form an elegant courtyard (*cour d'honneur*) with a uniform Louis XV façade after plans by Robert de Cotte. Today, this serves as the entry court for the Bibliothèque Nationale, at 58 Rue de Richelieu, which the mansion was expanded to house in the nineteenth century. A reading room by Henri Labrouste was opened in 1868—one of the most important early uses of structural iron.

St. Paul–St. Louis

99 Rue St-Antoine, IVe (illus. 20, page 76)

Next to the modest church of St. Joseph-des-Carmes (1613), St. Paul–St. Louis was the first church in Paris to renounce the medieval tradition and be patterned solely after contemporary Italian examples. The Jesuit order, which originated with the pledge taken by St. Ignatius and his friends at the foot of Montmartre, had had a branch in the Rue St-Antoine since 1580, which it was forced to abandon because of political entanglements under Henri IV. Under Louis XIII, however, the order's influence revived significantly, due especially to the support of Cardinal Richelieu.

As an expression of their newly won power, the Jesuits constructed this church (at first called St. Louis), for which Louis XIII himself laid the cornerstone in 1627. The plans were drawn by the Jesuit father Étienne Martellange, who kept close to the model of the mother church of the order, Il Gesù in Rome, not only in the plan of the interior but also in the façade. Father François Derrand, who had submitted a competing design in 1627, took control of the construction in 1629. He built the choir, the vaulting, and the crossing tower, which was the first in a long tradition of large cupola structures in Paris. The façade was begun in 1634, and the church was consecrated by Richelieu in 1641. The interior was embellished by Father Charles Turmel beginning in 1644.

Placed in the heart of the aristocratic Marais quarter, St. Louis came to attract the very best society, primarily because of its preachers; Marc-Antoine Charpentier and Jean-Philippe Rameau counted among its music directors. After the Revolution, St. Louis took over the role of parish church (and changed its name) because the church of St. Paul-des-Champs had been demolished, and the Jesuits' vocational house became the Lycée Charlemagne.

The façade of this church is effectively oriented to the Rue St-Antoine. Its three-story elevation resembles that of the nearby church of St. Gervais–St. Protais, whose façade had been designed by Salomon de Brosse almost twenty years before. But in contrast to the classical severity of St. Gervais–St. Protais, St. Paul–St. Louis is imbued with a Baroque sense of movement, intensified toward the center and upward, and covered with sculptural ornament of almost Flemish exuberance. The fragmented pediment contains the coat of arms of the alliance of France and Navarre. The coat of arms of Cardinal Richelieu originally graced the rounded pediment above the portal; it was the cardinal who largely financed the construction of the façade. The original central motif of Christ's monogram was replaced by the Baroque clock rescued from the ru-

ined church of St. Paul-des-Champs. The remaining sides of the church contrast sharply with the façade; above their simplicity and mass, the octagonal drum of the cupola rises. The interior follows the example of Il Gesù —a wide, barrel-vaulted nave rhythmically articulated by alternating tall Corinthian pilasters and round-arch arcades, above which a low gallery runs. Above the entablature and a deeply projecting cornice, the large openings of the clerestory windows cut deeply into the main vault. The transept projects only slightly beyond the nave, and it is dominated by the cupola, nearly 180 feet above the crossing. The resulting spandrels are decorated with reliefs of the four Evangelists. A semicircular apse with a choir bay completes the building. Along the long sides of the choir there are small side chapels, each with its own small dome, which are connected to each other and to the transept. Originally the church was richly furnished with altars and tomb monuments—including caskets for the hearts of Louis XIII and Louis XIV—but only a few paintings remain. In 1802, however, one of the major works by Germain Pilon, *Mary as Mater Dolorosa* (1586), was transferred here from the abbey church of St. Denis; it now hangs in the left-hand choir chapel.

Ste. Ursule-de-la-Sorbonne

Place de la Sorbonne, V^e

Richelieu became the director of the Collège de Sorbonne, where he himself had studied, in 1622. A short time later, he was named a cardinal, and he became prime minister in 1624. In 1626, he commissioned his architect, Jacques Lemercier, to plan a new building and chapel for this institution, which had been founded about 1254 by Robert de Sorbon, the court chaplain to Louis IX. The school provided theological training for secular priests, and in the late Middle Ages it became the seat of the theological faculty of the University of Paris. It was also here that France's first printing press was established in 1470 by Michael Freiburger, Ulrich Gernig, and Martin Krantz, from Colmar and Constance.

Lemercier designed a U-shaped structure around a courtyard, the fourth, southern side of which was to be closed by the chapel. The archbishop of Rouen, François du Harlay, laid the cornerstone for the academic building in 1626, and in 1635, when work on the chapel began, Cardinal Richelieu specified it as his burial place. The basic structure was completed by the time the cardinal died in 1642, and his executrix, the Duchesse d'Aiguillon, charged the painter Charles Le Brun to complete the interior (Lemercier had died as well). But not until 1694 was Richelieu's tomb, created by François Girardon, installed in the church choir. During the Revolution, the church was profaned and robbed of its sculptural ornamentation, and only on the initiative of the Duc de Richelieu was it restored to the faith under Louis XVIII. Meanwhile, the artists who had been evicted from the Louvre had settled into the college buildings. Starting in 1821, the central administration of the university was moved here, so that the name Sorbonne eventually became synonymous with the University of Paris.

Lemercier's U-shaped building was replaced, beginning in 1885, by a much larger and unattractive new structure, with paintings by Puvis de Chavanne in its large lecture hall, and the sculptural decorations of the chapel were restored. It is virtually unfurnished. Richelieu's tomb has been moved into the south transept, and religious services are held here only twice a year: on October 21, the feast day of St. Ursula,

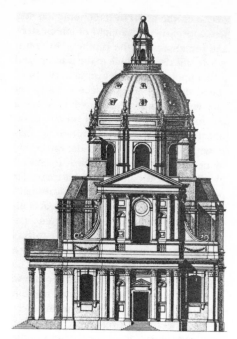

Ste. Ursule-de-la-Sorbonne: west façade and cupola.

and on December 4, the anniversary of Richelieu's death.

The chapel designed by Lemercier is the first completely Roman-influenced structure from the seventeenth century in Paris. Lemercier had been in Rome from 1607 to 1614 and there had become familiar with the façade of Il Gesù and with later sixteenth-century variations on it. He had also studied Roman solutions to the problems of integrating a central structure with a nave and of balancing cupola and façade to create a unified impression.

Although inspired by Roman models, Lemercier nonetheless created something highly original and utterly French—a structure that would be a great influence in the further development of church architecture in Paris. The church's central axis is accentuated on the north by a monumental portico approached by a flight of fifteen steps and reminiscent of the Pantheon in Rome. Above this rises the bulk of the transept and a tall cupola with an elegant lantern atop a round drum. There is a second façade at the western end of the nave, this one a measured, elegant variation on the traditional Roman two-story elevation: its narrower upper story is tied to the lower one by descending volutes; its bays are set off by pilasters and columns; and a triangular pediment, originally framing the cardinal's coat of arms, crowns the whole. To accompany the circular drum of the cupola, Lemercier devised four round stair towers that project above the bulk of the structure and also further set off the façades. The rhythmic balance and proportion of these structural masses, a precise differentiation between three-dimensional forms and mere reliefs, a wealth of ornamental sculpture, urns, and balustrades at the summits of the walls, and the extreme care with which the stonework was finished make this one of the most noteworthy churches constructed in Paris during this period and establish a tradition for other great Parisian churches of the seventeenth century, from Val-de-Grâce to the Dôme des Invalides.

Inside, a very short transept precisely bisects the nave, with a broad cupola above the crossing. The height of the cupola, 130 feet, is identical to the length of the nave. Lining the main space are side chapels that open onto it in large arcades. A cornice resting on tall, flat pilasters runs around the entire space and ties it together. The quite beautiful tomb of Richelieu was originally placed in the choir in such a way that the half-recumbent cardinal, supported by an allegorical figure representing piety, could gaze directly upon the altar, while an allegory of learning gave in to tears at his feet.

Notre-Dame-des-Victoires

*Place des Petits-Pères, II*e

This church, slightly hidden behind the buildings of the Place des Victoires, is one of the major shrines to the Virgin Mary in France. It was begun in 1629 as the church of the order of barefoot Augustinians— called Petits Pères—based on plans by Pierre Le Muet and with the patronage of Louis XIII. It received its name in commemoration of the king's defeat of the Protestants in La Rochelle in 1628. Finally completed around 1740 by Sylvain Cartaud, Notre-Dame-des-Victoires represents in its ground plan, façade, and interior the classical form of French church architecture in the seventeenth century, quite without any distinguishing vitality or movement. Notable in the second chapel on the left is the remnant of the tomb of Jean-Baptiste Lully, with an impressive bust of the composer by Jean Collignon. Lully's house is at 45 Rue des Petits-Champs, not far from the church, and is an important example of a Parisian residential façade before Jules Hardouin-Mansart.

In the choir, above some fine wooden paneling from 1688, there are seven paintings by Carle van Loo executed between 1746 and 1755. They depict scenes from the life of St. Augustine as well as Louis XIII's pledge before the Battle of La Rochelle that he would build a church to the Virgin if he succeeded in capturing the city.

Temple de la Visitation Ste-Marie

*17 Rue St-Antoine, IV*e

This is the first important building by François Mansart in Paris. It was built in 1632 to 1634, along with other convent buildings, for the order of the Daughters

Temple de la Visitation Ste-Marie: François Mansart's façade.

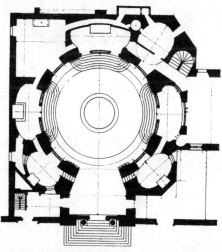

Temple de la Visitation Ste-Marie (ground plan).

of the Visitation, which was founded in 1610 by François de Sales and established in Paris in 1619. The convent buildings were for the most part destroyed during the Revolution; the church was consecrated to the Protestant faith in 1803.

The church has a cupola almost 108 feet high and 44 feet in diameter, with a drum supported by massive console pillars. The cupola rises above a low, nearly square pedestal story on a narrow lot. A monumental round-arch motif—similar to the one at the entrance to the Hôtel de Châlons-Luxembourg in the Rue Geoffroy-l'Asnier from around 1610—dominates the portal structure, into which have been set a small portico with doorway and a round window above.

The ground plan follows a circular scheme, uncommon in Paris before this time; it provides an early example of a Baroque concept of space. The circular central space is flanked by oval-shaped chapels on either side. A slightly larger oval comprises the chancel, flanked by the nuns' choir at one end and by a trapezoidal entry area at the other. These four smaller spaces open onto the central rotunda in great arcades. The remaining space is taken up by smaller side rooms and chapels.

Schemes such as this had been known in France previously only in palace architecture, in a simplified form in Philibert de l'Orme's chapel at Anet, for example. The actual model may have been Michelangelo's plan for San Giovanni dei Fiorentini in Rome. Characteristic of Mansart is the blend of simplified, monumental forms, a strikingly dynamic concept of space, and a nearly Baroque wealth of ornamentation.

OVERLEAF: *Val-de-Grâce: church, monastery, and square in the seventeenth century (Perelle).*

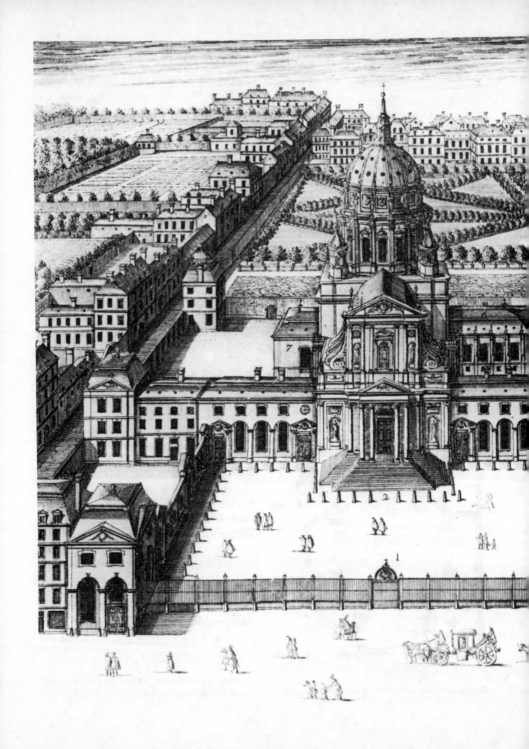

A Paris chez N. Langlois Avec Privil. du Roy.

Val-de-Grâce

277 Rue St-Jacques, V^e (illus. 24 and 25, pages 79 and 80)

Val-de-Grâce is the most important Baroque ensemble in Paris, one in which the preoccupation with Roman models and Spanish influences culminated. It owes its existence to a pledge made by the wife of Louis XIII, Anne of Austria, who after a long childless marriage gave birth in 1638 to Louis le Désiré, later Louis XIV. After the death of her husband in 1643, the queen, as regent, decided to build a church to celebrate the birth of her son and to erect a cloister for the Benedictine nuns whom she had brought to the Rue St-Jacques from Bièvre in 1621. François Mansart was given the commission. There could be no question of using his rival, Jacques Lemercier, who had served as architect to Richelieu, the queen's archenemy.

Mansart's designs were the most ambitious that Paris had seen since the first plans for the Louvre. They provided for a central church structure with the cloister on one side and a palace for the queen, with multiple parallel and projecting wings, on the other. Combined with the church front, these were to form a varied, rectangular square, a layout reminiscent of the Escorial in Spain, where Anne of Austria, sister of the Spanish king, had spent her early years.

The seven-year-old Louis XIV laid the cornerstone for the church in 1645. A year later, Mansart was dismissed, possibly because he refused to agree to changes desired by the queen mother. Lemercier took over the direction of the building.

Struggles with the Fronde interrupted construction in 1648, and work could not be resumed until 1655, now directed by Pierre Le Muet in place of the deceased Lemercier. The cloister was begun, but plans for the queen's palace as a counterpart to it had to be abandoned. The large square that had been planned was reduced to an elongated forecourt in front of the church, with low wings extending out on either side, blind arcades, and corner pavilions. The nave of the church was completed in 1662 and the cupola a year later. Following Anne of Austria's death in 1666, Louis XIV entrusted the decoration of the church to Michel and François Anguier and Philippe de Buyster. The architect Gabriel Le Duc designed the high altar and baldachin after Bernini's in St. Peter's (illus. 24). Construction was again suspended in 1667, although the side chapels along the nave were still unfinished. The church was not consecrated until 1710.

The cloister was turned into a military hospital in 1796 and was not returned to the faith until 1827. The sculptural grouping of the birth of Christ by Michel Anguier from the high altar had been transferred to the church of St. Roch during the Revolution and was not replaced by a copy until 1869. Extensive restoration of the exteriors of the cloister and the church has been done in recent years.

The existing church structure is the result of planning by two quite different architects. Mansart's conception most clearly remains in the ground plan, for which he completed the final design in 1645. The building rests on a cryptlike lower chapel that was to serve as the burial place for the House of Orléans and where the hearts of French kings were interred until the Revolution. The church itself is without antecedents in France, for it combines a nave and the three-apse design of a centrally oriented building; scholars tend to compare it with Il Gesù in Rome or with the churches of Palladio. The three apses lie within a square block whose corners make up the massive pillars of the crossing and into which small oval chapels have been set. A gallery, resting on corbels, connects the nuns' choir (adjacent to the south apse) with the sacrament chapel (on the north side of the central apse) and the St. Anne chapel (also on the north side). The queen mother's residence was to have been connected to this last chapel according to Mansart's original plan. Mansart's plans, had they been fully realized, would have here culminated in a cupola dynamically highlighted with narrow ribbing and treated as a *dôme percé*.

Lemercier, however, completely altered the form of the cupola. In place of the dynamic, steeply rising and open form that Mansart had envisioned—and that anticipated the cupola of the Dôme des Invalides —Lemercier used, in the interior, a hemisphere above a tambour surrounded by columns. On the exterior, these same forms are enlarged (illus. 25), and they dominate the appearance of the church, especially from a distance. The massive drum rises above the closed cube of the east end of the church, flanked by the four round stair towers and surrounded by sixteen closely placed and dramatically projecting pilasters. Standing above the entablatures of the pilasters are male allegorical figures supporting flaming urns. Behind these figures, broad volutes support a frieze that encircles the drum and is embellished with Bourbon lilies (fleurs-de-lis) and royal monograms. The ribs of the cupola extend upward from the frieze to a lantern encircled by a pierced balustrade. This monumental cupola is one of Lemercier's greatest achievements and one of the most impressive in France. The exterior of the nave is harmoniously joined to the cupola; the roof of the nave is also supported by massive volutes in a variation of one of the basic motifs of the façade.

A medal that was struck when the cornerstone was laid in 1645 reveals that various essential aspects of the elevation do indeed go back to Mansart: the fundamental decision in favor of a Roman church façade; the emphatic entry—a projecting portico with a large triangular pediment above two massive pairs of columns; and the contrapuntal setback of the central façade on the floor above this portico. On the whole, Mansart's design was more restrained than Lemercier's. It did not include the frieze between the floors and did not draw out the volutes into such broad curves, a touch that gives the existing façade a very Roman, Baroque appearance.

The design of the interior, except for the actual ground plan, is the work of Lemercier, his successors, and their colleagues. In place of a very complex vaulting, which would have tended to unify the space according to Mansart's way of thinking, Lemercier gave the structure a barrel vault that is cut into by the deep secondary vaults above the windows. An extremely rich sculptural ornamentation covers this vault: the spandrels above the arcades are filled with reliefs of allegories of the virtues; and the pendentives of the crossing carry medallions of the four Evangelists. This display is uncommonly Baroque by French standards and reveals the Roman schooling of its creator, the sculptor Michel Anguier. It would also appear that the creator of the ceiling fresco in the cupola, Pierre Mignard, studied in Rome as well. This work was completed in 1665 and depicts God the Father in heavenly glory as Anne of Austria presents a model of this church to him. The plans for the baldachin above the high altar, often mistakenly attributed to Bernini, go back to Mansart, but the baldachin owes its final form to Le Duc.

In contrast to the Baroque exuberance of the church, the cloister buildings are extremely restrained. They comprise a square with a two-story gallery around a courtyard, calling to mind medieval covered cloisters, which continued to be built for French monasteries as late as the seventeenth century. The elegant façade of the east wing, facing the garden, is flanked by two pavilion structures. The right-hand one, provided with an unusual porch in the style of Salomon de Brosse, served as a residence for Anne of Austria.

St. Sulpice

Place St-Sulpice, VI *(illus. 26, page 113)*

The "cathedral" of the aristocratic Faubourg St-Germain is the most important of the long series of Parisian churches of the classical period, structures that are somewhat arid yet remarkable for the clarity of their ground plans and the logic of their conception. St. Sulpice was begun in 1645 on the site of a smaller structure from the twelfth century, in response to the growing needs of a parish that extended as far as Vaugirard, Vanves, and Grenelle. In its ground plan, designed by the architect Christophe Gamard, it translates Notre-Dame into the forms of classicism, with a continuous side aisle, accompanying chapels, round choir apse, and only slightly projecting transept.

Construction began on the east end but soon was suspended because of the unrest during the Fronde. In 1649, Louis Le Vau took over the project. He enlarged its scale to one that rivaled that of Notre-Dame. After Le Vau's death in 1670, work was continued by Daniel Gittard. In 1678, it was again suspended—this time for lack of funds. By then, the choir, ambulatory, chapels, and a portion of the north transept were complete. It was not until forty years later that construction resumed. The regent's architect, Gilles-Marie Oppenord, completed the tran-

St. Sulpice and the Faubourg St-Germain.

sept in 1722 and worked on the nave until 1736. Oppenord was one of the founders and chief proponents of the Rococo style. He designed a façade that would have been among the most original Rococo structures in Europe and might have led French architecture in a different direction. But it was never built; nor were the ebullient Rococo decorations he envisioned for the interior, except for the high altar, which was destroyed during the Revolution. A design competition for the façade was won by a Florentine, Giovanni Niccolò Servandoni, who had distinguished himself primarily in the field of theater and stage design. His design was the decisive step that moved Parisian monumental architecture toward classicism.

Construction of the façade, consisting of a two-story portico flanked by towers and topped by a triangular pediment, began in 1733. The pediment, not completed until after Servandoni's death in 1766, was demolished a short time later when it was struck by lightning; it was not rebuilt. The upper stories of the towers were still unfinished. Jean-François Chalgrin began to construct the northern tower in harmony with the rest of the façade in 1777. The southern one remained unfinished, in spite of various experiments. Servandoni's plan provided for setting off the façade by developing a semicircular square in front of it, but only one of the buildings he envisioned was constructed—No. 6, directly north of the church. The remainder of the square dates from the nineteenth century.

The church was secularized by the Revolution, and in 1799 it served as the scene of a lavish banquet for 750 people given for Napoleon on his return from Egypt. It is the burial place of some of the most brilliant families of France—the Condés, the Contis, and the Luynes—and of the architect François Blondel, the painter Jean Jouvenet, and Molière's wife, Armande Béjart.

The façade unites the portico and towers into a single block of monumental severity. Only the upper stories of the towers rise above it. Two rows of columns, which become double pilasters on the towers, support the continuous entablatures that give the building its broad, horizontal appearance. On the ground floor, narrow flights of stairs lead up between the bases of the columns to an open vestibule, while the arcades of the second story—now open as well—were originally intended to be glazed; it was envisioned that a library would be housed behind them. The crowning balustrade, in place of Servandoni's destroyed pediment, was constructed in 1869.

The interior, with the extraordinary dimensions of 386 by 186 feet, appears quite homogeneous, despite the long period of construction. The spatial impression is defined by tall arcades alternating with fluted pilasters, the continuous band of the entablature with a deeply projecting cornice, a

St. Sulpice: façade, after Giovanni Niccolò Servandoni and Jean-François Chalgrin.

high barrel vault interrupted by the lesser vaults of the broad windows, an unpronounced crossing, and the round rear wall of the choir. Touches of rich decoration, especially in the crossing, go back to Oppenord and were executed by Michel-Ange Slodtz, who also created the very Baroque embellishment for the Lady Chapel on the central axis behind the choir. This is the oldest part of the church, but its present-day form derives from plans by Charles de Wailly in 1774.

Although the church has lost the greater part of its original furnishings, there are still a number of noteworthy objects to be seen. The organ was designed by Chalgrin in 1776 and stands on the balcony built in 1750 from plans by Servandoni. Two fonts in the form of giant shells—a gift to François I from the Venetian Republic—stand on Rococo bases by Jean-Baptiste Pigalle. A pulpit with a double staircase was executed by de Wailly in

1788. Frescoes of Jacob wrestling with the angel and of the story of Heliodorus in the first chapel on the south side are late works by Eugène Delacroix, dating from 1858 to 1861. The fifth chapel on the south side houses the tomb of the Curé Languet de Gergy, by Slodtz; its theatricality was scathingly criticized by contemporaries during the Enlightenment. In the sacristy, some rich wooden paneling by Oppenord dates from 1731.

Institut de France (Collège des Quatre-Nations)

23 Quai de Conti, VIᵉ (illus. 28 and 29, page 114)

In 1657, Cardinal Mazarin began to think of erecting a residential college, combined with a public library and a chapel that would contain his tomb. At Colbert's urging, a commission was given to the architect Louis Le Vau, who was simultaneously working on the Louvre. Le Vau suggested placing the new building along the Seine opposite the Louvre, on the site of the medieval Tour de Nesle—not, as had been intended, near the Sorbonne. The king supported this plan, although the city was opposed to it, and he had a new quay constructed along the Seine at his own expense. In his will dated March 6, 1661, only a few days before his death, Mazarin bequeathed a great sum of money to the project, specifying that the college was to be for young noblemen from the territories that had fallen to France as a result of the Treaty of Münster in 1648 and the Peace of the Pyrenees in 1659: Alsace, Flanders with Artois, Pignerol and Piedmont, Roussillon and Sardinia. The cornerstone for the chapel was laid in 1663. In 1665, the Tour de Nesle was torn down and construction began on the library. The chapel was completed in 1674, although the frescoes

planned for the cupola were not executed for lack of funds. In 1684, Mazarin, who had died in Vincennes, was placed in his tomb with great ceremony (illus. 29). The college opened in 1688. Although its official name was the Collège Mazarin, it was popularly called the Collège des Quatre-Nations because of the nationalities of its student body. In 1793, the institution was dissolved and a prison established in the buildings. In 1805, Napoleon turned over the chapel and portions of the other buildings to the newly founded Institut de France.

The Institut was essentially an amalgamation of the old royal academies: the Académie Française, which had been founded by Louis XIII at Richelieu's urging in 1635, and wherein thirteen (later forty) *Immortels* were charged with upholding the purity of the French language; the Académie Royale de Peinture et de Sculpture, founded in 1648; the Académie d'Architecture (1717); the Petite Académie (1663), which reviewed texts that glorified the king on monuments and medals—known after 1716 as the Académie des Inscriptions et Belles-Lettres; and the Académie des Sciences (1666). Until the Revolution, all these academies had met in the Louvre. Antoine Vandoyer altered the chapel of the Collège des Quatre-Nations to accommodate the meetings of the Institut in 1806, but thorough renovation in 1960 to 1962 restored its original condition. To this day, the Institut's induction ceremonies take place beneath the cupola of the chapel.

Le Vau's design was determined by the college's orientation to the Louvre. The chapel of the college was placed on an axis with the middle pavilion of the palace's south wing—for which Le Vau originally envisioned a cupola as well. The architect intended to further emphasize this axis by constructing a connecting bridge, an idea

Collège des Quatre-Nations, from the Seine (Perelle).

that was eventually realized by Napoleon's engineers in 1802 with the Pont des Arts, the first iron bridge in Paris.

The main structure of the chapel (illus. 28) is set well back from the quay, where two large corner pavilions mark the beginning of the complex. Concave curved wings connect the chapel with these pavilions to create a semicircular square. This square is dominated by the projecting portico of the chapel, which boasts Colossal pilasters and columns, a triangular pediment richly adorned with sculpture, and the elegant cupola atop a tall tambour. A richness of architectural detail makes the façade of the Institut one of the most exuberant and elegant in Paris. Notable are its colonnades, Colossal pilasters on the corner pavilions, smaller columns on the two-story wings, flaming urns above deep cornices, statues of Latin and Greek church fathers and the

Evangelists above the chapel frieze, gilt ribs of the cupola, and graceful lantern, which was completed—after plans by Le Vau—in 1875. The arcades have been closed in; they originally housed shops, the rents from which helped to finance the college.

The library and student residences, clustered around courtyards, stretch behind the more formal main structure between the Rue Mazarine and the Hôtel de la Monnaie. The first of these inner courts is dominated by the pilaster-ornamented front of the library on one side and a portico on the other.

The interior of the chapel comprises, in addition to the central space beneath its oval-shaped cupola, two side chapels, a square choir, and a rectangular narthex just behind the portico that projects into the square. A restrained alternation of fluted Corinthian pilasters and high arcade openings into the side rooms, with smaller blind arcades beneath round-arch windows, underscores the strict rationality and clarity of the ground plan. Mazarin's tomb, designed by Jules Hardouin-Mansart and executed by Antoine Coysevox and Jean-Baptiste Tuby in 1692, is one of the most important examples of seventeenth-century French sculpture. On top of the sarcophagus is the kneeling figure of the cardinal, in white marble, and leaning against the base are three allegorical figures representing wisdom, peace, and faith.

Hôtel Lambert

2 Rue St-Louis-en-l'Ile, IVe

The Ile aux Vaches, behind the Ile de la Cité, was used by the canons of Notre-Dame as a pasture for their cows. Then, in the early seventeenth century, it was renamed the Ile St-Louis and divided into building lots by the developer Christophe Marie. It soon became a favored building site for wealthy Parisians who wished to escape the confinement of the busy city. The first to build here was the Sieur de Bretonvilliers, who

Collège des Quatre-Nations, at the edge of the Quartier Latin (Plan Turgot).

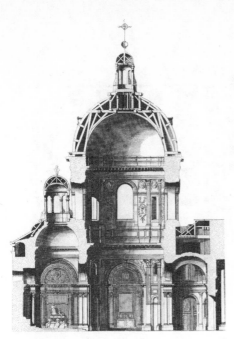

Collège des Quatre-Nations: chapel
(longitudinal section).

commissioned Jean Androuet Du Cerceau to build him a large mansion on the eastern tip of the island in 1633 (this edifice was destroyed in 1840). A councilor to the king, Jean-Baptiste Lambert de Thorigny, bought a lot adjacent to it, for which he asked Louis Le Vau to design a luxurious town house. Le Vau's family owned neighboring property as well as several other lots on the island. In quite a short time, between 1640 and 1642, the Hôtel Lambert was constructed, but its owner died shortly after he moved there in 1644. His brother Nicolas, who was president of the auditing office, completed the decoration of its interior.

Le Vau did a brilliant job of meeting the dual requirements of grandeur and comfort. On the ground floor, around a courtyard facing the island's main street, he grouped everything needed to run a great house: kitchens, servants' quarters, coach houses, and stables. Above this low, pedestal-like ground floor he created a two-story, lavish array of public rooms and living areas. An unusual open stairwell stands at the back of the courtyard, which has rounded corners. Abutting this staircase, there is a long gallery wing extending toward the Seine; it forms' with the right-hand wing another courtyard at the second-story level. This upper court is a terrace garden, from which one can enjoy a view of the river. The fronts of the two wings facing the garden have the Colossal pilasters that Le Vau was so fond of, and the second-floor windows are French doors that open onto the terrace. The gallery wing, with a rounded end facing the Seine, contained a library on the lower floor and the so-called Galerie d'Hercule on the upper floor. This gallery had high windows facing the garden and trompe l'œil landscape paintings by Jacques Rousseau on the opposite wall. The young

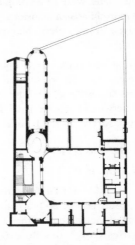

Hôtel Lambert: étage noble *(ground plan)*
(Mariette).

199

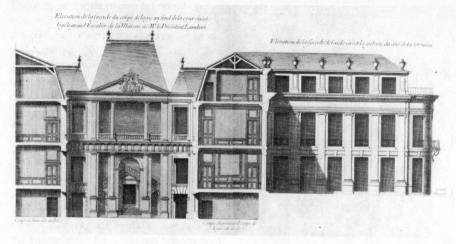

Hôtel Lambert: courtyard façade and gallery (cross-section through the wings) (Mariette).

Charles Le Brun painted its ceiling with a fresco depicting the labors of Hercules. Galleries of this type, quite popular in France since the Renaissance as reception rooms or banquet halls, were to be found in well over a hundred Parisian mansions. Another has survived in the Galerie Mazarine (see page 185).

The wing perpendicular to the gallery structure was the main residential section, which was lavishly decorated by Eustache Le Sueur between 1646 and 1655. Portions of his work survive in the Louvre.

Hôtel de Lauzun

17 Quai d'Anjou, IVe

In 1656 to 1657, not far from the Hôtel Lambert, Louis Le Vau built a mansion for the commissioner general of the Light Cavalry, Charles Grüyn des Bordes. It was bought in 1682 by the Duc de Lauzun and was later owned by the Richelieu family. In

the nineteenth century, both Théophile Gautier and Charles Baudelaire lived here; since 1928, it has belonged to the city, which has had it thoroughly restored.

Typical of most of the *hôtels* on the Ile St-Louis is its reversal of the usual Parisian scheme; the *corps de logis* faces the quay and the Seine, and the courtyard and secondary buildings stand behind it. By adding a mezzanine, Le Vau managed to raise the level of the *bel-étage*, whose decoration was extraordinarily lavish, in sharp contrast to the simple façades. The façades are marked solely by the rhythm of the window bays, the side portal, the dormers, and a handsome balcony in front of the two center windows.

Very few other Parisian mansions still provide such a complete picture of a townhouse interior before the development of the Louis XIV style. The ornamentation has recently been attributed to Jean Lepautre, the brother of Antoine and one of the most important decorative designers of the period. The frescoes were created by a follower of Charles Le Brun.

Hôtel Salé

5 Rue de Thorigny, IIIe (illus. 30, page 114)

Louis Le Vau's influence is also apparent in one of the most lavish *hôtels* in the Marais. It was built in 1656 by the otherwise obscure architect Jean Boullier for Aubert de Fontenay, collector of the salt tax (hence the disparaging name Hôtel Salé). The tall, two-story *corps de logis* is enhanced by an ornamental doorway with a triangular pediment in the center and a mezzanine that is practically a floor in itself. A rounded courtyard in front of the *corps de logis* faces the street. To the right of this courtyard, there is a low wing comprising the coach houses and leading into a second courtyard. The wall along the street curves inward to accommodate the small courtyard in front of the monumental portal, an arrangement that would come to be adopted for several Parisian mansions. The three central bays of the *corps de logis* are spanned by a large, curved pediment with abundant but undistinguished sculptural ornamentation. The façade, however, with its simple lines, tall French doors, and narrow sections of wall, is quite elegant. Narrow corner pavilions frame the façade on the garden side.

The interior is notable for its uncommonly large, three-flight staircase to the right of the vestibule, which opens onto this stairwell in three generous arcades. A vault with considerable sculptural ornament spans this stairwell, its cornice supported by caryatids. Portions of the interior furnishings have survived. The mansion will one day house the Picasso museum, but its restoration is still incomplete.

Hôtel Amelot de Bisseuil (Hôtel des Ambassadeurs de Hollande)

47 Rue Vieille-du-Temple, IVe

This building is an example of the still Baroque-influenced tendencies of Parisian architecture under Mazarin. It was rebuilt from an older mansion with two courtyards but no garden by Pierre Cottard in 1657 to 1660. The portal is splendid. On its street side is a round medallion between two goddesses of fame by Thomas Regnaudin. On its courtyard side is a relief with an allegorical figure of the Tiber and the discovery of Romulus and Remus. Beyond the small courtyard, there is a rusticated ground floor and an open passage to a second courtyard. On the central ornament above the flat wall panels of the second floor, *putto* caryatids support a triangular pediment with a coat of arms. The wings and the *corps de logis* are connected by a rounded gallery on the *bel-étage*. The second courtyard has not survived in its original state.

Hôtel de Beauvais

68 Rue François-Miron, IVe

This structure, which has not yet been restored, stands on the grounds of the town house of the abbots of Chaalis, whose Gothic cellar was recently excavated. It is the most unusual of the seventeenth-century Parisian mansions, and Bernini, who was otherwise ill disposed toward French architecture, fully approved of it. It was built by Antoine Lepautre between 1656 and 1660 for Catherine-Henriette Bellier, lady-in-waiting to Anne of Austria, and her husband, Pierre de Beauvais. Lepautre placed the residence on an irregular lot between the Rue St-Antoine—this portion of which is today the Rue François-Miron—and the Rue de Jouy.

It stands directly on the street, and the original façade, badly disfigured during the Revolution, was splendidly ornate. A passage led to the courtyard, a complicated combination of rectangle, trapezoid, and semicircle that masks the irregularity of the lot and gives an impression of spaciousness. The left-hand boundary of the courtyard is only a property wall; on the right and to the rear is a wing containing coach houses, servants' quarters, and stables. A second dwelling was attached to this wing on the Rue de Jouy. Lepautre filled the ground floor of the main house with shops, and the *bel-étage* above it extended over the wing as a long gallery, with a terrace garden above the stables. A chapel in a corner of the property had its own portico facing the courtyard. The complex form of the courtyard is held together by the rusticated stonework of the ground floor—a projecting cornice with large consoles that surrounds the whole and originally supported an iron railing—and a frieze

beneath it with beautifully sculpted rams' heads. The two floors above this are tied together by tall Ionic pilasters. Also uncommon for Paris is the circular vestibule supported by Doric columns and the very lavish staircase to the left of it, decorated with freestanding pairs of columns, snakes, sphinxes, *putti*, and so on, by the sculptor Martin Desjardin.

The mansion was completed in 1660, in time for the entry into the city of the young Louis XIV and his bride, Marie-Thérèse of Austria. The queen mother and the queen of England watched the procession from the central balcony of the house. Mozart stayed here in 1763.

Hôtel d'Aumont

7 Rue de Jouy, IVe

This is one of the most elegant Parisian mansions from the mid-seventeenth century, and a number of artists had a hand in its creation. It was built after 1630 by Louis Le Vau for the royal councilor Michel-Antoine Scarron. Scarron's son-in-law the marshal d'Aumont, appointed governor of Paris in 1662, had the house remodeled by François Mansart and decorated by Simon Vouet and Charles Le Brun in about 1660. Its splendid gardens, which no longer exist, were attributed to André Le Nôtre. After being requisitioned for other uses and allowed to fall into disrepair, the Hôtel d'Aumont was one of the first mansions in the Marais to be restored after World War II. It was remodeled to serve as the administrative court of the *département*, and the façade facing the garden was completely renovated.

Especially notable is the courtyard, with its five-bay *corps de logis* and wings of equal height. The whole is severely ordered by the regularly spaced windows with only nar-

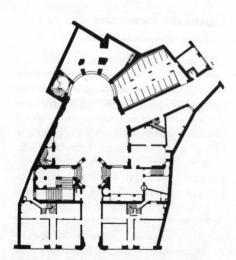

Hôtel de Beauvais: ground floor (ground plan).

row wall panels between them. The exterior walls have been painstakingly structured so that there is a perfect balance between horizontal and vertical lines. There are elegantly sculpted draperies, of the sort that Mansart loved, above the ground-floor windows, with somewhat less delicate scrollwork and masks above those of the upper story. Mansart's 1665 staircase has been destroyed.

Hôtel de Guénégaud

60 Rue des Archives, IIIe

This is the only fully preserved town house that can be ascribed with great assurance to François Mansart. He built it in about 1653 on the corner of the Rue des Archives and the Rue des Quatre-Fils for Jean-François de Guénégaud, who had been treasurer of France since 1632. The house has a very plain five-bay *corps de logis* that, together with its extending wings and a low gatehouse, surrounds a small courtyard. There is almost no architectural sculpture. The central axis is marked simply by a rusticated border and a console cornice. The ground-floor windows were lengthened downward in the eighteenth century. On the garden side, the outermost bays are extended forward as pavilions. The *hôtel* is an extremely stylish structure, impressive for its balanced proportions and exquisite stonework. Inside, there is an elegant staircase, dating back to Mansart, with an open flight of steps above corbels. Careful restoration in recent years has included refurbishing of the small garden and has turned part of the *hôtel* into the Musée de la Chasse.

A remnant of another residence by Mansart in the Marais has been preserved, although in poor condition—the garden front of the Hôtel de Chavigny, from 1642, at 7

Rue de Sévigné. This structure now serves as a firemen's barracks.

Hôtel de Mansart-Sagonne

28 Rue des Tournelles, IVe

Between 1667 and 1670, Jules Hardouin-Mansart remodeled his mother's house in the Rue des Tournelles, making it into a residence for himself. It was expanded in 1687 to 1692, with exquisite interior decoration by Charles Le Brun, Pierre Mignard, Allegrain, and Charles de Lafosse.

This is an early work of Hardouin-Mansart's that reveals the insecurity of a beginner as well as the influence of his grand-uncle François Mansart. The garden side facing the Boulevard Beaumarchais is notable. It boasts pairs of Ionic columns on the ground floor that support a balcony; a row of wall plaques on the second floor that were originally ornamented with busts; and third-floor bays accentuated with balconies, rusticated framing, and triangular pediments. The dormers in the mansard roof have been altered.

Hôtel Libéral-Bruant

1 Rue de la Perle, IIIe

After the Hôtel des Invalides and the chapel of the Salpêtrière, this is the most important work by Libéral Bruant in Paris. He built it as his own residence in 1685. Its quite lavish façade combines round-arch arcades with lower square openings and oculi above filled with busts of Roman emperors. A triangular pediment with cornucopias, *putti*, and a round window (in place of a coat of arms) ties the façade together. A small courtyard lined with blind arcades extends in front of it. After exemplary restoration, it now houses the Musée de la Serrure (a collection of decorative door hardware).

Hôpital de la Salpêtrière

47 Boulevard de l'Hôpital, XIIIᵉ (illus. 27, page 114)

In 1656, to care for the beggars and vagabonds of the city, whose numbers had grown to more than 50,000, Louis XIV established the Hôpital Général. Comprising facilities at various locations, this was to serve as a training center for the former vagabonds as well as a nursing home for invalids, the aged, and the mentally handicapped. A separate facility for women was planned on the grounds of a gunpowder factory outside the city, to the east of the Faubourg St-Victor, the so-called Salpêtrière (named after the main ingredient of the gunpowder, which consisted of six parts of saltpeter to one of sulfur and one of charcoal).

Construction of the Hôpital de la Salpêtrière was financed by grants and tax

Hôtel de Mansart-Sagonne: garden façade (Mariette).

surcharges. Louis Le Vau developed plans for an extensive complex, and his colleagues Charles Duval and Pierre Le Muet were responsible for executing them. Cardinal Mazarin donated 160,000 livres for the north wing, which was begun in 1660. In 1669, Libéral Bruant built a chapel. The south wing, patterned after the north one, was not added until 1756. Behind the wings, a number of smaller structures were grouped about various courtyards in a grid that is less rigid than that of the Hôtel des Invalides. In 1684, a prison was attached to the hospital. It was intended to hold prostitutes and women convicted of both misdemeanors and felonies.

The Salpêtrière constituted a small city in itself, administered by a directress and an array of *sous-officières*. Near the end of the eighteenth century, it had almost 10,000 occupants—the largest hospital in the world at that time. The prison was closed in 1794, after thirty-five women were raped and massacred by revolutionaries on the infamous night of September 4, 1792. In 1789, Viel de Saint-Maur established buildings to house the mentally disturbed, and in 1795, the physician Philippe Pinel instituted more humane treatment of the insane by releasing them from their iron chains. As a result of these reforms, the Salpêtrière became a center for neuropsychiatric treatment in the nineteenth century. It was there, for example, that Sigmund Freud attended the lectures of Jean Martin Charcot. Today, it constitutes a portion of the Pitié–Salpêtrière university clinic.

The Salpêtrière's severe wings with accentuated corner pavilions and monumental central portals are typical of the rational sobriety that also marks the Hôtel des Invalides. Between the two wings stands the church of St. Louis-de-la-Salpêtrière, dominated by an octagonal 196-foot cupola to

Hôpital de la Salpêtrière (Plan Turgot).

of the Port-Royal cloister, it was designed by Claude Perrault, the creator of the Louvre Colonnades. In the nineteenth century, an avenue was created to tie it to the Jardin du Luxembourg.

The heart of the structure is a closed two-story cube above a high pedestal that is obscured on the south side by a terrace. There is a rectangular porch on the north side, and octagonal pavilions stand on the corners of the south side. The building's main sides face in the four compass directions, and its central axis corresponds to Paris's meridian of longitude. The extreme precision of its stonework and the regularity of the masonry symbolize the rigor and earnestness of the exact sciences. There is no ornamentation except for two festoons composed of astronomical devices on the garden side facing the south. Originally the roof behind the surrounding balustrade was flat; observatory domes were added in the nineteenth century.

which the four arms of a Greek cross are attached. Between these wings, in turn, there are octagonal chapels opening onto the center in large arcades, creating eight separate spaces of considerable size in which the various categories of patients and prisoners—as many as 4,000 at a time—could take part in the Mass being celebrated at the central altar. The exterior of the building is almost without ornament and is of crystalline clarity. The interior is of impressive proportions and is also virtually unadorned; its impact, though, is destroyed by a wealth of badly preserved paintings from the seventeenth and eighteenth centuries, which give it the feeling of an art storeroom.

Observatoire

61 Avenue de l'Observatoire, XIVe

This prime example of French rationalism from the time of Colbert was built between 1667 and 1672 for the newly created Académie des Sciences as an observatory and an institute for chemistry. Situated to the south

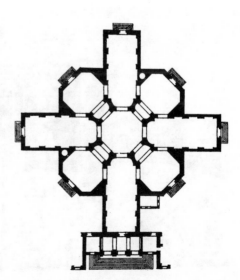

Salpêtrière: chapel (ground plan).

Port-Royal

Boulevard de Port-Royal, XIVᵉ

Along with the church of St. Jacques-du-Haut-Pas, this was one of the centers of Jansenism in Paris. Jansenism was a mystical movement that took its name from Cornelius Jansenius, bishop of Ypern, and exercised a considerable fascination on French intellectuals because of its ascetic stance. This cloister was founded in a mansion on the Rue St-Jacques in 1646 by the mother superior Angélique Arnauld as a colony of the Cistercian nunnery of Port-Royal-des-Champs in the Chevreuse Valley (see pages 491–492). In that same year, a church for the order was constructed after plans by Antoine Lepautre, who also completed its convent buildings by 1650. In 1648, the church was consecrated by the archbishop of Paris, and Port-Royal soon became the center of Parisian religious life, casting its spell on philosophers like Blaise Pascal, dramatists like Jean Racine, and artists like Philippe de Champaigne, whose daughter joined the convent.

Tensions between Jansenists and Jesuits—the latter supported by Richelieu, the king, and the pope—led to the expulsion of the nuns from the cloister as early as 1664, whereupon the archbishop filled it with Visitandines. Port-Royal-des-Champs and its Paris convent were separated. The cloister in the Chevreuse Valley, which continued to adhere to Jansenism, was virtually leveled in 1710. During the Revolution, Port-Royal was turned into a prison, and it has served as a maternity hospital since 1814.

According to Lepautre's plans, the extremely simple cruciform church structure was to have had an entry portico on the north side of the transept and considerable sculptural ornamentation inside. For reasons of thrift, the order refused both. Nevertheless, the building is impressive for the clarity of its conception and the balance of its

Observatoire, from the south (Perelle).

proportions. Inside, Ionic pilasters support the entablature and a surrounding cornice, above which rise the cupola and a barrel vault. The church originally was embellished with a number of remarkable paintings, chiefly by Champaigne; some of these are now in the Louvre. The western nave, set apart by a grille, served as the nuns' choir, and it was connected to the convent buildings, of which the simple but quite elegant cloisters, the chapter house, and two lively stairways with wooden balustrades have survived.

Notre-Dame-de-l'Assomption

263-bis Rue St-Honoré, Ier

The convent of the Assumption was originally a hospital for poor widows, but it later became a refuge for widows, abandoned wives, and women who wished to do penance. In 1622, it moved from the vicinity of the Hôtel de Ville into the worldly Faubourg St-Honoré. Its convent buildings, from 1632, were torn down in the nineteenth century, and the Cour des Comptes, the accounting office of the French government, stands on the site today. All that remains of the convent is the church, which was erected between 1670 and 1676 after plans by Charles Errard, the first director of the Académie de France in Rome. This massive cupola structure above a square base has been nicknamed *le sot dôme* (the ridiculous dome), for its proportions are so imbalanced that the tambour and cupola appear to almost squash the structure below. It was patterned after Bernini's Santa Maria dell'Assunzione in Arriccia, which had been completed only a short time before. The massive portico with smooth Corinthian columns and a triangular pediment is

Notre-Dame-de-l'Assomption and the Porte St-Honoré (Perelle).

a variation on the motif of the Pantheon.

Fluted double pilasters and eight arcades outline the large, circular interior, which is about 80 feet in diameter. A painting, *Mary's Assumption into Heaven*, by Charles de Lafosse, adorns the cupola. Rich decorations in marbled plaster are reminiscent of Roman models. Since 1850, the church has served Paris's Polish community.

Hôtel des Invalides

Esplanade des Invalides, VIIe (illus. 33, 41–43, and 50, pages 115, 120, 121, and 123)
As early as 1604, Henri IV had established a home for old and infirm soldiers who pre-viously had been left at the mercy of religious houses or had roamed the countryside as vagabonds. For a time, under Richelieu, the palace of Bicêtre was used as a hospital for infirm soldiers—scarcely a generous solution to a social problem that was becoming increasingly acute as a result of frequent wars. Finally, at the urging of his minister François Louvois, Louis XIV decided on a gesture unique in Europe at that time, and one that would at the same time glorify the king's military stature. Beginning in 1668, the religious houses had to make contributions to a new hospital, and a competition was held for its design. Libéral Bruant won the commission.

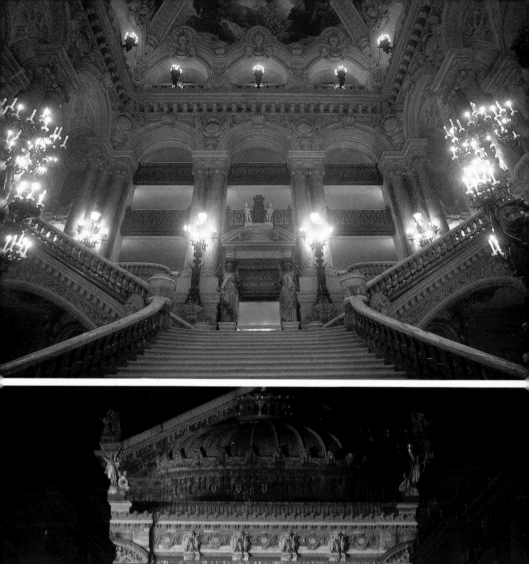

Bruant had just taken over the direction of building of the Salpêtrière from Louis Le Vau, and the parallels between this cloistered barracks for invalid soldiers and that hospital for indigents and beggars are obvious. The basic model for the layout, which clusters a series of wings in a rigid grid pattern around a number of courtyards, was the Escorial, which was also influential in the planning of Val-de-Grâce. It is possible that the Escorial's influence on Val-de-Grâce was effected by the Spanish Anne of Austria; for this project, the connection may have been the queen, Marie-Thérèse of Austria, one of the Spanish Hapsburgs. The Plain of Grenelle, outside the city on the edge of the new Faubourg St-Germain, was chosen as a site for the building. The king laid the cornerstone on November 30, 1671, and the huge structure was nearly completed by 1674. The dimensions of the entire complex, surrounded by trenches, were 1,471 by 1,275 feet. By 1676, almost 6,000 old and invalid soldiers, officers, doctors, and priests had moved in.

Bruant's plans for the church structure did not meet with the approval of Louvois, and in 1676, the minister commissioned Jules Hardouin-Mansart to prepare new ones. Louis XIV seems to have at least briefly entertained the notion of being buried among his soldiers, so Hardouin-Mansart was to build not only a church for the *invalides* but also a mausoleum for the king. The architect solved the problem brilliantly: between the south wings of the *hôtel* he placed a long, narrow, equally plain structure to serve as the soldiers' church (St. Louis-des-Invalides), with an entrance and façade facing the central courtyard. In place of a choir he then created, facing south, the splendid Dôme, which was attached to St. Louis-des-Invalides only by a common chancel. The purpose of the cupola structure was made

perfectly apparent because Hardouin-Mansart appropriated the plans by François Mansart, his great-uncle, for a Bourbon mausoleum on the north side of the abbey church of St. Denis.

The Dôme des Invalides, or l'Église Royale (illus. 41), was begun in 1680, and when Hardouin-Mansart died in 1708, it was not yet quite finished. This long period of construction can be explained only by the extreme care given by both the king and the architect to the interior. The cupola was erected in 1691, and work on the interior began then. By 1706, the church could be consecrated and given over to the king. The remaining work was carried out after plans completed by Hardouin-Mansart's brother-in-law Robert de Cotte. Instead of a projected forecourt, it was decided simply to frame the square by trenches, guard houses, and a broad *allée* leading to the church from the south. This avenue was laid out as early as 1680 and is known today as the Avenue de Breteuil. De Cotte, who in 1704 had developed the magnificent esplanade, an open space on the north side of the *hôtel* with grass and four rows of trees extending to the Seine, also added elegant low wings on either side of the Dôme to house the marshal and administration. These served to tie the tall blocks of the *hôtel* to the Dôme and to heighten the latter's effect. They were recently restored at André Malraux's initiative, and a number of barracks that were added in the nineteenth century have been removed.

Since it was first attacked by François Blondel, Bruant's design for the *hôtel* has been criticized frequently. Yet its rationality and sobriety and its mathematical rigor accurately represent the period of Louvois and Colbert. Behind the north wing, which is some 685 feet long, Bruant placed four perpendicular wings that form, together

Dôme des Invalides, with the forecourt design by Jules Hardouin-Mansart.

with the less imposing south wing, a central *cour d'honneur* and two smaller, secondary courtyards on either side, separated by cross ties. The two inner perpendicular wings continue beyond the south wing to frame the nave of St. Louis-des-Invalides.

The façade facing the esplanade is quite plain but powerful. Slightly projecting four-bay pavilions mark the corners, while the center is emphasized by a monumental round arch rising to the height of the roof ridge and supported by two pairs of Colossal pilasters (illus. 43). With its portal, this arch stretches across the middle bays, and on it, in relief, there is an equestrian statue of the Sun King of the type found in the pediments of French Renaissance palaces. This one was originally created by Guil-

laume Coustou in 1735; in 1815, after damage during the Revolution, it was replaced by a copy by Pierre Cartellier. In front of the pilasters are spirited allegorical figures of wisdom and justice by Coustou.

The entry arch juts out with a slight curve from the line of the façade. Otherwise, the only interruptions along the face of the building are two flat, one-bay ornamental surrounds on either side over entrances to the courtyards. The dormer windows are treated as trophies; these comprise the sole ornamentation. This north wing, consisting of three stories plus mezzanine, was originally reserved for the governor of the institution and his administration on the right side, doctors and orderlies on the left. The wings branching from it had kitchens and dining rooms on the ground floor and the soldiers' rooms on the floors above. The sick wards were in the low buildings on the east side of the church, grouped around four small courtyards and connected to the south side of the taller complex. There were laboratories and pharmacies here, as well as a central chapel.

The *cour d'honneur* displays a brilliant, virtually mathematical logic (illus. 42). It is surrounded by wings opening onto it in a double row of arcades, one above the other. In each corner, there is a projecting structure crowned by statues of horses, while the intervening bays are highlighted by unusual dormers in the form of trophies and suits of armor. The fifth of these from the right incorporates a wolf's head that appears to gaze down on the courtyard and is known as *le loup qui voit* (the wolf that sees all), a play on the name Louvois. Opposite the entrance portal is the portico, which consists of two stories of four pairs of freestanding columns leading into St. Louis-des-Invalides (illus. 33). In its central arcade is the statue of Napoleon by Seuvre that stood atop the

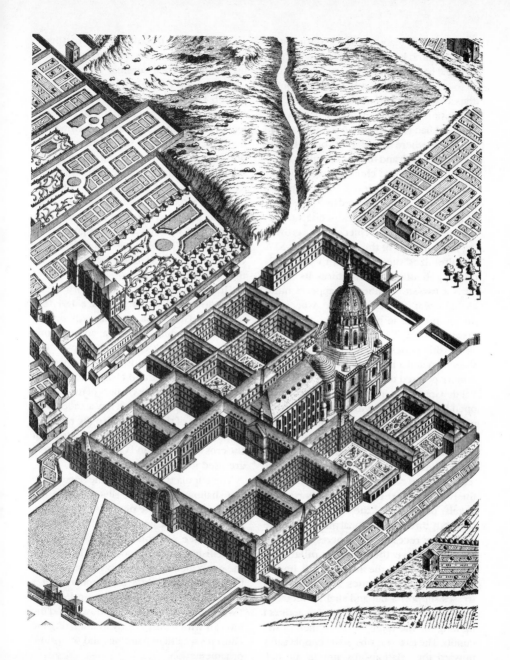

Hôtel and Dôme des Invalides (Plan Turgot).

column in the Place Vendôme until 1863.

This church is extremely plain, with nine identical bays and a continuous barrel vault. Its lower side aisles run beneath balconies draped with captured banners. Until the Revolution, the high altar had two fronts. (Mansart had used the same solution at Val-de-Grâce, where the altar stood between the main church and the sacrament chapel.) Since 1873, the two churches of Les Invalides, originally connected by a common chancel, have been separated by a glass wall.

The Dôme des Invalides is one of Hardouin-Mansart's masterpieces and a crowning achievement of the reign of Louis XIV. It epitomizes the seventeenth century's thinking about central structures. Its pedestal is a two-story cube that appears quite close except on the south side, where the deeply projecting portico over the entry breaks its lines. The cupola thrusts upward above this pedestal, supported by a massive drum and a high attic floor. This dome is more pointed than that of St. Peter's or of Val-de-Grâce and rises majestically to an open lantern topped with a cross. A harmonious balance among the components of the structure and a distinct emphasis on the horizontals of each floor belie the Dôme's extraordinary height; the cupola rises to 351 feet. The base culminates in the columns of the two-level portico, which supports a triangular pediment. At the level of the drum, distinctly three-dimensional pillars alternate with more recessed ones; here, the diagonal axes above the crossing pillars are emphasized while the main axes are underplayed. Graceful volutes above the buttresses support a tall and slightly recessed attic story whose windows provide indirect lighting for the topmost inner shell of the cupola. The exterior ribs of the cupola carry upward the relationships among the columns below. In the fields between these ribs are flat, military trophies of lead that have been gilded, as have the ribs themselves and the lantern at their summit.

Sculptures of eight Greek and Latin church fathers and of Virtues once enlivened the church's silhouette at the roof level. None of these has survived. However, in the niches on either side of the entrance, one can still admire two statues from the original complement: on the left is a St. Louis by Coustou after a design by François Girardon, and on the right is a figure of Charlemagne executed between 1700 and 1706 by Antoine Coysevox after a design by Martin Desjardin. There are also four Virtues by Coysevox on the second story, two on either side of the columns.

The interior floor plan consists of a Greek cross described within a square 184 feet on a side. The cupola rests directly on the walls surrounding a rotunda, and the four arms of the Greek cross end in apses; the northern one expands to form an oval-shaped chancel. Round chapels topped by smaller cupolas fill the corners of the square, and these connect through low arcades both to the arms of the cross and to the rotunda. Huge Corinthian columns stand in front of the crossing pillars, and Corinthian pilasters are used in the side rooms.

The cupola is a double dome. First there is a shallow dish whose ribs continue the spacing of the double pilasters of the drum; then, through a broad circular opening, one can see a second, overarching dome embellished with frescoes and lighted by the concealed attic windows. The wooden framing that supports the cupola's outer shell begins above this second dome. Twelve high rectangular windows flood the interior with light, brightly illuminating the church's wealth of paintings and sculptural ornamentation.

The original spatial feeling has been con-

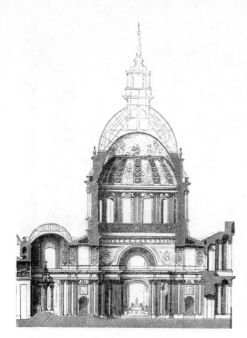

Dôme des Invalides (longitudinal section).

siderably compromised by the huge round opening that was cut in the floor of the rotunda. Through this, one gazes down into a crypt designed by Louis Visconti and containing the porphyry sarcophagus of Napoleon (illus. 50), whose body was brought from St. Helena in 1840 and interred here with great ceremony in the presence of Louis-Philippe.

Porte St-Denis and Porte St-Martin

After victorious campaigns in Flanders and in the Franche-Comté and the completion of national boundary fortifications by Sebastien Vauban, Louis XIV ordered that the old city walls, dating back to the time of Charles V, be demolished. Tree-lined promenades were created in their stead; this was the origin of the Grands Boulevards. The word *boulevard* derives from the Dutch *bolwerk*, meaning "rampart."

The old city gates were now to be replaced by triumphal arches designed to impress the grandeur of the capital upon visitors. The city commissioned François Blondel to design the first two of these on the most important routes leading to the north, the Rue St-Denis and the Rue St-Martin. Blondel was one of the most important theorists of rationalistic architecture in the Colbert era and a man who was highly respected as an engineer, a marshal, and a diplomat. He also served as the first director of the Académie d'Architecture.

Blondel patterned the Porte St-Denis after the Arch of Titus in Rome, but his triumphal arch is gigantic. On either side of its round-arch opening are massive pillars supporting a low entablature, a deeply projecting cornice, and a flat attic wall. Against the smooth, flat masonry surfaces of these pillars he placed steep pyramids resting on tall pedestals and richly festooned with trophies. Allegorical figures of the conquered Netherlands and the Rhine lie at their bases. It was only at the city's insistence that he created passageways through these side pedestals as well. The spandrels of the arch are filled with victory goddesses, and above them on the side facing the city there is a relief depicting the king crossing the Rhine. Another, on the side facing away from Paris, shows the capture of Maastricht. These sculptural embellishments were designed by Charles Le Brun and executed by the sculptor Michel Anguier. At the express wish of Blondel, they were based on the reliefs of Trajan's Column in Rome and the remains of the columns of the rostra in the Roman Forum. Blondel placed great value

Porte St-Denis (Perelle).

on strict mathematical proportions. His arch is described within a square; its components —arch and pillars—correspond to the division of the square into thirds. The numbers three and four govern all its further subdivisions. Begun in 1672, the arch was the first place to display the king's new title: Ludovico Magno.

Two years later, Pierre Bullet constructed the Porte St-Martin after plans by Blondel. This is a triumphal arch with two lower side arcades, all strongly rusticated to emphasize its military character. The upper half of the structure is embellished on either side of the arch with large reliefs depicting the capture of Luxembourg and the defeat of the German Empire on the side facing away from Paris, the conquest of Besançon and the victory of the king over the Triple Alliance on the side facing toward the city. The

Portes St-Antoine, St-Bernard (fig., page 59), and St-Honoré (fig., page 207) were built a short time afterward, but they have not survived.

Place des Victoires

(illus. 32, page 115)

In his design for the Place des Victoires, Jules Hardouin-Mansart revived the tradition of regal squares from the time of Henri IV. This square was a nearly closed circle, with two streets entering into it and a third tangent to it. Taking his cue from the nearby Hôtel Lully, by Daniel Gittard, from 1671, Hardouin-Mansart constructed a row of mansions with uniform façades: round-arch arcades on the ground floor that housed shops, a *bel-étage* and a shorter third story

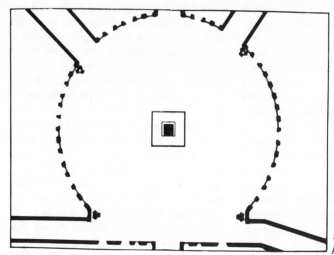

Place des Victoires (ground plan) (Mariette).

tied together by Colossal Ionic pilasters, a continuous entablature that underscored the curvature of the square, and an uninterrupted mansard roof with gracefully curved dormer windows. The nobility of these sandstone fronts, constructed (beginning in 1684) with municipal assistance, was destroyed due to various additions made to

Place des Victoires, with the statue of Louis XIV (Perelle).

the houses in the nineteenth century and demolition of some of the structures to accommodate new streets.

The square served as a setting for a monument to Louis XIV to celebrate the Treaty of Nijmegen. In 1679, the marshal de La Feuillade, the governor of the Dauphiné, had commissioned the sculptor Martin Desjardin to create a statue of the victorious king. Desjardin's marble statue pleased the king so much that de La Feuillade gave it to him and commissioned a second one in gilt bronze for the square. It showed the king stepping on three-headed Cerberus—an allegory of the Triple Alliance—and crowned by a goddess of victory atop a high pedestal with four bound warriors at its corners, representing the conquered nations of Spain, Holland, Piedmont, and the German Empire. The statue was dedicated with great ceremony on March 28, 1686; the façades of the surrounding houses were only beginning to be constructed. It was destroyed during the Revolution, although the four warriors are now in the park at Sceaux, and was replaced by an equestrian statue of Louis XIV by Astyanax Bosio in 1822.

Place Vendôme

(color plate, page 43)

The Place Vendôme, which would form the center of the Faubourg St-Honoré from a city-planning standpoint, originated in a bit of speculation in 1677 by Jules Hardouin-Mansart and five financiers, among them Crozat, who had funded the Canal du Midi. On the site of the Hôtel de Vendôme and its grounds, these men hoped to build city mansions and public institutions such as libraries, academies, and so on. After the death of Colbert, who had opposed these plans, Hardouin-Mansart and Louvois convinced Louis XIV that he should not leave

the establishment of a regal square to a private individual, as had been the case with de La Feuillade and the Place des Victoires. The king thus bought the Hôtel de Vendôme, and Hardouin-Mansart prepared the plans for a rectangular square opening onto the Rue St-Honoré. In its center, there was to be an equestrian statue of the king, and François Girardon received the commission for it. In the middle of one end of the square, a large triumphal arch was to open onto the façade of the church of the Capuchin monastery. The War of the League of Augsburg, which began in 1688, halted construction of the square, however, and in 1698, the king turned the site over to the city with the understanding that it would construct the façades of the square according to a new plan by Hardouin-Mansart and sell the building lots behind them to private individuals. The buyers were mostly speculators and financiers, but they also included Hardouin-Mansart himself and some of his relatives. They all had their own architects build them their mansions behind the uniform façades.

The king's statue was positioned in 1699, and the city began to construct the façades

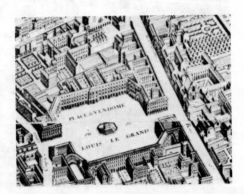

Place Vendôme (Plan Turgot).

Place Vendôme, with the Louis XIV monument and the church of the Capuchins (Mariette).

after Hardouin-Mansart's plans. The final version of these plans provided for a rectangle, with angled corners, that would run perpendicular to the Rue St-Honoré. The middle of each of the long sides and the angled corners are emphasized by Corinthian half-columns and triangular pediments. These serve to break up the otherwise continuous succession of identical bays that Hardouin-Mansart drew around the square: a ground floor with round arcades (originally planned to be open), pierced by rectangular windows; above these, an *étage noble* tied to the shorter third story by means of Colossal Corinthian pilasters; a continuous entablature; and a unifying mansard roof highlighted by dormer windows above each bay. This arrangement continues along the street that

connects the square to the Rue St-Honoré.

Sculptural ornamentation is limited to masks on the keystones of the arcades and coats of arms adorned with trophies in the pediments, thus underscoring the restrained elegance of the stone façades. Although individual builders had complete freedom to design the interiors behind these standard fronts as they chose, the final product was a grand setting for the king's statue.

The equestrian statue itself was destroyed in 1792. In its place, in 1806, Napoleon commissioned a 144-foot column modeled on Trajan's Column in Rome. Around it were reliefs of his campaign of 1805 and of the victory of Austerlitz. Known as the Colonne d'Austerlitz, it was constructed of melted Russian and Austrian cannon captured near

Place Vendôme: façade detail (Mariette).

church and set up in front of it the façade from the Barnabite church on the Ile de la Cité, which had to be dismantled in the course of Haussmann's renovation of that quarter. This façade had been constructed in 1703 by Sylvan Cartaud.

The interior of the church is quite uniform, with no transept. It has a continuous, relief-embellished entablature above Corinthian pilasters that emphasize the regular rhythm of the tall, narrow arcades. The plaster barrel vault, with intruding perpendicular vaults above the windows, is relatively shallow. Particularly notable is the pulpit from 1749, a superb Rococo creation with inlay work in pewter and ivory, which was purchased in 1864 at the Exposition de l'Art et de l'Industrie in Paris.

Austerlitz and was topped by a statue of Napoleon. The column was felled during the Commune and restored in the Third Republic. The painter Gustave Courbet was suspected of having masterminded the attack on the monument, and restoration was done at his expense. The present statue of Napoleon in antique costume is by Augustin Dumont and dates from the time of Napoleon III.

Notre-Dame-des-Blancs-Manteaux

Rue des Blancs-Manteaux, IVᵉ

A convent of mendicant Augustinian monks, whose white robes are recalled in the name of the spot, had been established here in the thirteenth century. The site was owned by the Benedictine congregation of St. Maur since 1618, and it was they who had a new novitiate and church constructed here, starting in 1685, after plans by Charles Duval. The monastery to the right of the church was demolished during the Revolution. In 1863, Victor Baltard added a bay to the

Hôtel Le Brun

47–49 Rue du Cardinal-Lemoine, Vᵉ

This is an early work by Germain Boffrand, the colleague of Jules Hardouin-Mansart and one of the most important architects—along with Robert de Cotte—in early-eighteenth-century Paris. It was built in 1700 for economic councillor Charles Le Brun, the nephew of the painter of the same name, who is memorialized in the pediment relief. The residential wing stands apart from its accompanying structures, as in the later Hôtel Biron and countless other eighteenth-century mansions. It is imposing less for its decoration than for the balance of its relative dimensions. The proportions of its center ornamental surround, for example, are in accordance with those of the golden section. Hardouin-Mansart had already used this ratio to determine the height of the pedestal story in relation to the overall height of the façades of the Place Vendôme.

Hôtel de Soubise

60 Rue des Francs-Bourgeois, IIIe (illus. 45, page 122)

The Hôtel de Soubise is one of the most lavish mansions in Paris, princely in the rich use of double columns as well as in the extravagant size of its deep, rounded courtyard. The palace was created by Alexis Delamair between 1705 and 1709 for François de Rohan, Prince de Soubise, through renovation of the medieval Hôtel Clisson, which had belonged to the Guise family. Delamair saved the portal structure of the earlier residence on either side of his new façade. Louis XIV facilitated the purchase of the *hôtel* in appreciation of the services rendered him by the princess, Anne Chabot de Rohan.

The courtyard ends in a semicircle toward the street, and Delamair lined it with twenty-four pairs of Corinthian columns. Corinthian columns continue along the front of the two-story palace, concentrated in the center of the façade, where there is one row of columns above the other to create a monumental portico with a triangular pediment. On either side, at the second-story level, there are allegories of the seasons on pedestals set above the double columns. Allegories of magnanimity and fame adorn the pediment. All of the sculptures are by Robert Le Lorrain.

On the occasion of his marriage with the young Marie-Sophie de Courcillon, Prince Hercule-Mériadec had the interiors renovated between 1735 and 1739 after plans by Germain Boffrand, who hired some of the best artists of his generation to collaborate on them: the painters Charles Natoire, François Boucher, Carle van Loo, and Jean Restout; and the sculptors Adam Lemoyne and Jean-Baptiste Lemoyne the Younger.

The decorations—those on the ground floor were recently restored—are among the best examples of the Rococo in Paris. Most striking is the princess's Salon Oval on the second floor, with tall mirrors that visually expand the space, a regular se-

Hôtel de Soubise: portal, courtyard, and corps de logis *(Mariette).*

quence of high arches for windows, doors, and mirrors, and eight paintings by Natoire that depict the fables of Psyche. A winding ring of gilt cartouches and *putti* is connected by a web of curved bands to the central ornament of the ceiling mirror.

Since 1808, the Hôtel de Soubise has been the home of the Archives Nationales, which has added a number of buildings in what was the garden and has also taken over the adjoining Hôtel de Rohan (see pages 477–478).

Hôtel de Rohan

87 Rue Vieille-du-Temple, IIIe (illus. 44, page 121)

The son of François de Rohan, Prince de Soubise, Armand-Gaston de Rohan—prince-bishop of Strasbourg, a cardinal after 1712, and *grand aumônier* of France—commissioned Alexis Delamair to build a *hôtel* in 1705 opposite his parents' and with a courtyard facing the Rue Vieille-du-Temple. Massive and closed, with a mezzanine story above the *étage noble* and a portico with double columns facing the garden, this severe structure derives its effect from the regularity of the window bays. Their tall openings largely suppress the wall mass, and the precision of the building's stonework emphasizes the subtle wall relief. On the north side of the courtyard are the former stables. Above the entrance to these is one of the masterpieces of eighteenth-century French sculpture, Robert Le Lorrain's *The Watering of the Horses of the Sun*.

Inside, the *étage noble* is given over to historical exhibits. Particularly remarkable is the Cabinet des Singes (Monkey Room), whose Rococo paneling boasts extremely delicate painting by Christophe Huet from 1749 to 1750, comparable to the chinoiserie and monkey fables in the châteaux of

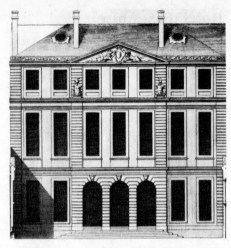

Hôtel de Rohan: courtyard façade (Mariette).

Chantilly and Champs (see pages 358–361 and 418–419).

St. Roch

296 Rue St-Honoré, 1er

St. Roch is one of the great Parisian parish churches, as important to the wealthy Faubourg St-Honoré as St. Sulpice is to the Faubourg St-Germain. In 1622, a separate parish was established for part of the congregation of St. Germain-l'Auxerrois because the population to the west of the city had grown so rapidly. But the cornerstone of its new church—on the site of an older chapel—was not laid until 1653. Plans for this classical, three-aisle structure with a slightly projecting transept and apselike choir were finished by Jacques Lemercier the year before he died. In 1660, construction was halted for lack of funds. Only the choir, the transept, and the first bay of the nave had been built by then, and these were covered with a temporary roof. In 1701, the king consented to the establishment of a lottery

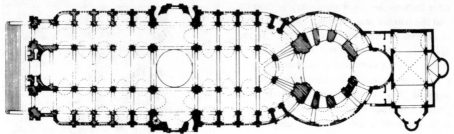

St. Roch (ground plan).

to finance renewed work on the church. Beginning in 1706, an oval-shaped Lady Chapel was built onto the choir after plans by Jules Hardouin-Mansart and was expanded, starting in 1717, by the addition of a small, round sacrament chapel. A donation of 100,000 livres from the Scottish financier and speculator John Law, who had converted to Catholicism, permitted the remaining bays of the nave and the half-barrel vaulting to be completed.

The sculptor René Charpentier, a student of François Girardon, embellished the church with a rich array of ornamental sculpture, making it the most splendid Baroque church in Paris, but most of his work was destroyed during the Revolution. The façade was begun in 1736 after plans by Robert de Cotte, who had died the year before. His son Jules-Robert oversaw its construction. This quite elegant, two-story façade, facing the Rue St-Honoré, was a forceful and ingenious variation on the classical Parisian scheme. Its Baroque ornamental sculpture was also destroyed during the Revolution. The façade still bears the bullet holes from the shots fired on October 5, 1795, by the young General Napoleon Bonaparte and his men at a group of royalists threatening the Convention in the nearby Tuileries.

The church was expanded one last time beginning in 1753, when the sculptor Étienne-Maurice Falconet attached a third chapel behind the choir, along the central axis, with the help of Étienne-Louis Boullée,

St. Roch: façade (Mariette).

237

later famous as a Revolutionary architect, and the painter Jean-Baptiste Pierre. Consecrated to the Crucifixion, this final space gives one a view from the choir through a series of spaces of varying brightness, as in a Baroque stage set. The congregation approved this effect enthusiastically, but Diderot sharply criticized it. Boullée was also responsible for the quite elegant redesign of the arms of the transept.

Even though the Revolution destroyed most of the church's celebrated ornamentation, St. Roch still displays—thanks mainly to the transfer of works from other Parisian churches demolished after 1819—an amazing wealth of seventeenth- and eighteenth-century sculpture and painting. Surviving from the original furnishings are the remarkable Rococo organ from 1752 as well as Simon Challe's sounding board above the pulpit from 1758, with the allegory "Truth Exposing Error."

The *hôtels* of the Faubourg St-Germain

The westward development of the city became more rapid on the Left Bank once the Hôtel des Invalides had been built. In 1672, Colbert fixed the new city boundary along the Esplanade des Invalides. Cross streets in the Faubourg St-Germain—the Rue de l'Université, Rue de Lille, Rue St-Dominique, Rue de Grenelle, and Rue de Varenne —were extended beyond the Rue du Bac toward the west. At first only a few religious orders, such as the *Missions étrangères* on the Rue du Bac, ventured to settle in this damp, marshy area. But beginning in 1700, it rapidly became a favored residential area for the nobility. Within thirty years, more than forty mansions arose here, often right next to one another. Given the similar standing and identical living habits of

Fontaine des Quatre-Saisons by Edme Bouchardon in the Rue de Grenelle: central façade (Mariette).

their builders, they are quite uniform. Almost all are placed between a courtyard and a garden. The structures consist of a *corps de logis* and wings for servants and horses, and they are closed off from the street by walls and a tall *porte-cochère*.

The social and political status of the nobility is revealed by this emphatically private architecture, which completely does away with "public" ornamentation of the façades. Even in the interiors, except for the vestibules, it places greater value on comfort and restrained elegance than on display, in spite of the spaciousness appropriate to this class of building. In the second phase of construction in the quarter, under Louis XVI, this restraint disappeared. These later *hôtels* competed with public buildings in their extravagant use of columns and Colossal pilasters. The Hôtel Biron (see pages 240–241) and the Hôtel de Salm (see pages 241–242) are typical examples of these two respective periods.

In spite of countless demolitions, remodelings, and additions, the Faubourg St-Germain is the best-preserved eighteenth-century ensemble in Paris. Most of the mansions are now ministries or embassies, so they are just as inaccessible to the public today as they were in the eighteenth century. We will therefore confine ourselves primarily to those structures that one can visit or whose façades one can at least admire.

Almost all the great architects of the time were commissioned to build in the Faubourg St-Germain. Surviving from the work of Robert de Cotte, the successor to Jules Hardouin-Mansart, is the Hôtel d'Estrées from 1713 (77 Rue de Grenelle), now the Soviet embassy. Its façade has been altered, unfortunately, by the addition of a fourth story in place of the original mansard roof.

Germain Boffrand, architect and builder, constructed the unusual Hôtel Amelot-de-Gournay (1 Rue St-Dominique) in 1712. It has an oval-shaped courtyard and Colossal pilasters in front of the concave, five-bay façade of its *corps de logis*. Also by Boffrand are the Hôtel de Seignelay from 1713 (80 Rue de Lille) and the Hôtel de Beauharnais from 1714 (78 Rue de Lille), which was built for Colbert's nephew, the Marquis de Torcy. The latter is most famous for its remodeling under Eugène de Beauharnais, the son of Joséphine de Beauharnais (Napoleon's first wife), who renovated its interior beginning in 1803 for the then-extraordinary sum of more than 1.5 million francs. It survives as the most brilliant example of Empire inte-

rior architecture in Paris. Beauharnais also placed an Egyptian-style portico in front of the façade facing the courtyard. Owned by Prussia (and later Germany) since 1817, the mansion was restored by the West German government in the 1960s and now houses its embassy.

The first of the great *hôtels* to be constructed in the Faubourg St-Germain was the Hôtel de Charolais (99–101 Rue de Grenelle), today the Ministry of Industrial and Scientific Development. Pierre Cailleteau, known as Lassurance, built it, beginning in 1700, for the Marquis de Rothelin. Next to the main courtyard, Lassurance created two secondary courtyards, resulting in a long front of seventeen bays facing the garden. The hôtel displays an unusual combination of a half-column portico and an iron grille. Equally unusual is the manner in which the round-arch window in the center of the second floor extends upward into the area of the triangular pediment. There is a similar motif in another of Lassurance's buildings, the Hôtel de Longueil-Maison, or Hôtel Pozzo di Borgo (51 Rue de l'Université). This one, constructed in 1707, boasted interior decorations created in part by Jean-Baptiste Leroux.

Lassurance also worked on the Palais-Bourbon, which Lorenzo Giardini had begun in 1722 for the natural daughter of Louis XIV and Mme. de Montespan, the Duchesse de Bourbon. Completed by Jacques-Ange Gabriel and Jean Aubert, the Palais-Bourbon was repeatedly remodeled and enlarged after 1764 so that the original structure is unrecognizable. It is now the seat of the National Assembly and appears to date from the age of classicism. Also by Lassurance is the Hôtel de Roquelaure from 1722 (246 Boulevard St-Germain), completed by Leroux in 1733. Today it houses the Ministry of Public Works.

Palais-Bourbon: portal and corps de logis *(Mariette).*

A particularly notable late-eighteenth-century *hôtel* is the Hôtel du Châtelet (127 Rue de Grenelle), today the Ministry of Labor, designed by Mathurin in 1770. Its courtyard side is quite severe, while the garden side is more informal, translating the scheme of the Hôtel de Matignon into the Louis XVI style.

The late eighteenth century's love of columns is especially apparent in the Hôtel de Gallifet (50 Rue de Varenne), which was begun in 1775 by Antoine-François Legrand for the Marquis de Gallifet. It has a tall peristyle of Ionic columns on the courtyard side and more Ionic columns, half buried in the wall, on the garden side. The passageways on either side and the windows also have smaller, embedded columns. The interior, with its staircase, vestibule, and Grand Salon, is one of the best examples of a Louis XVI ensemble in Paris. The mansion was completed only in 1792 for use by the Foreign Ministry; Talleyrand lived in it for ten years. Today, it houses the Italian embassy (cultural division).

Hôtel Biron

77 Rue de Varenne, VIIe

The location of this lot at the edge of the Faubourg St-Germain permitted the mansion and garden to approach the scale of a noble country house. The main building stands alone between the courtyard and the garden. It has a three-bay, pedimented central façade and two-bay corner pavilions that jut out slightly into the courtyard. Its garden side is more strongly emphasized. There, the corner pavilions project somewhat farther and display angled sides, the stonework accents the horizontal lines, and the pavilions have only a single bay; their round-arch windows correspond to those of the central façade. The Graces in the pediment are from a later date than the building itself, which was constructed between 1728 and 1730 by Jean Aubert, the architect of the Grandes Écuries of Chantilly, with assistance from Jacques-Ange Gabriel. The builder was the wigmaker Abraham Peyrenc, who had grown rich through speculation with John Law and had acquired the title of Sieur de Moras and the office of *maître des requêtes*. The interior arrangement—with a paired sequence of rooms on the courtyard and garden sides, a large vestibule, and an elegant staircase—further underscores the resemblance between this mansion and a country house.

In 1736, the mansion came into the possession of the Duchesse du Maine, who had it decorated in the style of Germain Boffrand. Beginning in 1754, the house belonged to the Duc de Biron, who gave it its name. During the nineteenth century, it served as a boarding school run by the convent of the Sacred Heart. It was then that the wainscoting was sold (but some of it has been repurchased and installed in the ground-floor salons) and that, in 1875, the chapel to the right of the entrance was built by Jean Lisch. After 1905, the *hôtel* was occupied by a succession of artists: Henri Matisse, Isadora Duncan, Rainer Maria Rilke, and Auguste Rodin. It was Rilke who introduced Rodin to the house, and the sculptor lived in its ground floor from 1910 to 1917. After Rodin's death, the Musée Rodin was established here, housing his most important works, his collection, and documentation about his *œuvre*. His larger sculptures in bronze are in the garden (see pages 481–482).

Hôtel de Matignon

57 Rue de Varenne, VIIe

This most lavish princely residence of the Faubourg St-Germain was begun in 1721 for the son of the marshal of Luxembourg, Prince de Tingry, after plans by Jean Courtonne. Before it was finished, it was bought by the Comte de Thorigny, Jacques Goyon de Matignon, who had it completed by Antoine Mazin. The young Jean-Honoré

Fragonard and various pupils of Christophe Huet contributed to its rich Rococo decorations.

A tall portal in a concave wall leads to the semicircular courtyard lined by low side wings. The *corps de logis*, with its richly sculpted central pavilion and its balustrade that masks the flat roof, has the look of a palace, especially on the long, thirteen-bay garden side. There, flanking corner pavilions extend forward, and a broad staircase leads down from the terrace into the expansive park—the largest private park in Paris. The Hôtel de Matignon has served as the official residence of the prime ministers of France since 1935.

Hôtel de Salm

64 Rue de Lille, VIIe (illus. 46, page 122)

This is the most important private *hôtel* from the time of Louis XVI, one in which public display on the street side contrasts with comfortable privacy on the garden side. Its gardens originally extended all the way to the Seine. It was built between 1782 and 1787 for Prince Frederic III de Salm-Kyrburg, who ruined himself by spending over 600,000 francs on it and died, totally impoverished, on the gallows. In 1804, it was designated as the seat of the Legion of Honor. After a fire during the Commune, it was painstakingly restored.

It is obvious that the architect, Pierre Rousseau, fashioned the street side after the École de Médecine (see pages 249–250). A stern triumphal arch leads into the very deep inner courtyard, which is surrounded by colonnades. At the end of this courtyard, a tall portico with six composite columns and a flat entablature nearly conceals the residence behind it.

The garden façade, however, is charming and elegant. Here, the mansion appears as a long, low building with a projecting central pavilion. This pavilion is surrounded by half-columns and crowned by a cupola with statues around its base. The length of the front is accentuated by subtle horizontal joints in the stonework, and the niche-like windows and round niches above them, containing busts, soften the severity of the façade. Above the French doors of the central pavilion are bas-reliefs. The sculptures and reliefs were created by Jean-Guillaume Moitte, Boguet, and Philippe-Laurent Roland.

École Militaire

43 Avenue de la Motte-Picquet, VIIe

The idea of founding a school for training military officers originated with Louis XV's mistress, the Marquise de Pompadour, who also wanted to erect a major monument to the king in Paris that would rival the Hôtel des Invalides. The approval for this project was signed by the king on January 22, 1751. A site on the Plain of Grenelle was chosen, not far from the Hôtel des Invalides, whose orientation toward the Seine was intended for this complex by the king's architect, Jacques-Ange Gabriel (fig., page 96).

Construction had begun on the secondary buildings when a shortage of funds and the onset of the Seven Years' War brought the project to a halt. Only in 1768 was work resumed, now after less ambitious plans by Gabriel. The main building, the château, was completed in 1773, and a year later the main courtyard was finished. No longer oriented toward the Seine, this courtyard was flanked by two long galleries and faced what was originally to be the back. It was linked to the Hôtel des Invalides by new squares and avenues. Gabriel's successor, Alexandre

Brongniart, built two lower additions onto the main structure facing the Champ-de-Mars in 1782, which were further extended in 1856 and 1865.

The school was originally planned to accommodate 500 cadets, but it was dissolved by 1787. Its most famous student was Napoleon Bonaparte, who attended in 1784 and 1785. Since 1878, the site has been the home of the École Supérieure de Guerre.

Gabriel's second plan made the main building a palacelike, U-shaped structure opening onto the courtyard, its façades quite markedly differentiated. The side facing the Champ-de-Mars was designed to be seen from afar. It is a long structure with twenty-one bays, whose center projects forward as a portico with four Colossal columns and a triangular pediment. The bays on either side of the portico are framed by pairs of columns. Above the pediment is a tall frieze and a massive, square cupola—an arrangement reminiscent of Louis Le Vau's south wing of the Cour Carrée at the Louvre.

On the courtyard side, there is a similar arrangement of the central pavilion. However, the portico is placed directly in front of the wall and is flanked by two floors of open galleries with columns, which are in turn contained between plain, projecting wings. Colonnades with double columns extend outward from these wings on either side of the courtyard, and an elegant wrought-iron fence, after a design by Gabriel, closes off the space. A statue of Louis XV by Jean-Baptiste Lemoyne the Younger was placed in the center of the courtyard in 1773, but it was destroyed in 1792.

The interior is almost completely preserved, but can be seen only with special permission. It is one of the brilliant achievements of the Louis XVI style, with a wide staircase and a chapel in the left wing of the château.

Hôtel des Monnaies (Mint)

11 Quai de Conti, VIe

In 1648, François Mansart erected the Hôtel de Conti on this site, but it was torn down beginning in 1768. Only the façade of the Petit Hôtel de Conti is preserved today in one of the courtyards of the Mint. Between 1771 and 1775, Louis XV had a new mint constructed after plans by Jacques-Denis Antoine, a major representative of the developing classicism. The Mint is the first monumental example of this style in Paris.

The main building, 382 feet long, faces the Seine, and conceals a number of secondary structures grouped about the main and various smaller courtyards. A high foundation floor with deep joints in the stonework supports the *bel-étage* and a mezzanine capped by a cornice supported by a narrow band of consoles and creating a seemingly endless horizontal. Only the central five bays are developed, with Colossal Ionic columns and a raised frieze that do not diminish the horizontal sweep of the building. Antoine completely avoided additional subdivisions, preferring a subtle rhythm created by the small balconies and console cornices on every third bay of the *bel-étage*. The central bays are provided with round-arch arcades on the ground floor, although above them, as everywhere else in the building, there are only rectangular windows. The arcades lead into the vestibule in the form of a three-aisle peristyle, which serves as both a passageway into the main courtyard and an anteroom to the grand staircase. Fluted Doric columns support a coffered barrel vault in the central passage. The semicircular back wall of the main courtyard has a portico like a triumphal arch that leads into a second peristyle from which one can reach the various workshops of the Mint.

The dimensions and the cool elegance of the staircase, built completely of stone and with a coffered vaulting supported by double columns, make it one of the most magnificent eighteenth-century examples in Paris. The adjacent salon, with tall Corinthian columns, and a gallery that develops into an octagonal ceiling from a square floor plan are also highlights of early classical interior architecture in Paris.

Under Charles X, a numismatic museum (Musée de la Monnaie) was established in the Mint. It continues to mount regular exhibitions on the *bel-étage* (see page 480).

Place de la Concorde

(color plate, pages 34–35)

After the Treaty of Aix-la-Chapelle in 1748, countless French cities built statues and laid out squares in honor of Louis XV. Paris did not wish to be outdone. The *prévôt des marchands* and the assessors commissioned Edme Bouchardon to create an equestrian statue of the king, and an architectural competition was held in 1748 for the design of a suitable square in his honor. More than fifty artists participated, and their projects involved locations throughout the city. Their one common feature was that extensive purchases of land and buildings would be required; therefore, the city postponed its decision. However, the king then announced that he would place at the city's disposal a piece of his property between the Jardin des Tuileries and the Champs-Élysées. Planning began anew.

The plan by the royal architect Jacques-Ange Gabriel was finally accepted in 1755. His proposal provided for setting the equestrian statue in a rectangular square at the intersection of two axes: one, the east–west line leading from the Tuileries across the Champs-Élysées and up to the heights of Chaillot; the other, a new north–south street, the Rue Royale, that would extend from the church of the Madeleine to the Palais-Bourbon via a bridge to be built across the Seine. The square was to have angled corners and would be surrounded by a moat bridged only along these axes and the diagonal ones to the west. As a boundary for the square, Gabriel suggested low balustrades with small guard houses at the corners, so that the sight lines would remain completely open. Only on the north side, facing the Faubourg St-Honoré, did he envision a uniform bank of buildings. The statue of the king was to be flanked by two fountains along the north–south axis.

Work began in 1757 and continued for twenty years. Bouchardon's statue, completed by Jean-Baptiste Pigalle, was set in place in 1763. As was done for the Place Vendôme, the architect designed the façades for the north side of the square, but private investors could buy the lots behind them and construct whatever they wished. These façades were begun in 1757, and it was not at all clear what they would be used for. The property to the west of the Rue Royale, today the Hôtel Crillon, ultimately came to house four private mansions. The lot to the east, now the Hôtel de la Marine, served as the Garde-Meubles, a storeroom for royal furniture and other objects. It was completed in 1768. Construction on the lots behind the façades of the Rue Royale, which were part of Gabriel's plans, continued until the early nineteenth century, by which time the façades themselves had been partially altered.

The design of the two main façades that were required to anchor the otherwise open square is based on regal precedents. It borrows from the Louvre Colonnades, which Gabriel had restored and completed with Jacques-Germain Soufflot. It also incorporates the rusticated pedestal story with rounded arches that Jules Hardouin-Mansart had used at Versailles and in the Place des Victoires and the Place Vendôme. Gabriel framed these references on either side by pavilion structures of the same height. These have porticos and triangular pediments between broad expanses of wall set with niches containing figures and medallions. They also have a second façade facing the Rue Royale, a flush portico with six columns that serves as an upbeat to the richly varied street front beyond.

Between the fluted, Colossal Corinthian columns of the colonnades, the actual structure appears to be set back and of two stories; the windows of its *étage noble* are emphasized by means of console cornices. The buildings are topped by a balustrade *à l'italienne*; one cannot see the roof behind it. Only the pediments of the pavilions are flanked by trophies, and the pediments themselves are embellished with sculptures by Michel-Ange Slodtz and Guillaume Coustou the Younger. The magnificence of these façades was anticipated by the fronts of the Rue Royale and by two palaces flanking them on the side facing the square —the Hôtel de la Vrillière on the right, and the Hôtel Grimod-de-La-Reynière on the left; the latter was replaced in the 1930s by the American embassy, whose design was inspired by the still-standing Hôtel de la Vrillière.

The guard houses, which today boast the somewhat stiff female allegories of eight French cities, were not in fact filled with soldiers. Rather, they were rented to private individuals who planted gardens in the surrounding trench. In 1852, Napoleon III had the trench filled, thereby obscuring the

Place de la Concorde, north side, with Jacques-Ange Gabriel's structures and the church of Ste. Marie-Madeleine, by Pierre Contant d'Ivry, in the background.

original excellent balance between the architecture and the design of the square itself.

The equestrian statue of Louis XV, whose name initially graced the square, was demolished in 1792, and the square became the site of the Revolution's executions On January 1, 1793, Louis XVI was b headed here by the guillotine. Until the death of Robespierre and his colleagues, there followed 1,343 additional victims, including Marie-Antoinette, Mme. Du Barry, Charlotte Corday, and Danton. After the Reign of Terror, the square and the bridge, opened in 1790, that led to the Palais-Bourbon were optimistically renamed "Concorde."

Under Louis-Philippe, the square was filled out with two large fountains, after plans by Jacob Hittorf, and the obelisk from Luxor that the Egyptian governor Mahmed Ali had given to the king in 1829. This 75-foot column, dating from the thirteenth century B.C., contains a dedication to the god Ammon and the pharaoh Ramses.

Panthéon

Place du Panthéon, Vᵉ (illus. 47, page 123)

As early as the seventeenth century, Claude Perrault had drafted plans for a new church of Ste. Geneviève to replace the structure built about 1180. This old church stood next to the church of St. Étienne-du-Mont, on the site of the present-day Rue Clovis. When

it was finally demolished in 1802, its so-called Tour Clovis was preserved as part of the adjacent convent building to the south, today the Lycée Henri IV. Perrault's planned church was not undertaken for lack of funds, and not until 1754, when Louis XV determined to build a new church for Ste. Geneviève in gratitude for his recovery from a dangerous illness, did the project get under way. A number of architects, including Jacques-Ange Gabriel, took part in the competition for its design. But the Marquis de Marigny, who was superintendent of buildings, awarded the commission to his friend Jacques-Germain Soufflot. Marigny and Soufflot had gone to Italy together in 1750, and their trip was decisive in turning French art and architecture toward classicism.

Soufflot's design was extremely ambitious. It called for a new location for the church, on the top of the Mont Ste-Geneviève. Moreover, the church was to sit on a rectangular square that would be connected by a new street to the Jardin du Luxembourg. The church itself would vie with St. Peter's in Rome, St. Paul's in London, and Paris's own Dôme des Invalides. On top of a base in the shape of a Greek cross, Soufflot envisioned a cupola that would tower above the whole quarter and be visible all over the city, marking the spot where its patroness was buried. Soufflot devised a number of variations on this idea, and even during construction he repeatedly altered his plans.

Preparations began in 1756: the colleges that had settled on the top of the hill were closed; the new street was cut through, at first only as far as the Rue St-Jacques; and construction of the foundation was started. This last task proved exceedingly difficult because excavation revealed a number of Gallo-Roman tunnels that had once been sources of clay. The king could finally lay the cornerstone on September 6, 1764. Funds were short, however, and construction was anything but rapid. By 1774, only the portico was complete. In 1778, the drum that was to support the cupola above the crossing was begun, but the columns developed cracks, and the supports for the cupola had to be strengthened. Soufflot died in 1779, and his co-workers Maximilien Brébion, Guillaume Rondelet, and Soufflot Le Romain completed the building in 1790. In the same year, the congregation of Augustinians that owned Ste. Geneviève was dissolved.

At the suggestion of the Marquis de Villette in the Jacobin Club, therefore, Ste. Geneviève was transformed into a mausoleum. The first person to be buried there in an elaborate ceremony on July 11, 1791, thirteen years after his death, was Voltaire. Next was Honoré Mirabeau, who was removed after his contacts to the royal family had been revealed.

It was the archeologist and art critic Quatremère de Quincy who suggested call-

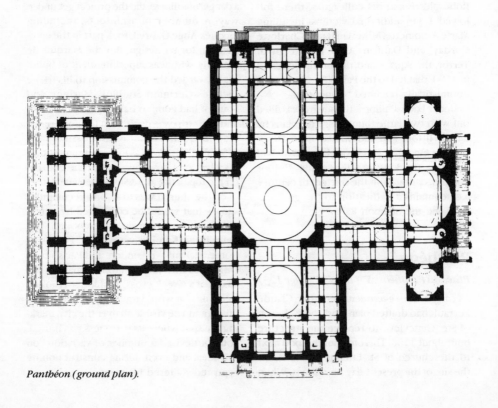

Panthéon (ground plan).

ing the building the Panthéon, and he was given the task of remodeling the church to make it suitable for its new role. As a church, the building had been flooded with light, but Quatremère de Quincy proceeded to wall up the forty-two tall windows that illuminated the interior. The cross and all sculptures with Christian themes were removed, as were the two towers on the east side of the church. Their lower floors were preserved, however, and still reveal the old window openings designed by Soufflot.

The history of France can be traced through the constant rededications the structure experienced during the nineteenth century. In 1806, Napoleon restored the church to the faith but designated the crypt as a necropolis for distinguished men from the army, politics, and cultural life so that the inscription placed on the portico in 1791 by the Constituent Assembly—"Aux Grands Hommes la Patrie reconnaissante" —could remain. But in 1823, on the occasion of the consecration of the church, Louis XVIII had the inscription replaced with a dedication to Ste. Geneviève and Louis XV. In 1830, Louis-Philippe once again turned the church into the Panthéon, restoring the old inscription and commissioning the sculptor Pierre-Jean David d'Angers to create a pediment relief in which an allegory of France disposes wreaths upon its heroes.

In 1851, shortly before being elected Napoleon III, Louis Napoleon elevated the Panthéon to the status of a "National Basilica." The Commune established its headquarters there; the Third Republic saw the building restored to its original use as a church; and only in 1885, after the death of Victor Hugo, was it decided, this time for good, to restore the structure to its role as a national necropolis. Since then, a number of prominent Frenchmen have been buried here—among them, Émile Zola, the assassi-

Panthéon, from the west.

nated president Sadi Carnot, and the Socialist leader Jean Jaurès.

To his contemporaries, Soufflot's church exemplified perfect architecture. According to his own thinking, it combined the lightness of Gothic construction with the forms of ancient Greece. The structural elements are not the walls but the columns. The changes made during the Revolution, however, altered the appearance of the structure considerably.

Fifty-two fluted columns surround the entire space like a peristyle. Together with seventy-six wall columns of equal height, they support the vaulting above a continuous entablature. In each of the arms of the cross, there is a flat cupola above a narrow vault. Only in the crossing are the massive pillars supporting the cupola provided with pilasters. Tall windows originally stood between the wall columns. Today, the interior receives its light solely from the skylights above the entablature (they are not visible from the outside).

Following the example of the Dôme des Invalides, the cupola consists of three separate shells. On the outside, it is ringed by thirty-two smooth Corinthian columns surrounding the drum lighted by large windows and its tall attic supporting the slightly pointed cupola with its lantern. Within, a coffered lower shell opens in a wide oculus onto a second dome ornamented with paintings.

The absence of an elaborate system of buttresses, pillars, and wall masses, a concept requiring incredible precision in its execution, produced a brilliant construction hailed by contemporaries. It also led to the collaboration between Soufflot and Rondelet toward the development of a new material that would be of prime importance to modern architecture: reinforced concrete. This medium was first used here, in the construction of the portico. This portico, with its 72-foot fluted columns—a touch of the Pantheon in Rome—gives the building, whose other faces are identical and less elaborate (the vestibule built on the east side as the entrance to the crypt dates from the nineteenth century), an orientation underscored by the layout of the square. Soufflot rounded off the corners of the west side of the square with two buildings whose façades describe the quadrants of a circle. Only the northern one, the Faculté de Droit, was completed during his lifetime, between 1771 and 1783. Its counterpart was constructed, in careful adherence to Soufflot's conception, as a mayor's office by Jacob Hittorf in 1844 to 1846. With Ionic porticos, a tall pedestal floor, and emphasis on the corners in the form of accented horizontal stonework, this building corresponds more strongly to the French eighteenth-century tradition than does the church itself.

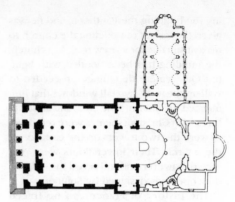

St. Philippe-du-Roule (ground plan).

St. Philippe-du-Roule

153 Rue du Faubourg St-Honoré, VIIIe

Until 1750, the rapidly growing congregation of the genteel Faubourg St-Honoré had to use the chapel of the leprosarium du Roule for its services. Then, at last, the minister de Saint-Florentin commissioned the architect Jean-François Chalgrin to plan a new church for the quarter. Chalgrin submitted his proposal for St. Philippe-du-Roule in 1764, but it was executed only between 1774 and 1784. It represented a further step toward the appropriation of antiquity—the use of a building style similar to that of the early Christian basilicas—that would be typical of many nineteenth-century Parisian churches. The three aisles—the central one is twice the width of the side ones—are separated by two rows of convex, fluted Ionic columns. Above the smooth architrave, there is a barrel vault into which the caps above the tall, round-arch windows are deeply cut. Chalgrin had planned a continuous coffered stone vault, with only a single cross vault where the side aisles end in chapels, but tall windows in the outside walls of the side aisles to create a dramatic lighting effect. For financial reasons, however, a wooden vault was actually constructed and simulated coffers were merely painted on it.

The choir originally ended in a semicircular masonry apse, with the Ionic columns continuing in front of it. Then, in 1845, the architect Étienne Godde added an ambulatory and chapels to the choir, thereby destroying the spatial effect of this portion of the church. The painting on the half-dome of the apse was also a later addition; this is a late work of the painter Théodore Chassériau, *Descent from the Cross* (1855).

A portico, with four plain Doric columns, an entablature, and a heavy triangular pediment, dominates the façade. Within the field of the pediment is an allegory of religion by Duret. The pediment's deeply projecting cornice continues around the whole blocklike front of the church. A frieze pierced by a semicircular window conceals the beginning of the nave roof.

In 1775, while St. Philippe-du-Roule was still under construction, Chalgrin was given the commission to complete St. Sulpice. For that church he designed the organ, the decoration of the tower chapel, and the final form of the north tower.

École de Médecine (College of Surgery)

12 Rue de l'École-de-Médecine, VIe

As important as Jacques-Denis Antoine's Mint to the beginning of classicism in Paris, but even more radical in its consistent use of antique columns, was the École de Médecine, for which Jacques Gondoin submitted plans in 1771, when construction of the Mint began. Gondoin's scheme proposed, along with the college, a great new square on the grounds of the monastery of the Cordeliers that would be bordered by a prison and a church consecrated to St. Cosmas, the patron saint of surgeons. The monks, however, refused to surrender their land, and only the college was built, beginning in 1774.

Gondoin arranged the building in four wings around a nearly square courtyard. Along the side facing the street, he designed a façade that captured the attention of his contemporaries: sixteen Ionic columns support a plain frieze with a sharply incised cornice, above which there is a low story like an attic with square windows, topped by a balustrade. In spite of the strict emphasis on the horizontal lines and on the regular arrangement of the columns, the effect is not cold. The front of the building can be seen behind the columns, and in the three end bays on either side, the windows of the side wings appear in round-arch arcades; the center is developed into a triumphal arch. The two bays on either side of the high arcade of the central bay are closed. In the attic above the three bays, there is an elongated relief instead of windows.

The junctions between the central structure and the wings are treated as open peristyles, with a second, inner row of columns between which one can see into the courtyard, where wall columns alternate with rounded arcades.

The center of the wing opposite the entrance is emphasized by a portico, with a triangular pediment, that ties together the two floors with tall Corinthian columns. The wall behind the portico is closed, and in place of upper windows there are medallions like those on the east side of the Louvre.

Along the central axis, a portal leads into the amphitheater, a semicircular hall with a coffered half-dome that can accommodate

1,400 students. Light falls into this hall through an oculus in the middle of the dome. The relief of "Theory and Practice Joining Hands" in the pediment of the portico is by Pierre-François Berruer, who also created the relief on the street side, "Louis XV [altered during the Revolution to an allegorical figure of charity] Commissioning the Construction of the School." The college, which is still part of the medical faculty, was expanded between 1878 and 1900 after plans by Ginain.

Palais-Royal

Place du Palais-Royal, Ier

The Palais-Royal, today the seat of the State Council (Conseil d'État) and various cultural agencies, faces the Louvre across a small square on the Rue de Rivoli. The Palais-Royal played a central role in the social life of Paris around 1800, mainly because of its garden and the shops, restaurants, and cafés surrounding it. During and following the Revolution, the garden was a center of public life; now it is a quiet oasis in the middle of a teeming metropolis.

The beginnings of the Palais-Royal go back to Richelieu, who, between 1627 and 1629, commissioned his architect Jacques Lemercier to build him a mansion in the vicinity of the Louvre. Once the city walls from the time of Charles V had been torn down— they formed one of the boundaries of his property—Richelieu expanded the mansion, between 1634 and 1639, into a princely residence with a *corps de logis* and four wings, forming the *cour de l'horloge* on the Louvre side and the *cour d'honneur* toward the north. The latter opened onto a very large park that stretched far beyond the former line of fortifications. Of this Palais Cardinal, where Richelieu lived until his death in 1642

and which he willed to Louis XIII, nothing has survived except for an exterior wall on the east side of the main courtyard, the Galerie des Proues. The palace was at various times the residence of Anne of Austria and the young Louis XIII. After 1692, it belonged to Gaston d'Orléans, the younger brother of the king, and thus became the ancestral seat of the Orléans branch of the House of Bourbon. Repeated fires resulted in a number of renovations. The last of these was in 1763, when the structure was given essentially its present form by Pierre Contant d'Ivry. Portions were burned during the Commune, and once again it had to be restored.

The Palais-Royal experienced its first period of brilliance after the death of Louis XIV in 1715, when Philippe d'Orléans, the regent, refused to move to Versailles and made the Palais-Royal the center of court life.

The society that gathered around the Palais-Royal after 1790 was of quite a different sort. In order to deal with his oppressive debts, Philippe d'Orléans, the regent's great-grandson, agreed to an extraordinary piece of speculation in 1780. He commissioned the architect Victor Louis, a Freemason like himself who had just built a highly successful opera house in Bordeaux, to build sixty houses around the edge of his huge garden, each with three bays and with an identical façade facing the park. Three new streets were laid out to provide access to them; these were named after the duke's three sons: the Rue de Valois on the east, the Rue de Beaujolais on the north, and the Rue de Montpensier on the west. These changes reduced the size of the garden considerably, and it took on the character of an enclosed square similar to the *plaza mayor* found in Spanish cities, for Louis provided the houses with an open gallery and spaces for shops on the ground floor around the

Palais-Royal in the late seventeenth century, from the south (Perelle).

open square. These soon came to be filled with cafés and restaurants. The galleries, with a lantern in each arcade, were open to the public and did not close until 2:00 A.M.; because they belonged to the duke, they were outside the jurisdiction of the police. The speculation was a complete commercial success. Although he originally planned to rent the houses, the duke sold them at a flat rate of 50,000 livres per arcade—that is, for each shop and the three floors above it.

The south side of the square as it was originally planned, which would have bordered on the main courtyard of the Palais-Royal, was never completed. In its place, there developed the so-called Galerie des Bois, a fairlike emporium that attracted the

most unusual acts and became one of the attractions of the Palais-Royal. It also became a meeting place for the thieves, defrauders, and other criminal types of Paris. Since the police could not supervise the garden, the cafés and gaming halls, the garden and galleries, became the center for a freewheeling life style that was unthinkable elsewhere in Paris before the Revolution (fig., page 83).

It was here that Camille Desmoulins called upon his fellow citizens to take up arms on July 13, 1789. After the cancellation of titles of nobility, the duke took the name Philippe-Égalité, but he was guillotined anyway, and the palace was confiscated. At the Restoration, it was returned to the Orléans family, and between 1814 and 1830, Louis-Philippe, later the Citizen King, ordered substantial renovations. The architect Pierre Fontaine provided the main courtyard with its colonnades and constructed the Galerie d'Orléans in place of the Galerie des Bois in 1829 to 1831. This is a peristyle composed of Doric columns that was originally covered with glass and housed a number of shops—an early example of the popular covered streets, or *passages*, that Paris developed in the nineteenth century.

In 1836, the gaming casinos were closed, and the garden began to decline as a social center. It developed more and more into a quiet residential quarter, especially prized by artists and intellectuals, and so it remains today. Colette and Jean Cocteau are among those who have lived here.

A number of the cafés and restaurants at the Palais-Royal had their moments in history. There was the Café-Glacier Corazza, which was the headquarters of the Jacobins. There was the Café du Caveau, where "Gluckists" came to blows with "Piccinnists" —Christoph Willibald von Gluck was named director of the Opéra by Marie-Antoinette in 1774, angering those who favored Niccolò Piccinni. There was the Café Février, where the guard Pâris stabbed Le Pelletier de Saint-Fargeau for voting for the death of Louis XVI on the eve of the monarch's beheading. And in the gaming rooms above, Gebhard Blücher managed to lose 150,000 francs in a single evening. The only one of the noble restaurants to have survived is the Grand Véfour, on the northwest corner of the park.

The south side of the Palais-Royal appears today in the form given it by Contant d'Ivry in about 1765: a U-shaped structure surrounding the *cour d'horloge*, which is closed off on the side facing the Place du Palais-Royal by an arcaded wall with portico. Its

Théâtre Français by Victor Louis, next to the Palais-Royal.

central pavilion is emphasized by double columns, a curved pediment (the coat of arms of the House of Orléans formerly stood in place of the clock), and a three-bay passage to the main courtyard on the north side. This courtyard is more lavishly ornamented, with columns on either side of the recessed center of the façade. The fourth story was built by Fontaine in the early nineteenth century. He also added the galleries and colonnades—a typical example of the "column frenzy" of classicism.

In contrast to Fontaine's rather dry additions, the Victor Louis façades surrounding the park on three sides are extremely elegant. Tall Colossal pilasters separate the narrow bays, in which an *étage noble* is tied to a mezzanine above a tall, open arcade. The third-floor windows are cut into the frieze, and the whole is capped by a continuous cornice, above which a balustrade, embellished with vases, half-conceals the set-back attic floor. Louis provided the façades with rich ornamentation—reliefs in the spandrels of the arcades and above the windows of the *bel-étage*, fluting on the pilasters, fancy capitals, vases, and artistic wrought iron—

all of which gives the palace a splendid air.

The Théâtre Français also goes back to Louis. He built this structure just west of the Palais-Royal between 1787 and 1790 to take the place of the theater in the right wing of the palace that had burned in 1763 —one in which Molière, Jean-Baptiste Lully, and Jean-Philippe Rameau had performed.

In 1799, the Comédie Française moved into this building, and in 1812, under Napoleon, it became the official state theater. Its exterior dates from the creation of the Avenue de l'Opéra by Prosper Chabrol in 1863. Its interior, recently restored, is from the turn of the century. Along with busts of famous poets, the foyer contains the marble statue of the aged Voltaire that was done in 1781, three years after the philosopher's death, by Jean-Antoine Houdon.

Odéon (Théâtre de France)

Place de l'Odéon, VIe

In 1770, the actors of the Comédie Française were forced to abandon their traditional home at 14 Rue de l'Ancienne-Comédie, so the king purchased the grounds of the Hôtel de Condé near the Palais du Luxembourg for them in 1773. Construction of a new theater began there in 1774 after plans by the city's architect Pierre Moreau, though the Marquis de Marigny, the superintendent of royal buildings, had already commissioned the architects Marie-Joseph Peyre and Charles de Wailly to draw up plans for a theater in 1767. In 1779, Moreau's plans were abandoned, construction having progressed slowly, and Peyre and de Wailly were given the job of completing the theater. The new structure was dedicated in 1782 with a performance of Racine's *Iphigenia in Aulis*. Twice the building was burned out, in 1799 and in 1818, but each time it was re-built in accordance with the original plans.

The architects planned the freestanding theater together with a number of other buildings that were to make the grounds of the Hôtel de Condé the center of this quarter. The exterior is remarkably geometric and massive, an appearance that is heightened by the original, pyramid-shaped roof. (As such, it has much in common with the so-called Revolutionary architecture of Claude-Nicolas Ledoux and Étienne-Louis Boullée.) The façade of the closed, blocklike theater is ornamented solely by the horizontal seams of its stonework, a continuous cornice, and a monumental portico with eight Doric columns. In front of it, to the north, is a semicircular square serving as the nexus of five streets that were constructed at the same time as the square. The architects controlled the façades of the buildings surrounding this square, dictating a tall, rusticated pedestal floor with round arcades, a low second story or *entresol* (half-story above the ground floor), three floors above it, and a mansard roof.

The theater was attached to its two neighboring structures by means of broad arches across the intervening streets. These arches

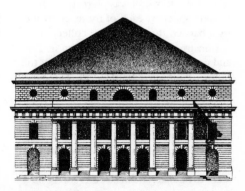

Odéon: façade.

provided audiences with sheltered entrance to the theater in rainy weather. Along the sides of the building, the ground floor opens out in arcades that formerly housed bookshops. With its 1,913 seats, the semicircular auditorium was the largest in Paris. On April 26, 1784, *The Marriage of Figaro* by Pierre-Augustin de Beaumarchais was premiered here, which led to the arrest of the author. In 1797, the theater became known as the Odéon, and it was used primarily for musicals. After World War II, for about twenty years until 1968, the theater, renamed the Théâtre de France, enjoyed considerable success under the direction of Jean-Louis Barrault. In 1965, the auditorium's ceiling was repainted by André Masson in the style of lyrical abstractionism.

Ledoux's Tollhouses

(illus. 49, page 123)

After the city walls were torn down under Louis XIV, it became increasingly difficult for the tax collectors—the *fermiers-général*—to collect the duties levied on goods being brought into the city. In about 1780, they convinced Louis XVI that the city needed to be surrounded by a wall to facilitate the control of all imports. Almost fifteen miles long, this wall was pierced by streets in sixty spots. At each of these, controlled by a barrier, the taxes were collected.

Construction of the wall began in 1784 and was completed in 1787. Work on its tollhouses continued until 1790. These had been designed by the architect of the Ferme, Claude-Nicolas Ledoux, who conceived of them not merely as practical structures but as impressive touches, in the form of ancient temples and pavilions, at the entrances into the capital. No two adjacent ones were to be alike, and in fact there were forty-five separate designs, providing a broad spectrum of free and unorthodox interpretations of antique models, often with Palladian touches. Along with Ledoux's work in the salt-producing town of Chaux, in the Franche-Comté, these represent the most important examples of the so-called Revolutionary architecture, which did not actually differ from the architecture of the last phase of the *ancien régime*.

Indeed, these tollhouses symbolized one of the causes of the Revolution, for the tax wall was deeply despised. Countless epigrams of the period treat it with scorn. The most famous of them, with a play on the word *mur*, was:

Le mur murant Paris rend
Paris murmurant.
[The wall hemming in Paris has
Paris murmuring.]

Even before the storming of the Bastille, some of the tollhouses had been set on fire, and the wall was breached on July 12, 1789. Nonetheless, the toll barrier persisted into the nineteenth century. Only when a law was passed on May 26, 1859, to extend the city limits out to the defense ring did the barriers become superfluous. And, in the course of time, all but four of Ledoux's tollhouses were torn down.

This wall was of extraordinary importance for the development of Paris, however. In addition to the 11-foot wall, there was a 40-foot-wide guard strip inside and a nearly 200-foot-wide boulevard outside. Moreover, any building outside the wall had to be at least 325 feet from it. Thus the ring of Boulevards des Maréchaux could be developed in the swath that remained when the wall was torn down.

Ledoux's surviving structures are the Rotonde de la Villette; the Rotonde de Chartres, next to the Parc Monceau; the Barrière de l'Enfer, on the Place Denfert-

The customs wall tollhouses of Claude-Nicolas Ledoux.

Rochereau; and the Barrière du Trône, on the Place de la Nation. The Rotonde de la Villette is the most important of these. It has recently been restored and now houses the archeological administration of the region. It was more than a mere tollhouse, containing a number of offices for the tax collector and his accountants, rooms for the guards, and storerooms. Its ground plan combines a Greek cross and a circle. A high cylinder rises above this base. Colonnades with double columns support the smooth exterior walls and the massive ring of the cornice. The only openings in the wall are a row of small mezzanine windows. Each arm of the cross ends in a broad portico, topped by a low triangular pediment, with steps between its Doric columns. These severely geometric forms are not softened by any ornamentation.

The small Rotonde de Chartres is equally austere. It is a variation on Bramante's Tempietto, with a ring of Doric columns without bases around a cylindrical core. Rising above these columns is a low cupola.

The two pavilions of the Barrière de l'Enfer are the farthest removed from accurate reconstruction of antique forms. The round-arch arcades of the ground floor are interspersed at regular intervals with square blocks and wedge-shaped stones that continue as bands around the corners. The forbidding, military character of the ground floor contrasts markedly with the elegant frieze, ornamented with female figures, that runs beneath the cornice forming the eaves.

The Barrière du Trône (Barrière de Vincennes) provides the best idea today of Ledoux's classical concept. Two tall, closed, cubelike pavilions face each other, each with a high arcade. Between the pavilions, on either side of the street, there are smaller

pavilions with a cruciform ground plan. These served as guard houses but are also the bases of two 98-foot Doric columns that marked the city limit and are visible from a considerable distance. In 1845, these were topped by statues of Louis IX and Philippe Auguste.

The Barrière de la Rapée, which was not the work of Ledoux, has also survived.

Madeleine (Ste. Marie-Madeleine)

Place de la Madeleine, VIIIe

In the Middle Ages, there was a chapel consecrated to St. Mary Magdalene in the Couture-la-Ville-l'Évêque, a garden outside Paris that belonged to the bishop. In 1722, this area was incorporated into the city, and in 1763, Louis XV began construction of a new church here after plans by Pierre Contant d'Ivry. This church, with a flight of steps and a portico on the south side, was to form the termination of the new Rue Royale and serve as a perspective for the Place Louis XV (Place de la Concorde), which was under construction. Work on the church proceeded slowly; after Contant d'Ivry's death in 1777, its direction was taken over by Couture, but by the outbreak of the Revolution, only portions of the south portico were completed. In 1806, after the Battle of Jena, Napoleon decided to build a temple glorifying the Grande Armée in place of the church. The architect Pierre Vignon designed a structure of imperial dimensions and in slavish imitation of classical examples. It was to be 353 feet long and 140 feet wide. It would have 52 Corinthian columns 49 feet tall on a 13-foot pedestal. Broad steps would lead to it on the north and south, and the interior was to include a register of the names of the soldiers who had accom-

panied the emperor on his campaigns. In 1813, Napoleon decided to change the so-called Temple of Glory back to a church, and Vignon was required to redesign the interior. The structure was finally completed in 1842 by Jean-Jacques Huré, Vignon's successor.

From the exterior, only the inscription on the frieze and the pediment relief of the Last Judgment, created in 1833 by Philippe Lemaire, indicate the building's Christian use. Low and massive, the Madeleine dominates the square on which it sits, and its pedimented front dominates the view up the Rue Royale from the Place de la Concorde. Its counterpart at the opposite end of this axis is the façade—also commissioned by Napoleon—that Bernard Poyet placed in front of the Palais-Bourbon in 1806, across the Pont de la Concorde.

The interior of the Madeleine is a rectangular hall whose three bays, roofed by low cupolas, are defined by inset Corinthian columns. Colonnades that are half the height of the space continue around the semicircular apse. On the high altar of white marble is Carlo Marochetti's *Elevation of Mary Magdalen into Heaven* (1837).

Arc de Triomphe

Place Charles-de-Gaulle–de l'Etoile, VIIIe (color plate, page 212; illus. 53 and 54, pages 125 and 126)

After the battles of Marengo and Austerlitz, Napoleon commanded that triumphal arches be erected in Paris to the glorious French armies. Charles Percier and Pierre Fontaine promptly designed the Arc de Triomphe du Carrousel (illus. 52, page 124), after the arch of Septimius Severus in the Roman Forum. This was built between the Louvre and the Tuileries, where the emperor lived.

A second arch was to have been placed in the Place de la Bastille, but it was finally decided to set it in the star-shaped square on the heights of Chaillot, halfway between the Place de la Concorde and Neuilly. This square had been laid out under Louis XV, at which time the top of the hill was cut down by some 16 feet so that the slope facing the Champs-Élysées would roughly correspond to the one on the Neuilly side. For the toll wall that ran along the east side of the square, Claude-Nicolas Ledoux had designed two pavilions and barriers across the Champs-Élysées in 1787. The elderly Jean-François Chalgrin, the architect of St. Philippe-du-Roule, was given the commission for the arch after a design competition. He had chosen not to copy a Roman arch; rather, he borrowed from the Porte St-Denis from the time of Louis XIV. In translating that monument to this new situation as a focal point of both the city's east–west axis and the star-shaped square, he enlarged the arch to gigantic proportions. The new structure was to be 164 feet high and 148 feet wide, with a huge arched opening along the main axis and smaller arches perpendicular to it. Thus, Chalgrin introduced a new and important city-planning motif. The broad pillars have smooth wall surfaces, and there are no columns. However, the proportions have been precisely calculated, so that the individual elements balance one another and stand in a pleasing relation to the whole, and the entire structure fits into the larger urban context.

The Arc de Triomphe and the destruction of Claude-Nicolas Ledoux's tollhouses.

Preparation of the foundations of the arch was extremely difficult. By 1810, at the time of Napoleon's marriage to Marie-Louise of Austria, the walls had scarcely risen above the ground. Chalgrin was therefore required to construct a full-scale model of canvas stretched on scaffolding for the pair's triumphal entry into the city. This facsimile nevertheless provided a foretaste of the monument's ultimate effect. Work on the arch was resumed under Louis-Philippe in 1832, and it was completed in 1836. Of the four large groups of sculptures on the main faces, only the so-called Marseillaise—the *Departure of the Volunteers in 1792*—by François Rude is noteworthy.

La Bourse

Place de la Bourse, IIe (illus. 51, page 124)

In 1808, Napoleon initiated construction of a templelike building for the stock exchange, which had been founded in 1724 and during the Revolution had been housed at Notre-Dame-des-Victoires. The new structure was built on the grounds of the former Dominican cloister of the Daughters of St. Thomas. The architect Alexandre Brongniart surrounded this rectangular, two-story building with a peristyle of smooth Corinthian columns—twelve across the ends, twenty along the sides. These rise above a high pedestal and are topped by an unornamented entablature, above whose projecting cornice a low attic conceals the roof structure.

Leading up to this freestanding "Temple of Money" on its newly created square, there are broad flights of steps. These are flanked by low walls that serve as pedestals for four seated allegorical figures: justice, commerce, industry, and agriculture. The building was finally dedicated in 1826; between 1902 and 1907, two wings were added so that its plan assumed the form of a Greek cross.

Chapelle Expiatoire

29 Rue Pasquier, VIIIe (illus. 48, page 123)

In the marshy area of Ville l'Évêque, there had been a cemetery attached to the convent of St. Mary Magdalene since 1720. This was the closest cemetery to the Place Louis XV (Place de la Concorde). In 1770, it had served as the burial place of the 133 people crushed or trampled to death during a fireworks display on the square celebrating the marriage of Louis XVI and Marie-Antoinette. Here, too, were buried the Swiss Guards who were killed during the attack on the Tuileries on August 10, 1792. And it was to this cemetery that all those beheaded in the square between August 26, 1792, and March 24, 1794, were brought—among them, Louis XVI and Marie-Antoinette, Charlotte Corday, Philippe-Égalité, and the Comtesse Du Barry. In 1815, Louis XVIII had the bodies of his brother and sister-in-law exhumed and placed in the royal necropolis at St. Denis. He then commissioned Pierre Fontaine to erect an expiatory chapel on the site of their original graves, and the entire cemetery was restructured in the form of medieval charnel houses to accommodate the bones of the more than 1,000 people guillotined during the Revolution. The chapel cost more than 3 million francs, a sum shared between the king and the Duchesse d'Angoulême, who, although imprisoned, had survived the guillotine. With the cupola structure of this chapel and the rectangular cemetery square, Fontaine and his associate Le Bas created an unequivocal testimony to the Restoration, one that glorifies the victims of the Revolution as Christian martyrs.

Behind the chapel's severe Doric portico, there is a central, coffered chamber flanked on three sides by semicircular apses that are illuminated, like the cupola, by round

La Bourse: Alexandre Brongniart's stock exchange.

openings in the top of the vaulting. In the side apses are statues of the royal pair. Louis XVI, by Astyanax Bosio, is being conducted into heaven by an angel (with the features of the abbot Henry Essex Edgeworth, who accompanied him to the guillotine). Marie-Antoinette, by Jean-Pierre Cortot, is being supported by Religion (with the features of Élisabeth, the king's sister, who was also executed). On the bases of these sculptures are the royal couple's testaments. A sarcophagus-like altar in the crypt marks the spot where the king's corpse was buried for twenty-one years.

St. Vincent-de-Paul

Place La Fayette, X^e (illus. 60, page 162)

This is the masterpiece of Restoration Paris. It was begun according to plans by Jean-Baptiste Lepère in 1824 and completed by his son-in-law Jacob Hittorf, the builder of the Gare du Nord. The church was consecrated in 1844.

Situated on a slight elevation, St. Vincent-de-Paul draws on Hittorf's reminiscences of Rome, which he had visited in 1822 to 1824, especially the church of the Trinità dei Monti with its two towers and the Spanish Steps in front of it. But this influence is combined with the Parisian tradition of the portico façade (St. Sulpice, the Panthéon).

The interior, a five-aisle, flat-roofed basilica, re-creates the early Christian basilica, as does St. Philippe-du-Roule. The clerestory of the nave is fitted with colonnades of Corinthian columns, with a straight entablature supporting the open roof timbers.

The extraordinary wealth of polychrome painting was designed by Hittorf, who also called for painted stucco on the exterior walls. A 556-foot frieze, by Hippolyte Flandrin, portrays saints and church fathers

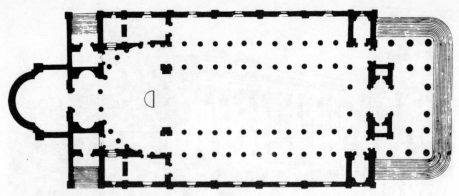

St. Vincent-de-Paul (ground plan).

against a gold background. The choir stools are by Jean-François Millet, with depictions of the members of the House of Orléans in the garments of their patron saints. In the apse cupola is Picot's *Christ as World Judge*, and beneath the baldachin of the high altar is a bronze crucifixion group by François Rude, from 1852.

The church was considered by its contemporaries, among them Jean Auguste Dominique Ingres, to be the most beautiful modern building in Paris. It was shelled during the Commune.

The *Passages*

(illus. 62–64, pages 163 and 164)

More characteristic of nineteenth-century Parisian architecture is the *passage*—a shopping street lined with small boutiques, generally no wider than 15 to 18 feet, and roofed with a thin sheath of glass to protect against bad weather. This style is closely associated with the industrial boom of early capitalism in France and the resulting mass production of consumer goods. Its heyday was the Restoration, although the oldest examples (Passage de la Reine-de-Hongrie,

1775; Passage du Caire, 1798) date from the late eighteenth century.

The *passages* were undoubtedly inspired by the bazaars of the Orient and the rows of shops in the galleries of the Palais-Royal. The façades of the shop rows were regarded as artistic achievements of the architects, while the roofs were considered engineering accomplishments of the builders. The aesthetic value of these light, weblike structures did not come to be appreciated until the age of functionalism—as is the case with all the technological, utilitarian architecture of the nineteenth century.

For decades, the *passages* were focal points in the life of the city, surrendering their importance only with the rise of the great department stores after 1870. Of the twenty-five *passages* still in existence, some clustered together as interior corridors between long blocks of buildings, most are in very poor condition. Even the most exclusive, the Passage des Panoramas, now offers little of the luxurious fashion salons, delicatessens, cafés, and entertainment centers that once attracted the cream of Parisian society. Some of the *passages* are still of interest because of their particular collections of often highly specialized dealers in antiques, coins, firearms, or instruments (the Passage Véro-Dodat, for example, illus. 62). The most interesting glass roofs are found in the Passage du Caire, from 1798; the Galerie Vivienne (illus. 63), from 1823; the Passage du Grand-Cerf (illus. 64), from 1825; and the Passage Brady, from 1828.

L'Opéra

Place de l'Opéra, IXᵉ (color plates, page 213)

The Opéra stands as a symbol of the Second Empire: the "cathedral" of the Parisian bourgeoisie in the nineteenth century, and the quintessential example of the Napoleon III style. And despite the excess of its decor, the unprecedented richness and color of its materials, and the confusion of its historical styles, Charles Garnier's opera house nonetheless distinguishes itself quite favorably from most of the buildings erected in Paris under Napoleon III. Thanks to its masterful arrangement of spaces and structural masses and its subtle orchestration of details, it far outranks, for example, Hector Lefuel's additions to the Louvre (illus. 35, page 116), Joseph-Louis Duc's monumental and exotic façade of the Palais de Justice, and Théodore Ballu's insipid Tribunal de Commerce. Admittedly, the Opéra also benefits from Haussmann's insistence on axially symmetrical street lines: its front dominates the Avenue de l'Opéra as far as the Louvre and serves as its end point; and its secondary façades dominate the intersections of the side streets.

Garnier was virtually unknown before 1861, when his design won out over 170 others in a competition, including that of the "pope of architects," Eugène Viollet-le-Duc, the empress's favorite. In 1862, the cornerstone was laid. The dedication cere-

monies took place on January 5, 1875; the estimated cost of 34 million francs had not been exceeded.

In his design, which was inspired by Victor Louis's opera house in Bordeaux, Garnier combined the requirements of the theater with that of Second Empire society to display itself. In front of the core consisting of the stage and auditorium, he called for a showy staircase, reminiscent of Baroque designs, a vestibule, and a grand foyer. His façade recalls the Louvre Colonnades as well as Jacques-Ange Gabriel's imposing buildings at the Place de la Concorde. But it surpasses these in the architectural and ornamental motifs and in the colorful variety of its materials. On the right side of the auditorium, he placed a pavilion with a covered approach for subscribers; on the left, a similar one with a Baroque, curved double ramp for the emperor. This led to the sovereign's private salons on the second floor, from which there was direct access to his box. Today the Opéra's library and museum occupy the emperor's suite. Behind the stage, Garnier constructed the much more severe and massive complex that housed administrative offices, storerooms for wardrobes and sets, and rehearsal spaces.

The diverse functions of the separate sections of the building are reflected quite admirably in the arrangement of the structural masses. Above the flat-roofed block containing the foyer and the staircase, which is concealed behind a tall attic wall, rises the low, round, copper-green cupola of the auditorium, surrounded by golden garlands and topped by a crownlike golden lantern. Behind this towers the triangular gable front of the stage structure; from its summit Apollo holds his lyre aloft. This powerful figure by Millet, like the rest of the building's ornamentation—winged horses, allegories of harmony and poetry, busts of famous composers and writers—is interesting more for its placement within the whole architectural context than for its individual excellence. An exception is the sculpture representing the dance—one of four allegorical groupings: lyric poetry, music, dance, and lyrical drama—in front of the arcade of the ground floor of the main façade. This work by Jean-Baptiste Carpeaux (replaced in 1964 by a copy by Paul Belmondo), the original of which is in the Pavillon de Flore of the Louvre, exhibits a freshness of movement that breaks through the academic rigidity of the remaining sculptures. Also by Carpeaux is the quite lifelike bust of Charles Garnier on the left side of the Opéra, in front of the drive leading to the imperial pavilion.

In the interior Garnier expended the greatest abundance of precious, multicolored materials on the ensemble of the Grand Escalier and Grand Foyer, a space quite as large as the auditorium itself. The theater seats only 2,158 people and is thus considerably smaller than comparable houses; Milan's La Scala seats 3,600, for example. The staircase, with steps of white marble and a balustrade of Algerian onyx, begins in the center at a width of some 32 feet. At the first landing it divides and continues upward in two flights of steps to the second floor. Here, a gallery surrounds the rectangular stairwell, and slightly curved balconies project between tall arcades that rise to the fourth floor, supported by double columns of pink marble.

The height of splendor is attained in the Grand Foyer. This room is suffused in a heavy shade of old gold. A wealth of architectural detail and decorative motifs dissolves the wall surfaces into picturesque masses: pairs of Corinthian columns support female statues, and massive ornamental frames surround the doorways. The ceiling vaulting includes sculpted cartouches and frames for numerous paintings.

The auditorium is encircled by five tiers of loges and is decorated in warm red and gold. In 1964, at the urging of André Malraux, a brightly colored painting by Marc Chagall was hung in place of the illusionist ceiling fresco by Jules-Eugen Lenepveu. Chagall's ceiling incorporates depictions from a number of famous operas and ballets: *Tristan and Isolde, Romeo and Juliet, The Magic Flute, Pelléas and Melisande, Daphnis and Chloe, The Firebird, Giselle*, and *Boris Godunov*. The stage is 170 feet wide, 120 feet deep, and 196 feet high. Behind it is the Foyer de la Danse (depicted in many of Edgar Degas's paintings), which is reflected in a monumental mirror.

Hôtel de Ville

Place de l'Hôtel-de-Ville, IVe (illus. 61, page 162)

The city government has occupied the same site ever since 1357, when Étienne Marcel purchased the Maison aux Piliers on the Place de Grève for the administrators of the municipality of Paris. The Place de Grève was the site of public executions from 1310 until 1830. It also has been the spot where jobless workers tend to assemble, hence the expression *faire la grève* (to strike).

At the urging of François I, the medieval city hall here was replaced beginning in 1533 by a Renaissance structure in the style of a Loire château. Its plans were provided by the Italian Domenico da Cortona, known as Boccador, who had been active at Blois and Chambord. Its southern section was completed by 1551; the northern part, following the same plans, was not constructed until 1606 to 1628.

The Revolution did away with the office of *prévôt royal*, the king's appointed governor of the city. Napoleon replaced it with the post of *préfet de la Seine* as head of the city administration and representative of the central government. This official was to reside in the Hôtel de Ville, and in 1803 and again between 1837 and 1841, wings were added onto the existing Renaissance structure for his use.

The Republic was proclaimed here on September 4, 1870, and the Commune made the building its central headquarters. When the uprising collapsed on May 24, 1871, the Hôtel de Ville and the municipal archives went up in flames.

The Tuileries, the imperial palace, was also torched by the Commune, and through the 1870s, the citizenry of the Third Republic was unable to agree on its reconstruction; finally, its ruins were cleared in 1882. But the Hôtel de Ville was rebuilt in 1873; a crude copy of the Renaissance building was designed by the architects Théodore Ballu and Edouard Deperthes. The central por-

tion comes closest to being a precise rendering of Boccador's original. The interiors of the new structure were created by Jean Formigé beginning in 1885, and they provide countless reminders of historical events in Paris, glorifying the sensibilities and virtues of its citizens. They are a fine example of the pomposity and self-importance of the citizenry during the Belle Epoque.

Sacré-Cœur

Parvis du Sacré-Cœur, XVIIIe (color plate, pages 46–47; illus. 58, page 128)

Unanimous condemnation by architecture critics has done nothing to prevent Sacré-Cœur from becoming one of the favorite tourist attractions in Paris. Its popularity stems in part from its commanding position at the top of the hill of Montmartre; from its terraces, one can enjoy an overwhelming panorama of the city. But its appeal can also be attributed to its gleaming

Place de Grève and the Hôtel de Ville: Paris's Renaissance city hall by Domenico da Cortona.

white structural masses that combine Byzantine influences with the Romanesque style of Aquitaine. It is paradoxical that this least Parisian of churches should have become one of the symbols of the city and the center of a quarter that exemplifies a specific image of Paris. For here, deliberately marketed for tourists, the Paris of the Belle Epoque—of amusements in garden taverns (*guinguettes*), in cabarets, at the Moulin Rouge, and in the Place Pigalle—lives on; so does the Paris of artists' studios.

The motives behind the founding of this church, however, stand in sharp contrast to the bohemian life style its surroundings have come to symbolize. In response to the French defeat at the hands of Germany—which some interpreted as a sign from God and a call for moral revolution—and as atonement for the "crimes" of the Commune, the Catholic movement known as the Voeu National au Sacré-Cœur began to agitate, in 1871, for a national church of expiation on the highest elevation in Paris. In 1873, the National Assembly approved the plan and the fund drives required to realize it.

The designer was Paul Abadie, who had worked as a diocesan architect in Périgueux, whose church of St. Front provided the crucial inspiration for this new structure. It is a square building to which a choir with ambulatory and *chevet* has been attached. The main space is a Greek cross with a tall cupola above the center. Shorter cupolas crown the secondary spaces in the corners. A tall campanile, set off to the side, was added in 1904 by the architect Lucien Magne. In October 1919, the building was consecrated to the Most Sacred Heart of Jesus. The two huge equestrian statues above the vestibule by Hippolyte Lefebvre, depicting St. Louis and Joan of Arc, were set in place in 1927.

Tour Eiffel

Quai Branly, VIIe (color plate, page 224; illus. 71, page 170)

The first principle of architectural aesthetics prescribes that the basic lines of a structure must correspond precisely to its specified use. And what laws did I have to consider in the tower? The laws of wind pressure. Well enough, I maintain that the curvature of the four pillars, just as my calculations called for, will communicate a distinct impression of strength and beauty, in that it will make visible the audacity of the entire composition. In the same way the countless open spaces in the various parts of the structure will reveal my constant desire to avoid surfaces that would allow the force of the wind to endanger the stability of the structure.... The geometric form of the 984-foot tower was primarily determined by mathematical considerations dependent on the force of the wind. To a certain extent the tower was formed by the wind itself.

Gustave Eiffel

The expression of a functional, technical aesthetic was bound to be a shock to a city where the Beaux Arts style reigned supreme, and the construction of the Tour Eiffel in 1887 to 1889 did produce a phalanx of prominent opponents: Charles Garnier, Charles Gounod, Paul Verlaine, Guy de Maupassant, Émile Zola, and others. Soon, however, they were silenced by a general admiration for the technical achievement the structure represented and by pride that France had realized the dream of a 1,000-foot tower before any other country in the world.

The broad arch between the tower's slanting pillars served as the gateway to the world's fair of 1889 on the Champ-de-Mars.

This event, marking the centennial of the Revolution, was France's first opportunity to display itself internationally since its defeat in the Franco-Prussian War, and it was an overwhelming success. In the Palais des Beaux-Arts, designed by Jean Formigé, France exhibited its art of the past hundred years, and in the gigantic Galerie des Machiens by Dutert, Contamin, Pierron, and Charton, French industry showed its preeminence. This hall of steel and glass, 156 feet high, 1,373 feet long, and an extraordinary 376 feet wide, was one of the most important engineering feats of the nineteenth century. It was broken up for scrap in 1909, making way for the formal gardens in front of the École Militaire. Only the nonutilitarian Tour Eiffel survived from the exhibition—a symbol of progress and a new Parisian landmark.

Above a 408-foot-square plot, the tower rises, a steep pyramid whose four sides curve inward slightly. There is a platform 187 feet above ground level, a second at 377 feet, and a third at 899 feet. The angle of inclination of the four iron pillars decreases from 80 degrees at the bottom to 54 degrees at the top. Above the second platform, the pillars unite to form a single shaft that narrows to a width of 33 feet. The topmost floor is a cabin whose roof can serve as an open terrace and where, among other things, the scientific measuring devices installed by Gustave Eiffel are located. A television antenna was placed on top of the tower in 1957, increasing the total height to 1,051 feet. Even in the strongest winds, though, the structure has never swayed more than 4.5 inches from the vertical. The extraordinary lightness of its construction is evidenced less by its total weight of 7,000 tons than by its pressure on the ground of 57 pounds per square inch, or roughly that of a man sitting in a chair. This amazing reduction of material outlay was the result of Eiffel's long engineering experience, particularly in the building of bridges; before constructing the tower, he had made a name for himself with the Douro Bridge at Porto, in Portugal, and the Garabit Bridge in the Massif Central. A bust of him, created by Antoine Bourdelle, was placed at the foot of the north pillar in 1930.

Grand Palais, Petit Palais, and Pont Alexandre III

Avenue Winston-Churchill, VIIIᵉ (color plates, pages 33 and 42; illus. 70, pages 168–169)

This group of structures is the most significant city-planning project from the Belle Epoque. It is effectively oriented along the axis that connects the Champs-Élysées with the Hôtel des Invalides. Its site, adjacent to the Cours-la-Reine, had been used for the first Parisian world's fair. Since 1855, the Palais de l'Industrie, a 650-foot structure of iron and glass by Jean Viel, had stood here, but this was demolished in 1897 to make room for a pair of palaces with which the Third Republic intended to demonstrate the glory of French art at the world's fair of 1900.

The eastern building, the Petit Palais, by Charles Girault, presents, on the street side, a central cupola structure, to which a long flight of gracefully curving steps leads through a monumental, round-arch portal—a variation on the central ornamental surround of the Hôtel des Invalides. Extending from either side of this central structure is a wing of colonnades with elegant Ionic columns and a wealth of Rococo-influenced sculptural and architectural ornamentation. The western building, or Grand Palais, by contrast, is cast in the heavier Louis XVI style. It too boasts colonnades, behind which a frieze depicts the great epochs in art. Despite the fact that there is a central portal, the beveled ends of the wings are the actual entries—a deft stroke from a city-planning point of view—with tall flights of steps and crowning bronze sculptures of charging quadrigas. In the Petit Palais, the Baroque idiom has been consistently preserved, even in the back portions of the building, which surround a semicircular inner court, and in the interior. However, the stone architecture of the Grand Palais serves only as the outer layer of a most elegant and spacious structure of iron and glass. This feat of engineering is based on a cruciform ground plan and has a low cupola in the center, spanning the open space in a broad arch. Unfortunately, it has been largely obscured by partitions put up for temporary exhibitions. The building was created under the direction of Girault by Henri Deglane, Louis-Albert Louvet, and Albert Thomas. In front of the simpler north face, there is a lovely fountain with nymphs by Raoul Laroche.

The Petit Palais houses the Musée des Beaux-Arts de la Ville de Paris and also has temporary exhibitions (see page 481). The Grand Palais was modernized in the Fifth Republic, and, with more than 54,000 square feet of floor space, it is one of the most important exhibition centers in Paris. The south wing is part of the University of Paris; since 1937, the west wing has housed the Palais de la Découverte, a science museum.

The Pont Alexandre III seems virtually to epitomize the Belle Epoque. It is one of the most elegant bridges in Paris, spanning the river in a single low arch of nearly 353 feet. Its steel structure is draped with garlands, and massive candelabra with dancing children punctuate its splendidly ornamented railing. Four tall pylons mark the approaches to the bridge and support goddesses and winged horses. Before each pylon sits an allegorical figure of France at a given high point of its history.

The bridge is a monument to the alliance struck between France and Russia in 1892. Russia's imperial coat of arms is displayed next to Paris's, and a figure representing the river goddess of the Seine is matched by one symbolizing the Neva's. The cornerstone for the bridge was laid in 1896 by both President Félix Faure of France and Czar Nicholas II.

Art Nouveau

(illus. 72–78, pages 171–173)

The first line of the Paris Métro was opened in time for the world's fair of 1900, and with one stroke, Hector Guimard—an architect whose work undoubtedly comprises France's most important contribution to European Art Nouveau style—became world famous.

Guimard's Métro entrances (illus. 76) were exotic, colorful, and highly stylized. Transparent glass roofs spread above these entrances, providing the emerging passenger with a steady crescendo of light. These Métro entrances became a familiar part of the Parisian street scene, but when they were first erected they met with violent disapproval, not only from academic traditionalists but also from the populace at large. So great was the resistance to them that they were discontinued in 1904. After the completion of the entrance in front of the Opéra, only much more neutral, noncommittal balustrades were used.

Guimard provided the most important stops with enclosed entry pavilions. These, along with all his other stations—except for a single example at the Porte Dauphine—have fallen victim to modernization and a general disdain for the Art Nouveau style.

These same impulses destroyed some of Guimard's most important buildings in Paris and the surrounding area—for example, the concert hall in the Rue St-Didier, the Hôtel Nozal facing the Jardin du Ranelagh, and the Villa Castel Henriette in Sèvres. However, his surviving structures in Auteuil and Passy, in the southern sections of the Sixteenth Arrondissement, constitute a veritable open-air museum of the architecture of about 1900. Here, one can trace the most important stages in Guimard's development. He began as an academically trained eclectic who mixed the most disparate styles and materials in an unorthodox manner, as in the Roszé block (34 Rue Boileau); the Villa Jassedé (41 Rue Chardon-Lagache); and the studio building for Mme. Carpeaux (39 Boulevard Exelmans). Next came his constructivist experiments under the influence of Eugène Viollet-le-Duc—Lycée Sacré-Cœur (9 Avenue de la Frillière)—and then his personal artistic manifesto, the Castel Béranger (14 Rue La Fontaine) (illus. 75). Guimard was under the influence of the Belgian Victor Horta while planning this apartment building, and his design broke away from historicism once and for all. He had discovered his own formal idiom, which he defined as a "blend of logic, harmony, and feeling." The building's façade consists of a variety of materials—notably, careful brickwork, distinctively formed cast iron, and glass bricks, which were very uncommon at that time—that provide for a colorful and lively interplay between interior and exterior. Guimard designed not only the structure itself but the interior furnishings as well, creating a work that consciously imitated nature in the soft flow of its lines. It also borrowed from the native French Gothic and Rococo traditions, without imitating specific details. In 1897 to 1898, the Castel Béranger was named the most beautiful

façade in a competition held by the city of Paris; this prize first brought recognition to Guimard.

A series of commissions was subsequently awarded to the architect. Most of these were in the Sixteenth Arrondissement, a district that had been linked closely to downtown Paris by various of Haussmann's projects and was becoming one of the most important residential areas for the bourgeoisie around the turn of the century. Here, Guimard had an opportunity to further develop and refine his architectural concepts. Among his works are the residence at 142 Avenue de Versailles (illus. 72 and 74); the villa at 8 Grande Avenue de la Villa-de-la-Réunion; the residence at 11 Rue François-Millet; and the small Hôtel Mezzara at 60 Rue La Fontaine (illus. 78). His own residence (illus. 77), constructed on a triangular lot at 122 Avenue Mozart, demonstrates his mastery of difficult ground-plan problems and his ability to give a sculptural quality to his façades. His apartment buildings at 8 and 10 Rue Agar, 17–21 Rue La Fontaine, and 43 Rue Gros display his experimental uses of standard elements. And, in the apartment blocks at 18 Rue Henri-Heine and 36–38 Rue Greuze, he assimilated aspects of the post-World War I Art Déco. The Musée des Arts Décoratifs owns an impressive collection of Guimard's furniture, interior appointments, and drawings (see pages 474–475).

Compared with Guimard's sublimely elegant forms, the structures by the other Art Nouveau architects in Paris seem slightly vulgar—for example, the apartment house on the Place Félix-Faure by Wagon, the Maison Potin on the Rue de Rennes by Auscher, and the structures of Charles Plumet, Xaviar Schoellkopf, and Tony Selmersheim. One other Art Nouveau architect, Jules Lavirotte, is nonetheless fascinating because of his rich creative fantasy. Especially notable are his erotic, symbolist decorations on the residence at 29 Avenue Rapp (illus. 73); his experiments with colors and materials—a collaboration with the ceramicist Alexandre Bigot—at the Céramic-Hotel (34 Avenue de Wagram); and his Baroque exuberance at the Lycée Italien (12 Rue Sédillot).

Of extraordinary quality are the luxurious Art Nouveau interiors that have survived in a number of Parisian restaurants. None of these are economy-class establishments, unfortunately. The most notable are Maxim's, Rue Royale, by Louis Marnez (1899); the Julien, Rue du Faubourg St-Germain, by Trézel (1899); and the Lucas-Carton, Place de la Madeleine, by Louis Majorelle (1905).

Auguste Perret

Shortly after Hector Guimard's Métro entrances were installed but before most of his structures in Auteuil and Passy were designed, there arose, also in the Sixteenth Arrondissement, a structure that stood in direct contrast to Guimard's blend of rationality and romanticism but that was perhaps even more strongly tied to the French tradition of classical art. This was the apartment house at 25-*bis* Rue Franklin, which was built by Auguste Perret and his brothers in 1903. It was the first building in Paris in which reinforced concrete dictated not only the method of construction but also the exterior appearance of the structure. Built on a narrow lot, Perret's apartment house had ten stories, each containing a single apartment whose five rooms all enjoyed light from the street, thanks to a quite complicated floor plan. A reinforced-concrete skeleton made it possible to do away with walls to a great extent; windows and panels of colorful ceramic tiles largely replaced them. Perret eschewed any sculptural ornamentation, preferring to let his building speak for itself through the rational and symmetrical arrangement of its parts. Nevertheless, he made sure that his arrangement respected certain of the traditional laws of aesthetics that he had studied at the École des Beaux-Arts. Perret's work is characterized by the attempt to harmonize the possibilities and requirements of modern concrete construction with classical French aesthetics. He said:

> The conditions imposed by nature are lasting; those imposed by man are transitory. The vicissitudes of climate, the characteristics of materials, the laws of statics, the distortions of optics, a universal sense of line and form—these have permanence. The great buildings of our time are provided with a framework, a structure, of steel or concrete. This framework is to the building what the skeleton is to the animal; just as an animal's harmonious, balanced, symmetrical skeleton envelops and supports organs that are quite unalike and quite differently placed, so must the structure of a building be carefully designed, harmonious, balanced, and also symmetrical.

Following the apartment house on the Rue Franklin and the famous garage on the Rue Ponthieu from 1905, which was one of the first purely functional buildings in Europe, the classical component of Perret's work became more and more apparent, yet he continued to conceive of the new system of reinforced concrete as one of loading and bearing elements.

In 1922 to 1923, Perret constructed his sensational church of Notre-Dame in Raincy, a suburb to the east of Paris. Together with the painter Maurice Denis, he created a structure of extraordinary, almost mystical transparency. After this, he came to be more and more one of the official state architects. His views—despite his use of reinforced concrete—were compatible with the tastes of the dominant bureaucrats. His Théâtre des Champs-Élysées, designed before World War I, in 1911 to 1913, anticipated the classicism of the 1930s. This style is apparent in Perret's Palais du Mobilier-National (1 Rue Berbier-du-Mets) from 1935 and his Musée des Travaux-Publics (Place d'Iéna) from 1937. It also characterizes the Palais de Chaillot and the Palais de Tokio, also from 1937, although more conventional forms and materials are used in these structures.

Robert Mallet-Stevens

(illus. 79, page 173)

A kind of purist antithesis to Hector Guimard's work was created by the architect Robert Mallet-Stevens in the Sixteenth Arrondissement beginning in 1927. While Guimard's buildings represented the most imaginative products of French Art Nouveau, the Rue Mallet-Stevens, a private street —virtually a small neighborhood—consisted of cubistic structures with white masses and clearly defined surfaces. The project was designed for an exclusive clientele comprised of painters, film directors, architects, and composers, and each structure was carefully attuned to the life and work of its inhabitants. This individual tailoring is evident even in the exteriors of the architecture. In its refusal to make decorative compromises, the ensemble of the Rue Mallet-Stevens stands in refreshing contrast to the Art Déco style that had recently been touted at the great exhibition of 1925. But it also differed from the return to the classical tradition that characterized official architecture of the time. The austerity of the ensemble's straight lines and right angles is lightened, in contrast to other con-structivist movements, by an almost playful delight in the complex interlocking of the cubes.

Le Corbusier

At the 1925 exhibition, Le Corbusier (Charles-Edouard Jeanneret) had shocked Paris by suggesting that the old center of the city on the Right Bank be torn down and replaced by a double row of cruciform skyscrapers, a radical solution to both housing and traffic problems, with a logical separation of layers of traffic. Le Corbusier was too revolutionary to be given public commissions in Paris, but he was able to demonstrate his architectural ideas in a number of private projects—for example, the strictly cubistic villas for Raoul Laroche (10 Square du Docteur-Blanche) and for the painter Amédée Ozenfant (53 Avenue Reille), both from 1923; Le Corbusier had collaborated with Ozenfant on the manifesto of purism, the polemic *Après le cubisme*, in 1918. The architect himself lived in the apartment house he designed in 1933 at 24 Rue Nungesser-Coli.

The two most important pre-World War II buildings by Le Corbusier in Paris are at the southern edge of the city. One is the Quartier Général de l'Armée-du-Salut from 1932 to 1933, a headquarters and residence for the Salvation Army, which uses exposed concrete and glass bricks. The other is the Pavillon Suisse dormitory from 1930 to 1932 at the Cité Universitaire, where a short time before, in 1929, the Dutch De Stijl architect Willem Dudok had designed the Pavillon Néerlandais as a manifesto of the most orthodox constructivism. Near the Pavillon Suisse is a later work by Le Corbusier, the Pavillon de Brésil of 1959. This building places a stronger emphasis than does his earlier work on the three-dimensional qualities of concrete.

In the Rue Villa-Seurat, not far from the Cité Universitaire, is another ensemble of cubistic architecture. Here, in 1924, André Lurçat constructed a series of dwellings with studios for his artist colleagues. (The house at No. 7, built for the sculptor Chana Orloff, was, however, the work of Auguste Perret.) Lurçat also built the studio residence for the painter Georges Braque in 1927, at 6 Rue du Douanier, in the same district.

Maison de l'UNESCO

Place de Fontenoy, VIIᵉ

Between 1955 and 1958, the headquarters of the United Nations Educational, Scientific, and Cultural Organization (UNESCO) was built in Paris as a symbol of international cooperation. The plans were produced by architects from three countries: Marcel Breuer (United States), Luigi Nervi (Italy), and Bernard Zehrfuss (France); and their work was reviewed by an international jury. The interior decorations were created by artists of the UN's member nations, and they constitute a rich sampling of the art of the 1950s: Pablo Picasso, Henry Moore, Jean Arp, Joan Miró, Jean Bazaine, Isamu Noguchi, and Alexander Calder.

The main building, the Secretariat, consists of three wings in the shape of a Y. Its daring construction, attributed to Nervi, was much admired in its day. The seven-story office building rests on a row of elegant concrete supports whose very shapes manifest the play of the forces of thrust and tension. Because of subsequent additions on the ground floor, the structure has lost much of its original lightness and transparency. The differences among its façades result from a failure to integrate the quite different visions of the architects involved.

By contrast, the conference building is totally the work of Nervi, and it uses a bold concrete construction with a span of almost 230 feet, its beams supported by six pillars in the center. There is a remarkable interfolding of the side walls and the roof, giving the building the appearance of an accordion. Plenary sessions of UNESCO and committee meetings take place here. A third, almost cubist structure placed at the edge of a Japanese garden and decorated by Noguchi houses the permanent delegations to UNESCO. In 1963, an additional office complex was added to the center by Zehrfuss, a well-designed subterranean structure with open patios that admit light into it. On the piazza in front of the main entrance (on the west side between the Avenue de Suffren and the Avenue de Lowendal) is a concrete shelter that rises in an unbroken curve from two points, a typical product of the 1950s.

The works of art here include a large *Reclining Figure* in travertine by Moore; two ceramic walls executed by Artigas after plans by Miró—*Wall of the Sun* and *Wall of the Moon*; a large mobile by Calder; a painting on wood by Picasso, *The Victory of the Forces of Light and Peace over the Powers of Evil and Death*; and a large abstract bronze relief by Arp. The décor of the seventh floor, which contains common rooms, a cafeteria, a restaurant, and so on, is the work of the painters Afro (Italy), Karel Appel (Holland), and Roberto Matta (Chile), and of the photographer Brassaï (France).

Les Halles

(color plate, pages 220–221; illus. 68, 69, and 83, pages 167 and 176)

No topic had so preoccupied public opinion in Paris for years. Victor Baltard's Halles (illus. 68; fig., page 95) were demolished in 1972, and the use of the area that this legendary market had occupied—which became known as "le trou (hole) des Halles"—was uncertain for some time.

Removing Les Halles and a number of the surrounding buildings created an open site of about 106 acres, the largest city-planning opportunity since Haussmann's redesign of the city. But it also meant the destruction of an institution that dated back to the Middle Ages and the sacrifice of some of the finest early examples of steel construction. The market was transferred out of the city to Rungis in 1969, and until they were torn down, the buildings proved useful in hundreds of ways—for cultural and social events and for spontaneous "happenings," for example. The intensity of the debate over Les Halles made it clear that here a vital city nerve was struck. These buildings not only represented "le ventre (belly) de Paris," as Zola referred to them in 1873, but they appealed to the Parisians' nostalgia for their own past.

After the demolition, there was a period in which all manner of different proposals were made for the site. Finally, a compromise was reached between the state and the city, between the crassest kind of exploitation and a respect for the needs of the populace. The result is a highly intensive use of the site, especially for the purposes of mass transit and traffic. The largest underground train station in the world, connecting the RER and the Métro, was opened here in 1977. There are also underground traffic intersections and gigantic parking garages. Lastly, there is the Forum des Halles, an underground shopping center whose core resembles an inverted, open pyramid accessible from the eastern portion of the site. This was opened in late 1979. The whole is to be surrounded by a number of apartment blocks whose final form is yet to be determined. The western side, facing the church of St. Eustache, is to be left as a green park, but its final design has occasioned still another battle between the president and the mayor.

The Bourse du Commerce (illus. 69) is the only structure to have survived the general demolition. It is a massive circular building topped by one of the loveliest surviving cupolas of iron and glass in Paris (compare the cupola of the Galeries Lafayette and the glass hall of the Grand Palais). Constructed by Paul Blondel in 1887, it replaced the Halle aux Bleds (Grain Hall) put up by Nicolas Le Camus de Mézières in 1767. A 124-foot-wide cupola of iron and glass had been added to that earlier building by François Bélanger and Brunet in 1811. It was the first of its kind, and Blondel used it as a pattern for his own. The Halle aux Bleds had been built on the grounds of the Hôtel de Soissons, once a residence of Catherine de Médicis. The sole remnant of this *hôtel* is the 101-foot fluted column that Jean Bullant constructed as a viewing tower for astrological research in 1575. It still stands right next to Blondel's Bourse.

The centerpiece of this development is the startling Centre National d'Art et de Culture Georges-Pompidou, which is more commonly known as the Centre Beaubourg (see page 476). It was conceived by President Georges Pompidou, and it is considered to be his legacy to Paris and to France.

The design of the building has been a cause of controversy ever since it was selected from among the 681 proposals suggested for the site. For the architects, Richard Rogers and Renzo Piano, chose to celebrate the functional parts of a building rather than mask them under the typical glass skin of modern construction. It is a steel framework 542 feet long, 196 feet wide, and 137 feet high, with five floors. In order to guarantee the most flexible use of

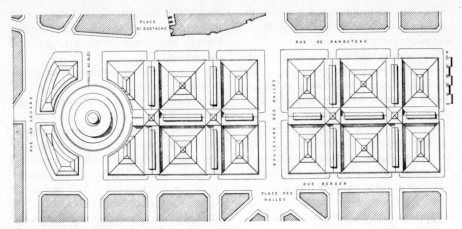

Les Halles: the layout of Victor Baltard's pavilions.

the interior, all service elements—stairways, elevators, air conditioning and heating units, and electrical wiring—were placed outside. Their huge surfaces were left free of pillars and are supported by steel beams attached to the exterior frame.

Only a bit more than half of the available site between the Rue St-Martin and the Rue Beaubourg was used. The structure itself was placed right up against the Rue Beaubourg, so that a broad piazza was created on the west side (illus. 83). This not only provided a perspective from which to view the structure, but also created an excellent meeting place and an immensely popular setting for jugglers, acrobats, and street theater.

On the east side of the building, along the narrow Rue Beaubourg, the blue, red, and green pipes and boxes containing the technical service systems dominate. The more inviting west side has been given a futuristic touch—a diagonal escalator that

rises in front of the white framework of the building and is enclosed in transparent plexiglass. The high-tech result has been described by its detractors as a scaffolding in search of a building or a child's toy, and applauded by its supporters as the only true "modern" building.

The materials and design of this structure stand in complete contrast to the architecture of the surrounding area; they belong rather more to the tradition of ephemeral structures from nineteenth-century world's fairs. But one must concede that, from a city-planning standpoint, the Beaubourg's integration into its setting is a success. And, in fact, the stylistic contrast was expressly desired.

The Beaubourg houses the Centre de Création Industrielle, the Institut de Recherche et de Coordination Acoustique/Musique, and the Bibliothèque Publique d'Information, as well as the Musée National d'Art Moderne. But the main attraction has been the build-

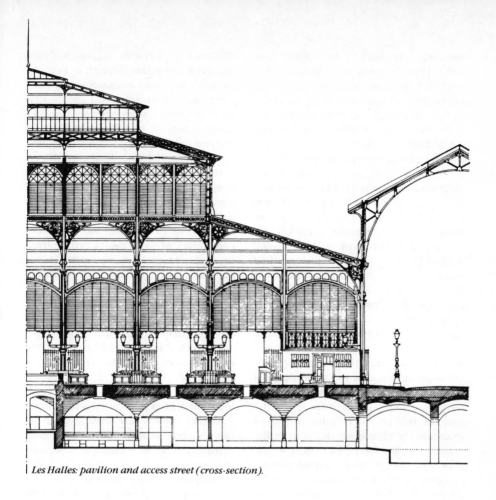

Les Halles: pavilion and access street (cross-section).

ing itself, which has drawn nearly 8 million visitors a year.

La Défense

(illus. 57, page 127)

La Défense is the most extensive city-planning project in the *banlieue*, with which Paris reaches out into the Ile de France. The site occupies portions of Courbevoie, Puteaux, and Nanterre, and comprises about 320 acres in Sector A, around the Place de la Défense, and about 1,600 acres in Sector B, in Nanterre.

In 1955, it was decided to develop an office complex in the *banlieue* to relieve congestion in the city. The Place de la Défense was selected as the site for this project. It stood at the intersection of the important routes from St. Germain-en-Laye and from Pontoise with the Avenue de la Défense, which led into Paris and was the most heavily traveled thoroughfare in the *banlieue*. Planning and building of La Défense were entrusted to the Établissement Public pour l'Aménagement de La Défense in 1958. This agency was charged with easing the traffic situation, creating office space, and constructing a new residential quarter.

The exhibition hall of the Centre National des Industries et Techniques (CNIT) was already constructed here between 1957 and 1959, and in 1961, work began on an underground express train (RER) to connect La Défense with the banking quarter of Paris, around the Opéra. A model of the future office quarter was submitted in 1964. It provided for thirty towers of roughly the same height (325 feet) and one of just over 650 feet to serve as a major focal point at the end of the great east–west axis, from the Louvre and the Champs-Élysées. Traffic was to be routed beneath a massive concrete slab, completely separate from a pedestrian zone connecting the towers. After a number of initial difficulties, improving economic conditions in the 1960s led interested investors to press for a less symmetrical development and more intensive use of the site. The final project calls for 16 million square feet of office space, or five times the original specification of 3.2 million. At the same time, the limitation on heights of the proposed buildings was removed. In 1972, the people of Paris watched in horror as a 542-foot concrete tower arose to the west of the Arc de Triomphe. Public protest finally forced the government to impose new limitations in 1974. By 1980, some 9.4 million square feet of office space had been constructed, almost 120,000 people were coming into the quarter every day to work, and roughly 20,000 had moved there.

The center of the complex is the Dalle, surrounded by a monorail system and connected with the surrounding network of streets. The Dalle is an immense platform three-quarters of a mile long and between 800 and 1,400 feet wide. It consists of various levels and plazas. Beneath it, multiple levels accommodate various modes of transportation. Stations of the SNCF and the RER are underground, as are a bus station and a complex network of highways and streets. The very lowest levels contain garages with space for 35,000 cars. In the northwest corner is the Centre Commercial, with branches of the department stores Printemps and Samaritaine, 150 boutiques, 20 restaurants, and a number of cinemas. At the west end of the Dalle, and thus at the end of the east–west axis of Paris, Aillaud has designed a semicircular residential building made up of two tall, curved towers whose façades will consist entirely of mirrored glass so as to reflect the axis and the nearby towers. The present recession has made it questionable whether this showpiece will be built, just as it has slowed the completion of La Défense in other ways as well.

About fifteen residential and commercial towers have been constructed at La Défense. A number of them have adapted American designs, thus signaling France's ultimate departure from its national architectural tradition.

Compared with the glitter of the bronze, mirrored glass, and polished granite of the new towers, the CNIT exhibition hall already seems dated. Its vast roof stretches like a sail above the gigantic hall in a flat curve, supported at only three points on the ground yet spanning almost 720 feet. Its interior encompasses 1 million square feet, and this structure from 1957 to 1959 by Zehrfuss, Camelot, and de Mailly is an extraordinary engineering achievement.

Sector B in Nanterre is reserved primarily for residential structures (28,000 apartments are projected); cultural institutions like the Maison de la Culture, École d'Architecture, Maison des Jeunes Musiciens, École Nationale des Arts Décoratifs, and University of Paris X; small industries; and a large 60-acre park.

Construction in this sector is by no means complete. It began in the early 1960s with the buildings for various institutes of the University; their isolation within the run-down *banlieue* contributed significantly to the unrest of 1968. Some of the finished buildings are highly questionable, such as the fifteen (of a projected twenty-five) round residential towers in garish colors.

The new towns

Municipal authorities were astonishingly late in attending to the development of the *banlieue*. The first large industrial settlements arose in St. Denis during the Second Empire. By the turn of the century, with the advent of heavy industry and automobile manufacturing, the area around Paris had become a chaotic, unplanned jumble of residential, industrial, and commercial areas. These simply developed along the transportation routes: the rivers, railroads, and major highways. The problem was fully recognized only in the 1920s, when the ring of fortifications around Paris was finally removed, and by which time the population of the *banlieue* was higher than that of the city itself. Still it took almost thirty more years before the state could come up with any solutions, and meanwhile the problem had grown far more acute. In the 1930s, and during and after World War II, immigration into the Paris region continued in full force; the combined pressures of this growing population and the housing shortage had become unbearable.

Beginning in 1955, and without any comprehensive plan or coordination, the economic upswing brought about the construction of the Grands Ensembles. These were large complexes of standardized, federal housing structures—spiritless barracks on inexpensive sites. They lacked any appropriate educational facilities; they were simply bedroom communities for commuters who worked in Paris.

Then in 1958, the model communities of Massy-Antony, Stains-Pierrefitte, and Sarcelles came into being. These were vast projects housing between 30,000 and 50,000 people each. These satellite cities were so dreary—the name "Sarcelles" came to stand for a life of unrelieved drabness—that at last there began to be more general discussion about the planning of humane cities and about guidelines that France ought to follow in dealing sensibly with its population growth. How could the growth of Paris and its surrounding region be brought under control? Was it possible to correct the imbalance between Paris and the rest of the country?

In spite of its announced commitment to decentralize, the government's ultimate answer was not in favor of a calculated boost to the regional metropolises. It chose rather to accept further growth of the Paris region, hoping only to channel and structure it. In 1961, Paul Delouvrier was commissioned to draw up a developmental scheme for the whole Paris region. The result continues to be the guide to all planning and development around the city.

Instead of a *banlieue* spreading shapelessly out into the Ile de France, Delouvier's plan calls for a developmental axis, stretching to the northwest and the southeast, along which five completely new cities are to develop. Each will have its own character, and each will be provided with everything that makes up a metropolis. Each will have an administrative center with a city hall, law courts, and in some cases a prefecture. There

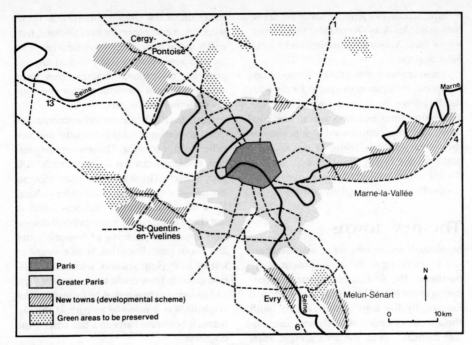

Developmental scheme for the "new towns" in the Paris region.

will be shopping centers, cultural institutions such as libraries, theaters, and museums, and residential quarters with individual characteristics and a variety of dwelling types. Sufficient jobs will be provided by the industries, trades, and administrative organizations attracted to these cities. Lastly, they are to be generously provided with recreational facilities.

The five cities are Cergy-Pontoise in the northwest, between the Oise and the Seine; Marne-la-Vallée in the east, along the valley of the Marne; St. Quentin-en-Yvelines in the southwest, an extension of Versailles; and Melun-Sénart and Evry in the southeast, along the Seine. Although it is not officially recognized as a new town, one must add to these the new city of Créteil. Planners of

these communities have been able to avoid most serious mistakes by drawing on the experiences of other countries in creating complete new satellite cities. For example, even before the first residents moved in, the necessary transportation facilities were in place: highways, trains, and in some cases the new RER express line to Paris (though this admittedly encourages commuting to the capital). Where possible, municipal centers were begun before the residential districts.

Residential areas are being completed in stages. Services—from schools to parking spaces and parks—are constructed along with the apartment buildings, so that inhabitants need not feel that they are living for years on a construction site. An insistence

276

on architectural diversity has prevented the monotony of older complexes, and the design of these outer areas is often exemplary. Aillaud, the only architect of the Grands Ensembles to apply a great deal of imagination and formal skill to this problem, was an influential precursor. His contributions in favor of more humane communities are manifest in his La Grande Borne in Grigny, the Cité de l'Abreuvoir in Bobigny, and the Quartier des Courtillières in Pantin. Yet many of these quarters seem to have been created by designers rather than by architects; they are all too trendy in their use of colors and forms, too futuristic, too overdone to prevent their inhabitants from feeling nostalgic for the Paris of old.

Originally planned for populations of from 300,000 to 1 million each—in 1965, it was still assumed that the total population of the Paris region would level off at 14 million —the cities have by no means come close to completion. Yet in the most advanced of them—Evry, Créteil, and Cergy-Pontoise— one can already recognize their future form and structure, and appraise their plusses and minuses.

Créteil

Developed out of the Grands Ensembles, which was started in 1956 as a complex of 5,500 dwellings, Créteil had grown into a city of some 125,000 inhabitants and 25,000 jobs by 1980. As the main population center of the new *département* of Val-de-Marne, it has profited considerably from special federal commitment. Its overall design was the work of Dufau, who also planned the city center. This includes the prefecture (by Badani), shopping center (Goldenberg), courthouse (Badani and Roux-Dorlut), cultural center (Faugeron), and central clinic (Riedberger). Various architects were as-

signed to the individual residential quarters; in each case, a variety of clearly differentiated dwelling forms, from detached houses to apartment towers, has been created.

Evry

This is the most spectacular new town, with a population density that in certain sections surpasses that of Paris—and all in the middle of endless fields of beets. The city is laid out as an X. Between each pair of arms of the X is a park of roughly 32 acres. The center of the city is an Agora planned by Jean Le Couteur, made up of the city administrative center (by Lagneau, Weill, Dimitrijevic, and others), the prefecture of the *département* of Essonne, a courthouse, a gigantic shopping complex, branches of the University, sports facilities, and underground garages. Pedestrian walks and bridges connect the city with the various neighborhoods. The first of these to be completed, Evry I, consists of complicated pyramidal mountains of dwelling units (by Andrault and Parat)—7,000 apartments and 270,000 square feet of office space—producing a concentration of almost 750 inhabitants per acre.

Nearby Melun-Senart contains the prefecture of the *département* of Seine-et-Marne and is basically only the metropolitan area between the old cities of Melun and Corbeil. One can assume that it will one day merge with Evry.

Cergy-Pontoise

Planned for 350,000 inhabitants, this city lies in a charming landscape on a bend of the Oise River, along which an extensive recreation area will provide a main attraction. Here, another municipal center, or Forum, has been developed—this one built around the prefecture of the *département* of Val-d'Oise, an intriguing structure in the form of an inverted pyramid by Henry Bernard, the architect of the ORTF building in Paris. This Forum includes a shopping complex, administrative buildings, and so on. Nevertheless, the city has been envisioned as polycentric, with sections of widely divergent character, including the old village of Cergy, the city of Pontoise, and ultimately the city of St. Ouen as well. Of interest here is the Le Ponceau quarter, with complex, interlocking apartment structures from one to four stories high, nicely varied vistas, and small squares—a clear example of the rejection of the residential tower that began in about 1970. Also notable is the Evagny quarter, where this trend is taken still further and combined with a regional style that echoes the traditional settlement forms of the preindustrial era.

St. Quentin-en-Yvelines

This newest of the new towns is not centered around a new administrative and shopping core—the prefecture of the *dé-* *partement* of Yvelines is in Versailles—but rather around a transportation nexus, including a station of the SNCF and a number of bus terminals. A first residential quarter has been constructed near these in Elancourt-Maurepas by Coulomb and Lagneau. The true centers of this developing metropolis will continue to be the old town of Versailles and the university town that has developed between Orsay and Palliseau due to the transfer of a number of large academic departments out of Paris. The Arcades du Lac quarter by the Spaniard Ricardo Bofill has recently attracted considerable attention because it represents an attempt to revive the classical architectural tradition in the context of government housing.

Marne-la-Vallée

Conceived as a "landscape city," like Melun-Sénart, and projected as four metropolitan units of from 100,000 to 180,000 inhabitants each, Marne-la-Vallée is actually more like an elongated zone of dense population along the new line of the RER between Paris and Meaux.

ILE DE FRANCE

THE
GREAT
CATHEDRALS

St. Denis
The Abbey Church

(illus. 88, 89, 130, and 131, pages 291, 292, 369, and 370)

St. Denis is an industrial city in the *banlieue* north of Paris. Today, it radiates little brilliance. Yet the abbey church of St. Denis (since 1966 a cathedral; its restoration is still incomplete) is one of the most important monuments of French history and of Western architecture. It was here that the French monarchy began to renew its strength in the twelfth century, and it was here that Abbot Suger (1081–1151) laid the foundations of Gothic architecture.

According to Gregory of Tours, St. Dionysius (St. Denis), the first bishop of Paris, had fallen victim to the persecution of Christians under the consulate of Decius and Gratus in about A.D. 250. He was beheaded, together with his colleagues Rusticus and Eleutherius, at the foot of Montmartre. Through the centuries, the legend arose that the saint had taken up his severed head, tucked it under his arm, and walked to the village of Catoliacus, where he finally collapsed and died.

An oratory was erected above his grave as early as the fourth century. Ste. Geneviève restored this structure in 475 and added a priory to it. Dagobert I furnished the monastery with rich benefices and ordained that the new church he had built there in about 630 was to be his burial place. This began a tradition: since Hugues Capet, all the kings of France have been buried at St. Denis except Philippe I, Louis VII, and Louis XI.

In 754, while Fulrad was abbot, Pope Stephen II anointed Pepin le Bref and his sons Carloman and Charlemagne kings of the Franks—the beginning of the Carolingian dynasty. St. Denis became the place where the kings were anointed and enthroned. Even though Reims later became more important for the consecration of the French kings, the regalia, or royal insignia, remained in the treasury at St. Denis until the Revolution. The remains of these are now in Paris in the Bibliothèque Nationale and in the Galerie d'Apollon of the Louvre.

Abbot Fulrad set about building a new church in 750. In 775, it was consecrated in the presence of Charlemagne. It was one of the founding structures of Carolingian architecture, and remnants of it have been preserved in the crypt of the present building.

Rich gifts of land, art works, and reliquaries from a succession of kings made the abbey the most powerful in France. The so-called Lendit, a market held next to the abbey on the plain between Paris and St. Denis, had developed into one of the most important in the Ile de France during the eleventh century. It attracted great crowds, encouraging the development of a municipal parish around the abbey.

St. Denis came into its fullest flower under Suger, who became abbot in 1122. Suger was a friend and adviser to Louis VI and Louis VII, the regent of France during Louis VII's absence on the Second Crusade (1147–1151), and one of the most important figures of the Middle Ages.

Since the Frankish period, there had existed a close connection among St. Denis, his monastery, and the royal house. Therefore, the kings could buttress their claims to power by declaring themselves vassals of the saint. In 1124, Louis VI made a ceremonial vow and took the feudal banner of the Vexin, a dependency of the monastery, from the altar of the abbey church. The people considered this flag to be the legendary oriflamme of Charlemagne mentioned in *The Song of Roland*. With it, Louis VI gave the signal to the assembled French knights to do battle against the German emperor Henry V, who was threatening to attack Reims.

Among other benefices, Louis VI commanded, in 1124, that all the income from the Lendit was to go to the abbey of St. Denis. (Previously, this money had been shared with the chapter of Notre-Dame in Paris.) With the sizable financial resources that the abbey now had, it was decided to replace the Carolingian church with a new structure.

The architect of this new church is unknown, but it is certain that Abbot Suger played a major part in its design and thereby helped to create the French Gothic cathe-

St. Denis: schematic reconstruction of the original façade.

dral style (illus. 89). After 1130, work began on a structure with two towers in front of the Carolingian building; the tower chapels were consecrated in 1140. In a second and quite brief period of building between 1140 and 1143, the choir was erected, with a double ambulatory and chapels above a crypt. It was this structure that actually established the Gothic style (illus. 88). The Carolingian church continued to stand between this choir and the new structure. It was not until a hundred years later, under Abbot Eudes de Clément in 1231, that it was demolished to make room for a new nave and transept. Pierre de Montreuil began to influence the building of these in 1247; they were finally completed in 1281. The upper portion of Suger's choir was sacrificed to this thirteenth-century construction.

The lower portion of Suger's western front is closed and blocklike, almost square, like a Roman city gate, with three broad portals and strong vertical division by buttresses. It culminates in a crenelated wall that conceals the bases of the recessed towers, which are even more fully developed with window openings (the northern tower was inaccurately restored early in the nineteenth century and removed in 1846). The various elements of the façade reflect the differing heights of the central stories and the lateral ones. Here, for the first time, a rose window appears above the central three-part window—its tracery added in the thirteenth century—a major motif in cathedral façades from then on.

Except for minor remnants (a zodiac on the north portal, signs of the months on the south portal), the doorway sculptures were destroyed by modernization in the eighteenth century and by inaccurate restoration in the nineteenth. This is a highly regrettable loss, for St. Denis was the first church to have a Gothic figure portal with jamb figures in front of the columns, as they were to appear at almost the same time on the Portail Royal of Chartres—a row of sibyls, prophets, and Old Testament kings who were later thought to represent the Frankish kings. The tympanum of the taller center portal still belongs to the tradition of Romanesque Last Judgment reliefs. Among the figures of the resurrected is Abbot Suger, who is commending himself to Christ. This tympanum was heavily restored in the nineteenth century.

At the same time as the façade, a structure two bays deep was erected, with chapels above the portals. Here, the first experiments toward a Gothic manner of building were made tentatively. Massive bundles of columns were gathered together, with heavy ribs branching from them at various levels to support the huge pointed arches of the vaulting. A somewhat illogical construction and a heaviness of form suggest that this western structure was not the work of the same architect who produced the choir. For it is precisely the logical plan and the intelligent transformation of massive structure into skeletal structure by pointed arches, ribs, and partial columns that distinguish the choir. Twelve columns—an allusion to the twelve apostles—circle the apse, around which there is a double ambulatory. The

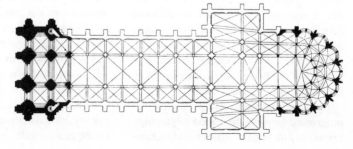

St. Denis (ground plan of the cathedral, with portions from the time of Abbot Suger shown in black).

283

outer row opens onto semicircular chapels. The apse is a wonderfully modulated complex of partial walls, pillars, half-columns, and protruding ribs that is filled with colored light from large, pointed-arch windows without tracery.

The idea of a *lux continua*, a wall filled with openings that bathe the interior of the church in a supernatural light, was technically possible only after the wall had been freed from the system of cross-ribs supported by pillars and half-columns. It is of central importance to Suger's concept of the cathedral as a symbol of the heavenly Jerusalem. His thinking combined neo-Platonic ideas of order, which also define the geometric structure of the church, with a metaphysics of light based on the writings of Pseudo-Dionysius. Pseudo-Dionysius was a mystic of the Eastern church who had lived in Syria in the fifth century A.D., but who was commonly held to be the Athenian Dionysios who, according to the Acts of the Apostles, had been converted by Paul. Since the early Middle Ages, it was also common to identify the Gallic St. Dionysius (St. Denis) with these two figures, so the writings of Pseudo-Dionysius were highly revered in the monastery.

Suger himself designed the iconography of the fourteen glass windows of the ambulatory, filling them with Christian symbols of the relationship between the Old and New Testaments. Only in the central chapel do fragments of these survive. Polychrome painting of the sculptures and of the architecture itself, not to mention the colorful mosaics of the floors, only added to the effect of the colored-glass walls.

The nave that Suger had planned never progressed beyond the barest beginnings. It was only during the major building campaign begun in 1231 that the existing structure was completed. It introduced a number of innovations, such as the continuous fenestration of the outer wall behind the triforium.

The ground plan of the church is unusual because of the addition of two side aisles to each of the transepts to accommodate the royal tombs, at the wish of St. Louis. Otherwise, it follows the classic scheme of tall, pointed-arch arcades, triforium, and clerestory, whose tracery windows fill the entire space between the wall pillars up to the arcaded arch of the vaulting. Decorative half-columns rise along the clustered pillars from the floor to the beginning of the vaults. The rose windows in the transepts are masterworks by Pierre de Montreuil, described in rectangles whose lower corners are glazed so that, together with the illuminated triforium, they produce the impression of a conservatory adorned with lacework tracery. At 36 feet in diameter, these rose windows are larger than the transept roses of Notre-Dame in Paris, for which they served as models.

The structure has remained essentially unchanged since the late thirteenth century. In the early fourteenth century, Charles IV had six chapels added onto the north side aisle, and Catherine de Médicis commissioned Jean Bullant and Jacques Androuet Du Cerceau the Younger to build a central structure to the north of the transept in 1572 as a mausoleum for the Valois kings. This mausoleum was never fully completed and was removed in 1719. François Mansart's proposed mausoleum for the Bourbons to the east of the choir was never constructed, but it did somewhat influence Jules Hardouin-Mansart's conception of the Dôme des Invalides in Paris. The abbey to

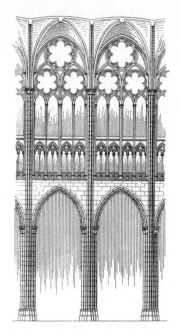 

St. Denis: the thirteenth-century nave (including cross-section).

the south of the church was rebuilt in the eighteenth century. Robert de Cotte designed this elegant new structure in about 1700. Its construction, which Jacques V. Gabriel superintended for a time, dragged on until 1786.

The Tombs

Louix IX confirmed the importance of this church as the necropolis of the French kings by providing new tombs for his ancestors in the crossing. He also ordained that in future only kings were to be buried here—a decree that was soon abandoned. As a symbol of the *ancien régime*, St. Denis was a favorite target for attack and vandalism by

Revolutionary mobs in 1793. The tombs were profaned, and forty-nine recumbent bronze figures were melted down. Alexandre Lenoir, however, succeeded in saving the stone monuments for his Musée des Monuments Français in Paris. In 1806, Napoleon designated St. Denis as the burial place for the new imperial dynasty. Restoration undertaken at that time by the architect François Debret did more damage to the structure than it had previously suffered.

The fabric of the building was saved only by the appointment of the young Eugène Viollet-le-Duc as caretaker. He saw to it that the royal tombs were returned to their original locations and that a number of tombs from dissolved Parisian churches were added; these comprise roughly half the present inventory. A national memorial thus came into being, one that is also a museum of the development of French funerary sculpture, from the simplest of incised slabs to the templelike mausoleums for François I and Henri II. In these latter, the dead are depicted twice: above, humbly kneeling but in their full regalia; below, as pitiful, naked corpses. The tradition of royal tomb monuments in St. Denis ends with the Bourbons; after Henri IV, these sculptures were replaced by the numerous equestrian statues on royal squares in Paris and in the provinces.

The part of the basilica that contains the tombs, which are not in chronological order, is separated from the rest of the church by a grille. The entrance to it is in the right-hand side aisle, and one can see it only with a guide (open daily, except during services on Sunday and holidays, 10:00 A.M.–12:00 M. and 2:00 P.M.–6:00 P.M., between April 1 and September 30). The following listing corresponds to the accompanying plan:

1. Charles, Comte d'Étampes, died 1336. Reclining figure from the monastery of the Cordeliers in Paris.
2. Louis d'Orléans, died 1407, and Valentine Visconti, died 1408. Commissioned by their grandson, Louis XII, from Italian sculptors in Genoa in 1502 for the church of the Célestins in Paris. One of the first Renaissance tombs.
3. Marguerite de Flandre, died 1382, the daughter of Philippe V.
4. Urn containing the heart of François I, who died in 1547 in Rambouillet. Created by Pierre Bontemps in 1556.
5. François I, died 1547, and Claude de France, died 1524, with their children François, died 1537; Charles, died 1545; and Charlotte, died 1524. Created between 1548 and 1558, after designs by Philibert de l'Orme, in the form of a triumphal arch. Sculptures by Pierre Bontemps and his associates. A masterpiece of the French Renaissance (illus. 131).

6. Statue of Béatrice de Bourbon, died 1338, the wife of the Bohemian king John of Luxemburg.
7. Column that supported the urn for the heart of François I. After a design by Francesco Primaticcio. From the church of the Célestins in Paris.
8. Isabelle d'Aragon, died 1271, the wife of Philippe III le Hardi (Philip the Bold). One of the earliest marble tombs at St. Denis.
9. Philippe III le Hardi, died 1285. Created between 1298 and 1307 by Jean d'Arras with the assistance of Pierre de Chelles, an architect of Notre-Dame. The beginning of individual, true-to-life portrait statues.
10. Philippe IV le Bel (Philip the Fair), died 1314. Created between 1327 and 1329 in the same workshop that produced the tombs of his sons Louis X (No. 39), Philippe V, and Charles IV (No. 34).
11. Charles Martel, died 741. Like Nos. 12, 13, 15, 16, 17, 37, 38, 39, and 40, this is an idealized portrait commissioned in 1263 by Louis IX, who wished to immortalize his forebears. The costume is that of the thirteenth century; the work originally stood in the transept.
12. Clovis II, died 656.
13. Carloman, died 884.
14. Louis III, died 883.
15. Berthe, died 783, the wife of Pepin le Bref (Pippin the Short).
16. Pepin le Bref, died 768.
17. Dagobert I, died 638. Tomb with tabernacle for the Merovingian king who was once held to be the founder of St. Denis. Heavily restored by Viollet-le-Duc. Next to it, *Madonna and Child*, a masterpiece of French wood sculpture from around 1160, originally in St. Martin-des-Champs in Paris.
18. Louis de Sancerre, constable of France, died 1402, comrade-in-arms of Bertrand Du Guesclin.
19. Charles V le Sage (Charles the Wise), died 1380. Realistic portrait of the king created in 1364, while he was still alive, by André Beauneveu. Next to him is his wife, Jeanne de Bourbon, a reclining figure from the tomb in the monastery of the Célestins.
20. Charles VI, died 1422, and Isabeau de Bavière, died 1435. Created with great compassion by Pierre de Thury in 1429.
21. Bertrand Du Guesclin, died 1380, the commander-in-chief under Charles V. Strongly re

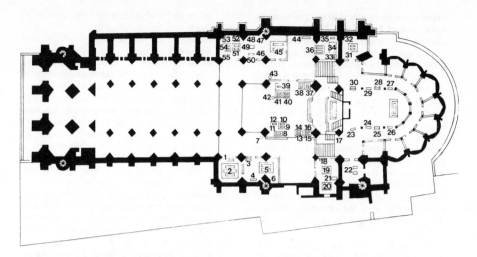

St. Denis: arrangement of the tombs (Nos. 1–55) in the eastern portion of the church.

alistic re-creation of his facial expression. This
slab and reclining figure are all that survive
from what was a quite lavish monument created by Thomas Privé and Robert Loisel
under the direction of Raymond Du Temple,
the architect of the Louvre under Charles V.

22. Louis XVI, died 1793, and Marie-Antoinette,
died 1793. Mediocre statues by Gaulle and
Louis Petitot, commissioned by Louis XVIII
in 1816.

23. Léon de Lusignan, died 1393, the last Latin
king of Armenia. When pursued by the
Saracens, he found refuge in Paris (hence
the gloves in his hands rather than a scepter).
From the monastery of the Célestins.

24. Unknown child, fourteenth century.

25. Charles de Valois, died 1346, and Marie
d'Espagne, died 1379. Attributed to Jean de
Liège; from the monastery of the Jacobins
in Paris.

26. Blanche de Bretagne, died 1327?

27. Blanche, died 1243, and Jean, died 1268, the
children of St. Louis. The copper slabs with
Limousin enamelwork come from the monastery of Royaumont, their father's foundation.

28. Robert d'Artois, died 1317. A work by Jean
Pépin of Huy for the monastery of the
Cordeliers.

29. Frédégonde, died 597, the wife of Chilperic
I. The slab with mosaic inlay from the mid-

dle of the twelfth century comes from St.
Germain-des-Prés in Paris.

30. Clovis I, died 511, and his son Childebert I,
died 558. Clovis's grave slab from the middle of the thirteenth century from the demolished church of Ste. Geneviève in Paris,
founded by this king. Childebert's grave slab
from the middle of the twelfth century was
moved here, like Frédégonde's, from St.
Germain-des-Prés.

31. Henri II and Catherine de Médicis. Reclining figures in coronation regalia by Germain
Pilon, created for the former Valois chapel.

32. Marie de Bourbon, died 1538, the aunt of
Henri IV. From the abbey of Notre-Dame in
Soissons.

33. Philippe VI, died 1350, and his son Jean II le
Bon (John the Good), died 1364 in English
captivity. Commissioned from André Beauneveu in 1364 by Charles V, their grandson
and son, respectively.

34. Philippe V, died 1322; Charles IV le Bel
(Charles the Fair), died 1328; and the latter's
wife, Jeanne d'Evreux, died 1371.

35. Blanche de France, died 1392, the daughter
of Charles IV. A work by Robert Loisel for
the monastery of the Cordeliers.

36. Henri II, died 1559, and Catherine de Médicis,
died 1589. The last major tomb monument
created for St. Denis. Based on plans by Prima-

ticcio, it originally stood in the center of the Valois chapel built for it by Catherine de Médicis. The king and queen are kneeling in coronation regalia on the rectangular *tempietto* (the figures are bronze, and the accompanying prie-dieus were melted down during the Revolution). Inside it, the two are shown lying in death and scarcely clothed, the queen (at her command) as a beautiful young woman. These figures are in white marble. On the corners are large bronze allegories of the four Cardinal Virtues, and on the base are the Theological Virtues. The sculptures were done by Germain Pilon and his associates, who also created the other sculptures for the Valois chapel that are now scattered. (The *Resurrection*, for example, is now in the Louvre; the *Pietà*, in St. Paul–St. Louis in Paris.)

37. Carloman, died 771, king of Burgundy and Austrasia and brother of Charlemagne, and Ermentrude, died 869, the first wife of Charles le Chauve (Charles the Bald). The tomb was commissioned by Louis IX.

38. Philippe, died 1131, the son of Louis VI, and Constance of Castile, died 1160.

39. Louis X le Hutin (Louis the Quarreler), died 1316. The tomb dates from 1327, as do Nos. 10 and 34. His children Jeanne, died 1349, and Jean, died 1316, whose death five days after his birth meant the passing of the crown to the Valois line.

40. Henri I, died 1060, and his grandson, Louis VI le Gros (Louis the Fat), died 1137.

41. Robert II le Pieux (Robert the Pious), died 1031, and Constance d'Arles, died 1032.

42. Column for the urn containing the heart of Henri III. Created by Jean Pageot in 1635.

43. Column for the urn containing the heart of Louis de Bourbon, died 1556, abbot of St. Denis.

44. Guillaume du Chastel, died 1441, the confidant of Charles VII.

45. Louis XII, died 1515, and Anne de Bretagne, died 1514. One of the masterpieces from the early Renaissance in France. Commissioned from Giovanni Giusto in Tours in 1516 by François I. The first dual portrait of a royal couple. Below, in pitiless realism, are the naked corpses, while above, on a slab supported by rounded arcades, the pair appears in coronation regalia. The Cardinal Virtues are at the corners; the reliefs on the base depict the king's Italian campaign.

46. Philippe-Dagobert, died 1235, the brother of St. Louis, who had this and the following tombs built for the monastery at Royaumont.

47. Louis, died 1260, the oldest son of Louis IX.

48. Blanche de France, died 1243.

49. Louis and Philippe, died 1272, the grandsons of Louis IX.

50. Charles d'Anjou, died 1285, king of Sicily and brother of Louis IX. Buried in Naples, his tomb in the church of the Jacobins in Paris contained only his heart.

51. Jeanne de France, died 1371, and Blanche d'Evreux, died 1398.

52. Charles de Valois, died 1325, king of Aragon and son of Philippe III le Hardi.

53. Clemence de Hongrie, died 1328, the second wife of Louis X.

54. Louis, Comte d'Evreux, died 1276, the son of Philippe III le Hardi, and Marguerite d'Artois, died 1311.

55. Unknown queen. Grave slab in black marble from the abbey of Maubuisson, founded by Blanche of Castile, St. Louis's mother, whose grave this has long been thought to be.

84. MORIENVAL: Romanesque masterpiece in the Ile de France. ▷

85. ST. LOUP-DE-NAUD: robust cousin of the Portail Royal at Chartres.

86. ST. LOUP-DE-NAUD: heads of kings and saints on the jamb.

87. JOUARRE: Merovingian sarcophagi in the crypt.

88. ST. DENIS: ambulatory from the time of Abbot Suger.

89. ST. DENIS: west façade of the basilica (before restoration).

90. ST. LEU-D'ESSERENT: the abbey church above the Oise.

91. LUZARCHES: the choir apses.

92. CHAMPEAUX: side aisle of Early Gothic church.

93. SENLIS: cathedral and bishop's palace. ▷

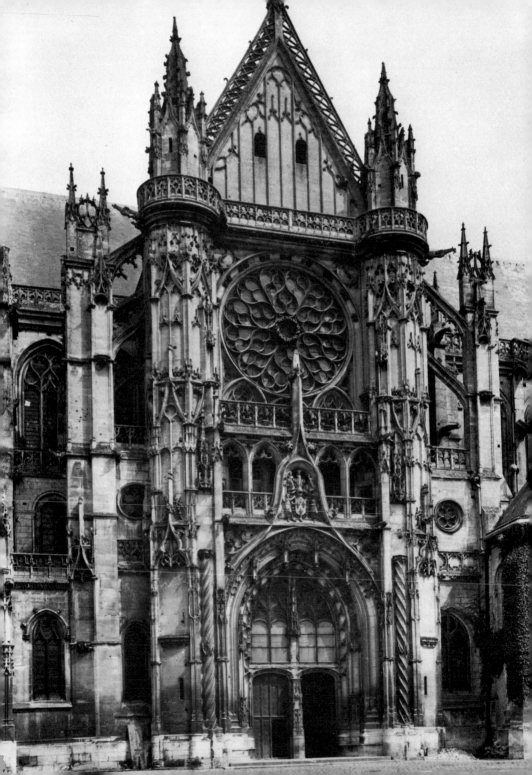

◁ 94. SENLIS: façade of the south transept.

95. SENLIS: coronation of the Virgin on the tympanum of the main portal.

96. NOYON: choir and north transept.

97. NOYON: view from the nave toward the choir.

98. MANTES: nave and west wall. ▷

99. LAON: view from the crossing into the nave.

100. LAON: west façade and south transept tower. ▷

102. CHARTRES: south transept.

101. CHARTRES: west façade with the Portail Royal. ▷

103. CHARTRES: Portail Royal, Christ as World Judge.

104. CHARTRES: Portail Royal.

105. CHARTRES: portals of the north transept.

106. CHARTRES: buttressing of the cathedral choir.

Senlis

Former Cathedral of Notre-Dame

(illus. 93–95, pages 293–295)

Of the Early Gothic cathedrals in the tradition of St. Denis and Sens—Senlis, Noyon, Laon, and Paris—Senlis is the smallest (inside length, 229 feet; height of the nave, 59 feet; width of the nave, 30 feet) and the one that has preserved the least of its original form. However, it is still quite rewarding. It was begun in 1153 by Bishop Thibaut as a three-aisle basilica without transept (under the influence of Sens) and with a twin-towered west façade in direct imitation of St. Denis's but with only a central portal. The sculptures of this portal, created around 1170, likewise derive in style from St. Denis. But here, for the first time, the Last Judgment has been replaced with motifs that relate to Mary. On the tympanum (illus. 95) is the coronation of Mary, as a symbol of Christ's devotion to his church, and below it on the lintel are Mary's death and assumption. Adorning the jambs are figures from the Old Testament, and in the archivolts are the Tree of Jesse and various prophets. In spite of damage during the Revolution and clumsy restoration in the nineteenth century (the heads of the jamb figures are restored), these comprise one of the most impressive Early Gothic figure ensembles. Its range of themes was extremely important for all of the later cathedrals until Reims. The south tower was provided with a tall, octagonal spire of great lightness and elegance in the middle of the thirteenth century, and it became the model for a whole series of French church towers.

The building was consecrated in 1191. However, the interior is largely character-ized by changes made in the following centuries. In about 1240, a transept with a broad crossing was introduced. And in 1504, after a terribly destructive fire demolished the roof and the vaulting, all of the church above the balcony was rebuilt and heightened in the Flamboyant style. The high clerestory windows now descend into the area of the old triforium so that only the lower parts of the church reveal the original arrangement. Bundles of half-columns alternate with round pillars as a result of the six-part vaulting, much like that at Noyon and at Laon, that spans the bays in pairs. A broad balcony runs above the side aisles, with a continuous cross-ribbed vaulting, and opens onto the nave in a simple, pointed-arch arcade. The circuit around the choir is narrower than the side aisles, and the two radial chapels that flank the neo-Gothic central chapel are relatively shallow. From the outside, there is a sharp contrast between the impressive compactness of the Early Gothic semicircular choir (with the *chevet* and the balcony level above it) and the airy, richly ornamented sixteenth-century upper part of the church (illus. 93).

The Flamboyant style also characterizes the exteriors of the transepts. The façade of the south transept was planned as a splendid display facing a new square. Between 1530 and 1534, Pierre Chambiges, the son of Martin Chambiges, the architect of the transepts of Beauvais and of Sens, constructed the south transept and its façade (illus. 94), breaking up solid forms into a web of delicate and highly complicated decoration. The simpler façade of the north transept was completed in 1560. Above its portal is the salamander device of François I, who supported the rebuilding of the church. It forms a charming ensemble with the buildings of the chapter house and the library from the end of the fourteenth century.

The City

Only a very few towns around Paris have been able to preserve their old appearance as well as Senlis, which until the Revolution was a bishopric. The Gallo-Roman town wall, with sixteen towers surviving from the original twenty-eight, is one of the best preserved in France. It wraps around the core of the city in an ellipse more than 2,600 feet in circumference. The second, larger ring of medieval town walls has largely given way to boulevards, which offer an array of picturesque views into the old town.

Major portions of the Château Royal from the Romanesque and Gothic periods have survived next to the square donjon. Excavations on this site have unearthed portions of the Roman *praetorium*. Later, it was the residence of the Frankish kings. Here, in 987, the archbishop of Reims proposed to the assembled barons the election of the duke of Francia, Hugues Capet, as the new king. It was only in the late Middle Ages that the kings abandoned Senlis in favor of Compiègne and later Fontainebleau. Henri IV was the last French monarch to live here.

In the palace park there are remnants of the old priory of St. Maurice, a foundation of St. Louis's from 1264 intended to house the relics of the saints of the Theban legion. The prior's house from the eighteenth century now houses a unique hunting museum (Musée de la Vénerie; open daily, except Tuesday and Wednesday mornings, 10:00 A.M.–12:00 M. and 2:00 P.M.–5:00 P.M.; in summer, to 6:00 P.M.).

Like the Château Royal, the bishop's palace backs up against the Gallo-Roman town

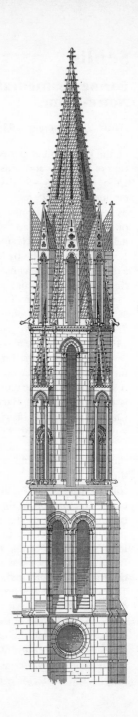

Senlis Cathedral: south tower.

306

wall. It stands to the southeast of the cathedral on the Place Notre-Dame and dates to the twelfth century, with some sixteenth-century remodeling. Also standing against the wall is the former church of St. Frambourg. This collegiate church from the late twelfth century has been restored by the composer Giorgy Cziffra, who hopes to establish an international music center here.

Outside the Roman wall, to the east of the cathedral choir, is the former church of St. Pierre. It was founded in 1029 and expanded by the addition of a crossing and a choir in the thirteenth century. In 1516, a new façade was built; it is ascribed to Pierre Chambiges. Not until 1615 was a classical tower constructed on the south side as a counterpart to the north tower, whose lower portions date from the eleventh century and whose spire was built in 1432. For centuries the church has been secularized and used as a market; there are plans to restore it as a municipal cultural center.

Senlis is extraordinarily rich in medieval and classical secular buildings, especially along the Rue du Châtel, the Rue de la Treille, and the Rue de Beauvais. In the last street are also the remains of the former church of St. Aignan, presently a movie theater. On the Place Henri IV, there is the city hall from 1495.

Less than two miles southeast of the town are the remains of the Abbaye de la Victoire, a memorial to Philippe Auguste's victory at Bouvines in 1214. Of the other great royal monastic foundations here, only the former abbey of St. Vincent has survived. This was endowed in 1062 by Anne of Kiev, the wife of Henri I. Its church has been heavily restored, but it preserves a tower from the twelfth century and extremely important monastic buildings from the seventeenth century, including a cloister in the classic style from 1680 (today used as a school).

Noyon
Former Cathedral of Notre-Dame

(illus. 96 and 97, pages 295 and 296)

Situated in the border area between the Ile de France and Picardy, the cathedral of Noyon belongs among the seminal structures of the Early Gothic period. In spite of damages, alterations, and restorations since the eighteenth century—most recently following World War II—it presents an extremely pure image of the Early Gothic cathedral.

The dates of its building are uncertain. It appears, though, to have been begun by Bishop Baudouin II in about 1150, after a fire struck the earlier church in 1131 and after the separation of the bishoprics of Noyon and Tournai. (Baudoin was a friend of St. Bernard of Clairvaux and of Abbot Suger of St. Denis.) By 1165, the choir, crossing, north transept, and first bay of the nave were complete; in 1183, the south transept and the chapel of the bishop's palace on the south side of the cathedral were finished. Construction of the nave, the façade and vestibule, and the south tower continued until 1220. The north tower was in place by 1231. A fire destroyed the roof and vaulting of the church in 1293. When they were restored, the cathedral's nearly square, six-part vaults spanning two bays each were replaced by diamond-shaped, narrow cross-ribbed vaulting. The wall elevation remained essentially the same. The alternation of broad and narrow transverse arches in the vaulting is a reminder of the earlier system. A wide cloister with a two-aisle chapter house and library was added on the north side.

Chapels were added between the buttresses of the building from the fourteenth until the seventeenth centuries. In the eight-

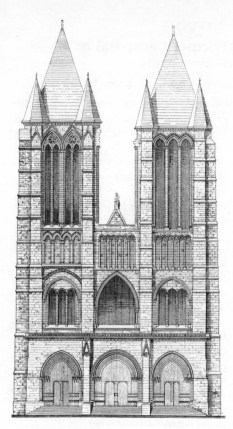

Noyon Cathedral: façade.

balconies and a clerestory above the arcade floor. In the choir at Noyon, though, the blind arcade of a triforium, still somewhat tentative in form above the balcony, continues in the nave as a true triforium with a corridor behind it. The temporal discrepancy between the choir and the nave (illus. 97) can be observed in their respective balconies; the apse has simple, pointed-arch arcades, while the nave has double arcades beneath an overarching one.

The transepts are uncommon both in ground plan and in elevation. Closed and with semicircular ends, they form—together with the choir—a three-apse arrangement. It is possible that Noyon's connections to the north, specifically to the Rhineland, may have influenced this layout. The transepts have only a single aisle, but the clear layering of their elevation gives the impression of depth. Above tall blind arcades, there is a triforium and a second row of blind arcades that suggest balconies, and—highest of all—the narrow clerestory windows. This is an early example of a diaphanous wall structure in superb, Early Gothic forms. Stressed wall pillars alternate with unstressed columns with slender half-columns that rise above them. This feature of the nave's wall arrangement reflects the original six-part rib structure of the vaulting. As at Laon, modern glass windows fill the church with an extraordinary amount of light. They allow the warm color of the sandstone to be seen to its best advantage, but they convey none of the medieval lighting effects.

Uncommon for the Ile de France—reminiscent, rather, of the architectural style of Burgundy—is the three-aisle, open vestibule in the west façade. The façade itself, with its two towers, reveals the basic pattern of St. Denis, adapted to the somewhat dry fourteenth-century reconstruction. In place

eenth century, these buttresses were modernized into curving volutes with urns, giving the choir end a totally un-Gothic appearance (illus. 96). The Revolution demolished almost all of the façade sculptures. The only piece to survive is a splendid fragment of a seated Madonna from about 1180. This was placed on the trumeau pillar of the west portal sometime before 1918. It is now in the cloister.

Noyon seems to be the earliest example of a four-story interior, for one must assume that Suger's church at St. Denis had only

Noyon Cathedral: transept, crossing, and choir (longitudinal section).

of a central rose window, there is a simple window composed of three lancets beneath a broad arcade. With the adjacent façade of the chapter house to the north, this window dominates a lovely, semicircular square surrounded by elegant curia buildings with eighteenth-century façades and portals.

Laon
The Cathedral

(illus. 99 and 100, pages 298 and 299)

Historically a part of the Ile de France, Laon today is more often considered a part of Picardy. It stands on a high plateau that drops off steeply on all sides. The Revolution and the two world wars cruelly decimated the architectural monuments of this region. Laon, happily, is one of the few medieval ensembles to have survived.

The cathedral is famous for both its incomparable location and its unusual structure, which diverges clearly from the other buildings of the Early Gothic. Although the dates of its construction are uncertain, it seems that it was begun under Bishop Gautier de Mortagne (1155–1174). It is a three-aisle basilica with a distinct crossing that opens into a tower, a short choir, and a transept with lavish façade structures. The cathedral has four stories, with wide, open balconies, triforium, and clerestory. Each pair of bays is spanned by a six-part vault. The west façade was under construction by 1190. After 1205, it was decided to extend the choir to the east by adding three double bays and to close it with a flat wall. The towers of the transept façades were begun in about 1220 and must have been completed in about 1235. However, the western towers had risen only as far as the

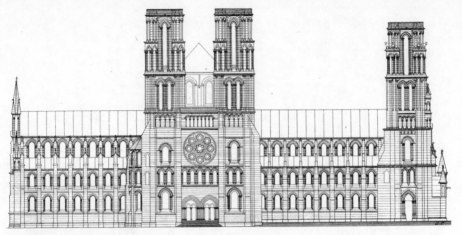

Laon Cathedral: north side with choir, transept, and façade tower.

beginning of the turrets; the spires were never added. With its seven towers (two above each façade plus the crossing tower), Laon would have very closely resembled the ideal Gothic cathedral as Eugène Viollet-le-Duc envisioned it.

The exterior of the cathedral is astonishing for the differentiation of its parts and the sculptural treatment of each of its elements. The west façade (illus. 100) begins with a deeply projecting vestibule that shelters the portals. The walls between the doors were originally open; this was the model for the similar transept façades at Chartres. The gables and baldachins of this vestibule extend upward across a transition zone, with its simple arrangement of lancet windows, into the monumental middle area of the façade. Here, the buttresses, connected by broad round arches, take up the triumphal arch motif from below. The wall proper is deeply recessed. It has a large rose window in the center and richly ornamented lancet windows under the towers. A triforium-like gallery that is somewhat raised across the central section completes the façade. Behind it, flanked by buttresses, the towers rise in two stories, changing after the first story from squares to octagons. At the corners of the top story are airy baldachins with oxen emerging from them like fabulous beasts. The significance of these animals is still unexplained. A surrounding balustrade masks the beginnings of the turrets that were never completed. In about 1230, Villard de Honnecourt sketched one of these towers with the comment that he had never seen a comparable one anywhere. The towers of the transept façades are lighter by several degrees, both in their columns and in their architectural decoration. Their design affected architecture as far away as Germany.

The deep modeling of the structure, which produces a dramatic interplay of light and shadow, continues on the long sides as well, where the interior structure is apparent in the regular alternation of deep buttresses and rows of windows between them. The clarity of the interior (illus. 99) has always been celebrated, in spite of the loss of nearly all the original glass.

The spaces immediately behind each of the transept façades are treated as crossbars with their own bays and with polygonal chapels on their eastern ends. In the early fourteenth century, these façades began to be transformed into tall glass walls, but only in the south transept was this modernization completed; work on the north transept barely got under way. In the windows of the choir wall, which were created in about 1225, the old panes have been preserved, with the life of Christ in the center, the life of Mary on the right, and the martyrdom of St. Stephen and the Mary miracle of Theophilus on the left. The rose window is dedicated to Mary.

Almost none of the cathedral's original furnishings have survived. However, there are some quite beautiful Renaissance doors that close off the chapels from the side aisles. Likewise, only very little of the sculpture of the west façade remains in place. This work was extremely important because it marked the first use in cathedral sculpture of the "antique" figure style, which had been developed by goldsmiths in the Meuse region. Photographs that predate the restoration begun in 1853, and casts preserved in the Musée des Monuments Français in Paris (see pages 480–481), suggest something of the quality of the original figures. The central subject of the façade was no longer the Last Judgment but rather the glorification of Mary. On the tympanum of the central portal, Christ is crowning her. In its archivolts (some of which are old), the Tree of Jesse and various prophets are depicted. The tympanum of the Christ portal contains the Adoration of the Magi, the Annunciation, and the Nativity, with shepherds depicted in the lintel below. The Last Judgment appears only on the right-hand

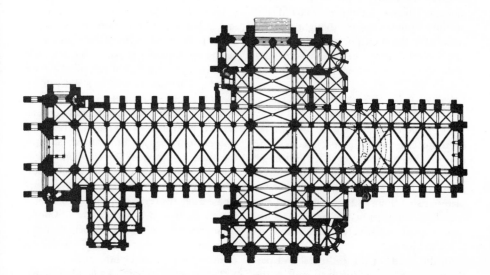

Laon Cathedral (ground plan, with dotted lines indicating the extent of the original choir).

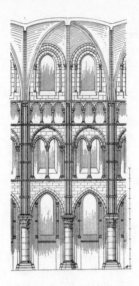

Laon Cathedral: nave (elevation, cross-section, and exterior of a single bay).

portal. The jamb figures of all three are nineteenth-century creations. In the Laon municipal museum, there are two old statues of prophets that are thought to have come from the west portal. If this attribution is correct, they can provide some idea of the style of the original jamb sculptures.

The City

Victor Hugo once exclaimed, "In Laon everything is beautiful: the churches, the houses, the surroundings—everything." The surroundings have suffered, but Hugo's praise is otherwise still deserved. Laon, its plateau rising almost 325 feet above the surrounding countryside, has retained its historical center relatively intact within its walls and gates.

To the north of the cathedral and partially incorporating the city wall is the bishop's palace (today the Palais de Justice), which includes a two-story chapel from the twelfth century. To the west of this edifice is its restored forecourt, surrounded by Romanesque and Gothic structures. To the south is the Gothic Hôtel-Dieu, and a bit farther on is the municipal museum, which boasts an important collection of Greek vases and statues as well as a diptych by the Master of the Rohan Book of Hours, one of the masterpieces of fifteenth-century French painting. An octagonal Templar chapel from the twelfth century stands in the museum's garden. The city library preserves treasures from the Cistercian abbey of Vauclair, east of Laon, which was secularized during the Revolution and almost completely destroyed in World War I. Among these treasures are highly important miniatures and manuscripts, some of which date from as early as the eighth century.

The inner city contains a number of private residences from the Gothic and Renaissance periods, with oriels, towers, and entrance carriageways. On the main square, next to the nineteenth-century Hôtel de Ville, there is a remarkable Baroque façade of a former pastoral church that will serve as a cultural center for the city once its restoration is completed.

At the western edge of the old town is the abbey church of St. Martin, whose transept towers are reminiscent of those of the cathedral. Its thirteenth-century west façade is topped by uncommonly slender pointed spires and was also inspired by the cathedral, echoing its choir façade. Inside, St. Martin's lacks both triforium and balconies, and the back wall of its choir is flat. It has some notable tombs, including those of Jeanne de Flandre and the Seigneur de Coucy. The adjacent wings of this abbey are from the seventeenth and eighteenth centuries.

Mantes
Collégiale Notre-Dame

(illus. 98, page 297)

This is the most important structure to have been directly influenced by Notre-Dame in Paris. It was developed under the patronage of Louis VII and Philippe Auguste, both of whom served at times as titular abbots of its college of canons. Philippe Auguste here launched his campaigns into Normany and the Vexin.

The west façade was begun in about 1170. Originally, the church was built on a quite simple ground plan, with a three-aisle nave, a choir, and an ambulatory, but no transepts. The chapels on the sides and in the choir are fourteenth-century additions in the Rayonnant ("radiant") style of the High Gothic, which attempted to make an architecture out of line and light, as in the Sainte-Chapelle in Paris. In its interior elevation,

Mantes reveals a number of Parisian characteristics. There are six-panel vaults, and thus wall pillars alternate with pilasters and round columns. There is a balcony story with three small arcades beneath an overarching blind arch in each bay (oddly enough, the balconies do not continue into the bay immediately adjacent to the west end). Even the oculi from Paris are present, illuminating the balconies. There is no triforium. Rather, the large clerestory windows begin immediately above the balcony. The carving of the partial columns and the delicacy of the sculptural decorations are quite close to those of Notre-Dame in Paris.

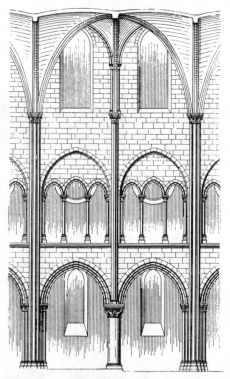

Mantes, nave of the Collégiale Notre-Dame: two bays with six-part vaulting.

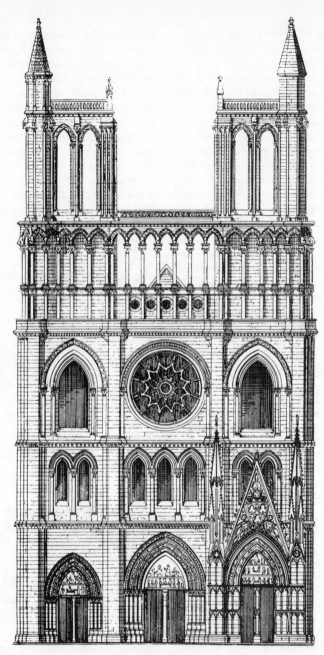

Mantes, Collégiale Notre-Dame: façade.

The nave is 98 feet high, and the broad, six-panel vaults virtually appear to float.

The façade, too, is reminiscent of the Parisian model. It has two towers, three portals between prominent buttresses, and a balance between horizontal and vertical elements. Above the portals, there is a row of simple lancet windows; above this, a central rose window. The open arcade connecting the two towers was added in the nineteenth century as a means of increasing the stability of the tower level. The portal sculptures are of high quality despite the damage they sustained during the Revolution. The left portal depicts the Resurrection, and it appears to be the oldest, from about 1170. On its lintel are the three women at the tomb guarded by an angel; above this, the resurrected Christ is accompanied by angels and attributes suggestive of his return. This portal is stylistically related to the north transept portal at St. Denis. The central portal, dated to about 1180, takes up the theme of Senlis, the coronation of Mary, which is accompanied by scenes from the life of Mary on the lintel. As at Senlis, the archivolts depict the Tree of Jesse as well as patriarchs and prophets. The right portal, with scenes from the life of Jesus, was created only in about 1300, under the influence of the cathedral at Rouen. That structure also served as the model for the Late Gothic decorations of the chapel here.

Chartres
Cathedral of Notre-Dame

(color plate, page 222; illus. 101–106, pages 300–304)

Chartres is considered the quintessential French cathedral. Not only has its architecture survived the centuries virtually unharmed, but its portal sculptures and medieval stained-glass windows are also almost completely preserved. Furthermore, Chartres offers a unique display of medieval iconography and cooperation among the various types of artists involved in the creation of a Gothic cathedral. But Chartres became a key structure in the Gothic tradition primarily because the later cathedrals of Reims and of Amiens (and ultimately most of the Gothic cathedrals in northern France and beyond) followed its cruciform layout, strong accentuation of the ends of the cross, and use of huge window surfaces between the triforium and the window vaults. Chartres was the initiator of a type that managed to maintain itself through countless modifications up until the late Middle Ages and out into the most remote fringes of the known Western world.

The cathedral as we know it was begun in 1194. But even before this, Chartres exercised an influence far in excess of its role as the capital of a rich grain region, the Beauce. In pre-Roman times, one of the great Druid temples was here, and in the Gallo-Roman period, there was a temple to a goddess here. Christian missionaries later allowed her statue to be worshipped as one of the Holy Virgin. The preeminence of Chartres as a sanctuary of Mary worship was fixed in 876, when Charles le Chauve (Charles the Bald) presented it with Mary's tunic.

After the fourth century A.D., a succession of churches was erected on the spot of the Roman temple. In 1020, an extensive Romanesque complex was completely destroyed by fire. Bishop Fulbert used its walls to construct a large crypt that still extends beneath the choir and the side aisles. The central nave of this structure was later razed, and its arcade openings were walled up. However, the old side aisles still serve as a crypt.

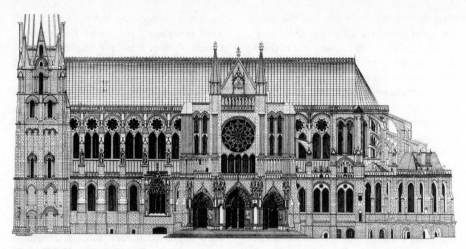

Chartres Cathedral: south side.

Work continued on Fulbert's building through the entire eleventh century. After a fire in 1134, the west façade had to be rebuilt. The north tower was begun in 1134. After a fire in 1506, its wooden spire was replaced by Jehan de Beauce with the richly detailed Flamboyant spire whose filigree stands in the strongest imaginable contrast to the restrained compactness of the south tower and the architecture of the structure below. The south tower was constructed between 1145 and 1165. Its square base becomes an octagon above the third story, where it is surrounded by dormer windows. Here, the crystalline lines of the masonry surfaces of the spire proper begin. Eugène Viollet-le-Duc considered this the most beautiful bell tower in France. Between the towers, the façade was raised only as far as the group of three windows. The rose window, above these, and the Galerie des Rois came into being only after 1200 (illus. 101).

A devastating fire in 1194 destroyed por-tions of the city, the bishop's palace, and all of the cathedral except the new west front. The relics of Mary, however, were saved. With encouragement from the papal legate, it was decided to build an even larger cathedral, and the entire population enthu-siastically contributed what it could to make this possible. The bishop and the chapter pledged three years of their income to help fund the project.

In little more than thirty years, a cathe-dral arose according to a unified plan; its architect is unknown. It both summarized the experiments of Early Gothic and laid the foundations for the masterpieces of High Gothic. The nave was completed in 1220, the choir with double ambulatory and *chevet* (above Fulbert's crypt) in about 1222, and work was done on the upper por-tions of the transepts in about 1230. The portal sculptures took considerably longer, however, so the consecration of the cathe-dral did not take place until 1260. Begin-ning in 1323, a chapter house was constructed behind the choir, but not along the central axis; and in 1349, the Chapelle St-Piat (today the cathedral treasury) was erected above it, reached by a lovely open staircase. Chartres is the only great cathedral that was not altered in later centuries. Except for the Chapelle de Vendôme from 1417 to 1421 on the south side, no chapels were added between its buttresses. Nor did it suffer major damage during the Revolution. A fire in 1836 required that only the roof be replaced.

Comparing it with the Early Gothic cathedrals, one is struck by the greater clarity, directness, and compactness that inform both its ground plan and elevation, its inner space, and its exterior. The basic form of the Latin cross is clearly apparent in the emphasis given to the transepts. These cross arms have been provided with their own façades (illus. 102 and 105). These are projecting porticos richly decorated with figures and reminiscent of triumphal arches. Each was intended to include twin towers, although they are not apparent from the inside. For unknown reasons, the towers were never developed beyond their foundations. Inside, the transepts display the same arrangement as the main church, with added depth provided by side aisles and stained-glass inner façades. With their dominant central rose windows, they correspond completely to the façade of the nave.

The nearly square crossing connects these two cross arms. A series of slender half-columns extends from the floor to the vaulting. It stands in front of the diagonally placed crossing pillars and effects the transition from the wall of the nave to the wall of the transept.

Clarity and simplicity characterize the wall elevation. The architect of Chartres chose to omit balconies—their structural necessity was obviated by the exterior buttressing—and instead increase the dimensions of the clerestory. The arcades and the clerestory windows are of nearly equal height. Between them, the dark triforium, with its succession of narrow arches, unifies the space. The wall of the clerestory is

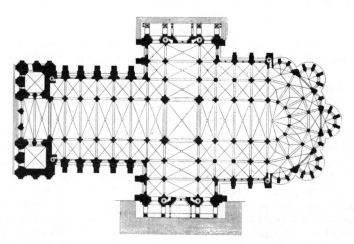

Chartres Cathedral (ground plan).

Chartres Cathedral: nave (two bays, cross-section, and exterior of one bay).

almost completely glass, with pairs of lancets and small roses forming window groupings that anticipate the tracery windows subsequently developed at Reims.

The single bays stand clearly defined as separate units; instead of six-panel vaulting arching over pairs of bays, each bay has a narrow, rectangular, four-part cross-ribbed vault. Harmonizing with this uniform rhythm of the vaulting is the succession of half-columns of different strengths, corresponding to their functions, which are clustered in groups of five and rise from the pillars of the arcades. These chamfered pillars have always been famed as a particular achievement of the Chartres master. The core of each is tied to four projecting columns that emphasize it. Round half-columns are placed around an octagonal core; octagonal half-columns, around a round one.

The spatial impression is one of clarity and balance. The height of the central nave is 119 feet, corresponding to its extraordinary width of more than 52 feet. The overall length of the church is some 425 feet. One has the impression that the space grows larger as one's gaze passes from the darker lower area, characterized by the heavy pillars, up into the lighter, almost insubstantial region of the windows. Abbot Suger's concept of *lux continua* is nowhere more clearly manifest than in Chartres. An unearthly, violet light transforms the space. Moreover, one must imagine the effect produced when the stone itself was painted with rich color. Chance has fortunately preserved most of the stained-glass windows, and, on the west side, restoration of them has begun —not without violent criticism because the cleaned panes, now much brighter and more radiant than before, no longer have the mystical obscurity to which visitors were accustomed. Of the roughly 160 windows, the majority were created between 1210 and 1240. Panes from the Romanesque structure, dating from about 1150, have survived in only three lancet windows on the west side: the one on the left depicts the life of Christ; in the center, the Passion; and on the right, the Tree of Jesse. Four additional twelfth-century panels, including Notre-Dame-de-la-Belle-Verrière, have been incorporated into a setting of thirteenth-century glass on the right side of the ambulatory.

Although it is impossible to trace a consistent program that underlies the entire inventory of stained glass, the main themes —as in the sculptural groupings of the exterior—can certainly be determined. The western rose window is dedicated to Christ and the Last Judgment; the northern one to Mary and the kings and prophets of the Old Testament; and the southern one to the exaltation of Christ. With these, the master of Chartres created the fundamental great cathedral rose window, combining radial spokes and concentrically arranged multifoil openings.

The windows of the clerestory, designed to be seen from a distance, contain large-scale figures of the apostles, saints, and prophets. In the more detailed windows of the side aisles and the choir, there is a wealth of scenes from the Old and New Testaments and from the legends of the saints. These are meant to be read in sequence from bottom to top and from left to right. The lower panels often depict donors—the various guilds of Chartres, merchants, craftsmen, churchmen—while the rose windows and those of the clerestory were generally commissioned by the nobility. The northern rose window was donated by the king.

The dissolution of the upper walls into window surfaces was made possible by an elaborate structural apparatus on the exterior. This construction, which functions as the decisive factor in the overall architectural design, brought to technical refinement the system of buttressing first developed in Paris (illus. 106).

The exterior of the nave of Chartres is uncommonly fascinating. The heavy forms of the side aisles and of the buttresses welded to them become lighter and lighter as one looks upward. The cross-brace emerging from each buttress is made lighter by a radial arcade that follows the line of its lower curve. And at the very top, there is a second, delicate flying buttress that translates the bracing system begun so massively below into a dizzying play of arcs. This topmost brace is often—doubtless incorrectly—considered to have been a later addition. The turretlike gallery that stretches along the edge of the roof serves as a weightless counterpart to the ponderous forms of the side aisles and provides a simple and serene termination to the complex structure.

On the façade of the south transept, the weight of the masonry has been softened by a network of slender bars that rings the massive buttresses like a veil (illus. 102).

The Portals

Portail Royal

Since the west portal of St. Denis has been essentially lost to us, the Portail Royal at Chartres (illus. 103 and 104) represents the known beginning of Gothic sculpture. The history of its creation is not entirely clear, but it was definitely conceived after the towers for the narrow central nave of the old Romanesque cathedral were begun. It was the model for the portal of the cathedral of Le Mans, which was dedicated in 1158.

Accordingly, it must have been constructed between 1145 and 1155, along with the chapel that originally stood above it and whose three lancet windows serve as the portal's culmination. Space limitations affect the portal's proportions. The three portals are packed close together—the central one taller than the other two—and all three have narrow, pointed arches. Originally, there was a succession of twenty-four slender, elongated jamb figures; of these, nineteen have survived. Above them are lintels and tympanums framed by archivolts, three in the center, two on either side.

The theme of the Portail Royal is the story of the Salvation. In the central tympanum (illus. 103) is Christ's return in majesty, accompanied by the symbols of the Evangelists, angels with scrolls, and the twenty-four elders of the Apocalypse. At the feet of Christ are the apostles, seated as jurors at the Last Judgment. The tympanums of the side portals are directly related to the central one. On the right are Mary and the Advent of Christ (the Annunciation, the Visitation, the Nativity, the Annunciation to the Shepherds, and the Presentation in the Temple on the bands of the lintel). On the left is the Ascension, beneath which angels assure the seated apostles of Christ's return. The capitals are tightly packed with additional scenes: from the center to the left, there are the ancestry and childhood of Christ from the meeting between Joachim and Anne to the slaughter of the innocents in Bethlehem; to the right are scenes from the life of Christ from the Presentation in the Temple to the dismissal of the apostles. Along with the signs of the zodiac and the corresponding signs of the months, the archivolts of the right-hand portal contain an unusual sequence of female allegories of the fine arts, each accompanied by an appropriate classical authority. It is possible that these were initiated by the chancellor of Chartres's Cathedral School, Thierry de Chartres.

Despite the unified concept behind the Portail Royal, it is apparent that various artists of different temperaments and backgrounds were employed in its execution. The master sculptor among them was the one to whom the central tympanum and the figures on the left jamb of the central portal are ascribed. His work combines delicacy and stringency, austere stylization and sensual vitality. The others were less forceful personalities who worked in his style. They are assumed to have come from St. Denis, and their artistic concepts may be related to the development of Late Romanesque sculpture in Burgundy. There was also one artist of a quite different stamp, the so-called archivolt master, whose approach emphasized the expression of character. His figures display highly compressed proportions and quite expressive physiognomies.

Transept Portals

The sculpture cycle of the two transept portals at Chartres is—along with those at Reims and at Amiens—the most comprehensive to be found on any Gothic cathedral. Firm dates are lacking, but the Comte de Blois's gift of the head of St. Anne to the cathedral in 1204 provides an approximate date for the figure of Anne on the trumeau column of the central portal of the north transept. In about 1240, when a screen—of which there are remnants in the crypt and in the Louvre—was erected inside the church, the sculptures of the portals and vestibules had been completed. The vesti-

107. SOISSONS: view into the south transept. ▷

320

108. SOISSONS: the cathedral, from the east.

109. SOISSONS: relief of the Last Judgment (detail) from the church of St. Yved in Braine, now in the municipal museum.

110. BRAINE: St. Yved, coronation of the Virgin, from the original middle portal.

111. MEAUX: nave and crossing. ▷

112. BEAUVAIS: façade of the south transept.

113. BEAUVAIS: view into the choir. ▷

114. CHAALIS: ruins of the monastery church.

115. SOISSONS: façade of the former abbey church of St. Jean-des-Vignes.

116. LONGPONT: ruins of the former abbey church.

117. LONGPONT: en-
trance gate to
the old monas-
tery precinct.

118. ROYAUMONT: refectory of the former Cistercian monastery.

119. ROYAUMONT: a thirteenth-century abbey; the abbot's palace is on the left.

120. RAMPILLON: main portal of the Templar church; pictures of the months from the base of the jamb.

121. AUVERS-SUR-OISE: thirteenth-century village church.

122. ST. GERMER-DE-FLY: Romanesque apse of the church and the Sainte-Chapelle, after the one in Paris.

123. PROVINS: three-aisle hall of the Grange aux Dimes.

124. PROVINS: city walls of the Vieille Ville. ▷

125. PIERREFONDS: something more than a French Neuschwanstein.

126. GISORS: a gate tower from the fortress of the English kings.

127. NEMOURS: twelfth-century castle above the Loing.

128. MAINTENON: a Late Gothic country seat, on the River Eure. ▷

129. The castle ruins of Château-Gaillard on white chalk cliffs, high above the Seine.

bules were not created at the same time as the portals, but their iconographic program appears, by and large, to continue that of the portals. The attribution of individual sculptures or of whole cycles to specific artists and workshops has been the object of scholarly discussion for decades. Close examination reveals a tremendous stylistic diversity, with links to the figures at Sens, Laon, Senlis, and Paris. Here, though, we shall present only a simple catalogue of the groups of works and their most important themes.

North transept. The tympanum of the central portal (c. 1205–1210) depicts the coronation of Mary. Mary's death and assumption are on the lintel, and her mother, St. Anne, is on the central pillar. The jambs present Old Testament figures, John the Baptist, and Peter; the archivolts are filled with angels, the Tree of Jesse, and prophets. The right portal (c. 1220) presents themes from the Old Testament: the story of Job on the tympanum; the judgment of Solomon on the lintel below it; on the jambs, Old Testament figures including Bileam, the queen of Sheba, and Solomon; and in the archivolts, the stories of Samson, Esther, and Tobias to the left, and of Gideon, Judith, and Tibias to the right. The left portal (c. 1220) concentrates on the birth of Christ. The tympanum depicts the Adoration and the Dream of the Magi; the lintel, the Nativity and the Annunciation to the Shepherds. On the jambs are the Annunciation, the Visitation, and prophets. In the archivolts are angels, along with the Wise and Foolish Virgins. In the north vestibule in front of the pillars (c. 1220–1230), there are priests and women from the Old Testament as well as saints; the archivolts contain the story of the Creation and allegories of the active life and the contemplative life.

South transept. The central portal (c. 1210–1215) presents the Last Judgment. Christ, intercessors, and angels are shown on the tympanum; the blessed and the damned on the lintel; Christ above a lion and a dragon on the trumeau pillar; and the apostles on the jambs. In the archivolts, heaven is depicted on the left, hell on the right, and the resurrected and choirs of angels above. On the right portal (c. 1220) are saints and believers. The tympanum and lintel present the legend of St. Martin on the left (his gift of his cloak and his dream) and the legend of St. Nicholas of Myra on the right (he is distributing gold, and cripples are gathered around his sarcophagus); a half-figure of Christ gives his benediction above these. On the jambs and in the archivolts are holy confessors, together with angels. On the left portal (c. 1210–1220) are martyrs. The tympanum and lintel present the martyrdom and vision of St. Stephen; on the jambs and in the archivolts are other blessed martyrs. The outermost jamb figures right and left, St. Theodore (presumably) and St. George, respectively, are from around 1230. In the south vestibule (c. 1230–1240), the pillars depict additional scenes of martyrdom, allegories of virtues and vices, and the elders of the Apocalypse.

In one of the chapels in the crypt, there are eight slabs from the rood screen created between 1230 and 1240. These contain scenes from the childhood of Christ and fragments of the Passion, as well as various keystones.

The City

Because of the overwhelming significance of the cathedral, which attracts more than 3 million tourists every year, it is easy to overlook the fact that Chartres itself is one of the most charming medieval cities in northern France. It is the only city in which the cathedral and its medieval quarter continue to stand in their original relationship. An impressive campaign to reclaim and restore the old town was begun more than ten years ago and is still in progress. It is well worth exploring the former quarter of the cathedral chapter to the north of the cathedral. One notable attraction in this district is the Cellier de Loëns, the chapter's gigantic three-aisle wine cellar; it has recently been restored and now contains a fascinating museum on the history of stained glass. Another is the former church of St. André from the twelfth century; its choir (demolished in the nineteenth century) was built out over the River Eure on supporting arches. In the crypt of this church, there are regular audio-visual presentations about the history of the city and the cathedral.

There is an extremely picturesque walkway along the Eure. It goes past ancient paved bridges, a number of preserved washing spots, the remains of the Porte Guillaume, and steeply climbing streets with old gabled houses, bringing one to the church of St. Pierre, the city's most important structure after the cathedral. The abbey of St. Père-en-Vallée originally stood outside the city walls. Its massive donjon, from around the year 1000, serves as the bell tower of the church. It also testifies to the need for fortifications at that time. The existing church structure was begun in 1150, when the lower portions of the choir were constructed. The extremely tall nave and side aisles were built at the beginning of the thirteenth century; rising on the exterior above the aisles, there is a double row of flying buttresses. Only toward the end of the thirteenth century was the choir completed. Its bright triforium and great clerestory windows make it a masterpiece of considerable elegance and lightness in the Rayonnant

style. Its importance is further heightened by the almost completely preserved cycle of stained glass from the fourteenth century, with depictions of Old Testament figures on the long sides and of Christ, Mary, saints, and bishops in the apse. This work enables us to observe stained glass in a later stage of development than in the cathedral. Some sixteenth-century panels from a demolished church have been set into the triforium.

A number of remarkable Renaissance structures also survive in the upper town. Among these are the church of St. Aignan, the Escalier de la Reine Berthe (a spiral staircase of carved oak), the Hôtel Montescot, the Logis de Claude Huvé, and a number of fifteenth- and sixteenth-century half-timbered houses near the Place de l'Étape-au-Vin and the market square (Maison du Saumon and Maison des Consuls).

Soissons
Cathedral of St. Gervais–St. Protais
(illus. 107 and 108, pages 321 and 322)

Scarcely any city in the environs of Paris has suffered the effects of war so heavily as the old Frankish royal city of Soissons, which has dominated the valley of the Aisne since Roman times. The Hundred Years' War, the

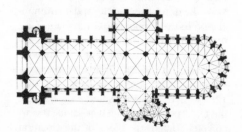

Soissons, cathedral of St. Gervais–St. Protais (ground plan).

338

struggle between the League and the Huguenots, the Franco-Prussian War, and most cruelly World War I all dealt crushing blows to the city. Its cathedral has suffered its share of damage as well. The remains of the cloister adjacent to the church on the north side were totally rebuilt in 1877. The most recent restoration, completed in 1937, is accurate but somewhat uninspired and tends to compromise the original effect.

The cathedral's dimensions are imposing (length, 376 feet; inside height, 98 feet), but its importance in art history owes to its early construction and to a change in its plans. It was begun under Bishop Nivelon in about 1177 as a three-apse structure like that of Noyon, but only the south transept had been erected by the end of the century. Then, after the rebuilding of Chartres began in 1194, the plan was altered. The building that arose after 1200, consisting of a nave, crossing, and choir, constituted the first reaction to the concept developed at Chartres. It combined in one structure extraordinary examples of both Early Gothic and High Gothic styles. The apse of the south transept (illus. 107) shows in its interior elevation some influence from Champagne; one thinks of the Gothic reconstruction of the choir of St. Remi in Reims.

Characteristic of Soissons is the extreme detail and the picturesque disintegration of its structural parts; an example is the leafy capital that here appears for the first time as a variant of the Gothic calyx capital. Also, the four-part elevation, with the usual succession of arcade, balcony, triforium, and clerestory, shows a much greater autonomy of elements than is typical. One field of vaulting corresponds to three arcades; the half-columns alternate in an *a-b-b-a* rhythm—a pattern that is repeated in the openings of the balconies and in the windows of the clerestory. A rhythmic unity is thus pro-

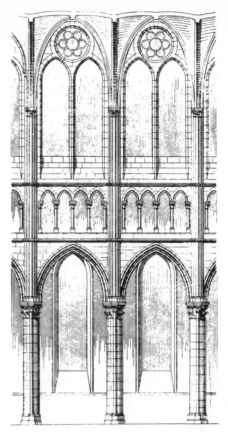

Soissons, cathedral of St. Gervais–St. Protais: two bays of the nave.

duced between each pair of pillars. The "veil of columns" emphasizes the diaphanous wall structure. Its picturesque effect also dominates the view through to the nearly circular Chapelle de la Résurrection, which extends off the transept to the southeast. Its two stories, punctuated by graceful half-columns, were doubtless constructed at the same time as the transept.

The High Gothic nave and choir show the same trend toward reduced wall surfaces as at Chartres and greater lightness in the pillars and half-columns than at Chartres. On the exterior (illus. 108), the buttressing has lost the mass of Chartres's bracing; inside, Chartres's chamfered pillars with their projecting half-columns have been abandoned in favor of round pillars with only single, delicate half-columns facing the nave. As a Chartres, the galleries have been omitted so that the elevation displays the harmonious three-story balance of High Gothic cathedrals. Above a tall arcade, with more pointed arches than at Chartres, there is a dark triforium with a passsage behind it and four small arcades in each bay. Above this, there are tall, narrow clerestory windows that comprise pairs of lancets topped by a small rose. A slight accentuation of the horizontal bands of the cornices, which continue out around the half-columns, produces, together with the carefully differentiated half-columns rising from the imposts of the round columns, an almost graphic structuring of the wall area.

The choir—with five bays, apse, ambulatory, and shallow radial chapels—was consecrated in 1212. The crossing and the seven bays of the nave appear to have been completed by the middle of the thirteenth century, as does the lower portion of the massive west front; the deep portal area of this stepped façade was robbed of its sculptural ornamentation by the Huguenots. In the early fourteenth century, before the beginning of the Hundred Years' War in 1337, the north transept was closed by means of a splendid glass wall consisting of slender shafts of tracery and a rose window whose stained glass has largely survived. Even more precious examples of thirteenth-century stained glass are to be found in the choir apse and chapels.

Although this church has frequently been ravaged and plundered, it preserves two notable art works. One, in the north transept, is a painting of the Adoration of the Shepherds by Peter Paul Rubens. It came from the former Franciscan church in Soissons and was a gift to the monks in gratitude for the care they had given the artist when he had fallen ill in Soissons en route to see Marie de Médicis. The other is a fifteenth-century tapestry in the north aisle with scenes from the life of the cathedral's patron.

The City

Even before the end of the Middle Ages, Soissons, had sunk in importance to a mere provincial capital. But it played a crucial role in the early history of France. Here was the residence of Syagrius, the last Roman governor of Gaul, whom Clovis, king of the Franks, defeated in 486. In 511, the city became the capital of the Frankish kingdom of Neustria, and the kings Clotaire I, son of Clovis, and Sigebert are buried in the crypt of the former abbey of St. Médard. Pepin le Bref (Pippin the Short) was anointed here in 751.

The Franco-Prussian War and World War I destroyed almost all of the city, and old photographs displayed in the nave of the cathedral reveal the extent of the devastation. A stroll through the reconstructed city is nevertheless rewarding.

Impressive remains of the abbey of St. Jean-des-Vignes stand in the quarter just south of the cathedral. The towers and façade of its church (illus. 115, page 327), as imposing as those of a cathedral, rise above the monastery grounds like a piece of stage scenery. This thirteenth-century church was not destroyed by the Revolution, oddly enough, but rather by a bishop of Soissons who needed its stones to repair the cathedral in the nineteenth century. He was prevented from razing its façade, with its elegant Flamboyant towers, only by the protests of the populace. To the south of the façade is the recently restored refectory from the thirteenth century, a two-aisle hall with elegant pillars and lovely cross-ribbed vaulting. Beneath it, there is a cellar with massive octagonal pillars. Two wings of the fourteenth-century cloister have survived, rich with architectural sculpture heralding the Flamboyant style. A second, smaller cloister displaying the forms of the early French Renaissance abuts the earlier one of the south side.

To the north of the cathedral, a municipal museum has been set up in the former abbey of St. Léger (open daily, except Tuesday and Friday, 2:00 P.M.–6:00 P.M.). After World War I, this abbey had to be almost completely rebuilt. It was founded in 1152; the choir and transept of its church date from the thirteenth century. Its nave was destroyed by the Protestants in 1567 and was rebuilt in a somewhat simplified form. The communal buildings date from the seventeenth century. In addition to documents relating to local history, the museum collections include important works by Jean-Antoine Houdon, Nicolas de Largillière, and Gustave Courbet, as well as two remarkable pieces of thirteenth-century sculpture —the head of Clotaire from the crypt of St. Médard and a large fragment (illus. 109, page 322) from the abbey church of St. Yved in Braine from about 1215, depicting Christ's descent into hell and the procession of the damned. The latter probably originated in a Laon workshop. It burlesque monstrosity is unparalleled in northern French sculpture from the Early and High Gothic periods. It has not been determined whether this work was originally part of a tympanum or came from some other context, perhaps a rood screen.

Another highly important work, depicting the coronation of Mary (illus. 110, page 322), has been preserved in situ in St. Yved in Braine, some thirteen miles east of Soissons at the edge of Champagne. Recently restored, it has been freshly mounted inside the church, together with surviving fragments of the church's central portal. The church of St. Yved, begun in about 1180 and consecrated in 1216, is generally associated with the Early Gothic tradition of architecture in Champagne. Its crossing, however, with its tall opening into the tower, shows a similarity to Laon.

St. Yved is well known to art historians for the ground plan of its eastern portion. As a transition between the choir and the transept, there are two pairs of chapels whose axes run diagonally to the crossing, a solution that not only was taken up in the surrounding Brie region but was copied as far away as Burgundy (Notre-Dame in Dijon) and Germany (the Liebfrauenkirche in Trier).

Meaux
Cathedral of St. Étienne
(illus. 111, page 323)

The old capital of the Brie, which belonged to the counts of Champagne until 1361, boasts an unusual, though now heavily restored, cathedral in which Early and Late Gothic elements blend. The early dates for this structure are unknown, but Marie de France, daughter of Louis VII and wife of Comte Henri de Champagne, was buried here in 1198. The choir appears to have been completed in about 1200. In about 1225, its ground plan was reproduced in the famous sketchbook of Villard de Honnecourt: a round apse with ambulatory and three radial chapels. It had four stories, including balconies in the Early Gothic tradi-

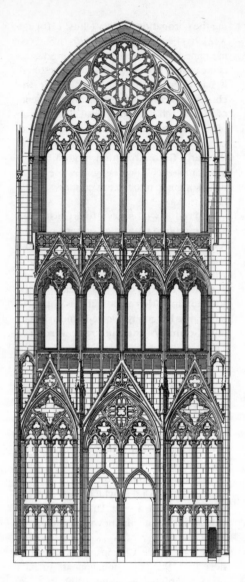

Meaux, cathedral of St. Étienne: interior wall of the north transept.

tion. The nave—which, it is assumed, was completed by 1240—preserved the four-story system of the choir by keeping a series of balcony arcades. But in fact the balconies were omitted; the walls of the nave rose directly behind these openings. Visual uniformity with the choir was thereby ensured, but the pillars of the nave were more structurally stable; quite early on, a considerable weakening of the structure threatened the completion of the church. In 1253, the architect Gautier de Varinfoy was summoned, and he decided to remove the balconies from the choir as well, raising the vaulting of the ambulatory to the height of the side-aisle vaults. In about 1335, two additional choir chapels were added. Near the close of the fourteenth century, two additional bays were added to the west end of the nave, and construction of the façade began. The north tower of this west front was completed in the Flamboyant style in around 1500, but the stump of the south tower was capped by a temporary roof that still stands today. In the fifteenth century, the mock balconies were removed, except for three on the right side of the choir, so that the arcades could rise higher without encumbrance. Traces of the line of the balconies remain, however, and a certain imbalance between the lower and upper portions of the central nave has resulted.

The spatial feeling of the church is strongly determined by these uncommonly tall arcades and the high side aisles behind them. Meaux, like Paris, has double side aisles, the outer one ending where it meets the radial chapels rather than continuing around the choir. The transept, which does not extend beyond the side aisles, divides the structure roughly in the center. Its façades are almost completely glass, with tracery that betrays the influence of the transept façades of Paris. Similarly, the portal of the south transept is directly patterned after the St. Stephen portal at Notre-Dame.

Despite the destruction wrought by the Huguenots in 1562, the portals still preserve a number of remarkable pieces of sculpture. In the main portal, from which the statues have disappeared, there is a Last Judgment tympanum in the center from about 1300. Within the side arches on the left are scenes from the life of St. John the Baptist; on the right, from the life of Mary. All are doubtless from the end of the fourteenth century. On the façade of the north transept, there is a lovely portal from the thirteenth century, with a statue of St. Stephen and scenes from his life on the lintel. Next to the choir are remnants of the twelfth-century chapter buildings, with round corner towers and a covered outside staircase.

The former bishop's palace, from the seventeenth century, was the residence of Meaux's most famous bishop, Bossuet, who served as pastor to Louis XIV. It now houses the Musée Bossuet (open daily, except Tuesday, 2:30 P.M.–6:30 P.M. in winter, 10:00 A.M.–12:00 M. and 2:30 P.M.–4:30 P.M. in summer).

Beauvais
Cathedral of St. Pierre
(illus. 112 and 113, pages 324 and 325)

Beauvais Cathedral has been called the Icarus flight of Gothic architecture. The history of the building is one of a desperate desire to surpass in height everything previously existing and of resulting collapse. Through the centuries, its builders took the same risks, and the cathedral repeatedly suffered the same fate.

In 1227, Bishop Milon de Nanteuil laid the cornerstone for a new cathedral that was to replace the Carolingian cathedral of Notre-Dame, which had become too small. It was not immediately possible to initiate the ambitious construction of a cathedral larger than Amiens, which was then being built. Work on the structure appears to have

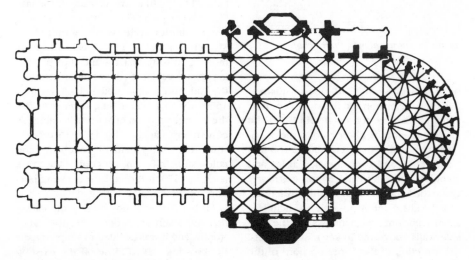

Beauvais, cathedral of St. Pierre (ground plan, with completed portions shown in black).

343

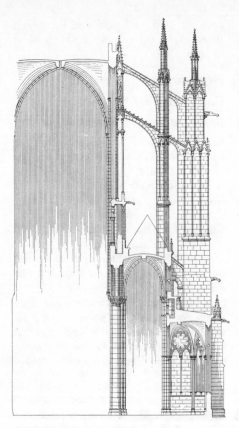

*Beauvais, cathedral of St. Pierre: choir
(cross-section).*

been delayed until 1248, due to quarrels between the bishop and the king. The choir and the apse were consecrated in 1272. The central aisle of the choir rose to the previously unheard of height of almost 160 feet (illus. 113), and even the side aisles and ambulatory rose 65 feet; Beauvais was nearly twice the height of Early Gothic cathedrals. This height made it possible to include a small triforium and windows on the outside walls above the lower radial chapels. Construction of the upper portions of the center aisle may not have been painstaking

enough, or perhaps the distance between the pillars in the choir bays was too large for the extraordinary height. In any case, the vaulting of the choir collapsed in 1284. Instead of building the crossing and the nave, it was now necessary to stabilize the choir. This was accomplished by cutting in half the distance between the pillars. Six new pillars were placed between the original eight so that closer placement of the pillars in the apse now continued into the choir bays. This rapid succession of supports, with their half-columns soaring upward into the reconstructed vaulting, only added to the impression of dizzying verticality. This reconstruction was completed in about 1325, but the choir continued to be embellished until nearly the end of the fourteenth century, when the roof was finally done.

There could be no thought of expanding the structure until the end of the Hundred Years' War. The cornerstone for the crossing and transept was laid in 1500. Over the next forty-eight years, Martin Chambiges and Jean Vast constructed the south transept (illus. 112) with a lavish façade in the late Flamboyant style. The north transept, in a much simpler style, was completed by Michel de Laliet in 1537. Instead of next moving on to the nave—and thus providing greater stability to the whole structure— the builders concentrated their efforts after 1550 on planning a crossing tower. Jean Vast the Younger, the son of Martin Chambiges's co-worker, managed by 1569 to erect a stone tower more than 490 feet high—the tallest spire in Europe. But only a few years later, in 1573, it too collapsed, taking portions of the crossing with it.

All hope of ever completing the cathedral was finally abandoned after this catastrophe, and it was decided to simply repair the crossing and to close off the existing torso to the west with a vast wall. The west end of the cathedral, the so-called Haute-Oeuvre, leads to the Basse-Oeuvre, the Carolingian church that still stands in place of the cathedral nave, and to the Gothic bishop's palace. Although the cathedral is only a torso, its interior dimensions are still impressive. Its longitudinal axis is 237 feet; its perpendicular axis, about 195 feet; its height, almost 160 feet in the south transept.

When the old town of Beauvais was completely destroyed by German bombs in June 1940, the cathedral suffered only minimal damage. Its stained-glass windows had for the most part been removed to safety.

The City

Beauvais was almost totally destroyed during the bombardments of 1940, and reconstruction has been rather desultory and unambitious. As a result, few points of interest are left in what was once an important bishopric. Next to the cathedral is the ninth-century Basse-Oeuvre (one of the few existing churches in France built before the eleventh century) and the remains of the bishop's palace, with a fortified portal structure from the fourteenth century and its central building from the sixteenth century. (This was heavily restored in the nineteenth century and converted into the Palais de Justice). The quite important Musée Départemental des Beaux-Arts (see page 489–490) has been recently established in this building (open daily, except Tuesday, 10:00 A.M.–12:00 M. and 2:00 P.M.–6:00 P.M.).

In the 1970s, the Galerie Nationale de la Tapisserie was constructed behind the choir of the cathedral, using in part the remains of the Gallo-Roman town wall. This is a remarkable structure architecturally and in its relation to its surroundings. Its lavish exhibits recall the heyday of manufacturing

in Beauvais. Since the Middle Ages, the town has been an important textile center. Its weavers and cloth merchants were in perpetual dispute with the bishop, who also exercised secular authority over the populace. One such bishop was Pierre Cauchon, who had to flee from the inhabitants' wrath to Rouen, where he was to play an infamous role in the trial of Joan of Arc. In 1664, Colbert declared Beauvais the seat of the Manufacture Nationale des Tapisseries, which was dependent on the Gobelins in Paris and worked exclusively for the king and his court. Under the direction of the painter Audry, this concern set the style for all of France in the eighteenth century. Demolished during World War II, the factory was never rebuilt, but its traditions are carried on by the Gobelins in Paris.

After the cathedral, the most important structure in the city is the church of St. Étienne, with a Romanesque nave and transept and a towering Late Gothic choir. One of the most significant ensembles of stained glass from the sixteenth century is preserved here. These windows were created by the Le Prince family, who were stained-glass artists in Beauvais; the most glorious panel is the Tree of Jesse by Enguerrand Le Prince. Inside, in the side aisles, there are archaic forms of Gothic rib vaulting. On the edge of an early rose window in the north transept, there is a remarkable depiction of a wheel of fortune, with five figures rising upward into bliss and five being cast down in torment. Also noteworthy, although in very poor condition, is the Romanesque portal of this north transept, which boasts highly fanciful sculptures.

To the north of St. Étienne is the beautiful façade of the Hôtel de Ville from the eighteenth century (Place Jeanne-Hachette). Its Colossal pilasters and elegant façade have been carefully restored.

MEDIEVAL CASTLES AND MONASTERIES

Pierrefonds

(illus. 125, page 334)

The château of Pierrefonds rises above the eastern edge of the Forêt de Compiègne like a fairy-tale vision. Napoleon III had it rebuilt from the ruins of a Gothic castle beginning in 1857, chiefly for the court at Compiègne, to whom a visit to this "medieval" site was a welcome diversion. Napoleon III's architect and director of restorations was Eugène Viollet-le-Duc, who had distinguished himself by his restorations of Vézelay and Notre-Dame and by his theoretical works on architecture, which revealed an understanding of Gothic art based on technical and structural considerations. Here, he was permitted to exercise his creative fantasy more freely than elsewhere; by the time the emperor was deposed, he had spent more than 5 million gold francs on the castle's reconstruction, decoration, and furnishings in the Imperial Gothic style. In fact, the ruins that he had started with were among the most complete remnants of late medieval feudal architecture and were imposing enough that Napoleon had acquired them in 1813. In 1832, they had served Louis-Philippe, the Citizen King, as a romantic setting for the marriage banquet for his daughter and Leopold I of Belgium.

The fortress of Pierrefonds had been given, together with all of the Valois, by Charles VI to his brother Louis d'Orléans in 1392. Immediately, the duke began to construct a castle here after plans by the royal architect Jean Le Noir of Senlis. It comprised a square donjon that served as a princely dwelling, with a chapel and various outbuildings within the high defense walls. These, in turn, were protected on all sides by eight tall semicircular towers and crowned by a double line of wall-walks with machicolations and battlements. The exterior of Viollet-le-Duc's castle resembles in all but some small details this original structure, which was nearly completed by 1407, when the duke was murdered by his brother Jean sans Peur (John the Fearless), Duc de Bourgogne. Not only could Viollet-le-Duc use the original masonry for the most part; he was also able to reconstruct from original fragments the eight statues of heroes from antiquity, the Bible, and the Middle Ages that ornamented the towers and niches: Hector, Alexander, Julius Caesar, Joshua, Judas Maccabaeus, Arthur, Charlemagne, and Godefroy de Bouillon. Between the towers of Caesar and Charlemagne he placed a relief of the Annunciation reminiscent of the one in the castle of La Ferté-Milon, which was also built by Louis d'Orléans to defend his newly acquired territories. In 1593, after having changed ownership a number of times, the castle was placed by Henri IV under the command of Antoine d'Estrées, the father of the king's mistress. D'Estrées's son aligned himself with the rebels in the quarrel between the king and his discontented nobles, and in 1616, the castle was placed under siege at the command of Louis XIII. A year later, the fortress was breached, and large portions of the defense walls were destroyed. Since then, local homebuilders have used the ruins as a quarry.

Although the exterior is largely authentic, Viollet-le-Duc gave free rein to his imagination in laying out the interior. Along the west side he constructed a 170-foot gallery called the Salle des Preuses (Hall of the Heroines) to parallel the heroes on the towers above. On its massive fireplace, the empress Eugénie and the ladies of her court are portrayed as heroines of the knightly epics. Living quarters and workrooms for the emperor were built into the old donjon, which was still largely intact, but in the courtyard the architect created a gallery and a grand staircase that were not part of the original layout. The only interiors to preserve an approximate idea of their original state are the guard room, below the Salle des Preuses, and the chapel. Viollet-le-Duc also designed the furnishings of the interior. In their indiscriminate use of the most varied Gothic ornamentation, they present a new hybrid style remotely reminiscent of the nearly contemporary designs of the English painter and designer William Morris. The extensive collection of weapons that Napoleon assembled here is now in the Salle Pierrefonds in the Musée de l'Armée of the Hôtel des Invalides in Paris (see page 474).

(Open daily, except Tuesday, 10:00 A.M.– 12:00 M. and 1:30 P.M.–6:00 P.M., between April 1 and September 30; 1:30 P.M.–4:00 P.M., between October 1 and March 31)

Chaalis

(illus. 114, page 326)

The "romantic" ruins of Chaalis were immortalized by Gérard de Nerval, who grew up here. They are the remnants of a large Cistercian monastery that was endowed by Louis VI le Gros in 1127 in memory of his brother Charles leBon, murdered in Bruges (hence the name: *Caroli Locus*, contracted to Chaalis). It was settled by monks from Pontigny. The Revolution left almost nothing of the extensive complex from the late twelfth and early thirteenth centuries, one of the first examples of Cistercian Gothic in the Ile de France. All that remain are traces of the cloister on the north side of the church, portions of the chapter house and the dormitory, and, most important, remnants of the north transept of the church. From these, it is possible to reconstruct the original layout. As in the first plans for the cathedral at Soissons, the choir section of the church was conceived as a three-apse structure, with a rounded polygonal closure in the choir itself and in the transepts, whose arcades opened into five radial chapels. Square chapels extended out from the crossing. The nave, of which nothing survives, was without side aisles and was covered by six-faced vaulting. The stair tower that provided access to the dormitory still rises behind the north transept.

Chaalis was converted into a prebend in the sixteenth century, and its first abbot appointed by the king was Cardinal Hippolyte d'Este, the son of Lucrezia Borgia, who had the abbot's chapel to the east of the church decorated with paintings by Francesco Primaticcio and his pupils. These works were heavily restored in the nineteenth century.

Even though the monastery housed very few monks in the eighteenth century, it was decided, in 1737, to build a new abbot's palace and cloister. Plans were provided by Jean Aubert, the architect of the Grandes Écuries of Chantilly and of the Hôtel Biron in Paris. Due to lack of funds, though, the abbot's palace was constructed with only short side wings; the plans had called for a four-wing layout. After a checkered history in the nineteenth century, this palace, as well as the entire grounds of the former monastery, came into the hands of Mme. André, who housed here a part of her collections from Roman antiquity, the Orient, the Middle Ages, the French Renaissance, and the eighteenth century. In 1912, she willed her entire estate to the Institut de France.

(Open daily, except Tuesday, Thursday, and Friday, 1:30 P.M.–6:00 P.M., between March and November)

Longpont

(illus. 116 and 117, page 328)

The founding of Longpont goes back to St. Bernard of Clairvaux. In 1131, he conducted twelve Cistercian monks into the marshy valley of the Savières, where Gérard de Chérizy was prepared to endow a monastery. At the behest of St. Bernard, Raoul, Comte de Vermandois, made a rich donation to the monastery as penance, making construction of an elaborate complex possible in the twelfth century. The young Louis IX and Blanche of Castile attended the consecration of the church in 1227. The size and magnificence of the monastery moved the saintly Louis IX to found his own abbey at Royaumont, with plans based on those for Longpont. A prebend since 1516, the monastery was modified and modernized in the eighteenth century. The cloister was plundered as a quarry after the Revolution. In 1831, it was saved from total destruction by the counts of Montesquiou, who moved into the abbot's wing, shored up the ruins, and continued to support restoration even after heavy damage to the buildings in the two world wars.

The church at Longpont was uncommonly large—343 feet long and 91 feet high. It had three aisles, with side aisles in the transept, and a false triforium and a clerestory in the manner of the cathedral at Soissons. Leading off the ambulatory were two square chapels and seven radial ones. Surviving are the façade and the greater part of the south wall, including buttresses; the walls of the side aisle (simultaneously the north wall of the cloister); and some of the clerestory windows. The rest can be determined on the basis of stumps of columns and wall foundations (illus. 116). The south wing of the cloister complex, originally containing cellars and quarters for the lay brothers, was converted into an abbot's palace in the eighteenth century; this was restored after destruction during the Revolution. Since 18`2, the former cellar has been used as a parish church. The casket of Jean de Montmirail, who died at Longpont in 1217, is here; it is made of red leather and displays fifty-three medallions of Limoges enamel from about 1250. From the former cloister, one has access to the monastery's unusual thirteenth-century warming room, a square chamber with four columns in the center that support a massive chimney. A protruding circle of stones contained the fire beneath it. All that survives from the original fortification of the monastery precinct is the entry gate with its round towers (illus. 117), to the north of the church square.

(Tours Saturday, Sunday, and holidays, beginning at 10:00 A.M.; the chapel is open continuously)

Royaumont

(illus. 118 and 119, pages 329 and 330)

Older than the Sainte-Chapelle in Paris, the former Cistercian monastery of Royaumont is the most important testament to St. Louis's building activity in the Ile de France. In founding this house in 1228, St. Louis was fulfilling a provision of the will of his father, Louis VIII. According to legend, during construction of the monastery, the sainted king carried stone and wheeled loads of sand, waited on the monks in the new refectory, and sat on the floor of the chapter house to follow their discussions. His royal donations permitted a generous layout: the church was 343 feet long and 91 feet high. It was consecrated in 1235 and became the resting place of five of the king's children and grandchildren. From 1516 on, it was ruled by prebendary abbots named by the king—among them Mazarin, who already enjoyed the income from fourteen other monasteries, and various members of the Lothringen family. One of the last of these, de Ballivières, commissioned the construction of a new abbot's palace in the park belonging to the monastery in 1785. His architect was Claude-Nicolas Ledoux's pupil Le Masson, and his palace was designed in the severe tradition of so-called Revolutionary architecture. The monastery was dissolved in 1791, and the abbey was sold. Its new owner, the Marquis de Travannet, went to great expense to raze the church and to set up a cotton mill in the remaining buildings. Since 1905, the property has belonged to the Goüin family, who has restored the dilapidated buildings at considerable cost and who established a cultural organization here in 1937. Since 1964, this group has tended the abbey as a foundation for the advancement of the study of mankind. Its seminars, music festivals, and other activities have made it one of the centers of cultural life in the Ile de France.

The church was almost completely destroyed; only the bases of the pillars, the south wall, and the north stair tower are still standing. Nonetheless, Royaumont remains the most impressive example of thirteenth-century monastic architecture in northern France. Some of its rooms—such as the two-aisle refectory, with its monolithic columns and stone pulpit (illus. 118)—are, in their severe Cistercian forms, among the most beautiful surviving from the period. Also surviving are the cloister—its sides 163 feet long, the eastern gallery restored—as well as the sacristy of the church (now a chapel), the chapter house, and the great hall.

The tomb of the marshal Henri de Lorraine by Antoine Coysevox was transferred to the refectory from the church. Among other art objects displayed in the adjoining kitchen is the unusual *Virgin of Royaumont* from the fourteenth century. The lay brothers' refectory (closed to visitors) boasts a fine portal from the thirteenth century with the Virgin and Child in the tympanum. A gallery of thirty-one arches lies along an arm of the Thève, the small stream that flows through the monastery grounds. Its water was used to keep the latrines clean and to operate the machinery that the monks had set up in various shops in this gallery.

(Open daily, except Tuesday, 10:00 A.M.– 11:30 A.M. and 2:00 P.M.–5:30 P.M., between March 15 and November 11; in winter, Saturday, Sunday, and holidays, 10:00 A.M.–11:30 A.M. and 2:00 P.M.–4:30 P.M.)

RENAISSANCE CHATEAUX

St. Germain-en-Laye

St. Germain-en-Laye is visited primarily because it houses the Musée des Antiquités Nationales (see page 492–493). Yet this castle is, along with Fontainebleau, a most important example of François I's passion for building, and it is a French royal residence that is particularly rich in tradition. Constructed in 1122 as a fortress to guard Paris to the west, it was located next to a small monastery dedicated to St. Germain and founded in about 1000 by Robert II le Pieux (Robert the Pious). Still surviving from this complex is the Sainte-Chapelle, built in about 1230 by St. Louis; it is attributed to the royal architect Pierre de Montreuil. Even though this chapel was very heavily restored in the nineteenth century (as was the whole palace) and no longer displays the warm glow of its original stained glass, it is nevertheless a significant early example of French architecture of the Rayonnant style.

The palace was largely destroyed at the start of the Hundred Years' War, and in about 1368, under Charles V, it was rebuilt by Raymond Du Temple as an irregular layout of five wings around a narrow courtyard containing a donjon from the original structure. In 1514, it served as the setting for the marriage of Claude de France and the Duc d'Angoulême, the future François I. Beginning in 1530, though, the Charles V building was completely razed and replaced by a new one after plans by Pierre Chambiges. However, this architect preserved the old moats, the fortresslike foundations, the chapel, and the donjon, on top of which he erected a small bell tower. Chambiges designed the new wings out of brick and light-colored cut stone from Chantilly. They had tall blind arcades bracketing two stories together, small round towers at the corners, and a flat terrace with balustrade—an uncommon feature at that time and one that contrasted sharply with the more characteristic tall roofs that typify Fontainebleau. In spite of this innovation, St. Germain-en-Laye owes its design to the first, and still quite tentative, phase of the French Renaissance, which adopted many of its decorative elements from Italy.

St. Germain-en-Laye: the original château in the sixteenth century (Du Cerceau).

François I made his residence here starting in 1543. St. Germain-en-Laye became the birthplace of a series of royal children, from Charles IX and Marguerite de Valois (La Reine Margot) up to Louis XIV, who first saw the light of day in the Château Neuf in 1638. Henri II had commissioned Philibert de l'Orme to build this palace in 1557. But the lavish complex had been scarcely begun when de l'Orme was dismissed. Francesco Primaticcio did some work on the terraces, but the Huguenot wars prevented any major progress. It was finally Henri IV who brought the palace to completion. Originally consisting of a *corps de logis* with corner pavilions, it now saw the addition of wings, six steplike terraces with grottoes and fountains, and extensive gardens and pavilions. This once-famous layout was largely demolished in around 1780 to make room for a new palace for the Comte d'Artois, later Charles X. All that survives from it are the Pavillon Henri IV (originally probably the oratory of Anne of Austria), the Pavillon Sully, and portions of the platforms and arcades.

Nineteenth-century restoration returned the original château to the state the sixteenth century intended for it, doing away with all of the rebuilding that had been done under Louis XIV. The Sun King was particularly attached to St. Germain-en-Laye, where he was born and where he found refuge during the Fronde. Before moving to Versailles, he commissioned Jules Hardouin-Mansart to renovate the original château, and in 1669, he commissioned André Le Nôtre to lay out the park. Le Nôtre's work has survived (or at least has been restored). It includes his large parterre on the north side of the palace and a terrace, a mile and a half long and supported by tall retaining walls, leading from the Château Neuf into the Forêt de St-Germain. From this terrace, one has a magnificent view of the Plain of Paris. Napoleon III added a very picturesque English garden to Le Nôtre's park; its priceless plantings of trees make it one of the most delightful places to stroll in the Paris area.

The town of St. Germain-en-Laye, which grew up around the palaces, still boasts a number of the *hôtels* of the high nobility. In one of the eighteenth-century buildings near the Place M.-Berteaux is the municipal museum, where—in addition to engravings and drawings illustrating the history of the palaces of St. Germain-en-Laye—one can admire the famous Hieronymus Bosch painting *The Cardsharper* (whose theft in 1978 made headlines) and a number of fine terracotta sculptures by Jean-Baptiste Lemoyne the Younger (open daily, except Sunday and Tuesday, 2:00 P.M.–7:00 P.M.).

Fontainebleau

(illus. 132–136, pages 371–373)

The stature and influence of Fontainebleau in the sixteenth century are revealed by a comment made by the Florentine art critic Giorgio Vasari. He wrote that with it, the French king François I had created a new Rome. This monarch was not a particular success politically. Nevertheless, once he had returned from his imprisonment in Madrid, he was especially eager to make his court the most brilliant in the Western world. And although he continued to build his gigantic hunting palace at Chambord in the Loire Valley, the main interest of the court shifted to Paris and the Ile de France. Here, in quick succession, the châteaux of Madrid (near Neuilly, destroyed in the Revolution), St. Germain-en-Laye and nearby La Muette, Challuau, Villers-Cotterêts, and Fontainebleau arose—even before the rebuilding of the Louvre began. Fontainebleau was not only a royal hunting lodge where François I loved to go; it also became the chief location for an elegant court life for which a whole colony of Italian artists—including Francesco Primaticcio, Il Rosso Fiorentino, Giacomo da Vignola, and Niccolò dell'Abate—worked to provide a suitably brilliant setting. In so doing, they surpassed even their imposing native models and created a source of inspiration for generations of northern European sculptors, painters, and decorators in the age of Mannerism. The School of Fontainebleau amalgamated the late Italian Renaissance with a French sense of form, thereby establishing one of the bases of modern French art. Although Fontainebleau has been called François I's Versailles, the austere, logical absolutism of the residence of the Sun King stands in dramatic contrast to the charming, picturesque hodgepodge of the structural groupings of Fontainebleau. From afar, it appears to be the silhouette of an entire city, and the ground plan is incomprehensible without some knowledge of the various phases of its building, its renovations, and its changes in planning.

In contrast to Chambord or the château of Madrid, but like St. Germain-en-Laye, Fontainebleau was not a totally new structure. The French kings had owned a hunting lodge here since the twelfth century; they added onto and frequently visited it before they withdrew to the Loire in the fifteenth century during their quarrel with the English. At first, François I wanted to modernize the old palace, but in 1527, he decided to have it torn down—all but the donjon —and to have the Parisian master mason Gilles Le Breton build a new one in its place. The old foundations were reused, for the most part, so that even this new palace continued to be an irregular layout of several wings grouped around a nearly oval courtyard. The old entrance in the southwest corner was also preserved, and in 1528, a three-story portal pavilion was constructed here with open loggias clearly patterned after Francesco Laurana's portal structures in Naples and Urbino.

To the west of the palace, the Basse Cour was laid out on what had been the grounds of a Mathurine monastery. This was an almost square courtyard with low wings on three sides. It was eventually closed off on the palace side by an asymmetrical tract punctuated by five-sided pavilions. A narrow gallery connected this tract to the palace, and it was this gallery that proved to be the most spectacular achievement of the new complex. Not only was it an uncommon structural element—although known in Italy—but its appointments, created under the direction of Il Rosso Fiorentino starting in 1533, were without precedent. It was the interior decoration of the palace and the collections that the king brought to it that elicited such high praise from Vasari.

The architecture of Le Breton is somewhat provincial and considerably indebted to traditional French building as it had developed in the Loire Valley on first contact with the Italian Renaissance. It places a strong emphasis on the verticals, with free use of classical motifs, such as pilasters and entablatures, to produce a grid of nearly graphic clarity. What brings the whole to life is the strong contrast between the light stucco surfaces and the hard, gray building stone of the Fontainebleau region. This stone could not be worked in great detail, and it was abandoned by Le Breton's successors.

A number of features still permit one to form an adequate impression of Le Breton's original structure. Among them is the Cour Ovale (even though it was extended to the

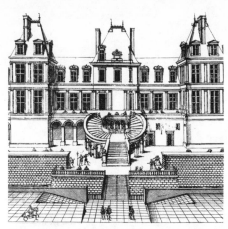

Fontainebleau: Cour du Cheval Blanc and Escalier du Fer-à-Cheval (Du Cerceau).

east and opened out under Henri IV), with the two short wings on either side of the old donjon that contained the royal apartments and were connected by a projecting row of columns supporting a walkway at the level of the second floor. (A larger, open, and strongly classical staircase in the Cour Ovale, which has survived in considerably reduced form as the Portique de Serlio, was the most significant architectural innovation in Le Breton's complex.) Other surviving elements of Le Breton's design are the Porte Dorée, the Galerie François I (which was later reworked), the north wing of the Basse Cour, and portions of its east side as well.

By contrast, the work of Philibert de l'Orme, the architectural director who succeeded Le Breton, has disappeared but for a few small traces. De l'Orme represented the first generation of schooled architects with theoretical training who would take the place of master masons throughout France, and he enjoyed the special patronage of Henri II. He completed the Salle de Bal, facing the Cour Ovale, which Le Breton had begun. Instead of the vaulting that Le Breton had envisioned for this room, de l'Orme designed a coffered ceiling, quite uncommon in France, that was executed in 1550 by the Italian Scibec de Carpi. The Chapelle de la Ste-Trinité, which de l'Orme built at the north end of the east wing of the Basse Cour, was completely remodeled under Henri IV. (The Basse Cour itself had meanwhile come to be known as the Cour du Cheval Blanc, after the plaster cast of the equestrian status of Marcus Aurelius set up in its center in 1540.) The large open staircase in front of this east wing, which almost turned this exterior into a second main façade of the palace, was replaced between 1632 and 1634 by the complicated twin-flight arrangement by Jean Androuet Du Cerceau that still survives. De l'Orme's version was more modest, developed out of two simple semicircles. The present one, by contrast, appears to be too large in relation to the narrow central pavilion.

With the construction of this east wing, which was connected with the south wing of the courtyard by means of a large pavilion on its south side, the Pavillon des Poêles, a third courtyard, the Cour de la Fontaine, was created between the Cour Ovale and the Cour du Cheval Blanc. The Cour de la Fontaine was closed off to the north by the Galerie François I; on the south, it opened out onto the carp pond. For its west side— that is, for the back of the east wing of the Cour du Cheval Blanc—de l'Orme proposed, in 1558, a façade with Colossal pilasters, probably the first example of its kind. A short time later, this idea would be adopted by Jean Bullant for his Colossal portico at Écouen (see pages 361–362).

After the death of Henri II, Catherine de Médicis entrusted Primaticcio, rather than de l'Orme, with the supervision of building. This architect closed off the east side of the Cour de la Fontaine in 1568 with the Belle

Fontainebleau: Cour Ovale and the Porte Dauphine (Perelle).

Cheminée wing. Its façade, with a monumental double staircase rising flush against the building from the center toward the sides and a tall central gable, introduced into France the severe Italian Mannerism of the imitators of Vignola. Under Louis XV, a theater was constructed in this wing; it burned down in 1856. The uninspired nineteenth-century restoration only strengthens the impression of forbidding coldness.

Work at Fontainebleau slowed down considerably during the religious wars, and came to a halt after the death of Primaticcio in 1570. It was Henri IV who finally commissioned a number of architectural undertakings that determine the appearance of the palace today. He was extraordinarily fond of the hunting lodge, and the style he applied to it displays the same severity and sobriety that characterize his building in Paris. He had the east wing of the Cour Ovale re-

moved and the two adjacent wings extended in a straight line toward the east. Between them, he placed a most remarkable portal, the Porte Dauphine, or Porte du Baptistère-de-Louis-XIII. (In front of it, in 1606, the dauphin was baptized with great ceremony.) The lower part of it, in heavy rusticated forms, originally formed the approach to a drawbridge leading to the Basse Cour, and its design derived from Primaticcio. The upper part—a compressed, open cupola structure with a triangular pediment containing victory figures and coats of arms celebrating the alliance of France and Navarre—was wholly the work of Henri IV.

The extensions added by this king emphasize the palace's orientation toward Paris. Opposite the Cour Ovale, but shifted to the north, rose the Cour des Offices. This is the most regular part of the palace, and originally it was separated from the rest of the complex by a moat. It is composed of three identical wings, rhythmically punctuated by central and corner pavilions, whose sole ornamentation is bossed stonework at the corners and around the windows. Its main axis, leading north toward the city, is marked by a tall portal structure with a monumental semicircular niche as a counterpart to the pavilion opposite. Unfortunately, this part of the palace, erected by Remi Collin in 1609, is in a very poor state of preservation.

Parallel to this extension, which was reserved for housekeeping functions, kitchens, and staff, another gallery was commissioned by Henri IV. It led from the queen's apartment and was closed off on the end facing the city by a perpendicular structure for the palace guard. Together with two additional wings that no longer exist, this gallery, the Galerie de Diane, enclosed the Jardin de Diane (illus. 136). Some 260 feet long, the Galerie de Diane became one of the showpieces of interior decoration from the so-called second School of Fontainebleau, thanks to its frescoes illustrating the story of Diana by Ambroise Dubois (altered in the nineteenth century). Beneath it, on the ground floor, the Galerie des Cerfs was decorated by Toussaint Dubreuil with hunting scenes and views of the royal hunting lodges. In addition to these new wings, Henri IV had large portions of the palace interiors modernized. This task brought legions of artists to Fontainebleau, chiefly from other parts of France and from Flanders. The chief contributions of this new Fontainebleau style were the remodeled Chapelle de la Ste-Trinité and the ceiling frescoes of Martin Fréminet.

No monarch after Henri IV devoted such

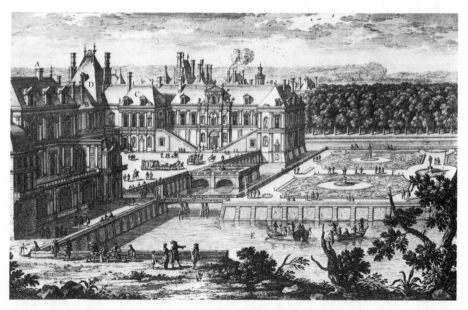

Fontainebleau: Cour de la Fontaine with the Belle Cheminée and garden parterre (Perelle).

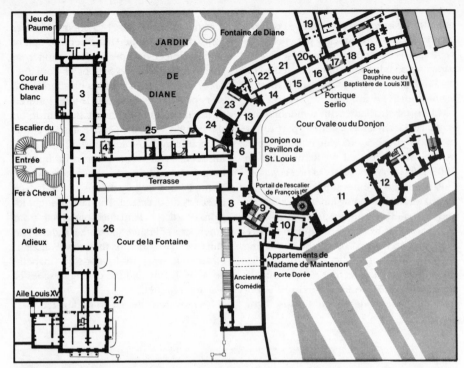

Fontainebleau (ground plan with second-floor rooms [only the most important are mentioned in the text]):
(1) Vestibule d'Honneur; (2) Tribune; (3) Chapelle de la Ste-Trinité; (4) Escalier de François I;
(5) Galerie François I; (6) Salon de St-Louis; (7) Salon des Aides-de-Camp; (8) Salle des Gardes;
(9) Escalier du Roi; (10) Salon; (11) Salle de Bal; (12) Chapelle St-Saturnin; (13) Salon Louis XIII;
(14) Salon François I; (15) Salle des Tapisseries; (16) Antichambre des Salons de Réception;
(17) Escalier des Chasses; (18) Appartements des Chasses; (19) Galerie de Diane (Bibliothèque);
(20) Salon des Dames d'Honneur; (21) Salon de Jeux de Marie-Antoinette; (22) Chambre
à Coucher; (23) Salle du Trône; (24) Salle du Conseil; (25) Appartements de Napoléon I;
(26) Appartements des Reines-Mères; (27) Appartements du Pape Pie VII.

interest to Fontainebleau. It was he who also had the grounds laid out in the grand style, with the central axis of a canal leading to the neighboring village of Avon. All the later kings used the palace for summer holidays and altered the interiors to adapt them to their own use, but by and large the exteriors were left as Henri IV had perfected them.

There were, however, two essential changes. In 1738, Louis XV razed the south wing of the Cour du Cheval Blanc—which since 1540 had contained the famous Galerie D'Ulysse, one of Primaticcio's masterpieces—as well as the Pavillon des Poêles. In their place, he commissioned Jacques-Ange Gabriel to erect a bland structure containing a series of apartments for his staff. Only its corner pavilion, whose two façades face the Cour de la Fontaine and the park, reveals Gabriel's mastery by its placement of columns and its marvelous proportions (illus. 133). In 1786, Louis XVI commissioned a suite of rooms along the north side of the Galerie François I, thus depriving the gallery of light from this direction. Not completed until after the monarchy fell, this apartment served as a residence for Napoleon, who preferred to stay at Fontainebleau rather than raise the powerful ghosts of Versailles; he had his throne room set up in the former king's bedroom. Napoleon had the west wing of the Cour du Cheval Blanc torn down and replaced by an iron fence. His leavetaking from his officers on April 20, 1814, occurred on this courtyard's grand horseshoe-shaped staircase (Escalier du Fer-à-Cheval) and gave the courtyard a new name, the Cour des Adieux.

The rooms at Fontainebleau represent one of the most important ensembles of French interior decoration of the period of François I to the Restoration, even though they do not exhibit the stylistic unity that distinguishes other palaces. Spectacular restoration, begun in 1964, has assured the stature conferred on many of the main rooms by art historians. One no longer enters the palace from the Cour Ovale but rather from the west, the Cour du Cheval Blanc, which Napoleon transformed into the palace's ceremonial courtyard. Thus, on arrival, one now immediately steps into the most important room in the palace, the Galerie François I. Beneath it were the king's bath and steam room, which were the talk of all Europe.

The gallery is a long, narrow corridor that Le Breton designed to link the royal apartments on the Cour Ovale with the Chapelle de la Ste-Trinité. It was decorated between 1533 and 1540 by Il Rosso Fiorentino, with a combination of painting, stucco, and paneling that was absolutely new to France. Previously, French palaces had been furnished with tapestries and only the most necessary furnishings for brief visits of the king and his itinerant court.

The room as a whole is divided into two levels; the lower one with rich wood paneling by Carpi; the upper one, between the windows, with pictures in cartouchelike frames, stucco, and painted allegorical figures. These juxtapose the king's reign with parallel themes from Greek mythology. The figures, whose style translates Michelangelo's figural innovations into the idiom of the contrived and decorative; the ornamentation itself, which combines early types of scrollwork with garlands of fruit and square and oval paintings; the freshness and variety of invention—all this was unprecedented in Europe and served to fix the ideal of beauty for Mannerism, which was just then coming into its own.

Through the Salle des Gardes, where portions of the famous fireplace that gave its name to Primaticcio's Belle Cheminée wing have been reassembled, one reaches the former Chambre de la Duchesse d'Étampes. This was decorated, beginning in 1541, for a favorite of François I. Here, Primaticcio further developed Il Rosso's system of ornamentation, creating elongated, fragile female figures of stucco holding paintings with scenes from the life of Alexander the Great. In 1748, Louis XV had this space converted into a stairwell (Escalier du Roi) leading to his own Grand Appartement. Gabriel, his architect, managed to preserve Primaticcio's decorations while installing his own lovely curving staircase (illus. 134).

Primaticcio is also associated with the decoration of the last important room from the sixteenth century, the Salle de Bal. This was begun by Le Breton and completed by de l'Orme. It is a huge banqueting hall, 98 feet long and 32 feet wide, with walls almost 10 feet thick into which tall window niches have been set. Dominating the space is a splendid fireplace (illus. 135) by Guillaume Rondelet after de l'Orme's designs, with caryatids based on Roman bronze models (only recently restored). Between the windows are frescoes on a rich variety of themes that go back in their design and invention to Primaticcio. They were executed by his followers, among whom was dell'Abate, summoned from Modena in 1552, who was clearly familiar with the latest trends in Italian Mannerism.

In contrast to these highly important French Renaissance rooms whose original character has been largely preserved or restored, the remaining suites in the palace appear to be less unified, especially the royal apartments, next to the Cour Ovale. Repeatedly modernized by their occupants, these display a mixture of interior-design concepts reaching from the Renaissance to the Empire period. One reaches them by way of the Salon des Aides-de-Camp (or Salle du Buffet) and the Salle du Donjon. (The latter occupies the twelfth-century tower and was the king's bedroom until the time of Henri IV. A large equestrian relief of Henri IV adorns its fireplace.) The adjoining Salon Louis XIII—named for the king who was born in it—has largely preserved its remarkable furnishings from the time of Henri IV. The Salon François I was originally the queen's bedroom, but it became the official dining room under Napoleon. The Appartements de la Reine (or Appartements de Marie-Antoinette) owe their present glory largely to modernization overseen by Marie-Antoinette, who added priceless wainscotting and furnishings by the best cabinetmakers of the time. The Salle du Trône, once the king's bedroom but converted into a throne room by Napoleon, and the Salle du Conseil, with its extraordinary Louis XV decorations, lead across to the Appartements de Napoleon I. These comprise the tract that was constructed along the north side of the Galerie François I. Its wall decorations date from the period of Louis XVI and its furnishings from the Empire. Legend has it that here in the Salon Rouge, the emperor signed his abdication announcement in April 1814.

On special Saturday tours one can also see the Petits Appartements de Napoleon et de Joséphine on the ground floor as well as the Appartements du Pape Pie VII. (Open daily, except Tuesday, 10:00 A.M.–12:30 P.M. and 2:00 P.M.–6:00 P.M., between April 1 and September 30; 2:00 P.M.–5:00 P.M., between October 1 and March 31. Grounds open from 9:00 A.M. until sunset.)

Chantilly

(illus. 138, pages 374–375)

Among the highlights of a tour through the Ile de France is the view from Vineuil, along the highway from Senlis, of the park and palace of Chantilly, which appears like a mirage in the tall forests. One recognizes the ordering hand of André Le Nôtre, who combined canals and round pools, stretches of lawn, terraces and gravel paths, ramps and open staircases, main and secondary axes into an exciting complex of relationships in which the palace appears to be only one of many bits of stage scenery.

Chantilly has always been associated with the great names of the Ile de France. It was originally the villa of a Roman citizen named Cantilius. In the tenth century, it came into the hands of the Le Bouteillers, the lords of Senlis. It was acquired in 1386 by Pierre d'Orgement, the French chancellor, who erected a three-wing, moated fortress whose ground plan and foundations determined the form of all the structures that succeeded it on this site. In 1450, it came by marriage

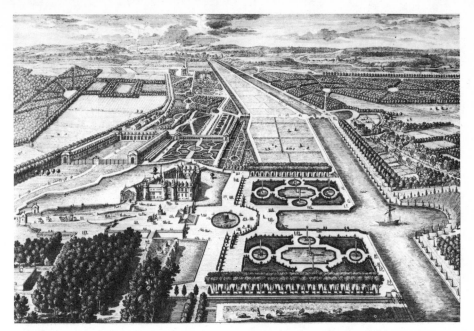

Chantilly: the château as it was in the late seventeenth century, with André Le Nôtre's gardens (Perelle).

into the possession of the Montmorency family, and between 1528 and 1531, Chantilly was completely rebuilt for Anne de Montmorency, the high constable, by Pierre Chambiges, who also worked on the nearby cathedral at Senlis and on St. Germain-en-Laye.

In 1550, the constable commissioned Jean Bullant, his architect in Écouen, to build the Petit Château, or Capitanière, on a nearby island. This is the only structure surviving today. The last Montmorency was beheaded in the Capitol Square in Toulouse in 1632 as an accomplice of Gaston d'Orléans and an opponent of Richelieu. But ten years later, the king returned Chantilly to the condemned man's sister, the Princesse de Condé. Through her, the palace fell to a collateral line of the French royal house.

Louis de Bourbon, the Grand Condé, hired Le Nôtre to lay out the park in 1666, after returning from Spain, where he had lived in exile because of his participation in the Fronde. He preserved Chambiges's Renaissance palace, however. In 1671, he entertained Louis XIV in the newly completed park. According to a famous story, the chef François Vatel took his own life in despair because the fish for this banquet was not delivered on time.

The Grand Escalier was constructed after plans by Gilard in 1682. It led down to the park that Le Nôtre had designed. Toward the end of his life, Condé commanded that a new palace be built—Jules Hardouin-Mansart erected this Grand Château on top of the foundations of Chambiges's palace—and that the gallery in the Petit Château be

Chantilly: the Grand Escalier and the château before Jules Hardouin-Mansart's reconstruction (Perelle).

ornamented with paintings of his battles and victories. Then starting in 1720, Condé's great-grandson, the Duc de Bourbon, who was Louis XV's prime minister, had the interiors decorated. In 1735, Christophe Huet began the interior decoration of the Petit Château, including the famous Salon des Singes, similar to the one at Champs. The duke also commissioned Jean Aubert to build the Grandes Écuries, which were completed in 1735. The duke's son was one of the first to emigrate after the storming of the Bastille. While he was busy abroad arming the Armée de Condé for the struggle against the Revolution, his property was confiscated. And in 1799, everything but the Petit Château was leveled.

In the nineteenth century, what remained of Chantilly fell by inheritance to the Duc d'Aumale, the son of Louis-Philippe, who began its restoration in 1844. He proceeded to assemble one of the most important nineteenth-century art collections, but was driven into exile in 1848. After the National Assembly returned his property to him in 1872, he had the architect Daumet construct a museum on top of the foundations of the Grand Château in the Historicist style of the period. In 1884, the duke, who was child-less, designated the Institut de France as his heir, charging it to preserve his collections as he had assembled them. His will became effective in 1897, making the Musée Condé at Chantilly the most important museum in France outside of Paris (see page 490).

Chantilly's fame derived only in part from

the collections of the Musée Condé and Le Nôtre's gardens—to which a small hamlet was added in 1774, a precursor of Marie-Antoinette's romantic village at Versailles. Equally impressive were Aubert's Grandes Écuries; contemporaries were wont to say that many a king was not so well housed as were the horses of the Duc de Bourbon. Set well away from the palace, at the edge of the great lawn on which the famous Chantilly horse races still take place, the palatial, 654-foot-long stables could accommodate 240 horses and their grooms, in addition to dog kennels and a riding school. The main building is a one-story tract with a mansard roof. A projecting central pavilion boasts an interrupted cupola and a monumental entry arch comparable to the entrance of the Hôtel des Invalides; its corners are developed into square pavilions. Facing the palace, the circular, open manège adjoins the corner pavilion. Its curved outer wall, with Ionic columns and rich coats of arms above the entablature, continues across the road in a tall arcaded wall that repeats the arrangement of the pavilion. The building planned to stand behind this wall was never constructed, so this wall seems a bit theatrical. An identical corner pavilion faces the town at the opposite end of the stables. The two pavilions embrace a lower central tract with a high, arched opening, elegantly decorated with hunting scenes, that forms the entrance to a number of courtyards and perpendicular wings extending between the main building and the town. Between these rises the church of Notre-Dame, planned by Hardouin-Mansart in 1687. The extraordinarily fine sculptures around the portals, windows, and pediments—the deer, boars, hunters, and hunting trophies that cover the structure—are the work of Bridault, Henry Bernard, and Brault.

(Museum and park open daily, except Tuesday, 10:30 A.M.–5:30 P.M.; in summer, to 6:00 P.M. Grandes Écuries open on Saturday and Sunday afternoons between Easter and November 1.)

Écouen

(illus. 141, page 377)

One of the most spectacular achievements of historic preservation in France is the renovation of the palace of Écouen. Only recently it was opened to the public as the Musée de la Renaissance, and a visit here, as to Fontainebleau, is essential if one wishes to understand the architecture and fine arts of the Renaissance in the Ile de France.

Because it was situated on a plateau dominating a broad plain in the heart of old France, Écouen had great strategic importance in the Middle Ages. A fortress here had belonged to the Montmorencys, the "first barons of Christendom," since the eleventh century. Anne de Montmorency, marshal of France and constable, had it replaced, beginning in 1535, with a four-wing palace of regal dimensions—a symmetrical complex with square corner pavilions, tall roofs, and richly ornamented dormer windows in the style of the François I wing in Blois. One Charles Billart is mentioned as the architect of the new structure. From 1545, the sculptor Jean Goujon and his assistants were in the employ of the constable. The decorations of the chapel (some of them now at Chantilly) are ascribed to Goujon. Its architectural design may be his, and it is probable that he also created the monumental equestrian statue above the entry in the portico, destroyed in 1787, along with portions of the ornamentation of the north and east wings. The three-story entry portico itself, which was torn down together with the entire east wing in 1787 but is depicted in an engraving by Jean Androuet Du Cerceau, would seem to date back to Jean Bullant, who beginning in 1556 carried on the construction for the constable, who had since become a duke after a time out of favor. The influence of Philibert de l'Orme's design for the central façade at Anet is quite obvious. Bullant, who had studied the buildings of antiquity in Rome in the 1540s, proved to be more independent in his execution of the north and south wings, placing a portico before the center of each in the strictest adherence to classical ordination. The north portico is a two-story structure. The south portico was inspired by Roman temples; its two stories are bracketed together, and it is closed off on top by a massive entablature. It was Bullant who transformed the austere castle into a dignified *palazzo*.

Here, for the first time in France, a dividing and ordering motif was introduced; its verticality had an extraordinary impact on French architecture. In the niches between the columns, Bullant placed the statues of the two slaves by Michelangelo that are now in the Louvre, a gift of Henri II.

After the death of the constable and until the Revolution, the palace remained in the possession of the Montmorencys and the collateral Condé line. Thanks to the intervention of the abbot Grégoire from Sarcelles, a member of the Convention, Écouen was spared from destruction by the Revolutionary mob. In 1806, Napoleon designated the palace as an educational establishment of the Legion of Honor, a function that it fulfilled until 1962.

Restoration has uncovered large portions of the original decorations, including splendid fireplaces in the Goujon style, tiles from Rouen, and reliefs and frescoes in the Fontainebleau style executed by French pupils of Francesco Primaticcio and Il Rosso Fiorentino. The majority of these works are now on display here. They include a series of tapestries illustrating the story of David and Bathsheba, furniture, jewelry, sculptures, and paintings that provide a remarkable glimpse of the culture of the French Renaissance.

(Open daily, except Tuesday, 10:00 A.M.–5:00 P.M.)

Villers-Cotterêts

As early as the twelfth century, the French kings owned a palace here in the middle of the rich forests of Retz. The English destroyed it in 1429, and François I replaced it, beginning in 1520, with the first great Renaissance building he constructed in the Ile de France. Jacques Le Breton and Guillaume Le Breton are thought to have been its architects. Henri II then had Philibert de l'Orme add a square pavilion, and Jean Androuet Du Cerceau included the structure in his book on the most famous buildings in France. Louis XIV had the park and garden redesigned by André Le Nôtre. Extremely important for French legal history was the Ordonnance de Villers-Cotterêts: in 1539, François I decreed that birth registries of all subjects be kept in French in their individual parishes. This was the beginning of an organized registry, a task that was not transferred to civil authorities until 1792.

The palace of Villers-Cotterêts is the least known of the royal palaces from the Renaissance in the Ile de France; its functions since the Revolution—first a home for beggars and then an old-age home—have contributed little to its state of preservation or its reputation. Surviving from the original palace is the main wing on the north side, with a very restrained articulation from the first phase of the Renaissance in the Paris region. A loggia with two niches opens above

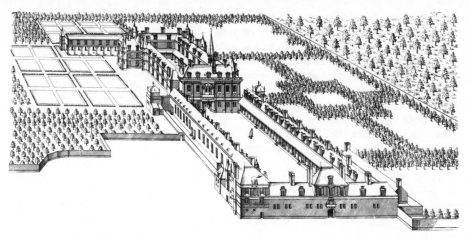

Villers-Cotterêts: the château of François I (Du Cerceau).

the entry leading to the Grand Escalier, whose richly sculptured coffered ceiling and straight flights anticipate the famous Henri II staircase in the Louvre, executed by Pierre Lescot in 1548. The Salle des États, transformed into a chapel before the end of the sixteenth century, boasts an elegant frieze composed of the salamander device of François I and the initials of the king. Unfortunately its high vaulted ceiling has been replaced by a modern flat one.

Projecting from the main structure is another courtyard with outbuildings, portions of which date to the sixteenth century. In its southeast corner is the square Pavillon Henri II, ascribed to de l'Orme. Of Le Nôtre's park, only the barest outlines of the original design have survived.

Villers-Cotterêts was the birthplace of the novelist Alexandre Dumas *père*. He is buried in the local churchyard, and a small museum commemorates him and his family.

About nine miles west of Villers-Cotterêts are the ruins of the fortress of Vez, a four-

teenth-century complex with a lovely donjon and a chapel housing a small museum. The museum displays artifacts from the earliest days of the Valois and from the region's prehistoric and Gallo-Roman periods, mostly from excavations at Champlieu.

(To visit the palace of Villers-Cotterêts, visitors must apply to the secretary of the old-age home.)

Anet

(illus 137, page 373)

Now it is in ruins, but Anet, more than any other work, still reveals the genius and imagination of Philibert de l'Orme. Indeed, because the Palais des Tuileries, his masterpiece, was completely destroyed, the remains of Anet and the tomb of François I at St. Denis (illus. 131, page 370) provide the only opportunities to recognize the significance of de l'Orme not only in the French Renaissance and its derivation from the Gothic tradition, but also in French classicism. But the visitor to Anet can form an adequate picture of the original complex only with the help of old plans and views.

Shortly after his coronation in 1547, Henri II made de l'Orme the royal architect, a post that put him in charge, much like the later superintendent of royal building, of all the royal building projects except the Louvre; this was still under the direction of de l'Orme's rival, Pierre Lescot. The coronation also meant that Henry II's mistress, Diane de Poitiers, nearly twenty years older than the king, became immensely powerful. She served as the king's most important adviser in all political, economic, and artistic matters. Later, she was even entrusted with raising the children of the king and his queen, Catherine de Médicis. Even before the coronation, Diane had begun rebuilding Anet, which was the country house of her husband, Louis de Brézé, seneschal of Normandy, who had died in 1531. But near the end of 1547, de l'Orme was commissioned to take over the project and transform the structure into a widow's residence appropriate to its owner's new exalted position. In 1559, after Henri II was killed in a tournament, Diane de Poitiers lost her palace at Chenonceaux, but the queen allowed her to keep Anet, to which she retired and where she died in 1566. In the seventeenth century, the Duc de Vendôme had the palace remodeled. During the Revolution, it was plundered and a speculator began its demolition. A rebellion by the inhabitants of Anet in 1811 finally brought an end to such destruction, but not before the *corps de logis*, the right wing, and a number of outbuildings had been razed.

Although not completely accurate, the engraving by Jean Androuet Du Cerceau provides some idea of the complex as de l'Orme created it (fig., page 365). Around a large courtyard, the architect placed three wings,

each of which was different. The main wing was open on the ground floor, taking the form of a gallery of paired Ionic columns and a smooth entablature. Its central axis was emphasized by a three-story façade; this was saved from destruction and has been reassembled in the courtyard of the École des Beaux-Arts in Paris. A beautiful example of the application of classical forms to a traditional architectural motif, its strict superimposition of elegant Doric, Ionic, and Corinthian columns transforms the façade into a first statement of French classicism. The quite un-Italian proportions, the extreme care taken with the relief ornamentation, the unorthodox fluting of the Ionic columns, and the delicate leaf ornamentation on the Corinthian columns are unique achievements. A statue of Louis de Brézé originally stood in the third-floor arcade. Diane kept in continuous mourning for her husband. Not only did she always dress in black (fully conscious of how becoming it was for her), but she also commissioned allusions to her widowhood in the architectural ornamentation; the most apparent were the fireplaces, which were built to resemble sarcophagi.

To the north, facing the garden, the *corps de logis* was flanked by two projecting pavilions, between which a raised terrace ran. From this terrace, an elegant, almost circular staircase led down to the garden, which was a flat surface divided into regular plots and bordered by arcades. A cryptoporticus opened onto the garden in broad arches and supported the terrace. Its highly ingenious vaulting was a masterpiece of stonecutting (in part preserved).

The right wing likewise had an open gallery on the ground floor, but this gallery had simple round-arch arcades and triangular openings in the center to mark the entry to the chapel behind it. The upper story

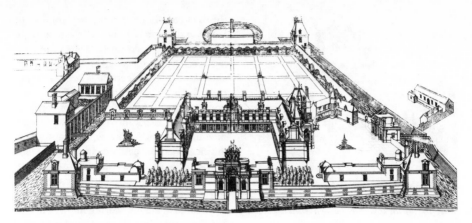

Anet: the château of Diane de Poitiers by Philibert de l'Orme (Du Cerceau).

was ingeniously organized by the interplay of windows, with alternating rounded and triangular pediments, and plain wall surfaces.

The left wing, the only surviving portion of the palace—and it survives in altered form—reveals a similar organization. But it was closed on the ground floor. This was where the housekeeping rooms were located.

An elaborate gateway structure closes off the courtyard to the south. It has been preserved virtually intact, and it is one of the most unusual surviving examples of French Renaissance architecture. From outside, it appears to be a variation on a triumphal arch, with a tall central arcade and two smaller ones on either side flanked by Doric columns.

A relief of Diana as Huntress by Benvenuto Cellini served as a tympanum in the half-circle of the central arch. (It was replaced *in situ* by a copy; the original is now in the Louvre.) It was originally created for Fontainebleau, but Henri II gave it to his mistress. Above the arch, there is a super-structure that appears to be more like a piece of furniture. It contains a clock, a niche, and a crowning, voluted pedestal for the grandiose sculpture of a stag being cornered by two hounds. Originally, these figures were connected to the clock by a complicated mechanism; the stag struck a bell with its hoof while the dogs barked out the hour. Semicircular structures supporting a terrace rise above the side arches, capped by a balustrade fashioned in a remarkable Renaissance version of Late Gothic patterns, similar to the ones that de l'Orme also used in his rood screen at St. Étienne-du-Mont in Paris (illus. 15, page 74). Single-story porter's lodges extend off the central portal structure on either side, so there is a crescendo upward from the sides to the dominating figure of the stag.

Corresponding to this progression on the outside is a sequence of setbacks on the courtyard side. From the central carriage portal with its severe arcades and coffered vaulting, low structures proceed in two steps to connect with the wings of the palace. The extraordinary sculptural quality of these structures is combined with a

Anet: the portal structure as seen from the court.

highly refined ornamentation. In its use of variously colored marbles, its combination of stone and bronze, and its highly imaginative individual motifs (like the pedestal beneath the animal group or the chimney pieces resembling sarcophagi), this ornamentation stands in complete contrast to that of the High Renaissance in Rome. Nor does it merely apply Renaissance forms to a basically Gothic structure, as in the châteaux of the Loire.

Quite as original as the portal structure is the chapel, which also has been preserved virtually unchanged. This is the first important central structure from the Renaissance in France. It consists of a rotunda with four short cross-arms whose ends are described within a second, concentric circle that is interrupted by the side rooms fitted between the arms. The cupola sits directly on the cylinder of the central space, and its network of diamond-shaped coffering, growing smaller as it approaches the opening of the lantern, serves to expand the space visually and belie the chapel's quite modest dimensions. De l'Orme may have seen this type of vaulting, repeated as a two-dimensional pattern in the design of the floor, in

the half-cupola of the antique temple of Venus and Roma in Rome. The side arms of the chapel are incorporated into the central space by means of tall arched openings, and they share the central space's arrangement—flat pilasters with entablature, and openings in the lower portion of the wall niches with figures above. Between the cornice and the onset of the cupola, another cylindrical wall area has been included. Reliefs of Victories grace its surface in the spandrels between the cross-arm arcades.

This sculptural ornamentation, along with the figures of angels bearing implements of martyrdom in the side vaults and statues of the twelve apostles, was formerly often ascribed to Jean Goujon. But these works now seem to have been created from designs by de l'Orme in the studio of the sculptor Pierre Bontemps, with whom de l'Orme also

Anet: chapel (longitudinal section) (Du Cerceau).

366

collaborated on the tomb of François I. (The most important surviving sculpture from Anet, a Diana resting on a sarcophagus-like pedestal, is now in the Louvre; originally, it stood atop a large fountain in the courtyard behind the left wing of the palace. It is also by Bontemps, or possibly the young Germain Pilon. It certainly is based on a de l'Orme design. Its somewhat morbid elegance is unthinkable without the aesthetic example of the School of Fontainebleau.)

As a model for the plan of this chapel, scholars have pointed to the Pellegrini chapel by Michele Sanmicheli at San Bernardo in Verona. It is possible that de l'Orme knew it. Conversely, though, his work at Anet seems to have exercised an influence in Italy: the chapel of the Villa Maser, a product of Andrea Palladio's old age from about 1580, reveals striking parallels with de l'Orme's design. Even though de l'Orme was the architect for the king's mistress, he nonetheless succeeded in gaining the queen's confidence in later years; in 1564, she commissioned him to plan the Palais des Tuileries.

(Open Sunday and holidays, 10:00 A.M.– 11:30 A.M. and 2:30 P.M.–6:30 P.M., between Easter and November 1; in winter, Wednesday, Thursday, Sunday, and holidays, 2:00 P.M.–5:00 P.M.)

PALACES
FROM THE
CLASSICAL PERIOD

Maisons (Maisons-Laffitte)

(illus. 145, page 379)

In 1642, François Mansart received the commission to build a palace in Maisons, above the Seine at the edge of the Forêt de St-Germain, for Robert de Longueil, president of the Parlement de Paris, governor of Versailles and St. Germain-en-Laye, and a short time later minister of finance. Longueil was exceedingly rich, and he gave his architect a free hand in planning the palace. More than 2 million livres were spent, an immense sum for that time, but the complex was never completed as designed.

Work began on the palace proper in 1646, and continued on the interiors until 1650. In 1651, Longueil was able to receive there the queen mother, Anne of Austria, and the thirteen-year-old Louis XIV, who lived nearby at St. Germain-en-Laye. The likelihood of the frequent presence of the king had played a large role in the design of the palace. But shortly after this reception, Longueil was to lose his post as minister of finance—paralleling Nicolas Fouquet's fate ten years later. The similarities between Maisons and Vaux-le-Vicomte, the two most important seventeenth-century palaces before Versailles, are quite obvious in other ways as well.

In the late eighteenth century, the palace came into the possession of the Comte d'Artois, the brother of Louis XVI, and later, during the Restoration, of Charles X. He saw to the modernization of a number of its rooms. After the Revolution, it was bought by the banker Jacques Laffitte, the unfortunate prime minister under Louis-Philippe, who was so deeply in debt that he had to break up the huge park in front of the palace into building lots (thus creating one of the earliest villa suburbs outside Paris) and tear down the palace's outbuildings.

Since 1905, the property has belonged to the state. It was restored after World War II. During the 1960s, the French preservation agency also managed to restore portions of the outer complex to Mansart's original conception, especially on the side facing the Seine.

Despite these efforts, it is still difficult to form a clear picture of Mansart's overall plan. Yet it was this plan, quite revolutionary in its day, that set the tone for palace architecture in the classical period. The palace was the focus of an axial system that cut across a vast sweep of the landscape and led the visitor along a mile-long *allée* from the Forêt de St-Germain to the palace. At the beginning of this axis, near the forest, there is a

130. ST. DENIS: the royal tombs in the north ▷
transept of the basilica.

131. ST. DENIS: tomb of François I and Claude de France, by Philibert de l'Orme.

132. FONTAINEBLEAU: the château from the west, the Cour du Cheval Blanc in the foreground.

133. FONTAINEBLEAU: Gros Pavillon by Jacques-Ange Gabriel on the Cour de la Fontaine and Louis XV's wing.

134. FONTAINEBLEAU: the Escalier du Roi in what was once the salon of the Duchesse d'Étampes.

135. FONTAINEBLEAU: fireplace in the ballroom.

136. FONTAINEBLEAU: Fontaine de Diane and Galerie des Cerfs.

137. ANET: portal structure by Philibert de l'Orme.

138. CHANTILLY: château and park of the dukes of Condé. ▷

139. ORMESSON: a typical manor house of the Ile de France, now in the *banlieue* of Paris.

140. RARAY: stag and boar hunts on the arcades of the main courtyard.

141. ÉCOUEN: residence of the constable Anne de Montmorency; today, the Musée de la Renaissance.

142. VAUX-LE-VICOMTE: André Le Nôtre's park, nature adapted to the Age of Reason.

143. BLÉRANCOURT: portal and pavilions of the château by Salomon de Brosse.

144. ROSNY: Sully's château on the Seine near Mantes.

145. MAISONS-LAFFITTE: masterpiece of French classicism.

146. VERSAILLES: Cour de Marbre, the core of the complex.

147. VERSAILLES: Petites Écuries, equestrian group above the entrance.

148. VERSAILLES: interior of the Chapelle Royale St-Louis. ▷

149. VERSAILLES: Petit Trianon.

150. DAMPIERRE: palace of the dukes of Luynes.

151. COMPIÈGNE: the last of the royal palaces in the
     Ile de France.

152. SCEAUX: Pavillon de l'Aurore by Claude Perrault
     in the park of the château.

153. CHAMPS: *maison de plaisance* at the edge of Paris.

154. PRÉMONTRÉ: a princely abbey near Laon, founded by St. Norbert.

complex consisting of portals, pavilions, and trenches around a sunken moat. From here, an *allée* with four rows of trees led up to the palace. A perpendicular *allée* with its own portal structures bisected this main one; these portals are partially preserved *in situ*. A second entry complex, with pavilions ornamented in Doric ordination, marked the beginning of the elongated forecourt that grew wider toward the palace and was to be flanked by the long, narrow stables and orangery. Bordering on this forecourt, there was a dry, square moat from which, as though on an island, the palace rose with its formal courtyard. On the garden side, a beautifully arched bridge crossed the moat, connecting the palace with a terrace from which one had a panoramic view of the broad parterre, *allée*, and formal gardens as far as the Seine; across the river, Paris was visible in the distance.

Today, this plan can be traced only in the lines of the streets of the residential quarter in front of the palace, the remains of the portal structures, and the restored portions of the east side of the palace. The splendid stables were almost as large as the palace itself. They comprised a single-story building with corner pavilions and a tall central pavilion and were prized in the seventeenth century as the most beautiful stables in France. Sadly, they disappeared under Laffitte. The orangery that was to stand opposite them was never constructed.

Even in its present condition, the palace of Maisons remains one of the main achievements of French classical architecture. In its layout, Mansart once again took up the tradition of the multipartite French palace. However, he added to it a new monumentality, thus preparing the way, especially in the disposition of the interior spaces, for Vaux-le-Vicomte, Versailles, and the structures that followed.

Mansart's scheme follows the standard layout of three wings that open onto a courtyard, but the ground plan reveals imaginative variation. The central structure consists of seven bays; the middle three project forward slightly to form a central pavilion with its own tall roof. The central bay is further emphasized by a three-story ornamental surround and a crowning pediment, a motif that had already been adapted to classicism in Philibert de l'Orme's façade at Anet. Corresponding to this emphasis, the wing structures were developed as pavilions, each with its own roof, central façade, and flat-roofed, one-story extension containing additional ground-floor rooms. This use of many elements and strong emphasis on verticality, enhanced by the tall chimneys towering in front of the roofs, is balanced by the horizontals of the surrounding cornices and entablatures. Together with the paired pilasters, these structure the façade into a kind of grid.

The trend toward simplification is more apparent on the garden side, where the wings do not project farther than the central pavilion. Moreover, the wings are here somewhat narrower than on the courtyard side, corresponding in breadth and arrangement to the three bays that comprise the central pavilion. The relief-like texturing of the wall is here emphasized by peristyles on the ground floor of the wings and corresponding full columns on the upper floors of the central ornamental surround. The calculated division of the wall into areas of light and shade, the rhythmic alternation of stressed and unstressed axes, the counterpoint of the dormer windows, the spare but effective architectural sculpture, and the uncommonly masterful stonework—all this makes Maisons one of the supreme structures of the seventeenth century.

The interior is equally imaginative. Here,

Maisons: the château from the west with gates and Communs.

Mansart connected an *appartement double* (two parallel suites of rooms) on the ground floor with a reception suite for the king on the floor above. A grand vestibule occupies the center of the structure. This is an elongated rectangle, whose four sides are all similarly treated. Its portal is flanked by free-standing columns (their highly polished steel grilles are now in the Louvre); flat pilasters frame high wall charts; and there is a deeply projecting cornice, above which arches the low, coffered ceiling. The cor-

ners beneath the vaulting are ornamented with eagles with widespread wings; these were a favorite motif of Mansart and also alluded to the palace's builder (Longueil evolved from *long œil*, meaning "far sight"). The tympanumlike semicircular spaces above the portals were decorated with bas-reliefs of Jupiter, Juno, Neptune, and Cybele by Jacques Sarrazin. Leading from the vestibule on the right is the staircase, executed entirely in light-colored stone. The manipulation of spatial relationships here is masterful; the clean lines of the repeatedly interrupted, cantilevered flights of stairs continue upward beyond the main floor and culminate in an oval gallery topped by a cupola and lantern. The amount of sculptural ornamentation increases as one ascends to the main floor, where there is a series of seated *putti* above the tall wall surfaces; allegories of music, science, the arts, poetry, war, and love; and a sequence of portrait medallions above the doors. These were executed by Philippe de Buyster and Gérard van Obstal after designs by Sarrazin.

This staircase topped by a cupola was the first of its kind, and it was extremely influential in the development of formal staircases even outside of France. It forms the prelude to the royal suite, whose décor builds up to the king's bedroom in the north corner, with its alcove like a triumphal arch. The first rectangular room is a ballroom with a musicians' balcony. A wide central archway flanked by lesser doorways leads from this room into the Salon d'Hercule, or Antichambre du Roi, which is dominated by a monumental fireplace with two nymphs beneath the Longueil coat of arms supported by eagles. These are the work of Gilles Guérin; the likeness of the king is a copy of the famous portrait of Louis XIV by Hyacinthe Rigaud.

Leading from the king's bedroom into the wing facing the courtyard are two quite remarkable salons; one is treated as a *salle à l'italienne*, ascending through a number of stories to a cupola supported by a pair of caryatids; the other is an oval cabinet with an exquisite marquetry floor. In the two ground-floor structures projecting from the wings were a chapel and a small vestibule (on the right) that gave access to the rooms of the south wing. The rooms on the ground floor have not survived in their original form or with their original decoration; Bellanger

gave them new and very fine Louis XVI decorations for the Comte d'Artois. The public rooms all extend across the full width of the building, receiving light from both sides. Mansart furnished them with a wealth of *entresols* (low rooms at the mezzanine level for the attendants) and *dégagements* (staircases incorporated into the thickness of the wall). Invisible from the outside, these features permitted servants to come and go inconspicuously. Such amenities were developed to perfection in the Parisian *hôtels* of the eighteenth century. Recent restoration of the interior at Maisons has attempted to reproduce its original state as much as possible.

(Tours Wednesday, Saturday, and Sunday, 3:30 P.M., between May and October; in winter, Sunday, 3:30 P.M.)

Vaux-le-Vicomte

(color plate, pages 36–37; illus. 142, page 378)

Even more spectacular than Maisons was the second great classical palace project— Vaux-le-Vicomte, near Melun, which was the direct inspiration for the expansion of Versailles. There were parallels between Vaux-le-Vicomte and Maisons. Once again, the builder, Nicolas Fouquet, was the president of Parlement. Fouquet was a favorite of Mazarin and, like Robert de Longueil, became minister of finance in 1653; he thus (together with Abel Servien, who developed Meudon) had an opportunity to enrich himself shamelessly. He soon wished to display his new wealth in a way that would surpass anything previously seen. Toward the end of 1655, Fouquet commissioned the royal architect Louis Le Vau, who was likewise championed by Mazarin and had built the Collège des Quatre-Nations after plans of the cardinal and the royal pavilions at Vincennes, to plan a sumptuous palace for his property at Vaux-le-Vicomte.

Fouquet largely left the design up to Le Vau, just as Longueil had done with François Mansart at Maisons. He stipulated, however, that the grounds were to be laid out by the architect of the royal gardens, André Le Nôtre, who had provided the queen mother with a novel park design for the Palais des Tuileries. Thanks to Le Nôtre, Vaux-le-Vicomte would be elevated to an entirely new plane. For the interiors, Fouquet engaged a man of great taste, the painter Charles Le Brun. Thus, a trio of the very best artists in France became responsible for the design and execution of this entire complex. Among them, they created within a very few years a new standard for the noble country house. On occasion, as many as 18,000 workers were employed at the site, although Fouquet dismissed them whenever important visitors—such as the king, Mazarin, or Colbert—appeared. Le Brun set up a local studio for the manufacture of tapestries; this was later transferred to Paris as the royal manufacturing center of the Gobelins. Records of the cost of Vaux-le-Vicomte are somewhat unclear, but it appears that well over 10 million francs were spent—an absolutely enormous sum at the time.

On August 17, 1661, Fouquet invited the king and queen to a ceremonial housewarming. Mazarin had only recently died, and Louis XIV had just begun to rule in his own behalf. The king's table was set with a solid gold service, and on the 80 other tables and 30 buffets, 120 dozen silver ser-

Vaux-le-Vicomte: the château from the north as it was in the late seventeenth century (Perelle).

vices glistened. This banquet took place shortly after the king had had to have his own tableware melted down to pay his remaining debts from the Thirty Years' War. For some time, Colbert had complained to the king that high state officials were using their positions to grow rich, and the king's irritation increased when the after-dinner entertainment began. The setting was the park, with its 1,200 cascades and fountains. First came a series of ballets, then a comedy— Molière performed *Les Fâcheux* with his troupe—followed by an elaborate fireworks display. The king declined to spend the night in the suite that had been prepared for him, and it was only with the greatest effort that his mother, Anne of Austria, prevented him from having Fouquet arrested on the spot. The king returned to nearby Fountainebleau that same evening. Three weeks later, he had Fouquet deposed, arrested, and placed in prison, where the ex-minister spent the rest of his life. Colbert then became finance minister, and a short time later, in 1664, he was put in charge of royal building as well. The young king determined to exercise the royal prerogative of splendid display that ministers like Fouquet had usurped. Accordingly, he commissioned the trio responsible for Vaux-le-Vicomte—Le Vau, Le Brun, and Le Nôtre—to design an even grander royal residence. They succeeded at Versailles.

Fouquet's possessions were seized, but the palace itself remained in the possession of his wife, who had become his creditor. In 1701, it was sold to the Duc de Villars. In 1875, it was acquired by the industrialist Alfred Sommier, who restored it and had the run-down gardens rebuilt. Today, the entire layout is in a state resembling its seventeenth-century condition, surpassing Versailles in its uniformity.

The stature of Vaux-le-Vicomte derives from the collaboration of the three great artists. Here, for the first time, architecture, landscape design, and the fine arts were completely integrated, thus helping to establish the dominance of French art for more than a century.

The palace complex is embedded in a system of axial relationships. The dominating main axis runs through the center of the palace and garden, and a sequence of perpendicular and parallel axes structures the grounds as a grid, extending the boundaries of the complex far out into the landscape. The actual palace area begins with a semicircular space centered on the main axis. A lovely grille with Hermes pilasters and two side portals separates this space from the Basse Cour, a nearly square forecourt inlaid with simple stretches of lawn. This forecourt is flanked by the Communs—low, three-wing complexes with beautifully articulated pavilions at their corners and in the center, arranged around secondary courtyards and closed off from the main forecourt by a blank wall. In spite of their severe arrangement, the Communs are quite picturesque due to their alternation of cut stone and brick, a combination extremely popular at the beginning of the seventeenth century; indeed, Le Vau had considered it for the main structure, but rejected it as less appropriate than pure stonework to the rank of his patron. The palace and its courtyard stand on an island in the middle of a rectangular basin as wide as the forecourt, so one can look past the palace from the forecourt into the far reaches of the park. "M. Le Nôtre n'aime pas les vues bornées" ["Monsieur Le Nôtre does not like limited views"]— the vast perspectives of a geometrically ordered landscape would from now on define the image of French garden design.

Le Nôtre had a masterful way of capitalizing on the natural terrain, amplifying changes in it to produce dramatic effects.

From the semicircular space outside the forecourt, the ground slopes downward to a small stream, the Augueil, which Le Nôtre transformed into a canal; then it rises once again. At the far end of the garden, Le Nôtre placed a grotto composed of seven arcades and a pool in front of it. Staircases on either side lead to the terrace above. From this level, a broad lawn, bordered by tall trees, leads to the summit of the hill, which is crowned by the Farnese Hercules in the center of a semicircular space from which the three rays of the *allée* stretch out into the distance. The changing terrain permits one to find endless new angles from which to view the park and its palace.

The area beyond the basin in which the palace stands constitutes a first zone of ornamental flowerbeds. This area is terminated by a round pool with a fountain and a perpendicular axis in the form of two elongated basins. A few steps lead down to the next zone, whose central *allée* is ornamented by a succession of fountains. Two rectangular stretches of lawn with curving pools flank this path. At the end of it, there is a rectangular pool that reflects the palace.

Le Vau's palace is not as polished as Maisons; its effect is one of greater compactness, and its proportions are entirely related to the landscape in which it is set. Its deep setbacks are meant to be visible from a distance, as are the Colossal pilasters that ornament the corner pavilions. The ground floor rests on a tall foundation story and has been treated as the main floor, to which open staircases provide access. The second story is not as high and is reserved for private rooms. Thus, Le Vau omitted an imposing central staircase. Instead, next to the splendid vestibule, he created along the central axis an oval *salle à l'italienne*, a high, domed salon extending through both stories and open to the garden through

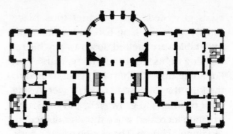

Vaux-le-Vicomte (ground plan of the ground floor).

three arcades. This innovation would become a typical feature of European palace architecture.

Le Vau's arrangement of rooms was more progressive than Mansart's. His *corps de logis* was wider, and he placed two suites of rooms in it. One faced the courtyard and one faced the garden, strengthening the corners by two pavilions on either end. This permitted him to create a profusion of rooms, which he connected by a complicated system of *dégagements*. The king's suite is located on the garden side; the dining room is on the courtyard side to the left of the vestibule. The courtyard side is the more highly differentiated. Here, the *corps de logis* is developed as a three-wing structure, with a projecting central pavilion and flanking corner ones, so that its façade is stepped back toward the center and then juts forward once more with the peristyle that serves as the entry into the vestibule. This was an important innovation in comparison with the three-story central façade that Mansart continued to employ. The wings are connected to the central pavilion on the ground floor by curving, concave extensions reminiscent of Mansart's work at the château at Blois. In fact, the depth of this façade owes a great deal to Mansart, especially to his design for the church of the Minimes in Paris. The garden side is dominated by the massive cupola with its lantern; the other roofs are clearly subordinate to it. Here, the corner pavilions scarcely project beyond the line of the *corps de logis*, thus producing a façade that is calm and monumental. The Colossal pilasters of the corner pavilions balance the two-story façade of the domed *salle à l'italienne* that curves outward from the main structure.

The interior arrangement of Vaux-le-Vicomte represents one of the first examples of the so-called *maison de plaisance*, which was the primary ground plan in the eighteenth century. Dominating this type of layout is the configuration of spaces along the central axis: a rectangular vestibule is connected by three arcades to an oval banquet room that lies perpendicular to the main axis. Adjoining these central rooms are almost symmetrical suites of rooms: on the left, an anteroom, a bedroom, and a sitting room for the king; on the right, the same succession of rooms for the lord of the house. The rooms on either side of the vestibule are clearly distinguished in size and arrangement: sitting rooms, dressing rooms, additional bedrooms, baths, dining rooms. The two basic principles behind the spatial arrangement of the *maison de plaisance* were clarity and rationality.

(Open daily, 10:00 A.M.–5:30 P.M., between March 20 and October 31; in winter, Saturday and Sunday afternoons. March to May and September and October, closed 12:00 M.–2:00 P.M. Fountain displays, 3:00 P.M.–6:00 P.M. on the second and last Saturdays of each month in season.)

Versailles

(color plates, pages 216–217 and 218–219; illus. 146–149, pages 380–382)

The palace of Versailles stands as the embodiment of absolutist royal power, and its history documents the development of Louis XIV from a young monarch, dependent on his ministers, into the godlike Sun King. The stages of its building are clearly tied to the political and military successes of the king. A small hunting lodge in a desolate marshland was transformed into the center of the most powerful country in Europe, and the country's elite, completely dependent on the king, attended the nearly liturgical ceremonies of his daily routine as though celebrating a Mass.

History

In 1624, Louis XIII commissioned the architect Philibert Le Roy to build a small, three-wing hunting lodge on a hill near the village of Versailles. During the night of January 5, 1649, the royal family left the Louvre to escape the danger of the Fronde in Paris; they settled in the old-fashioned St. Germain-en-Laye.

In 1661, the twenty-three-year-old Louis XIV experienced the luxury of Vaux-le-Vicomte, the palace of his finance minister, Nicolas Fouquet. He commissioned the three artists who had created Vaux-le-Vicomte—Louis Le Vau, André Le Nôtre, and Charles Le Brun—to modernize his father's old hunting lodge. Against the wishes of Colbert, who urged that the Louvre be expanded into the royal residence, the king invested increasing amounts of money in the expansion and beautification of Versailles, and he used this country seat more and more for hunting and for sojourns with his mistress Louise de La Vallière.

Le Vau had to preserve the structure built by Louis XIII, but he modernized the interior, provided the façades with elaborate decoration, and added outbuildings and an orangery in 1663. Le Nôtre designed

Versailles: garden façade before Jules Hardouin-Mansart's additions.

a preliminary garden layout that contained essentially all of the elements of the later plan. Beginning in 1663, huge fêtes were held in the garden and theatrical performances in the palace courtyard. In 1667, while he was still waging war against Spain and the Spanish Netherlands, Louis XIV asked Le Vau to plan the expansion of the palace into a residence; this work began after the Peace of Aachen in 1668. The old building was piously preserved, but it was surrounded by a monumental three-wing structure. The high foundation story of the new building faced the garden, and a wide terrace was built above it, flanked by two massive pavilions, in front of the garden side of the old structure. Inside, as in the Louvre, Le Vau developed an array of rooms designed to exhibit the highest degree of opulence, with a monumental staircase, the suite of rooms known as the Grand Appartement in the north wing, and another suite for the queen in the south wing. The building costs escalated—from 5 million livres in 1669, to more than 6 million in 1670, to 20 million in 1671.

Le Vau died in 1670, and his colleague François d'Orbay took over the execution of his plans. Le Brun planned the interior decorations and, together with Le Nôtre, the sculptural program for the park, which was increasingly adorned with fountains, pavilions, and statues. In 1667, Le Nôtre had been commanded to expand the dimensions of the park as befitted the enlargement of the palace itself. Given the marshy terrain, it was with the greatest difficulty that he managed to create a broad terrace in front of the garden side of the palace and a canal along the main axis. Beginning in 1669, the king maintained a whole fleet of pleasure vessels on this canal. Together with François Francini, who was a hydraulic engineer, Le Nôtre continued to add new pools, fountains, grottoes, and reservoirs. In 1668, the king acquired a village to the northwest of the park that contained the church of St. Maria-de-Trienno. He had this whole complex demolished and tied into the axial system of the park by means of a perpendicular canal. At the end of this canal, he commissioned Le Vau, in 1670, to construct a villa with adjacent pavilions and its own garden. This was the Trianon de Porcelaine. It was covered with faïence tiles and was the first manifestation of interest in the exotic culture of China in Europe.

In 1676, the king hired the young architect Jules Hardouin-Mansart, who had already executed small projects for various portions of the park, to build the Château Clagny near the palace for his mistress Mme. de Montespan and the eight children he had sired by her. Hardouin-Mansart rapidly won the king's confidence, and in 1677, he was given the contract to develop plans for still another expansion of the residence. It is not certain exactly when the king decided to transfer the court and the government to Versailles, but he was encouraging the nobility to build there as early as 1671. A plan, ascribed to Le Nôtre, conceives of the town as a foreground for the residence, with three broad *allées* converging on the palace.

France's triumph in the Treaty of Nijmegen in 1678 prompted the king to undertake the ultimate expansion of his residence to a size that would have been impossible in Paris. Its present state preserves this last burst of building. Between 1679 and 1689,

the largest and most splendid residence ever created by a European monarch rapidly took shape according to plans by Hardouin-Mansart and under the constant supervision of the king himself, an amateur architect. By 1690, almost 88 million livres had been spent. At times, as many as 36,000 workers and 6,000 horses were employed at the site. A squadron of sculptors, painters, stonecutters, carpenters, gilders, blacksmiths, and cabinetmakers worked on the interior furnishings under Le Brun and Hardouin-Mansart.

The most important planning decision had already been made in 1678—to enlarge Le Vau's palace by adding new wings on the north and south sides. These were to contain more than 100 apartments; those for the dauphin and the royal princes were placed in the south wing, built between 1678 and 1684, and others for the high nobility, as well as a palace chapel, were housed in the north wing, constructed between 1684 and 1689. When these were completed, the palace had an overall length of 2,224 feet. The terrace was removed from the central structure, and a long gallery was constructed in its place in 1680. This served to connect Le Vau's two pavilions. Hardouin-Mansart retained Le Vau's façade system, making only slight but decisive changes, and applied it to the new structures as well. The parterre in front of the central building was extended to the south, sacrificing Le Vau's orangery.

A new orangery was begun in 1682, after plans by Hardouin-Mansart. Placed beneath the projecting parterre, it helped support

OVERLEAF: Versailles: palace and park from the east as they appeared in the late seventeenth century (Perelle).

the south wing on the garden side. Beginning in 1679, Hardouin-Mansart modernized the Cour de Marbre, connecting the pavilions of the Avant-Cour to two wing structures for the king's ministers. But the king rejected his plan for remodeling the entire courtyard side so that it would conform to the architecture of the garden side. Hardouin-Mansart was permitted only to re-stucco the courtyards—Cour de Marbre, Cour Royale, and Avant-Cour—and provide them with splendid grilles (beginning in 1679). In the same year, construction began across from the palace—between the three main *allées* and beyond the new Place d'Armes—on the Grandes Écuries (for riding horses) and the Petites Écuries (for coach horses, carriages, and grooms).

In 1682, Hardouin-Mansart began, to the east of the south wing of the palace, the Grand Commun, a kind of giant kitchen and provision center for the bodily needs of the inhabitants of the palace, whose apartments, except for those of the king himself, had neither kitchens nor sanitary facilities. In the town, the king began in 1684 construction of the parish church of Notre-Dame for the newly arrived populace.

The addition of the large gallery connecting the Salon de la Guerre and the Salon de la Paix had markedly upset Le Vau's arrangement of rooms. Therefore, new suites of rooms were added facing the courtyard, and, as an analogy to the main staircase, the Escalier de la Reine was created on the south side in 1680. This also provided access to the king's Petits Appartements. The larger rooms of the state apartment were used primarily for social amusements, games, music, and refreshments.

Versailles became the official seat of the government in 1682, and the king received the foreign dignitaries on a precious throne at the end of the Grande Galerie, or Galerie des Glaces. Daily life was governed by the most rigid etiquette, beginning with the ceremonial *lever* (rising) of the king in the presence of his court and ending with the equally formal *coucher* (retirement). The Chambre du Roi was not only the physical center of the entire residential complex but also the center of the life of the court. Although the king had established such severe protocol himself, he withdrew from it increasingly often during the 1680s, sojourning instead at nearby Marly or at Fontainebleau. Beginning in 1687, he had the dilapidated Trianon de Porcelaine replaced by a minature palace, the Grand Trianon, for himself and his second wife, Mme. de Maintenon.

Following the Treaty of Ryswick in 1697, the king took up the plans for the construction of a large court chapel, but it was dedicated only in 1710; Hardouin-Mansart had died in 1708, and his brother-in-law, Robert de Cotte, had seen to the project's completion. After 1700, the king desired more comfort, and he had his apartments remodeled in a style that anticipated the coming Regency.

Louis XIV died in 1715. His son, the Grand Dauphin, had died in 1711, and his son in turn, the Duc de Bourgogne, in 1712. The Sun King's great-grandson, born in 1710, thus became Louis XV. His regent, Philippe d'Orléans, abandoned Versailles and returned to Paris.

Louis XV returned to Versailles to rule after 1722, but he made major changes to the palace. A grand proposal by Jacques-Ange Gabriel to modernize the courtyard façades was begun in 1771 but was soon dropped for lack of money. Beginning in 1736, the Petits Appartements were furnished for the king's personal use. For the marriage of his grandson, the future Louis XVI, with Marie-Antoinette, the king had Gabriel construct the long-planned Opéra at the end of the north wing in 1769.

To the north of the Petit Trianon, Jussieu had begun, in the 1750s, a botanical garden with pavilions and a small pleasure palace for the Marquise de Pompadour. The marquise died in 1764, however, and did not live to see it completed. Mme. Du Barry moved into it in 1769, but she was forced to turn it over to the new queen, Marie-Antoinette, in 1774. The queen made the Petit Trianon her chief residence, turning the botanical garden into an English park. At the end of the park, she commissioned, in 1783, a small farm village—Le Hameau—creating an illusion of rustic contentment. Not long afterward, in 1789, the Revolution drove the royal couple from Versailles.

Starting in 1792, all the palace furnishings were auctioned off, and in 1797, though there had been talk of razing the palace, it was made into a museum for French painting. Louis-Philippe, the Citizen King, rededicated the palace as a national history museum, with the motto "A toutes les gloires de la France," and had the Galerie des Batailles installed in the south wing after destroying the princes' apartments. The palace was temporarily the seat of the government during the Commune, and from 1875 to 1879, it housed the legislature; the Senate met in the Opéra, while a room for the Parlement was constructed in the south wing.

Major restoration of the exterior began with the assistance of John D. Rockefeller after World War I. The end of this war had been sealed with the signing of the Treaty of Versailles in the Galerie des Glaces on June 28, 1919. Since the 1950s, a considerable amount of thorough restoration of the interiors has been accomplished, and portions of the old furnishings have been returned. This work is still in progress.

The Grounds and the Exteriors

The overall plan of Versailles represents the quintessential rational, geometrically ordered landscape, in which even the palace, though the central focus of the layout, is merely one part of its logic. In spite of its history, the whole complex (except for the courtyard) displays a degree of uniformity that is the clear result of the close collaboration between Louis XIV and his artists, especially Jules Hardouin-Mansart and André Le Nôtre. It is this uniformity that made it symbol of an entire era.

The iconography of Versailles focuses on a single subject—the glorification of the king. The long axes that reach out across the landscape convey not only the sense of infinity that was characteristic of the seventeenth century, but also something of the concrete political postures of expansionism and absolutism. For, in contrast to the separatism of the feudal lords, absolutism, especially with its strong economic and military policies, was a step forward. Of course, it had its unsavory side; for example, the Edict of Nantes was revoked in 1685, leading to the expulsion of hundreds of thousands of Protestants.

The purely technical achievements in the creation of Versailles, from the engineering of the many fountains to the perfection of the stonecutting or the mere organization of such a giant building site, demonstrate the level of civilization that the country had reached. The strength of the new French glass industry was demonstrated in the Galerie des Glaces, and the *allées* revealed the nation's expertise in road construction. The artistic achievement of Versailles was viewed as a final victory over dependence on Italy. This latter triumph even led to the not-too-successful development of a "French ordination" by Charles Le Brun at Colbert's command; this was applied in the Galerie des Glaces.

The Place d'Armes, a semicircular square whose sides curve toward the palace, forms a prelude to the complex. Converging here are the three *allées*, from St. Cloud, Paris, and Sceaux, that flank the royal stables. The stable wings follow the course of the avenues and are connected by semicircular structures, so in ground plan the stables resemble horseshoes that open onto the square. Pavilions emphasize the center and the ends. The two-story façades reveal a very simple arrangement: there are round arches on the ground floor that are treated as open arcades in the central section; in the upper story, rectangular windows alternate with a plaque motif. Only in the central pavilion is the ornamentation more elaborate, with groups of charging horses above the entries (illus. 147), festoons of trophies on either side of them, and pediment reliefs. The Petites Écuries, to the south, culminate at the back in a rotunda whose entry boasts a 1685 masterpiece by François Girardon, *Alexander Taming His Charger Bucephalus*. The Grandes Écuries, to the north, housed a school for grooms and a manège, in addition to the riding horses; the manège was frequently used for balls and opera performances. The interior of the stables, whose vaulting rests on central pillars, reveals an exquisite combination of brick and stone. In general, one may say that the clarity of Hardouin-Mansart's architecture is most obvious in his utilitarian buildings (the Orangerie is another example).

The balustrade of the terrace of the Avant-Cour, the outer courtyard, curves outward, sloping down into the square, and is closed off by an elegant grille flanked by two small pavilions. Even here, the theme of the palace's iconography is evident. Above the entrance is the king's coat of arms, the crowned lily; in the grille is a stylized lyre with the symbol of the sun god Apollo; and on top of the pavilions are allegorical sculptures that depict French victories over Spain (on the right, by Girardon) and over the German Empire (on the left, by Balthasar Marsy).

The Avant-Cour slopes upward until it joins the second courtyard, flanked by the rather plain wings for the king's ministers. Hardouin-Mansart designed these in the picturesque combination of brick and stone that was commonly used for more informal structures. Where the two courtyards meet, there was originally a second grille, but today there is only a rather undistinguished nineteenth-century equestrian statue of Louis XIV.

The staggered architectural masses are set closer and closer together as they approach the Cour de Marbre (illus. 146), the inner courtyard of the old palace. Louis Le Vau was responsible for the façade arrangement, with its colorful alternation of materials and increasing ornamentation toward the center. However, the uniformity of his brilliant composition is disrupted by Jacques-Ange Gabriel's 1772 addition on the right—an attempt at modernization in the spirit of classicism that was soon abandoned for lack of funds. In the interests of symmetry, the corner pavilion of the left wing was altered between 1814 and 1829 to match Gabriel's work, but the remainder of the wing preserves Le Vau's arrangement. Hardouin-Mansart's changes to Le Vau's façades were much more cautious: he emphasized the center of the palace (the three bays containing the king's bedroom) with two Colossal pilasters and a portico comprised of four pairs of green-jasper columns that support a balcony ornamented with a priceless railing. He also raised the center of the

Versailles: Petites Écuries.

palace by adding a mezzaninelike attic, on top of which figures of Hercules and Mars support a central clock —which did not run but only indicated the hour of Louis XIII's death. The bedroom windows were heightened by semicircular arches, and gilt lead ornaments decorated the dormer windows and the peak of the roof. This very small courtyard was treated like an open salon; profuse ornamentation is generally to be found only inside. Five steps originally led up to the Cour de Marbre, but these were removed and the courtyard lowered under Louis-Philippe. This change destroyed the general sense of proportion, and in the summer of 1980, work began on restoring the courtyard to its original state. The courtyard floor was laid out like a parquet in black, white, and red marble. Busts of the Caesars were mounted on the walls between the windows, and, along the balustrade masking the eaves, allegories of the regions of the earth and of the virtues proclaimed the glory of the king.

Projecting from the Cour de Marbre and slightly set back from it are two wings with three arcades each. Furnished with gilt grilles, these arcades provided access to the two great staircases: on the right, the Escalier des Ambassadeurs, by Le Vau, which was destroyed in 1752; on the left, the Escalier de la Reine, by Hardouin-Mansart, which still survives. In the center, beneath the Chambre du Roi, a vestibule led to a passageway through the garden. Today, one reaches the garden through arcades adjoining these wings. The northern ones now serve as the main entrance to the state apartments, the chapel, and the Opéra.

The garden side stands in direct contrast to the eclecticism of the courtyard. Here the king's concepts of *grandeur* and *unité* come to the fore, requiring a different architectural idiom. The closed mass of the Italian *palazzo* was to replace the fussier structures of wings and pavilions; this idea was part of a general shift in artistic concepts during the 1660s. Le Vau planned that the main building of the palace would project deep into the park. A single story containing the king's apartments rises above a high foundation floor, distinguished by Ionic columns and pilasters. A wide entablature emphasizes the horizontal, which is further stressed by an attic floor topped by a continuous balustrade, punctuated by trophies and torches.

Even though the façade is basically Le Vau's, the changes made by Hardouin-Mansart greatly determine its present-day appearance. On the one hand, he emphasized the mass of the design by closing the setback above the terrace between the wings of the west side; a slight recess distinguishes the inserted central section (between the pairs of pilasters) from the sides. On the other, he relieved it by adding the much longer north and south wings, making the façade an element of the park. The brilliant fusion of architecture and landscape into an almost abstract pattern is particularly clear from the views commanded by the parterre in front of the main structure. Hardouin-Mansart's smaller changes are also significant: he heightened Le Vau's rectangular windows with semicircular terminations, thus lightening the façade considerably.

Hardouin-Mansart supplemented the four-column porticos that Le Vau had centered in each of his wings with a six-column portico in the center of the entire façade. He also enlarged the porticos on his own longer wings to eight paired columns. The façade is given variety by these projecting porticos, whose entablatures support statues—allegories of the months—in front of the attic story. Their position is further stressed by the trophies that interrupt the roof line above them. The comprehensive program for these sculptural ornaments derives from Le Brun.

The Interiors

In 1952, a grandiose restoration of the interior was begun. This work was supported by a 1961 decree demanding that all state agencies return to the palace any objects originally from Versailles. In 1980, the Chambre du Roi and the Galerie des Glaces were reopened. Renovation of the Cour de Marbre began in conjunction with the work on the interior, and more is to come. The restored palace suites constitute one of the most splendid ensembles of seventeenth- and eighteenth-century interior decoration in Europe. Admittedly, it may be difficult to enjoy them: in this era of mass tourism, one must expect crowds like those that swarmed the palace during the reign of the Sun King. It is definitely inadvisable to schedule a visit on a weekend during the peak tourist season.

Unfortunately, this ensemble is lacking its ceremonial prologue, the Escalier des Ambassadeurs. This formal staircase was designed by Louis Le Vau and executed by François d'Orbay and Charles Le Brun by 1678 as an approach to the Grand Appartement. It was removed in 1752 at the command of Louis XV. An elaborate model of it can still be seen in the former Salon de l'Escalier des Ambassadeurs.

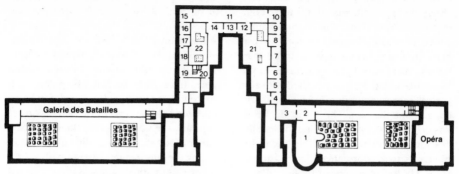

Versailles (second-floor ground plan):
(1) Chapelle Royale St-Louis; (2) Vestibule; (3) Salon d'Hercule;
(4) Salon de l'Abondance; (5) Salon de Vénus; (6) Salon de Diane;
(7) Salon de Mars; (8) Salon de Mercure; (9) Salon d'Apollon;
(10) Salon de la Guerre; (11) Grande Galerie; (12) Cabinet du Roi
(Chambre du Conseil); (13) Chambre du Roi; (14) Antichambre du Roi;
(15) Salon de la Paix; (16) Chambre de la Reine; (17) Salon de la Reine;
(18) Antichambre de la Reine; (19) Salon de Marbre;
(20) Escalier de la Reine; (21) Cabinets Interieurs du Roi;
(22) Petits Appartements de la Reine.

Today, one approaches the palace's main sequence of rooms through a quite prosaic vestibule and staircase at the junction of the main building and the north wing. One proceeds through the vestibule of the chapel (Chapelle Royale St-Louis, see pages 405–406) into two salons that do not themselves belong to the main suite of rooms but lead to them: the Salon d'Hercule and the Salon de l'Abondance. The Salon d'Hercule, the largest in the palace, was created in 1710, after the chapel was completed. Its dignified marble pilasters, after designs by Robert de Cotte, were a last, almost belated reflection of the high style of the royal apartment, which had become outmoded after it was remodeled beginning in 1701.

The room was conceived around Paolo Veronese's *Banquet at the House of Simon*, which the Venetian Republic had presented to Louis XIV in 1665. Above the fireplace,

in a priceless frame that anticipates, like the rest of Jacques Verberckt's decorations here, the coming Rococo style, there is another painting by Veronese, *Rebecca and Eliezer*. On the broad ceiling is the painter François Lemoyne's masterpiece, *The Apotheosis of Hercules*, which gave the room its name.

The Salon de l'Abondance, originally the anteroom for the Cabinet des Médailles du Roi, boasts a ceiling fresco by Houasse. Beginning in 1682, this room was used for the *soirées d'appartements*. "These so-called apartment evenings," wrote Saint-Simon, "involved the entire court from seven in the evening until ten, when the king went to table. There was much music, and tables were available for all manner of games. Behind the billiard tables there was a room in which refreshments were served. Everything was brilliantly illuminated." Three times a week, the king gave a reception for his court here in the Grand Appartement. Until 1682, when the Appartements du Roi were completed, the king actually lived in this suite, which Le Vau had begun in 1668. It was decorated in precious, multicolored marble and had heavy Baroque ceilings in the Italian manner, their frescoes filled with allegorical representations of the planets circling about the sun. The Salon de Vénus was originally a vestibule behind the Escalier des Ambassadeurs. In a marble niche between its two doors, there is a statute of Louis XIV in Roman armor by Jean Warin.

The Salon de Diane is a second anteroom behind the grand staircase; it was used as a billiard room in Louis XIV's day. In it are busts of Roman emperors and geometric marble paneling by Le Brun. A bust of the young Sun King stands in the center, an important work from 1665 by Gian Lorenzo Bernini. Above the fireplace, there is a small marble relief, *The Flight into Egypt*, by Jacques Sarrazin; above this is *Diana Freeing Iphigenia* by Charles de Lafosse. The ceiling frescoes are by Gabriel Blanchard, de Lafosse, and Audran.

The Salon de Mars, formerly a guardroom with military décor, served as a concert room during receptions. Today, it is embellished with the large portraits of Louis XV by Hyacinthe Rigaud and Maria Leczinska by Carle van Loo, as well as Savonnerie tapestries depicting the deeds of Louis XIV.

The Salon de Mercure was the first formal bedroom. It comprises, with the adjacent Salon d'Apollon, the core of the suite. Here, in 1715, the king lay in state for a week after his death. Gobelins tapestries illustrating the king's achievements; Jean-Baptiste Champaigne's 1671 painting, *Mercury with His Chariot Drawn by Roosters*; the famous musical clock made by Antoine Morand in 1706; and two commodes by Charles André Boulle—all these survive from the original

furnishings. The room's silver furniture had to be melted down by 1689 to pay war debts.

The Salon d'Apollon was the throne room and thus the center for the Grand Appartement. It originally contained a silver throne beneath a high baldachin. The painting on the ceiling is *Apollo in His Chariot in Company with the Seasons* by de Lafosse; on the walls are the portrait of the king from the atelier of Rigaud and Gobelin tapestries depicting the king's achievements in his youth.

The Grand Appartement was not finished until 1681. And in 1678, following the Peace of Nijmegen, the king determined to convert the terrace that Le Vau had laid out on the garden side of the palace into a grand gallery between the two corner pavilions, transforming the rooms in these structures into flanking salons. Jules Hardouin-Mansart drafted the plans, but the interior decoration of the gallery was the work of Le Brun. The new gallery was completed in 1686. It became the center of court life, and it was here that the king received foreign ambassadors.

The three rooms—gallery and adjoining salons—are unified by a single pictorial program. In the Salon de la Guerre, also known as the Salon de Jupiter, Le Brun's painting on the domed ceiling depicts a victorious France subduing its enemies Holland, Spain, and the German Empire. Above the fireplace is an oval stucco relief of the king, dressed as a Roman emperor on horseback, by Antoine Coysevox. The entire room is paneled in marble and bristles with emblems of war.

Le Brun and his assistants also did the paintings on the barrel vault of the Grande Galerie (also known as the Galerie des Glaces). They were executed as a series of works of various sizes, tied together in the Italian High Baroque manner by a uniform system of richly stuccoed frames. They depict the most significant events of the first seventeen years of the king's reign, from his accession to power in 1661 to the Peace of Nijmegen in 1678. The number seventeen also governs the layout of the room: seventeen arcade windows open onto the garden, and seventeen mirrored arcades reflect them on the opposite wall.

The ceiling of the third room, the Salon de la Paix, portrays the apotheosis of France as the peacemaker of Europe—another work by Le Brun. A slightly later oval painting above the fireplace takes up the same theme; it was painted by François Lemoyne in 1729 and depicts Louix XV as a bringer of peace.

The lavish use of exquisite materials—multicolored marble, fire-gilt bronze, crystal chandeliers, and, originally, silver furniture—takes these three spaces into the pompous and theatrical. Only the Grande Galerie (238 feet long, 34 feet wide, 42 feet high) bears any relation to the exterior, displaying a sequence of arcades and niches between pilasters of red marble with bronze bases and capitals. These are in the "French ordination" designed by Le Brun, incorporating the rooster, the lily, and the sun, and were executed by Jean-Jacques Caffieri. Above the heavy cornice of gilt stucco, groups of playful *putti* (by Coysevox) accompany coats of arms and cartouches containing the titles of the paintings—that is, the great deeds of the king. The king had his most precious antique statues placed in the niches; several of these were returned here from the Louvre after 1954. Still in the Louvre, however, are *Venus of Arles* and *Diana as Huntress*. The female figures in gilt bronze supporting candelabra come in part (the rest are copies) from the priceless furnishings that Louis XV commissioned for the wedding of the dauphin and Marie-

Antoinette in 1770.

The Appartements de la Reine were created at the same time as the Grand Appartement. Today, one enters them from the Salon de la Paix, which was incorporated into the queen's suite as a music room in 1710. In fact, one ought to approach the queen's apartments from the east, from the Escalier de la Reine. This staircase was begun by François Mansart in 1679 as a less extravagant counterpart to the Escalier des Ambassadeurs. It has preserved its original form, although it was expanded in 1701 by the addition of an open loggia leading to the Appartements du Roi. (Once the Grand Appartement had been abandoned, this staircase also served as the main approach to the king's suite.) The heavy polychrome marble paneling in the queen's rooms corresponded to that of the Grand Appartement. But since these rooms were occupied by every queen until the Revolution, they underwent a series of modernizations.

All the windows in this suite face south, toward the garden parterre. The Salle des Gardes de la Reine, or Salon de Marbre, largely preserves the decorations created for it by Le Brun in 1681, with the ceiling painting of a Jupiter allegory by Noël Coypel and scenes from ancient history in allusion to the monarch's virtues. The Antichambre de la Reine, where the royal couple occasionally dined in view of the public, is thus also known as the Antichambre du Grand Couvert. All that survives from its original furnishings are the ceiling, with its paintings in the vaulting and its stucco military trophies in the corners. The central painting has been replaced by Le Brun's *The Tent of Darius*. In this room, the young Mozart was presented to the royal couple in 1764. On the walls are Gobelin tapestries after Le Brun designs.

The Salon de la Reine, the queen's reception room, has preserved only its original ceiling with an allegory of Mercury by Michel Corneille from 1671. In 1785, Marie-Antoinette had the marble paneling removed and the walls refurbished with low wainscotting and a covering of green silk. Many of the original furnishings of the room—including pieces by Johann Riesener, Marie-Antoinette's favorite cabinetmaker, and gilt bronzes by Gouthière—have been recovered.

The Chambre de la Reine is the heart of the apartment. Here, the queens gave birth to their children in full public view (Louis XV and Philip V of Spain, among others, were born here). It was modernized in 1729 after plans by de Cotte, and now that it has been carefully restored, it constitutes one of the most splendid ensembles in the Louis XV style in France. The balustrade was reproduced from old drawings, its precious silk fabrics were newly woven in Lyons, the original carving of the bedstead reproduced, and so on. In the vignettes on the ceiling are grisailles with allegories of the queen's virtues by François Boucher. Next to the queen's bed stands a priceless gift from the city of Paris to Marie-Antoinette, a jewel chest made in 1786, a masterpiece by the German cabinetmaker Schwerdtfeger. In 1770, Marie-Antoinette had the coats of arms of the houses of France-Navarre and Hapsburg added to the corners of the ceiling.

De Cotte's modernization of this salon took place in response to a radical change in taste, a reaction against the heavy decorative style of the Grand Appartement. This change had already begun under Louis XIV in the furnishing of the Appartements du Roi, the king's rooms around the Cour de Marbre, as early as 1684. Instead of marble paneling and complicated ceilings with inset paintings, the preference now was for a simple wall arrangement based on pilasters or wainscotting, wood paneling either painted white or gilt, a continuous cornice, and a white ceiling with a minimum of stucco decoration. The only accents in the walls were the windows, doorways, and fireplace, above which a tall mirror was commonly placed. This simpler type of decoration persisted until the end of the *ancien régime*.

The Appartements du Roi can scarcely be perceived as a suite of rooms today because the anterooms next to the Escalier de la Reine are no longer accessible. Instead, one generally steps directly into the king's Chambre du Conseil from the Galerie des Glaces. The three rooms, facing the Cour de Marbre, that form the king's chambers have been thoroughly restored. They now appear approximately as they did at the end of the reign of Louis XIV.

The Antichambre du Roi, or Salon de l'Oeil-de-Bœuf (named for its small, "bull's-eye" window), was given its form in 1701, when the king established his bedroom in the adjacent center room. Everyone who attended the king's *lever* had to wait here first. Usually one had to wait a long time before being admitted to the bedroom, whose door was watched by a guard. The first to be granted entrance were the king's legitimate sons and daughters and princes of the royal blood. They were admitted after the king had been visited by the doctor, the surgeon, and the old nursemaid who came to embrace him each morning until 1688. There then followed the grand entry of the high officers of the Crown.

The Chambre du Roi is the geometric center of the palace and of the entire complex. Its gilt pilasters date from around 1679, and its gilt woodwork, in which the paintings are set, from 1701. In that same year, the bed-recess was remodeled with its balustrade, mirror, and supraporte. The bed itself was the monarch's "holy of holies."

It was guarded constantly by a servant who made sure that all approached it with the proper reverence and that no one touched it.

For a century, the Cabinet du Roi, or Chambre du Conseil, was the center of French politics. Here the council of ministers met each morning around a table—the ministers on stools, the king in an armchair —that has been restored. The present furnishings date from a remodeling by Jacques-Ange Gabriel in 1755 for Louis XV.

In addition to these formal rooms for the king and queen, there are the so-called Petits Appartements. These are arranged around the dark inner courtyards of the two wings, where the monarchs could lead a relatively private life apart from the gaze of their courtiers. The Cabinets Interieurs du Roi were begun in 1738; those of the queen were largely modernized for Marie-Antoinette (Petits Appartements de la Reine). Altogether, they constitute one of the most priceless ensembles of French interior decoration from the eighteenth century as well as from Louis XV and Louis XVI styles. They may be seen only on special guided tours, as is true for the Petits Appartements du Roi, which Louis XV had built for himself on the top floor, and for the rooms on the ground floor, where, in the eighteenth century, a number of apartments were created in place of the Sun King's baths.

(Open daily, except Monday, 10:00 A.M.– 5:30 P.M.; in winter, to 5:00 P.M. One may explore at leisure the Grand Appartement, the Appartements de la Reine, the Galerie des Glaces, the oratory, and the Chapelle Royale St-Louis. Guided tours of the Opéra and the remaining apartments are available; the times for these tours are posed in the entrance hall. For special group tours, phone 950–36–22. The fountains in the park play on the first and third Sundays of the month beginning at 4:30 P.M., from May to September. A self-service restaurant is located to the right of the entry.)

Chapelle Royale St-Louis

The king attended Mass daily, and various smaller rooms in the palace saw temporary service as chapels. Only under the influence of the pious Mme. de Maintenon did Louis XIV decide to construct a separate church, the last major building project at Versailles during his reign. Jules Hardouin-Mansart submitted the plans for this chapel in 1699, but work was postponed because of the War of the Spanish Succession. It was finally completed by Robert de Cotte in 1710.

This tall, narrow building, whose exterior is scarcely integrated into the massive structures of the palace wings, is essentially a Baroque version of the Sainte-Chapelle in Paris (illus. 148). It adopts from that model the principle of a two-story palace chapel, with a low bottom floor for the court staff and a tall, light, upper story containing the king's loge. Here, though, the two stories are not separated by an intervening ceiling, so that an interior space of extraordinarily lofty proportions is created. Slender, fluted Corinthian columns enhance the impression of elegance and delicacy, rising as an inner colonnade above the lower story and supporting a continuous cornice. Bright light floods through the colonnade from tall windows, falling on the white stone of the rounded arcade of the ground floor, whose spandrels and pillars are rendered less severe by splendid reliefs with allegories of religious themes. Contrasting with this dazzling architecture are the colored marble inlays in the floor and the rich color of the paintings on the ceiling. These serve to represent the Trinity, with *The Ascension of Christ* by Charles de Lafosse in the apse, *God the Father in Glory* by Antoine Coypel in the nave, and *The Dove of the Holy Spirit Descending to the Apostles* by Jean Jouvenet in the vestibule.

The organ stands in the apse directly above the altar, and the two are tied together by their lavish gilding. De Cotte designed the altar composition of the adoration of the angels of the Holy Name, and it was executed by Corneille van Cleve, Guillaume Coustou, and Antoine Lepautre. The organ was decorated by Clicquot; François Couperin played it at ceremonial Masses.

Opéra

As early as 1685, a royal opera was planned for the north wing. But construction was postponed, at first for lack of funds and later in favor of the Chapelle Royale St-Louis. The project was not actually begun until 1749, when Louis XV delegated its planning to Jacques-Ange Gabriel. Before it was built, Gabriel made extensive studies, together with the machinist Arnoult, of the newest technical advances and of the most recent concept of auditorium and stage as developed by Benedetto Alfieri for the theater in Turin. The Opéra was finally constructed in 1769 for the dauphin's marriage to Marie-Antoinette, and it is one of the most beautiful theaters in Europe. It was completed in less than two years, painted wood being used in imitation of precious materials. The auditorium is elliptical, with two sloping tiers, above which, adopting a motif from the chapel, there is a third gallery containing the king's loge in the center. This loge is at the level of the royal apartments; behind it, there is an elegant vestibule facing the garden.

The proscenium is flanked by Colossal columns. By means of a complex mechanism, the stage and auditorium could be brought to the same level, and a wooden wall set into the stage could transform the theater into a formal ballroom; its chandeliers were reflected in the gold of the decorations and the mirrors of this back wall. Careful restoration begun in 1952 has reproduced the exquisite original coloring of the room, dominated by greenish blue and gold; the coat of red that was added during the reign of Louis-Philippe has been removed. Restoration has also done away with the alterations made after 1871, when the Opéra was adapted to house the National Assembly and the Senate.

Gabriel's Opéra is one of the first signs that the Louis XV and Rococo styles were falling out of vogue in favor of the return to antiquity that paved the way for classicism. The ornamental reliefs by Augustin Pajou and his assistants and the ceiling painting *Apollo and the Arts* by Louis Durameau both reflect this more sober style.

The Park

The palace park was just as important as the royal chambers to the king. A drive or a stroll through the *allées* was a part of his daily ritual. In 1697, Louis XIV actually wrote a little memorandum, entitled *Manière de Montrer les Jardins de Versailles*, explaining how he wished the park to be understood. The following suggestion for a walk through the park represents the Sun King's own instructions (see page 408 for a plan of the park).

The terrace in front of the central structure of the palace offers a view out over the Parterres d'Eau. The terrace is decorated with four bronze statues—of Bacchus, Apollo, Mercury, and Silenus—cast by the Keller brothers. At the corner, below the Salon de la Guerre, is a marble vase, *La Guerre*, by Antoine Coysevox; below the

Salon de la Paix, a marble vase, *La Paix*, by Jean-Baptiste Tuby.

The Parterres d'Eau contain two pools that mirror the façade of the palace; they are by Jules Hardouin-Mansart and André Le Nôtre. Each is ornamented with four allegorical river figures, six nymphs, and four groups of children after designs by Charles Le Brun. The north pool includes the Garonne and the Dordogne (by Coysevox) and the Seine and the Marne (by Le Hongre); the south one, the Loire and the Loiret (by Thomas Regnaudin) and the Rhone and the Saône (by Tuby). The rivers that are grammatically feminine are represented by female figures; the masculine ones, by male figures.

From the steps of the Parterres d'Eau, one can view the Bassin de Latone, the ramps, the Allée Royale, the Bassin d'Apollon, and the Grand Canal. The steps leading down to the Bassin de Latone (Marches de Latone) are flanked by two fountains with allegories of the elements.

To the left of the Parterres d'Eau is the Parterres du Midi, which rests on the Orangerie. Built between 1684 and 1686, this structure replaced the small Orangerie by Louis Le Vau. It consists of a long, vaulted gallery beneath the Parterres du Midi and side galleries, underneath the Escaliers des Cent-Marches, which lead down to the south entry portals. Across the Route de Ste-Cyr is the Pièce d'Eau des Suisses, a long, narrow lake (2,230 by 766 feet) that was dug between 1678 and 1682 by a regiment of Swiss Guards, many of whom died of malaria during its construction. At the end of it, scarcely recognizable, is Gian Lorenzo Bernini's equestrian statue of the Sun King; the king had François Girardon change it into a likeness of Marcus Curtius.

South of the Marches de Latone are the Bosquet de la Reine, a glade that replaced an earlier labyrinth in 1775; the oval Bassin de Bacchus designed by Le Brun and executed by Balthasar Marsy in 1675; and the Salle de Bal from 1681 to 1683, an open amphitheater decorated with a shell motif.

The Parterres de Latone is set between gently sloping, semicircular ramps, along which stand copies of antique statues from the Académie de France in Rome. In its center is the Bassin de Latone, created in 1670 by Marsy. Latona is accompanied by her children, Apollo and Diana, and is beseeching their father, Jupiter, to turn the Lycaean peasants who have insulted them into frogs and lizards (the latter are shown in the two side fountains). The vases are likewise copies of Roman originals, most of them made by scholarship students at the Académie de France.

The Tapis Vert, or Allée Royale, connects the Bassin de Latone (to the east) with the Bassin d'Apollon (to the west). It is 1,095 feet long and 209 feet wide. Along it are twelve vases and twelve statues, also by students at the Académie de France in Rome.

The Quinconce du Midi, at the southeast end of the Tapis Vert, occupies the site of the former Girondole. It boasts eight marble herms created for Nicolas Fouquet at Vaux-le-Vicomte, after designs by Nicolas Poussin. They were purchased by Louis XIV in 1683.

The Bassin de Saturne was created by Girardon after Le Brun's design in 1675: It depicts the aged Saturn lying down and surrounded by children.

The Jardin du Roi and the Bassin du Miroir were moved to their present site from the Ile Royale under Louis XVIII.

The Salle des Marronniers was laid out in 1704 on the site of the Salle des Antiques. It has eight antique copies of marble busts.

The Colonnade, at the southwest end of the Tapis Vert, was erected in 1685 by Jean

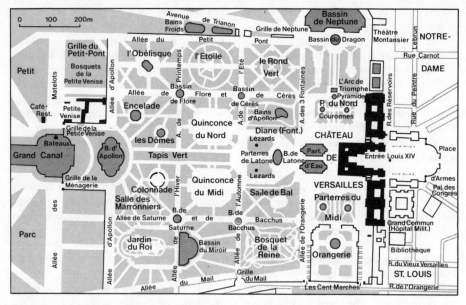

Versailles: plan of the main section of the park.

Lapierre from plans by Hardouin-Mansart. This circle of arches is constructed of red, white, and blue marble. The sculptural group *The Rape of Persephone* by Girardon originally stood in the center of the circle; it is now in the Orangerie. The Colonnade was used for banquets and concerts.

The Bassin d'Apollon lies in the center of a semicircular espanade, and constitutes the iconographic and visual focus of the whole complex. The sculpture *Apollo in His Sun Chariot*, by Tuby (1671) after a design by Le Brun, glorifies the Sun King. From here, there is a splendid view of the palace back along the Allée Royale.

The Bosquet des Dômes, at the northwest end of the Tapis Vert, was created between 1675 and 1678 by Hardouin-Mansart. It originally included two pavilions. Along the balustrades are forty-four reliefs by Girardon, Gilles Guérin, and Pierre Mazeline, coats of arms of various nations, and statues by Jean-Jacques Caffieri.

The Fontaine d'Encelade is by Marsy. It includes a lead sculpture (originally gilt) of Enceladus, the mythical giant who piled the world's three highest mountains on top of one another in order to reach the sky and was then buried under the masses of rock.

The Obélisque was created by Le Nôtre in 1706 after a design by Hardouin-Mansart. It replaced an earlier grove. The action of 230 jets of water creates an obelisk 82 feet high.

The Bassin de Flore is by Tuby (1675) after Le Brun. Flora lies on a carpet of flowers, surrounded by winged cupids.

The Quinconce du Nord, at the northeast end of the Tapis Vert, contains eight marble herms, six of them after designs by Poussin.

The Bassin de Cérès depicts the harvest goddess in the center of an octagonal pool. It was executed by Regnaudin after Poussin.

The Ile aux Enfants contains eight cupids created by Jean Hardy for the Trianon de Porcelaine and moved here in 1710.

The Bains d'Apollon was created in 1778, after Hubert Robert had turned the earlier Bosquet du Marais into a landscaped garden in the English-Chinese style. In stone caves at the edge of a small lake is the palace of Thebes, with sculptural groups from the grotto that was sacrificed when the north wing was built. In the center of the basin is *Apollo Attended by Nymphs* by Girardon and Regnaudin; to the side are the *Horses of the Sun* by Marsy and Guérin. Both allude to the Sun King relaxing after the daily effort of his reign.

The Bassin de Neptune, the largest fountain-pool in the park, was created by Le Nôtre between 1679 and 1684, then altered by Ange-Jacques Gabriel in 1738 to accommodate the huge sculptural grouping that Louis XV had commissioned. Neptune with his trident and Amphitrite with her scepter are the work of Lambert-Sigisbert Adam. They are accompanied by Proteus (by Edme Bouchardon) and Oceanus (by Jean-Baptiste Lemoyne the Younger), as well as dragons being tamed by cupids (by Bouchardon). The vases go back to the seventeenth century. On the north side is the marble group *The Glory of the King*, created by Domenico Guidi in Rome in 1686.

The Bassin du Dragon has sculptures by Tony Noël from 1899, after drawings by Marsy.

The Allée de l'Eau, or Allée des Marmousets, consists of twenty-two small pools in which *putti* hold basins of water. These were designed by Claude Perrault in 1668.

The Bassin des Nymphes includes a group of bathing nymphs by Girardon.

Along the *allée* that leads to the Parterres du Nord is a series of statues commissioned in 1674.

The Fontaine de la Pyramide was executed by Girardon (1669) after a design by Le Brun. Basins of decreasing size are stacked atop one another, supported by tritons, crabs, and dolphins.

The Parterres du Nord was laid out by Le Nôtre in 1668 and contains the Bassins des Couronnes by Le Hongre and Tuby.

Grand Trianon

In spite of the protocol and the regimen that Louis XIV imposed on official court life, he also had a great desire for privacy and intimacy, for places to which he could retire with his mistress of the moment. This wish motivated the construction of a number of "summer houses" in the park, at an appropriate distance from the palace. The Grand Trianon is the oldest of these.

Louis Le Vau had already planned a *maison de plaisance* here on the site of an earlier village, and it had been constructed in 1670 to 1672 by François d'Orbay. Consisting of a main pavilion and two smaller ones, it was known as the Trianon de Porcelaine, for its roofs were covered with faïence tiles (painted blue in imitation of Chinese designs) and the roof balustrades were decorated with pieces of blue and white faïence. The interior was ornamented with Chinese porcelain, lacquer work, and silk—a first manifestation of the China craze that was to sweep all of Europe in the eighteenth century.

Built from quite impermanent materials, this summer house rapidly fell into disrepair. In 1687, it was torn down to make

Versailles: Grand Trianon, one bay on the garden side.

the floor gives the peristyle the character of an open banquet hall. The transparency of the architecture reflects the king's desire to enjoy André Le Nôtre's garden to the full. French doors provided direct access to the parterres. The vivid colors of the gardens were reflected in the marbles of the exterior, producing an appearance of unparalleled splendor. The interiors, by contrast, must have seemed all the more startling; here, everything was attuned to the desire to find relief from the ceremony and lavish display of the nearby residence. The rooms were completely white, with only a few small, framed paintings to enliven the walls.

The Grand Trianon was restored between 1963 and 1966 under André Malraux and Charles de Gaulle, but no attempt was made to re-create its original state. Rather, it was decided to allow the later history of this palace to show as well. Almost completely unused under Louis XV and Louis XVI, it lost the majority of its furnishings during the Revolution. However, Napoleon had it renovated for Josephine and himself, and they used it frequently after 1810. Then, when the palace of Versailles had been converted into a national museum, Louis-Philippe moved into the Grand Trianon. A fair number of the furnishings, therefore, date from this period, so the salons display —in addition to late-seventeenth-century woodwork and stucco—a wealth of priceless objects from the Empire period and the Restoration.

(Open daily, except Monday, 2:00 P.M.–5:00 P.M.)

Petit Trianon

In 1749, Louis XV had a farm constructed behind the Grand Trianon to satisfy Mme. de Pompadour's countrified tastes. It in-

room for a new structure by Jules Hardouin-Mansart, in collaboration with Robert de Cotte. This new building was placed in part on the foundations of the earlier structure, and it became known as the Grand Trianon, or Trianon de Marbre. It is an uncommonly long, flat-roofed structure, with an open peristyle in the center and side wings that enclose a formal courtyard protected by grillwork and a moat. The garden façade emphasizes the horizontal even further. It does not extend only across the peristyle and wings, but it also incorporates a gallery that extends at a right angle to the north, presenting a regular succession of uniform bays —round-arch French doors between flat Ionic pilasters. This horizontal band was originally enlivened by vases and *putti* on top of the roof balustrade. The use of precious, colored marbles for the columns and

cluded a dairy, a cow barn, a henhouse, a poultry yard, and a small pavilion (still surviving) for refreshments. This pavilion contains a central salon with four adjoining rooms arranged in the shape of a cross. Jacques-Ange Gabriel decorated it with the motifs that he loved: jointed stonework, garlands above the round-arch doors, and a balustrade masking the roof. The structure is known as the Pavillon Français.

Ten years later, the king decided to build a more sophisticated retreat, the Petit Trianon, for himself and his mistress. It was constructed, according to Gabriel's plans, between 1762 and 1764, and decorated and furnished between 1764 and 1768. Mme. de Pompadour died in 1764, so it was her successor, Mme. Du Barry, who dedicated it.

The Petit Trianon was to become one of the key structures of European classicism. It is a simple square block topped by a continuous balustrade, without cupola, wings, or pavilions, embodying the most extreme clarity of design and purity of execution. It is without superfluous ornamentation, yet it is by no means arid. Rather, it radiates elegance and grace, and it was revered by generations of architects. Gabriel provided the structure with two distinct faces. One of these is oriented toward the main *allée* that leads from the Avenue St-Antoine. This façade centers around a courtyard enclosed by retaining walls. A rusticated foundation story contains a billiard room, the kitchen, service rooms, and the staircase leading up to the main floor. The main floor consists of five bays and tall French doors with cornices. Above it is a mezzanine with square windows. The three middle bays project slightly and are framed by pilasters that support the continuous entablature and balustrade. The foundation story connects with the retaining walls of the front courtyard.

These retaining walls mask the ground level of the adjoining park, to which the second façade is oriented. On this side, the *bel-étage* appears as a ground floor directly above a small terrace; the building's proportions look completely different here. Gabriel sank the terrace slightly toward the center below two broad staircases, thus suggesting a foundation for the massive portico. This portico, with fluted Corinthian columns, has no pediment. Rather, it supports a slight projection of the balustrade that masks the roof. Behind the portico, the wall is as flat as the one on the courtyard side, interrupted only by the windows. The north side of the pavilion takes up the arrangement of the garden side, although with pilasters instead of columns (illus. 149). The south side is quite plain; it is at the level of the courtyard side.

The balance and clarity that distinguish the exterior are also to be found inside, both in the arrangement and in the decorations, which are among the supreme achievements of the Louis XVI style (though they actually belong to the last years of the reign of Louis XV). Restoration of the interior is not yet completed.

(Open daily, except Monday, 2:00 P.M.–5:00 P.M.)

Le Hameau

Shortly after ascending the throne, Louis XVI presented the Petit Trianon as a gift to the queen. Marie-Antoinette had the palace refurbished and spent the greater part of her time here, away from the intrigues of the court. In accord with the taste of the time, she had the geometrical French garden transformed into a more "natural" park in the English manner. At the north edge of this landscape—which was complete with small brooks, rolling hills, and broad meadows—the painter Hubert Robert designed a small village, which was executed by the architect Richard Mique. In it, a hired farmer actually went about the business of farming, giving the queen the illusion of participation in the simple, wholesome life. Grouped around the large village pond, rather like the set of an operetta, were a mill, the queen's house—a farmhouse, complete with vegetable garden, that was connected by a gallery to a second farmhouse that served as a billiard room—a dovecote, the caretaker's house, a fisherman's house in the form of a tower (the so-called Tour de Marlborough), a large farmyard, and a dairy.

The rustic style of this little hamlet poses a certain contrast to the other buildings that Mique constructed for Marie-Antoinette in the park of the Petit Trianon. These structures reveal the last stage of refinement of the Louis XVI style. They include the Temple de l'Amour from 1778, whose open ring of columns houses one of Edme Bouchardon's masterpieces, *Love Carving His Bow from the Club of Hercules* (a copy by Bouchardon himself; the original is in the Louvre); a belvedere, with elegant arabesque decorations by Riquier; and an exquisite small theater decorated in blue and gold, where Marie-Antoinette herself used to perform.

It was in the park of the Petit Trianon that Marie-Antoinette was surprised by the news of the advance of the Parisian mob on Versailles on October 5, 1789.

Marly

Courtiers who felt that they deserved an extraordinary sign of favor from the Sun King would often whisper but two words as he passed: "Marly, Sire." During the last thirty years of Louis XIV's reign, no more than 800 people were privileged with an invitation to Marly.

In 1678, after the Peace of Nijmegen, Louis XIV commissioned his architect Jules Hardouin-Mansart to design a hermitage in this little valley above the Seine, a spot to which he could escape from the rigid etiquette of the court. Hardouin-Mansart's design, repeatedly imitated in the eighteenth century, combined privacy and a sublime princely splendor in an unusual way. For the king, the architect constructed a flat-roofed central pavilion; members of the family and guests were housed in twelve simpler pavilions arranged in two rows on either side of a long central pond. The décor of these pavilions was based on the symbolism of the sun in the middle of the constellations of the zodiac.

The king was able to move into the palace in 1686. Its white marble surfaces had no sculptural ornamentation for reasons of economy; they were provided with only trompe-l'œil paintings by Charles Le Brun. Each of the smaller pavilions contained two apartments, so twenty-four guests could accompany the king to Marly. Some 10,000 francs a day were spent on food, and peddlers sold leftovers from the table at the outer gates of the park.

The pavilions were set in a generous garden complex whose chief attraction was the Grande Cascade. Completed in 1699, this was a waterfall rising behind the king's pavilion. It consisted of sixty-three steps of green and red marble and was adorned by a wealth of statues and vases. A complicated machine (Machine de Marly) that made the whole world marvel pumped water from the Seine to the top of the hill, whence it splashed down the cascade into the Bassin du Grand Miroir. At the end of the valley was the Bassin de l'Abreuvoir. On either side of it stood the famous Marly horses (now

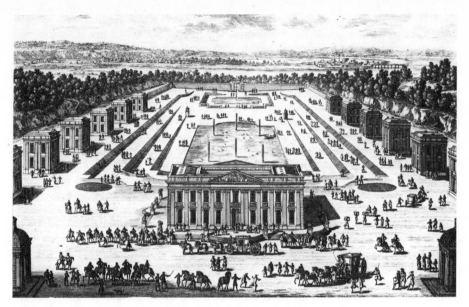

Marly: the overall layout in the late seventeenth century (Perelle).

in the Place de la Concorde in Paris), which set the tone for the entire layout.

By the time of the king's death, some 500 gardeners were required to keep up the park. The palace was seldom used in the eighteenth century, and Cardinal Fleury replaced the Grande Cascade with a simple lawn to save money. During the Revolution, the palace was sold to a manufacturer who set up a spinning mill in it. After going bankrupt, he sold it for demolition.

The grounds once more came into state ownership under Napoleon, but restoration of the complex did not begin until 1936. An esplanade of lime trees and some slabs in the ground now mark the site of the palace.

In the village of Marly-le-Roi, the church of St. Victor, built by Hardouin-Mansart in 1688, survives from the era of the Sun King. It still boasts its original furnishings as well as a high altar, in the Rococo style, that was originally in the court chapel at Versailles. Opposite the church is the former mansion of the superintendant of Marly, which belonged to Victorien Sardou, the author of *Madame Sans-Gêne,* in the nineteenth century. In 1843, Alexandre Dumas built himself a romantic castle in a curious mixture of styles on the road leading to Port-Marly. He called it the Villa Monte Cristo; hopelessly in debt, he was soon forced to sell it.

Meudon

Of the wreath of palaces surrounding Paris, Meudon and St. Cloud were two of the most important. Their loss was one of the tragic results of the Franco-Prussian War of 1870 to 1871. Meudon came into the possession of the Crown relatively late. In the sixteenth century, the small country place belonged to the Duchesse d'Étampes, the mistress of François I, and it was she who built the château. It was then owned by the cardinal of Lorraine, the Duc de Guise, who added a grotto and orangeries after plans by Francesco Primaticcio. In 1654, it was acquired by Abel Servien, the finance minister, who commissioned Louis Le Vau to renovate the old palace and create the first terraces.

François Louvois was the next lord of Meudon. While he owned it, André Le Nôtre laid out its gardens and park. Louvois's widow traded it to the Grand Dauphin in exchange for Choisy. In 1706, the dauphin commissioned Jules Hardouin-Mansart to construct a new palace on the site of the grotto. In their decorations for this so-called Château Neuf, Charles de Lafosse, Jean Jouvenet, Antoine Coypel, and Claude Audran III created the foundations of the Rococo style. The Grand Dauphin died here in 1711.

Meudon saw a number of famous visitors throughout the eighteenth century, among them Peter the Great. Used as an arsenal during the Revolution, it was the site of experiments with explosives by Choderlos de Laclos, Conté, and the chemist Berthollet. The old palace was set on fire by a blast in 1795; it was completely destroyed. The Château Neuf was refurbished by Napoleon. For a time, it was occupied by Marie-Louise and her son, and by Jérôme Bonaparte, the former king of Westphalia.

During the siege of Paris in 1870, the Prussians installed their batteries on the terrace of the palace, and the structure was burned out in the course of the fighting. Under the Third Republic, the ruined wings were reduced to a single story, and the central pavilion was fitted out with a huge revolving dome, where the astrophysicist Jules Janssen had his Observatoire d'Astronomie Physique. From this segment, one can form at least some idea of Hardouin-Mansart's last structure.

The observatory can be visited only with written permission. However, the terrace is open to the public, and from it, there is a magnificent view of Paris. Below the garden, in a house that once belonged to Armande Béjart, the wife of Molière, the museum of Meudon (11 Rue des Pierres) displays reminders of the town's famous inhabitants; Meudon was a favorite residence of a number of artists and intellectuals. Richard Wagner wrote *The Flying Dutchman* here, at 27 Avenue du Château; Rodin lived in the Villa des Brillants (today a museum) at 19 Avenue Auguste-Rodin; other notables who lived here include Jean Arp, Céline (Louis-Ferdinand Destouches), and Jacques Maritain. The Forêt de Meudon, bisected by the freeway to Chartres, is one of the favorite recreation areas around Paris.

St. Cloud

On July 15, 1871, Napoleon III surrendered to the Prussians at St. Cloud. The Germans occupied the palace on September 19; on October 13, it went up in flames. Its outer walls still stood, but they were torn down in 1891. So ended the history of what Corneille called the most beautiful palace in France.

The name St. Cloud derives from Clodoald, Clovis's grandson, who founded a monastery here. After Clodoald's death in 560, the cloister, along with dominion over the locality, passed to the bishop of Paris, who was thus permitted to call himself Duc de St. Cloud and Pair de France (the title *pair* was bestowed on the most notable princes of the country), titles that the bishops kept until 1839. In 1589, Henri III was murdered in the castle at St. Cloud, then the country seat of Bishop Gondi, by the Jacobin monk Jacques Clément. Cardinal Mazarin acquired the property in 1650 for Philippe d'Orléans, the brother of Louis XIV, who commissioned Jules Hardouin-Mansart and Jean Girard to construct a palace here for himself and his second wife, Liselotte, daughter of the Elector of the Palatinate. Antoine Lepautre designed its Grande Cascade, and André Le Nôtre drew up the plans for the gardens and the park, which Philippe d'Orléans expanded from 12 to 590 hectares. Marie-Antoinette acquired the château in 1785 and had it enlarged and refurbished by Johann Riesener, Weisweiler, Jacob, and others.

St. Cloud was a favored residence of Napoleon, and his marriage to Marie-Louise was celebrated here in 1810. In 1852, Louis-Napoleon was here proclaimed emperor.

Only the outbuildings of the residence have survived: the *cour d'honneur* with its eighteenth-century stables; the seventeenth-century Pavillon de Valois; and the Pavillon de Breteuil from 1743, St. Cloud's equivalent of a Trianon at the southeast end of the park, now the headquarters of the International Bureau of Weights and Measures. However, the landscaping is largely intact. It includes Lepautre's Grande Cascade from 1667; Hardouin-Mansart's adjacent Basse Cascade, with statues of the Seine and the Marne by the Adam brothers from 1734; the Bas Parc along the Seine; the Anciens Jardins Privés around the former château; and the Bassin du Fer-à-Cheval, designed by Girard in 1664. At the end of the broad parterre, a lawn connects the Bassin de la Petite-Gerbe with the center of the park, the Bassin de la Grande-Gerbe. On the south side of the parterre is the Bois des Goulottes,

with statues from 1734; on the north, the Jardin du Trocadéro from the Restoration. On the Rond-Point de la Balustrade, Napoleon had a tower, the so-called Lanterne de Demosthenes, erected after the model of the Lysikrates in Athens. Its light indicated to the people of Paris when the emperor was in residence at St. Cloud. The Prussians blew it up in 1870.

Adjoining the park on the southeast is the Sèvres porcelain factory, moved here from Vincennes in 1756. The original eighteenth-century building currently houses the Centre International d'Études Pédagogiques; the factory and the Musée National de Céramique are located in a châteaulike structure from 1876 (see page 493). To the west of the park of St. Cloud, in the community of Vaucresson on the other side of the Autoroute de l'Ouest, is the very lovely Pavilion du Butard, a hunting lodge that was built for Louis XV in 1750 by Jacques-Ange Gabriel. It boasts a splendid relief of a boar hunt on its pediment.

Sceaux

(illus. 152, page 383)

Colbert condemned Nicolas Fouquet's extravagance, and although he was more discreet, he was sufficiently conscious of his status to wish to acquire a suitable residence. Thus in 1670, he hired the architect Claude Perrault, whom he had championed in the building of the Louvre Colonnades, to expand a modest château in Sceaux to more princely proportions. Charles Le Brun, François Girardon, and Antoine Coysevox were charged with decorating it, and André Le Nôtre produced the plans for a generous garden layout that organized the sloping grounds into a network of axes, *allées,* canals, and terraces. Louis XIV was able to admire the completed residence in 1677.

Sceaux: Colbert's château in the late seventeenth century (Perelle).

Colbert's son sold the property in 1700 to the Sun King's illegitimate son the Duc de Maine, whose wife turned Sceaux into the setting for elaborate parties, the famous and scandalous *nuits de Sceaux* that Saint-Simon describes so scornfully in his memoirs. The château was torn down during the Revolution. A later owner, the Duc de Trevise, erected the present palace in its place in 1856. This structure has proved to be much too small for its setting. Since 1924, the property has belonged to the Département de la Seine, and the park has been carefully restored. The palace now houses the Musée de l'Ile de France, whose collection provides a splendid introduction to the history of the province.

The only surviving structure that offers a sense of Perrault's architecture is the Pavil-lon d'Aurore, in the park to the right of the entry portal. It is a round, domed building with two short wings and stands on a tall pedestal adorned with a balustrade. A wide staircase leads up to it on each end. Its sober design, precise forms, and exquisite proportions make it one of the most perfect structures of French classicism, a supreme expression of the period's ideal of nobility and grandeur. One of Le Brun's best ceiling frescoes, *Aurora Leaving Cephalus to Bring Light to the World,* graces the central domed space. Visitors may enter this building only with the consent of the director of the museum.

The outbuildings of the château survived the Revolution and have recently been quite splendidly restored. These include the entry pavilions; the Communs on the right,

416

after plans by Antoine Lepautre; and the Orangerie on the left, by Jules Hardouin-Mansart. The Orangerie is used for exhibitions and cultural events. On the north side of the palace are the bronze figures from the base of the monument to Louis XIV that once dominated the Place des Victoires in Paris, Martin Desjardin's 1686 allegories of the defeated German Empire, Holland, Spain, and Turkey.

Le Nôtre's park was essentially restored in the 1930s, but it is less lavishly maintained than Vaux-le-Vicomte's or Versailles's. Basic to its design is the intersection of two perpendicular main axes. One of these extends from the center of the palace, which stands at the top of the hill, down across various terraces and lawns far off into the landscape. The other governs the park's main orientation. It runs along the Avenue de la Duchesse, to the side of the palace, then descends across the Grandes Cascades to the Bassin de l'Octogone, and rises again as a lawn bordered by tall trees. Its chief highlight is the Grand Canal, which begins at the middle terrace behind the palace and runs through the entire park. This canal is part of an expansion of Le Nôtre's plans by the landscape architect François Leclerc after 1683. It is lined by two rows of Italian poplars, which give it an unusually melancholy quality. Along the lesser canal that connects the Bassin de l'Octogone and the Grand Canal, a small structure was added in 1832. This is the Pavillon de Hanovre, an elegant building with a semicircular façade and a wrought-iron balcony resting on consoles. The Duc de Richelieu commissioned the architect Jean-Michel Chevotet to build this pavilion in 1760 at the edge of his property in Paris. But it had to be moved to make way for the Berlitz building at the corner of the Boulevard des Italiens and the Rue Louis-le-Grand. It owes its name to the charge that the duke financed it with funds that he had extorted from the Hanoverians during the Seven Years' War. After the Revolution, the pavilion was one of the more fashionable ballrooms in Paris.

Dampierre

(illus. 150, page 383)

The château of Dampierre occupies an uncommon location. It and its outbuildings stand on the floor of the valley of the Yvette, and the park climbs up the slope behind it. It is, however, quite conventional in its architecture and not one of Jules Hardouin-Mansart's most impressive buildings (its quite clumsy restoration in 1840 has only contributed to its uninspiring appearance).

Dampierre was built in 1675 for the Duc de Chevreuse, whose wife was one of Colbert's daughters, on the site of a Renaissance complex, traces of which have been preserved in the smaller side buildings. The château is a two-story *corps de logis* with short wings facing the courtyard, a *cour d'honneur* with flanking Communs and two entry pavilions that frame a splendid wrought-iron gate. Since the ground slopes downward, a tall foundation story is visible on the garden side. The center of this garden façade is emphasized by bays that project slightly; a roof balustrade with urns ties them together. Further, the central bay is a two-story portico complete with triangular pediment. A grandiose open staircase leads down to the park, partially masking the ground floor. The park reveals the masterful hand of André Le Nôtre—a spacious arrangement of its parterres and basins, and a grand perspective along its main axis, which continues into the forest beyond. The architectural idiom of the château is that of the ministers' wings in front of Versailles—

a combination of red brick, light-colored limestone, and blue tiles.

The interiors are splendidly decorated and contain priceless furnishings. Some date from the time the palace was built; others are in the Louis XV style. The Salle des Fêtes displays the eclectic style of the Second Empire, including a fanciful reconstruction of Phidias's *Athena* and two colossal, unfinished paintings by Jean Auguste Dominique Ingres that depict the Golden Age and the Bronze Age.

(Tours daily, except Tuesday, 2:00 P.M.–6:00 P.M., between April 1 and October 15)

Champs

(illus. 153, page 384)

The palace of Champs is one of the earliest and most perfect examples of a *maison de plaisance,* the preferred type of country seat in the eighteenth century, combining comfort and a degree of display that varied according to the owner's status. The genteel, reserved elegance of Champs's exterior recalls the mansions of the Faubourg St-Germain or the Palais de l'Élysée. The disposition of interior spaces is highly inventive, including a wealth of *dégagements,* back stairs, and mezzanines designed to facilitate smooth and inconspicuous service.

Scarcely anywhere in Paris or the Ile de France does one have a better opportunity to sense how the nobility lived in the eighteenth century. Yet the history of this château is one of parvenus and social climbers and is instructive toward an understanding of French society in the *ancien régime.*

The builder of the house was Charles Renouard de La Touanne, who commissioned Jean-Baptiste Bullet to build it in 1699. Bullet's father, Pierre, had designed the château at Issy. La Touanne had grown rich as a military paymaster and treasurer of the light cavalry, but in 1701, he was forced to declare bankruptcy. According to Saint-Simon, when officers were sent to arrest him, he died of alarm on the front steps of his palace. The property was acquired by Paul Poisson de Bourvalais, a former footman who had made a fortune as a supplier to the army. He oversaw the completion of the château (in fact, other sources suggest that he actually built it and that La Touanne had left only plans) and its elaborate furnishing. It was also he who had Champs elevated to a barony.

Champs was completed in 1707; ten years later, its owner was arrested for embezzlement and taken to the Bastille, where he died in 1719. His palace went "for a song," as Saint-Simon wrote, to the Princesse de Conti, daughter of Louis XIV by his mistress Louise de La Vallière. In 1739, she left it to her nephew, the Duc de La Vallière, under whom significant additions were made. The gardens were laid out according to plans by Claude Desgots, a nephew of André Le Nôtre, and the interior decoration was finished. In about 1740, Christophe Huet painted the Salon Chinois and a boudoir with chinoiseries like those at Chantilly, and in the Cabinet des Singes of the Hôtel de Rohan in Paris. The duke, whose passion for the theater brought him to the verge of ruin, had to lease his palace in 1757. For six years, it was the country house of Mme. de Pompadour, who paid 12,000 livres a year in rent, but spent some 200,000 livres for "improvements."

The château then began to deteriorate, due to a combination of later owners, the Revolution, and use as a barracks in the nineteenth century. In 1895, however, a new owner, Comte Cahen d'Anvers, began its renovation. He restored the interiors and masked the stables and housekeeping buildings with colonnades like those of the palace. Most important, he restored the park from Desgot's original plans, extending the view down to the Marne. In 1935, the Cahen d'Anvers family gave the property to the government, which occasionally uses the château as a residence for foreign heads of state.

(Open daily, except Tuesday, 9:30 A.M.–4:30 P.M., between December and February; open later in the other months, and to 8:00 P.M. in July and August)

Compiègne

(illus. 151, page 383)

Compiègne has been the site of many major events: the capture of Joan of Arc by the Burgundians, who sold her to the English, in May 1430; the meeting of Napoleon and Marie-Louise in 1810; the series of receptions and balls under Napoleon III and Eugénie; and the armistice signed on November 11, 1918, in the adjacent forest by the Allies and Germany, ending World War I. This last ceremony was repeated on the same spot by Adolf Hitler on June 21, 1940; this time, though, France surrendered to the Third Reich.

Compiègne always has been one of the more important French royal palaces. The Merovingians had a residence at Compiègne, and Charles le Chauve (Charles the Bald) made it into his new capital. Charles V constructed a triangular castle here. Although it was demolished in the late seventeenth century, the castle's foundations influenced the layout of the present-day structure. It was Louis XV who began to modernize the layout and build a new palace. He gave the commission to Jacques Gabriel in 1738, but it was Gabriel's son Jacques-Ange, the architect of the Place de la Concorde, who in 1751 presented the grand plan for a completely new building, which was to be three times as large as the former palace. Work proceeded slowly—a portion of either the old or the new structure had to be kept open for the king's frequent hunting parties —and then it came to a virtual standstill during the Seven Years' War. After 1775, construction resumed under Gabriel's pupil Le Dreux de la Châtre, and the château was largely completed by 1786. The result, as seen from the town, is a symmetrical, three-wing layout with a deep courtyard that is closed off from the Place du Palais by an open colonnade with a portico. Gabriel also intended to incorporate the square itself, with colonnades and the ministers' palace, into the complex.

The building's façades are extremely sober. Above a high foundation story is the *étage noble,* whose sole ornamentation is the window frames. The next level is a mezzanine; above it, a continuous balustrade screens the roof. The ends of the side wings are pavilions with decorative flat pilasters facing the square. The *corps de logis* at the back of the courtyard has a portico with full columns. Outbuildings of uniform height extend outward on either side, creating a regular grid of secondary courtyards.

When one walks around the palace, one becomes aware that the garden façade does not lie behind the *corps de logis* but rather at an angle to it. It is extraordinarily long and lies at the level of the *étage noble,* facing the huge park across a series of terraces. This is the result of the preservation of the foundations of Charles V's castle, which followed the course of the old fortified walls on this side, thus suggesting a triangular ground plan for the new palace as well.

Marie-Antoinette had a hand in the interior decoration; the deposed Charles IV of

Spain took up residence in her former apartment in 1808. But it was Napoleon who first filled the palace with courtly life. Because the Palais des Tuileries was destroyed, his state apartment here now provides the best idea of the severity and the rather cold splendor of the Empire style. These rooms have undergone painstaking restoration with their original furnishings since 1945.

Compiègne was at its most brilliant under Napoleon III. He gave the palace a most splendid and radiant atmosphere, whose glitter is captured in the operettas of Jacques Offenbach and the waltzes of Métra. The empress loved this spot, where she had met her husband, and the imperial couple here held a series of receptions for the court, financiers, artists, and writers. These fêtes were the cause of jealousy and intrigue.

(Open daily, except Tuesday, 9:45 A.M.–12:00 M. and 1:30 P.M.–5:30 P.M.; in winter, to 4:30 P.M.)

OTHER POINTS
OF
INTEREST
IN THE
ILE DE FRANCE

Argenteuil

Almost nothing about this industrial city now suggests that it was the center of Impressionism more than a century ago. Claude Monet had a house here (in the Rue Port-St-Denis) from 1872 to 1878, and Edouard Manet, Auguste Renoir, Alfred Sisley, and Gustave Caillebotte also worked here, capturing the light of the Ile de France in their paintings of the Seine, its bridges, and its boats. At the same time, they documented the beginning of the industrialization of the north of Paris. The cubist Georges Braque was born in Argenteuil in 1882.

Auvers-sur-Oise

(illus. 121, page 331)

The little village church at Auvers has become world famous thanks to the painting of its choir (in the Jeu de Paume in Paris) by Vincent Van Gogh. It was built in the twelfth century and was altered in the thirteenth and again in the sixteenth centuries. Van Gogh spent the last months of his life here, being treated by Dr. Gachet until he committed suicide in 1890 in the fields outside the village. His grave is in the cemetery above the church; his brother Theo's is next to it. A monument to Van Gogh by Ossip Zadkine stands in the park.

After Barbizon and Argenteuil, Auvers was the most important artists' colony in the Ile de France. Jean-Baptiste Corot and Charles-François Daubigny were longstanding residents of Auvers. In 1872, Paul Cézanne followed his friend Camille Pissarro here for two years, during which he painted some of his most important works. Honoré Daumier and, later, Maurice de Vlaminck also worked here.

Barbizon

In the early nineteenth century, this little village at the western edge of the Forêt de Fontainebleau became one of the centers of the French *plein-air* movement, an artistic rediscovery of landscape influenced by the English painters Joseph Mallord William Turner and John Constable. Théodore Rousseau began to spend his summers here in 1835 and settled here permanently in 1847. He was followed by Jean-François Millet—who painted his famous *Angelus* (now in the Louvre) in nearby Chailly—Charles-François Daubigny, and his friend Jean-Baptiste Corot. The paintings that these artists created in and around Barbizon, chiefly in the summer months, were the forerunners of Impressionist works. Rousseau and Millet are both buried in Chailly. Their houses and the artists' pub Auberge du Père Ganne are virtually unchanged, although they are used, in part, for commercial purposes.

Blérancourt

(illus. 143, page 378)

The château of Blérancourt, between Noyon and Laon, was demolished, like most châteaux in the Ile de France, during the Revolutionary turmoil of 1793. Begun in 1610 for the Seigneur de Blérancourt, Bernard Potier, it was one of Salomon de Brosse's chief works before he built the Palais du Luxembourg in Paris. What remains of the château are the portals, the pavilions at the corners of the main platform, portions of the *corps de logis,* and the park. These were lovingly restored after 1918 by Ann Morgan, an American, who transformed them into the Musée de la Coopération Franco-Américaine.

The main structure, a *corps de logis* set between four corner pavilions of uniform height, was quite similar to the Palais du Luxembourg. The surviving entry pavilions are extremely elegant, with highly imaginative sculpture and ornamentation.

(Park open daily, 8:00 A.M.)

Champeaux

(illus. 92, page 292)

Under the direction of Guillaume de Champeaux, bishop of Châlons-sur-Marne and a theological opponent of Pierre Abélard, the seminary at Champeaux developed into one of the intellectual centers of the Ile de France in the twelfth century. Surviving from it is the stately, 222-foot-long church of St. Martin, whose six-part vaulting in its nave follows the examples of Sens and Paris. Its transept was completed before the end of the twelfth century; the nave and tower by the early thirteenth century; and the square-ended choir at the end of the thirteenth century. An angular ambulatory was added to the choir in the fourteenth century. In the crossing are choir stalls with bitingly satirical misericords created by Richard Falaize in 1522.

Champlâtreux

Just before reaching Luzarches, the N16 suddenly turns at an angle. This highway was laid out in the nineteenth century, and Mathieu Molé, the owner of the château of Champlâtreux and France's *grand voyer* (inspector of roads and bridges), saw to it that it did not cut through his park. The château had been built by his grandfather Mathieu-François Molé, the president of the Parlement de Paris, who had married a daughter of the wealthy banker Samuel Bernard. Its architect was Jean-Michel Chevotet, the builder of the Pavillon de Hanovre, now in the park at Sceaux.

Chevotet designed the château according to François Blondel's classical formula for a *maison de plaisance.* The center and sides are emphasized as slightly projecting pavilions with their own roofs and gables; the central axis is marked by a double ordination of columns and a wealth of architectural sculpture. This is particularly true on the garden side, where the central pavilion extends outward in a semicircle, its broken pediment displaying an allegory of the goddess Diana. The interior decorations were done by a follower of Germain Boffrand, and the arrangement of the rooms, like the exterior, follows the rules set by Blondel.

(Not open to visitors)

Chars

Near the end of the twelfth century, the small Romanesque church at Chars was provided with a lavish four-story choir. This choir follows the model of Notre-Dame in Paris, for it adopts the motif of the rose windows instead of a triforium above the galleries. The five radial chapels and the vaulting were renovated in the sixteenth century, when the bell tower between the south transept and the nave was built.

Château-Thierry

This town traces its name to the penultimate Merovingian king, Thierry IV, who died in 737 in the castle where he had been imprisoned by his powerful major-domo, Charles Martel. Expanded in the Middle Ages by the counts of Champagne, Château-Thierry became the most important fortification in the eastern part of the Ile de France, and it was repeatedly besieged by the kings of France, the English, the League, and the rulers of Lorraine. Here, in February 1814, Napoleon defeated the combined Russian and Prussian army under Gebhard Blücher, and in 1918, the area was the scene of fierce fighting between the German and the Allied armies. Despite its stormy past, the town preserves a number of picturesque lanes lined with middle-class houses and aristocratic *hôtels* at the foot of the former castle. The ring walls of the fortress and the massive gatehouses of the Porte St-Pierre and Porte St-Jean still dominate the ridge above the town. Of the castle itself, however, only remnants of the donjon have survived.

Château-Thierry was the birthplace of the seventeenth-century writer of fables Jean de La Fontaine. The house in which he was born, a Renaissance structure from 1559 at 12 Rue Jean-de-La-Fontaine, keeps his memory alive.

Courances

The château of Courances, set in one of the loveliest of André Le Nôtre's parks in the Ile de France, is a model of Louis XIII architecture. It was actually built in about 1550 by Gilles Le Breton, one of the architects of Fontainebleau, for Cosme Clausse, the secretary of state to Henri II and owner of nearby Fleury-en-Bière. Its present-day appearance, however, is the result of reconstruction done for Claude Gaillard, the president of the accounting office, who acquired the château in 1662. The double staircase that leads up to the *étage noble* and partially conceals the tall foundation story is a free imitation of the Escalier du Fer-à-Cheval at Fontainebleau. The *corps de logis* consists of nine bays and is executed in a combination of stone and brick. It is flanked by two narrower pavilions with their own steep roofs. Stone balustrades ring the island, surrounded by a moat, on which the palace stands. The park boasts 200-year-old plane trees, wide pools, and lawns. Among its numerous Baroque statues is a nymph by Poirier, originally in the park at Marly.

(Park open Saturday, Sunday, and holidays, 2:00 P.M.–6:00 P.M., between April and October)

Ermenonville

In 1763, the Marquis René de Girardin began to have the country around the château of Ermenonville, which he had just inherited, converted into a landscaped garden in the free English style and inspired by the ideas of Jean-Jacques Rousseau. It was to appeal to the feelings and the intellect. A series of symbolic monuments, memorials, and moralizing inscriptions invited strollers in the park to philosophical contemplation. In 1778, Rousseau himself came to Ermenonville at the marquis's invitation and was enraptured. On July 3, 1778, though, a sudden stroke took his life. The marquis had Rousseau buried on an island in the park's lake, the Ile aux Peupliers, and his grave became the goal of countless pilgrims. In 1794, his body was transferred to the Panthéon in Paris.

The château, an elegant three-wing structure from the eighteenth century with certain older elements, is a hotel today. Thanks to the Touring Club de France, the essential aspects of the park have been preserved. Its features, including the Temple de la Philosophie, the monument to the Strasbourg painter Meyer, and the Ile de Rousseau, poignantly reflect the sentimental ideal landscape of the Enlightenment.

(The park may be reached through the campground of the Touring Club; open daily, 9:00 A.M.–7:00 P.M.; in winter, to 5:00 P.M.)

Étampes

In the sixteenth century, the mistresses of the French kings made Étampes famous: Anne de Pisseleu, the Duchesse d'Étampes, for whom François I elevated the county into a duchy; Diane de Poitiers; Gabrielle d'Estrées; and others. But even in the Middle Ages, this royal town was associated with a woman, the unfortunate Ingeborg of Denmark, whom Philippe Auguste rejected immediately after their marriage. She was forced to spend more than ten years in the donjon of the castle, the Tour Guinette, an unusual structure whose ground plan is that of a quatrefoil. This tower is the only portion of the medieval fortifications that has escaped destruction.

Lying midway between Paris and Orléans and one of the gateways to the Beauce, Étampes always has been important both strategically and economically. Its wealth is reflected not only in its many stately merchants' houses (Ancien Presbytere, Maison de Diane de Poitiers, Hôtel de Ville, Maison d'Anne de Pisseleu, Hôtel St-Yon), but also in its churches, all of which date from the twelfth century.

Notre-Dame-du-Fort was built on an irregular ground plan, has one of the loveliest Romanesque bell towers in the Ile de France, and boasts a figured portal of around 1150 (damaged in the religious wars) that was directly influenced by the Portail Royal at Chartres. In the thirteenth century, embrasures and crenelation were added, giving the church a fortified appearance, unusual for the Ile de France.

Only the west portal (heavily restored) and the compact crossing tower of St. Basile remain from the Romanesque period. The remainder of its fabric dates to fifteenth-century construction.

St. Gilles was endowed by Louis VI le Gros in 1123. Its façade and nave date from the twelfth century, and its choir was built in the fifteenth and sixteenth centuries. The church suffered considerably under the bombardments of 1944, as did portions of picturesque Place St-Gilles, where there are still a few half-timbered buildings with stone pillars from the thirteenth century.

St. Martin attracts attention because of its leaning tower from the sixteenth century. The church was begun in about 1140 with the construction of its lavish choir, whose ambulatory and three radial chapels make it one of the most interesting examples of the transition from the Romanesque to Early Gothic in the Ile de France.

Farcheville

With its crenelations atop tall pointed-arch arcades, the almost square fortress of Farcheville, some six miles east of Étampes, is one of the few well-preserved examples of medieval feudal architecture in the Ile de France. It was begun in 1291 for Hugues II de Bouville, the chamberlain of Philippe IV le Bel, and it is rather more reminiscent of Provençal fortresses than of northern ones. Its walls enclose a broad courtyard, around which the chapel, tithe barn, kitchens, and dwellings for the nobility (from the seventeenth century) are picturesquely arranged. A rectangular tower with machicolation dominates the entrance, approached by a bridge across the old moat.

(Not open to visitors)

La Ferté-Milon

After Pierrefonds, the castle of La Ferté-Milon was Louis d'Orléans's largest building project. He began it in 1393, but he was murdered by Jean sans Peur, Duc de Bourgogne, in 1407, and it was left unfinished. Repeatedly besieged, the fortress was partially razed at the command of Henri IV in 1594. But even the remains of the castle are imposing: its façade is almost 300 feet long and 100 feet high, and in the center, between two slender towers, is the entrance portal with the beautiful relief of the coronation of Mary that served as a model for Eugène Viollet-le-Duc's decoration of Pierrefonds. In the tower niches are statues of the Greuses, medieval allegories of the virtues. In the courtyard are the remains of the rectangular donjon. La Ferté-Milon was the birthplace of Jean Racine, whose father was the local bailiff.

Fleury-en-Bière

Pierre Lescot, the builder of the Louvre, is thought to have been the architect of this palace, immediately adjacent to Fontainebleau, which was begun in 1550 for Cosme Clausse, secretary to Henri II. Even though the main building was radically modernized in the eighteenth century, the complex as a whole—its elongated Communs, their Mannerist division into sections of blank wall, its emphasized corner pavilions, the chapel, and the farm—provides an excellent picture of a noble mid-sixteenth-century manor, under the influence of the School of Fontainebleau. Actually, the large canal here is supposedly the model for the one that Henri IV constructed at Fontainebleau. It was in Fleury that Richelieu barely escaped an assassination planned by his opponent Gaston d'Orléans in 1626.

(Not open to visitors)

Gaillon

The unimposing ruins at Gaillon, rising above a picturesque village with half-timbered buildings (indicating the influence of nearby Normandy), would scarcely lead one to suspect that it was one of the earliest Renaissance palaces in France. It was commissioned shortly after Charles IX's Italian campaign by the archbishop of Rouen, Cardinal Georges d'Amboise. Jean Androuet Du Cerceau preserved the memory of this princely residence in his book on the most famous buildings in France. Since the Revolution, the building has been a prison and repeatedly disfigured, but until only recently, its main façade was set up in the courtyard of the École des Beaux-Arts in Paris. Restoration of the complex has been in progress for more than ten years.

Across the Seine, near Les Andelys and,

in fact, in Normandy, one can see the ruins of Château-Gaillard (illus. 129, page 336) atop a white chalk cliff. Built by Richard the Lion-Hearted in 1197 and taken over by Philippe Auguste in 1204, it was one of the most important fortresses during the Hundred Years' War. It was razed by Henri IV in 1603.

Gisors

(illus. 126, page 334)

Disputed for centuries by the Capetians and their rebellious vassals, the dukes of Normandy, the fortress of Gisors came to the Crown after the fall of Château-Gaillard in 1204. In the meantime, though, the Plantagenets, especially Henry II of England, had expanded it into one of the largest military complexes in France. Philippe Auguste enlarged the ring of fortifications even more. Surviving from his time are the Tour de Gouverneur, with its hall with pointed-arch vaulting, and the Tour du Prisonnier, a round, 90-foot-high dwelling tower that contains three vaulted rooms, one above the other. A park now occupies the site of the former royal residence, which has completely disappeared. But the polygonal donjon on its artificial hill—dating to 1097, when the fortress was enlarged by Guillaume le Roux (William Rufus), the son of William the Conqueror—still stands within the large Norman fortification ring. The twelve towers that guarded that ring have been reduced to the height of the wall.

(Open daily, except Tuesday, 9:00 A.M.–12:00 M. and 2:00 P.M.–6:00 P.M.; in winter, to 4:00 P.M.)

The historic center of the town of Gisors was largely destroyed during World War II. The church of St. Gervais–St. Protais has been restored. It is an important Renaissance structure whose eastern portions, a square choir and crossing with tower, go back even earlier to a bequest by Blanche of Castile in 1240. Its interior preserves some of the rich sixteenth-century furnishings, including stained glass by Enguerrand Le Prince and Nicolas Le Prince from Beauvais and an organ loft by Jean Grappin from 1578.

Gros Bois

The palace of Gros Bois is one of the most unusual buildings around Paris from the late sixteenth century. The center of the *corps de logis* curves inward; then the building expands stepwise, two pavilions on either side, to embrace the courtyard. It displays a picturesque alternation of brickwork and plaster; the bricks are used in those portions of the architecture that were usually executed in stone.

This palace, part of the transition from the Henri IV style to that of Louis XIII, was built in about 1580 for the royal treasurer, Raoul Moreau, by the architect Florent Fournier. In devising this remarkable ground plan, Fournier was inspired by the work of Jacques Androuet Du Cerceau the Elder. Beginning in 1625, a new owner, Charles de Valois, the son of Charles IX, commissioned Jean Thiriot to add two wings with corner pavilions on either side of the courtyard. Inside, the dining room, dating from 1644 and boasting frescoes ascribed to Abraham Bosse, has survived.

After a number of further changes of ownership, Gros Bois was acquired by the marshal Berthier, Prince de Wagram, in 1805. He refurbished the interior and constructed a large gallery with paintings of his battles. The elite of the Empire and of Europe gathered here for his hunting parties. On December 3, 1809, for example—in addition to the kings of Saxony, Württemberg,

Westphalia, and Bavaria and the queens of Naples, Holland, and Spain—Empress Joséphine appeared in public for the last time before her divorce. Since 1962, the palace has been owned by the French Horse Breeders' Society, which carefully maintains the property. Thanks to its interior appointments, Gros Bois is, second only to Malmaison, the most priceless surviving Empire ensemble in the Paris region.

(Tours Sunday, 2:00 P.M.–5:30 P.M.)

Guermantes

Marcel Proust had made the name of this palace world famous in his *Remembrance of Things Past* long before he himself first visited it.

The unpretentious structure in the Louis XIII style was built in the early seventeenth century for Claude Viole, scion of an ancient Parlement family and member of the privy council and the accounting office. After 1640, his son Pierre had additional pavilions and side wings built onto the *corps de logis*. In 1698, the palace was acquired by the tax collector Paulin Pondre, who modernized it after plans by Robert de Cotte and provided it with a long gallery with copies of famous paintings. André Le Nôtre planned the redesign of the park. After repeatedly changing hands, the palace was acquired by the Hottinguer family in the twentieth century, and they carefully restored it. Of particular interest in the interior are the rooms surviving from the time the palace was built and the 90-foot La Belle Inutile gallery, whose decoration was executed by Hanord after designs by de Cotte. (Its ceiling décor was created in 1852 by Andrien, a pupil of Eugène Delacroix.)

(Tours Saturday, Sunday, and holidays, 2:00 P.M.–5:45 P.M., between March 15 and November 15)

Jouarre

(illus. 87, page 291)

The burial chapel at Jouarre is one of the oldest examples of Christian art in France. As early as about 630, St. Ado, the brother of St. Ouen, bishop of Rouen, founded a double cloister here. It later became a Benedictine convent, and its buildings were rebuilt in the twelfth century. Jouarre continued to be one of the most refined cloisters in France, its abbesses coming from the high nobility. The present cloister buildings, except for the twelfth-century tower, date from the eighteenth century. But behind the parish church, the so-called crypt is preserved; it is a portion of the original seventh-century church with two rectangular burial chambers half-sunk in the ground. The masonry is Merovingian, and the porphyry and jasper columns and white marble capitals, which support Romanesque vaulting, are from the seventh century. The vaulting itself was reconstructed in the nineteenth century, when the east wall was strengthened and given windows. In the St. Paul crypt, there are a number of highly important tombs, including that of Ste. Théodechilde, or Telchilde, the first abbess, which is decorated with shells. Others contain the remains of St. Agilbert, Théodechilde's brother and bishop of Paris, and of St. Ado, the cloister's founder. On the tomb of Ste. Ozanne, a legendary Irish saint, there is a lovely recumbent figure from 1314.

In the second chamber are the tombs of St. Ebresigil, bishop of Meaux, and of Ste. Aguilberte, Ebresigil's sister and the second abbess of the cloister. The latter is embellished with a geometric design. This chamber was shortened by almost 20 feet in 1640; at its east end, there is still an apse with three Merovingian columns.

The adjacent parish church was completely renovated in the fifteenth century.

(Open daily, except Tuesday, 9:00 A.M.–5:00 P.M.)

Luzarches

(illus. 91, page 292)

In the middle of the fertile plain of ancient France, for which Luzarches was one of the grain markets, the remains of one of the oldest fortresses in the Ile de France have been preserved.

The church of St. Côme–St. Damien has a Romanesque choir, with several parallel apses, that was exposed and restored in 1957. It also boasts a twelfth-century tower whose top story dates from the sixteenth century, when the façade of the church was constructed. This work began in 1551 under the architect Nicolas de Saint-Michel, who also designed the church at nearby Mesnil-Aubry. The patron saints of this church were Cosmas and Damian, two Syrian doctors martyred in A.D. 303 under Diocletian and traditionally the patron saints of physicians. As a result, the fraternity of doctors in Paris used to treat the inhabitants of Luzarches without charge.

Maintenon

(illus. 128, page 335)

Françoise d'Aubigné, the widow of the comedian Michel-Antoine Scarron and governess to the children of Louis XIV and his mistress Mme. de Montespan, brought renown to the name Maintenon. In 1674, the king gave her the money with which to buy this ancient noble seat, and in 1688, he elevated it to a marquisate. Its owner, to whom he had been secretly married since 1683, became the Marquise de Maintenon.

It would be difficult to imagine a sharper contrast to the lavish monumentality of Versailles. The château of Maintenon consists of several elements. There is a massive, square twelfth-century donjon, to which a steep roof was added in the seventeenth century. A fourteenth-century *logis* was modernized at the beginning of the Renaissance, in 1521, by Jean Cotterau, who had been Louis XII's finance minister; Cotterau's coat of arms, a half-moon and lizard, can still be seen on the narrow, semicircular stair towers flanking the entrance. There are also three massive round corner towers in red brick. And in the inner courtyard, an irregular series of arcades gives the four-wing complex the feeling of a cloister. The new marquise did little to change the château, only removing the wing that faced the garden in order to have a view of the park. When restructuring the park, she summoned André Le Nôtre from Versailles in 1676 to ask his advice. She established her own apartment in a new tract connecting the main building with the old donjon.

In 1684, in order to alleviate the water shortage at Versailles, the king commanded that the River Eure, some thirty miles distant, be diverted there by a gigantic aqueduct. Sébastien Vauban and Lattière developed plans for the project, and François Louvois rounded up some 30,000 workers to bridge the valley of Maintenon with an aqueduct almost three miles long. Thirty-two arcades, spanning more than half a mile, had been completed when, due to a renewed outbreak of war in 1688, the workers were suddenly needed as soldiers. Construction was never resumed, and the unfinished aqueduct, used as a quarry in the eighteenth century, looms above the park like a Roman ruin.

In 1698, when her niece married the Duc d'Ayen, son of the marshal de Noailles, the marquise presented the property to the young couple as a wedding present. The château still belongs to the Noailles family.

(Tours daily, except Tuesday, 2:00 P.M.–6:30 P.M.; also Sunday, 11:00 A.M.–12:30 P.M., between April 1 and October 15. In winter, Saturday, Sunday, and holidays, 2:00 P.M.–5:30 P.M.)

Le Marais

Next to the château of Compiègne, this is one of the most important examples of the severe Louis XVI style, the "return to antiquity." The palace was built in 1778 for a treasurer of the artillery on the site of a small Renaissance palace whose dovecote and moats have survived. The new complex was created by the architect Barré, who also designed the château of Montgeoffroy in Anjou. He was influenced by the structures of Jacques-Ange Gabriel, but his forms are more rigid and his proportions less elegant. As at the École Militaire, the center of the *corps de logis* is crowned by a rectangular cupola that is masked on the garden side by an attic story above severe pilasters; the courtyard side takes the form of a peristyle of four Tuscan columns, incorporating a staircase that leads up to the *bel-étage*. The top story appears to be a bit too low. Four identical pavilions mark the corners of the island on which the palace stands. The large French park with its huge pool was restored in the nineteenth century.

After 1900, Le Marais became celebrated as the setting for stylish parties given for the cream of Parisian society by its owner, Boni de Castellane, one of the great dandies of the Belle Epoque. His wife, who had to finance these events, was the American Anna Gould, later the Duchesse de Talleyrand. She died here in 1962.

(Visitors may view the exterior on Sunday and holidays, 2:00 P.M.–6:00 P.M., between March 1 and November 1)

Méry-sur-Oise

The château of Méry, at the edge of the new town of Cergy-Pontoise, is a reminder of the *ancien régime*. The site was originally a monastery owned by the monks of St. Denis. In 1375, though, Charles V gave it to his chancellor Pierre d'Orgemont, who built a castle here. Claude d'Orgement, cupbearer to Henri II, had this structure modernized. The courtyard façades on the east and north sides date back to this remodeling. Beginning in 1597, the property belonged to the Saint-Chamans family, which owned it until only very recently. It was place of exile for the Marquis de Saint-Chamans, whom Louis XIV banned from court because of his affair with the queen of Spain. It was at this time that the south façade of the palace was erected. The unusual west façade was added in the eighteenth century, under the last Saint-Chamans, the wife of Mathieu Molé, who owned neighboring Champlâtreux. Its narrow central portal is topped by a triangular pediment; above this, the crowning balustrade continues uninterrupted (a wholly un-French motif, adopted from Italy). It also boasts a broad open staircase ornamented with sculpture. Mme. Molé had the gardens redesigned at the urging of the naturalist Georges Louis Leclerc, Comte de Buffon, and they were reworked again in the nineteenth century by Varé, the creator of the Bois de Boulogne. Today, the château is owned by the Compagnie Générale des Eaux and has been set up as a museum for the history of water management.

Montceaux

Standing high above the Marne in the Brie Française, to the east of Meaux, the château of Montceaux was one of the most important of the royal Renaissance palaces.

It was begun in 1547 by Philibert de l'Orme for Catherine de Médicis, whose creditors sold it to Henri IV in 1596. The king intended it to be the residence of his mistress Gabrielle d'Estrées, but she died in 1599. Jacques Androuet Du Cerceau the Younger, who had begun work on the Grande Galerie of the Louvre in 1594, submitted plans for the château's expansion in 1597. His associate in the project was his nephew Salomon de Brosse; Remi Collin, who constructed the Cour des Offices at Fontainebleau beginning in 1606, was the director of building. In 1601, Henri IV presented the still-incomplete structure to the queen, Marie de Médicis, on the birth of their third son. She commissioned extensive work on the project, but the elaborate complex, including a four-wing main structure with a stately entrance pavilion and a broad forecourt with chapel and Communs, was never fully completed. Louis XVI gave it to the Prince de Conti in 1783.

During the Revolution, most of the main building was torn down. What remains, in the middle of a well-tended park, are portions of the façades (with the Colossal Ionic ordination that also appears on the Louvre), the ruins of the entrance pavilion, richly ornamented small pavilions at the corners of the deep moat surrounding the main building, the chapel, and the stables.

(Open Saturday and Sunday, 10:00 A.M.– 12:00 M. and 2:00 P.M.–5:00 P.M.)

Montfort-l'Amaury

The town of Montfort and its castle came into the possession of the French Crown at a relatively late date. In the Middle Ages, it was the seat of the powerful barons of Montfort. The most famous, Simon IV, led the cruel crusade against the Albigensians and fell during the siege of Toulouse in 1218. In 1312, Montfort passed by marriage to the dukes of Brittany. The marriages of Anne de Bretagne, first to Charles VIII and then to Louis XII, brought it to the Crown.

Only ruins of the castle have survived above the picturesque little town. However, the church of St. Pierre, rebuilt toward the end of the fifteenth century by Anne de Bretagne, boasts important Renaissance windows and recalls the unusual situation of this enclave within the Crown domains. Also of interest is the Ancien Charnier (charnel house), with a Flamboyant portal and three cloisterlike wings from the sixteenth and seventeenth centuries.

From 1920 to 1937, Montfort-l'Amaury was the home of the composer Maurice Ravel. His house, Le Belvédere, has been turned into a memorial museum to him.

Moret-sur-Loing

Even before Alfred Sisley made it famous by his pictures and by his residence here, Moret-sur-Loing, at the edge of the Forêt de Fontainebleau, attracted streams of Parisians on summer weekends. Even today, Moret is best seen off-season and during the week. It is an extremely picturesque village with half-timbered houses along the bank of the Loing. Portions of the fortified town walls have survived, as have the massive Porte de Paris and Porte de Bourgogne, both from the fourteenth century. There are several points of interest here: the early-thirteenth-century church of Notre-Dame (consecrated to Thomas à Becket), which was completed in the fifteenth century; next to it, the Logis du Bon-St-Jacques, a fifteenth-century half-timbered hospice; and, not far away, at 9 Rue du Château, Sisley's house.

But the major attraction of Moret is the ruins of a most impressive fortress that goes back to Philippe Auguste. Before Champagne fell to the Crown, Moret was one of the most important border fortresses of the Ile de France, protecting the province against the counts of Champagne. Even later, during the Hundred Years' War, it proved to be of military importance to Charles VII in his battles with the English. Still standing is the donjon, the only part of the castle to have survived, where Louis XIV had his finance minister Nicolas Fouquet imprisoned until he could be brought to trial.

(Open daily, 2:30 P.M.–6:30 P.M., July and August; Saturday and Sunday, 10:30 A.M.–12:00 M. and 2:00 P.M.–7:00 P.M., between March 15 and November 11; in winter, Sunday, 2:00 P.M.–5:00 P.M.)

Morienval

(illus. 84, page 289)

Of the few surviving Romanesque structures in the Ile de France, the small monastery church at Morienval is the most important. Founded by the Merovingian king Dagobert and destroyed by the Normans, the monastery—including the church with its even older portions, such as the nave—was taken over by Benedictine nuns in the twelfth century. The exterior is imposing because of its three towers, a massive western one above the entrance and two smaller ones flanking the choir, which is stepped back above the ambulatory. In this ambulatory, which dates to about 1125, are the earliest ribbed vaults in France, placed above an irregular, curved ground plan. These rather ungainly ribs, which were imitated around 1130 in the ribs of the chapel to the right of the choir, and the cantoned pillars in the nave have led many art historians to speculate that Morienval was a precursor of Gothic architecture, predating St. Denis. But in spite of a number of pointed arches in the arcades, the overall impression of Mor-

ienval is wholly Romanesque. The nave and crossing received their present vaulting in the seventeenth century. Toward the end of the nineteenth century, the church underwent a thorough restoration.

Nemours

(illus. 127, page 334)

The castle of Nemours, above the Loing, with an almost square donjon and a twelfth-century gatehouse flanked by four round towers, was the seat of the counts, later dukes and *pairs,* of Nemours. It was here that Henri III negotiated with the leaders of the League in 1588 before he had the Duc de Guise murdered at Blois. From 1674 on, the castle was the seat of a bailiff. The portal and staircase on the street side were modernized in the eighteenth century. Today, the restored palace houses the municipal museum.

The town has partially preserved its medieval form, with narrow streets running parallel to the Loing and the church of St. Jean-Baptiste, a Gothic structure renovated in the sixteenth century. The Grand Pont across the Loing was dedicated when Pope Pius VII passed through on his way to Napoleon's coronation as emperor in 1804.

Associated with Nemours is the name of Pierre-Samuel Du Pont, who represented the town in the Estates General in 1789. A supporter of the king, he was forced to emigrate to the United States during the Revolution. There, in Delaware, his son, Eleuthère-Irénée, founded what was to become the chemical firm of Du Pont de Nemours.

Nogent-le-Rotrou

Two medieval castles in the borderland between the Ile de France and the Perche are associated with Henri IV's great minister, the Duc de Sully: Villebon and Nogent-le-Rotrou.

Sully inherited Villebon, built by the Estoutevilles in 1391, from the descendants of that Norman family in 1607. He soon made it the setting for his court life, which was regulated by the strictest protocol. He spent the greater part of the year there, scarcely visiting Nogent-le-Rotrou. Villebon presents a quite authentic picture of a late medieval feudal castle, with its round towers and its crenelations, restored by the duke. But Nogent-le-Rotrou is one of the few surviving examples of the early square donjons that were built under Norman influence. It was built by Rotrou III, Comte de Perche and companion-in-arms of El Cid Campeador (Rodrigo Díaz de Bivar) during the eleventh-century wars against the Moors in Spain. In the early sixteenth century, the daughters of the Duc de Nemours added to the fortress a comfortable *logis* in the Late Gothic style that became the setting for a bustling court life in the late sixteenth century under the new owners, the Bourbon Condé family. Sully acquired the castle in 1624, and it remained in his family, which restored it in the nineteenth century, until 1948, when the town of Nogent-le-Rotrou obtained it in order to establish a museum.

Ormesson-sur-Marne

(illus. 139, page 376)

The small manor house of Ormesson, which is reflected in a long pool, was built in about 1580 by Jacques Androuet Du Cerceau the Younger for Louis Picot de Santenay. It comprises a simple *corps de logis* that alternates stone, plaster, and brick. Flanking corner towers rest on corbels whose piers stand in the water. It has been in the Ormesson family since 1630. They commissioned André Le Nôtre to design the park, and in 1740, they added a second residential wing in the elegant Louis XV style.

Not far from Ormesson, in the middle of the industrial suburb of Sucy-en-Brie, is the château of Sucy, built by Louis Le Vau in 1641 for the jurist Jean-Baptiste Lambert de Thorigny. This is one of Le Vau's more important works prior to Vaux-le-Vicomte. After decades of neglect, it is now undergoing restoration. Its once-famous park is now the site of state housing.

Ourscamps

The Revolution and World War I have left only remnants, although highly interesting ones, of this important Cistercian abbey, founded in 1129. From the splendid entry gate, one first glimpses a long structure with a central portal. In its pediment is a sculpted bear, a play on the monastery's name. Two severely classical wings from the late eighteenth century extend forward from the main building and end in pavilions. The right one is a ruin, but the left one now houses a community of monks. The building's portal once concealed a thirteenth-century Gothic church that stood behind it. Its nave and transept have completely disappeared, but the choir survives as a skeleton of pillars, arches, and ribs—a startling view of the anatomy of a High Gothic structure.

Behind the choir stands an elegant three-aisle infirmary from the thirteenth century. Although in poor condition, it is almost completely unchanged. Today, it is a chapel, and the seventeenth-century choir stalls that were added spoil its spatial effect somewhat. Nonetheless, this infirmary is one of the most important medieval hospital structures surviving in France.

Pontchartrain

The brilliant days of Pontchartrain are past. But during the Second Empire, the infamous Marquise de Païva, a Parisian socialite, would gather Parisian society for parties that all but ruined her lover and later her husband, the Prussian Count Henckell von Donnersmarck. Later in the nineteenth century, the château was owned by Auguste Dreyfus; his wife, the Marquise de Villehermose, celebrated here the luxurious life of a seventeenth-century Spanish grandee. Today, the view from the avenue that branches off the road to Dreux and leads to the château is still startling and impressive: an extensive complex constructed of brick and stone; a *corps de logis* with corner pavilions, long side wings, lower outbuildings for the stables, and Communs; and a sizable park with a lake-size pool. The château dates from the mid-seventeenth century and is ascribed— probably inaccurately—to François Mansart. Its early history reflects the rise of a ministerial family of bourgeois origins, the Phélypeaux, to nobility and the highest state offices. The builder of the palace was president of the accounting office under Richelieu; his son was general inspector of finances and became the chancellor of France in 1699. The latter persuaded André Le Nôtre to help plan the park. The family continued to produce state secretaries and ministers until the end of the *ancien régime.*

The château's brilliant and eventful history in the nineteenth century was summarily ended when a fire destroyed portions of the building in 1901. Between the two world wars, a new owner considerably disrupted the harmony of the structure by constructing a huge arcaded passageway through the center of the *corps de logis.* For some time now, the property has been used as a boarding school for deaf children.

Pontoise

Today, Pontoise is only a portion of the new town of Cergy-Pontoise and is a largely modern part of the *banlieue*; most of its population works in Paris. Nonetheless, Pontoise has played a significant role in the history of the Ile de France. It was a fortress that protected the capital from the Normans and a market for a rich grain-producing area that was among the most densely populated agricultural regions of France in the Middle Ages. The importance of the old city of Pontoise can be judged from the fact that one of the first Gothic churches, St. Maclou, was built here. It was begun in 1140, only a few years after work started on St. Denis, with a choir, an ambulatory with early pointed-arch vaulting, and choir chapels. The capitals are still wholly Romanesque. The nave was renovated in the fifteenth and sixteenth centuries with a Flamboyant façade and three portals. The columns of the side aisles display the forms of the approaching Renaissance.

The municipal museum, in a fifteenth-century mansion in the Rue Lemercier (open daily, except Tuesday, 10:00 A.M.– 12:00 M. and 2:00 P.M.–6:00 P.M.), houses the last works of the German artist Otto Freundlich, whose importance in the history of nonrepresentational art is only gradually being recognized. Freundlich had lived in Paris since 1908 and belonged to the group "Abstraction-Création." He was murdered by the Nazis in 1943. At 17 Rue du Château, a small museum (open Wednesday to Sunday, 2:00 P.M.–6:00 P.M.) exhibits some works of Camille Pissarro.

Opposite Pontoise, on the other bank of the Oise, is St. Ouen, where important remains of the monastery of Maubuisson are preserved. This was founded by Blanche of Castile in 1236, and the queen took the veil here. She is buried in Maubuisson, a house that always had special ties to the royal family. It was here that a royal council ordered the arrest of the Knights Templar in 1307. After the Revolution, the monastery lost its church and cloister, but one can still view several important thirteenth-century buildings, including the chapter house, the four-aisle novitiate, the two-story latrine (beneath which a brook was led as a sewer), and the tithe barn.

(Visitors should apply at the bookshop of the Centre Commercial, St. Ouen.)

Prémontré

(illus. 154, page 384)

In a small valley nestled in the forests of St. Gobain, west of Laon, St. Norbert founded the reform order and the monastery of Prémontré in 1120. Only traces of the medieval complex have survived; in the eighteenth century, starting in 1720, Abbot Lucas de Marin had the old buildings replaced by a new, palacelike structure. This was completed in 1757 by his successor, Abbot Bruno de Becourt. The architect may have been Franque, who also built the abbot's palace at Villers-Cotterêts. Prémontré is one of the most important examples of eighteenth-century French monastic architecture, a highly interesting style. It resembles a princely residence. It has a massive *corps de logis,* from whose center a semicircular portal with a triangular pediment projects forward. (The side sections of the *corps de logis* were reduced to two stories in the nineteenth century.) Two freestanding structures of the same height lie perpendicular to the *corps de logis,* one on either side of it. These have narrower portals, but their pediments are also triangular. All three buildings have uncommonly narrow bays defined by Colossal Ionic pilasters that span their three stories. The courtyard is protected by a fence of lovely pillars ornamented with urns. This imposing and expertly restored complex is now a psychiatric hospital.

Provins

(illus. 123 and 124, pages 332 and 333)

The picturesque little country town of Provins owes its historic importance to the counts of Champagne, who took over the area from the Crown in the tenth century and governed it until the end of the thirteenth century. In Provins, they founded one of the largest markets of the Middle Ages; it attracted merchants and craftspeople from all of Europe, and the town expanded until it was, for a time, the third largest in France. At one point, it belonged to Edmund, duke of Lancaster, who introduced the cultivation of the red rose here and incorporated

Provins, St. Quiriace: choir bay.

it into his coat of arms when he married the widow of Henri, Comte de Champagne. Provins reverted to the Crown in 1296, upon Lancaster's death. Social tensions had already weakened the position of the market, and increasing centralization of the government in Paris and the Hundred Years' War hastened the town's economic collapse.

No city in the Ile de France except Senlis has preserved its medieval character as well as Provins. It is composed of two clearly different sections: the Ville Basse, the ancient mercantile town; and the Vieille Ville, on a ridge that is still almost entirely surrounded by a most impressive city wall (illus. 124) from the twelfth and thirteenth centuries. The best-preserved section of the wall stands between the Porte de Jouy and the Porte St-Jean; near the latter is the so-called Brèche des Anglais, through which the English invaded Provins in 1432 during the Hundred Years' War. Dominating the Vieille Ville are the remains of the old castle of the counts of Champagne. These include the town's foremost landmark, the so-called Tour de César. This is a twelfth-century donjon that is square at its base and octagonal above; it also contains a circular "collar" that was added by the English during their occupation of Provins as a platform for their cannon. Also dating from the twelfth century is the nearby Grange aux Dîmes (illus. 123). Originally it was doubtless a part of the fortified complex, but since 1445, it has been the tithe barn of the canons of St. Quiriace; it boasts a broad three-aisle hall and a Gothic façade.

To the east of the castle is the former collegiate church of St. Quiriace. Begun in 1160, it preserves a remarkable Early Gothic choir with a squared end, an ambulatory and rectangular chapels, and a triforium that continues into the transept. Only two bays of the nave were completed. In the choir,

one can see the eight-part vaulting that is characteristic of this portion of the Brie. The church has been repeatedly redesigned. The most recent modernization occurred after a fire in the seventeenth century, when the church was given a Baroque crossing cupola.

The Hôtel-Dieu, which leads to the Ville Basse, is the former palace of the countesses of Champagne. It has a huge subterranean hall, dating from 1160, and a lovely thirteenth-century portal that was heavily restored in the nineteenth century.

All the churches in the Ville Basse date to the twelfth century, but they were all altered in later centuries and now present anything but a uniform appearance. Most notable is the portal of St. Ayoul, with column statues (heavily damaged) closely related to those on the portal of St. Loup-de-Naud, not far from the town. Both the Ville Basse and the Vieille Ville have a wealth of medieval secular architecture; a Romanesque house in the Rue du Palais contains an archeological museum.

Some five miles north of Provins is the priory church of Voulton, built in three phases in the late twelfth and early thirteenth centuries. Its exterior reveals a crystalline style and a Cistercian severity; its proximity to Burgundy is readily apparent. As at St. Quiriace, in the Vieille Ville of Provins, the choir has eight-part vaulting. Its details are otherwise quite traditional, with massive pillars and uncommonly high vaults.

(The buildings in Provins are open 10:00 A.M.–12:00 M. and 2:00 P.M.–5:00 P.M., between April and September; in winter, 2:00 P.M.–4:00 P.M.)

Rambouillet

The château of Rambouillet, halfway between Paris and Chartres, is an irregular, gray stucco building, whose oldest portion

—the great round tower—dates from the fifteenth century. It was rather awkwardly expanded in the sixteenth and again in the eighteenth century. Although it is of slight interest to the art historian, it is rich with historical associations. It was here that François I died while hunting with the captain of his bodyguard, Jacques d'Angennes, whose family had owned the palace for centuries. Louis XIV bought the property for his illegitimate son the Comte de Toulouse, who renovated it and began to lay out its park in 1706. Louis XVI acquired it in 1783 because of its situation in the middle of an extensive hunting reserve. Near the park, he built a farm for breeding Merino sheep that he had obtained in Spain. For Marie-Antoinette, he commissioned Charles Thévenin to construct a "dairy" in 1785; it is a circular temple with an adjacent grotto. Napoleon had the château refurbished to suit his own tastes and had the governor's house, at the boundary between the town and the park, rebuilt as a palace for his son, the king of Rome. In 1814, Marie-Louise left Rambouillet to return to Vienna after a meeting with her father, Emperor Francis I. It was here that Charles X signed his abdication in 1830. Since 1897, the château has served as the summer residence of the president of France.

(When the president is not in residence, tours daily, except Tuesday, 10:00 A.M.– 12:00 M. and 2:00 P.M.–6:00 P.M.)

Rampillon

(illus. 120, page 330)

The simple, three-aisle church of St. Eliphe in Rampillon was part of a colony of Knights Templar. The nave is paved with the gravestones of members of the order and of Knights of Malta. It is most notable for its two portals, which were probably executed at about the same time as the Sainte-Chapelle in Paris, between 1240 and 1250.

The tympanum of the west portal shows Christ as World Judge between angels with the implements of the Passion. The sides portray the intercessors; the lintel, the resurrection of the Last Judgment with angels blowing trumpets, the weighing of souls, and Abraham's bosom. In niches on the jambs are the apostles; the figure on the trumeau pillar is not identified. In the blind arcades of the foundation area, there are charming reliefs of the months as well as of the Presentation in the Temple and the Adoration of the Magi.

The tympanum of the small south portal depicts the coronation of Mary with Christ blessing the praying Virgin, and accompanied by angels. Stylistically, the work closely resembles the sculpture at the Sainte-Chapelle in Paris.

Raray

(illus. 140, page 377)

The château of Raray, the setting of Jean Cocteau's film *Beauty and the Beast*, is less remarkable for its main building—a palace in the Louis XIII style to which an attic story was added in the eighteenth century—than for its courtyard. Two rows of arcades, in alternating round arches and niches containing busts of Roman emperors, extend out from the main building. Above these are sculpted hunting scenes—on the right, deer hunting; on the left, boar hunting— along with a wealth of imaginative though naïve sculptures.

The château and park were constructed in about 1610 under Nicolas de Lancy. His wife, Lucrezia de Landusi, the daughter of an Italian banker, may have brought with her a taste for Mannerist gardens with heathen gods and allegorical allusions. Although the layout of the park goes back to plans by André Le Nôtre, it contains, for example, the Porte de Diane, with most unusual hermaphrodites. And the nearby Parc d'Ognon has a completely Italian complex consisting of pool, statues, sculptures, and pavilions.

(Not open to visitors)

La Roche-Guyon

In the tenth century, the castle of La Roche-Guyon became a border fortress between the Vexin and the duchy of Normandy. High on a cliff above the Seine, the ruins of its donjon, renovated in the twelfth century, still stand. Below it, and partially built into the steep chalk cliff, is the residential building, which was built from the twelfth to the eighteenth centuries. Carefully restored after damage during World War II, when La Roche-Guyon was Rommel's headquarters, the château offers a picturesque conglomeration of elements from medieval feudal architecture (the machicolated towers), the early Renaissance, and the Louis XV style (an elegant portal that faces the courtyard). The stables also date from the early eighteenth century. Simpler than the Grandes Écuries at Chantilly, their large halls are an attractive setting for exhibitions and cultural events. Since the seventeenth century, La Roche-Guyon has belonged to the La Rochefoucauld family; the seventeenth-century thinker François La Rochefoucauld wrote some of his works here.

Rosny

(illus. 144, page 379)

The château of Rosny, seriously cramped by the expanding industrial and residential sections of Mantes, is the very model of a noble house in the Louis XIII style. It was constructed in 1595—before Louis XIII came to the throne—by Maximilien de Béthune, a strict Protestant and champion of Henri IV. He replaced the old Béthune family seat with a princely residence, even before the king made him his minister and named him the Duc de Sully. Louis Métezeau has, without proof, been credited with the design of the château.

Sully here created the prototypal elegant French country house: a *corps de logis* with corner pavilions that are emphasized by their separate roofs and their slight projection from the line of the main structure. He used the typical materials of the Louis XIII style—brick, stone, and slate—which already had made their appearance in Paris under Henri IV (Place Dauphine, Place des Vosges, Palais Abbatial of St. Germain-des-Prés). Facing the courtyard and forming a *cour d'honneur* are two lower wings. Sully stopped construction on these in 1610 as a sign of mourning for the death of Henri IV.

Sully himself laid out a large park with avenues of elms (some date back to his time) and extensive plantings of mulberry trees.

The property remained unchanged until the nineteenth century. In 1818, the Duchesse de Berry had the wings of the château completed in accordance with the original plans. By 1840, they had to be torn down because of poor workmanship. She also constructed a flat-roofed, one-story structure in front of the *corps de logis*, facing the courtyard. The duchess furnished a number of the rooms, notably her own boudoir and the grand salon, in the Charles X style. But thanks to careful restoration, Rosny today presents a fine picture of a princely residence from the time of Henri IV, not only in its exterior but also in some of its largely authentic rooms: the Salon Henri IV, the vestibule, and especially the Chambre de Sully on the second floor.

(Open daily, 2:00 P.M.–6:00 P.M., between July 20 and August 30)

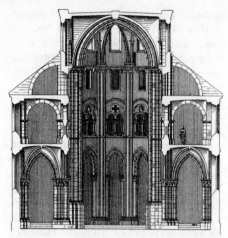

St. Germer-de-Fly (cross-section with choir).

St. Germer-de-Fly

(illus. 122, page 332)

St. Germer-de-Fly is one of the most important examples in the Ile de France of the transition from the Romanesque to the Early Gothic. The abbey was founded by St. Germer in 650. Beginning in 1150, its church was rebuilt in imposing dimensions (206 feet long, 95 feet wide, 62 feet high in the nave). It includes a transept and an impressive choir with galleries, triforium, and radial chapels. A walkway surrounds the whole interior at the level of the clerestory windows. The central chapel has been replaced by a vaulted corridor, some 30 feet long, that leads to the so-called Sainte-Chapelle. This was a donation of Abbot Pierre de Vessencourt in 1160 (completed in 1167) and is a direct imitation of the Sainte-Chapelle in Paris, although without a lower chapel and smaller in size. In the chapel's west façade, there is a lovely rose window with sixteen rays, and two of the choir windows still preserve their thirteenth-century glass. The façade of the abbey church was destroyed during the Hundred Years' War and was not rebuilt until 1640. The bell tower above the crossing was constructed in 1754.

The church contains a number of important furnishings: a choir grille from the thirteenth century, an interment grouping of eight figures in the south transept, and a twelfth-century Romanesque altar in one of the choir chapels.

St. Leu-d'Esserent

(illus. 90, page 292)

Built on a steep slope high above the Oise, the church of St. Leu-d'Esserent is astonishingly large (251 feet long, 68 feet wide, 88 feet high). Its size is explained by the importance of the Cluniac priory to which it belonged. Portions of the house, including two wings of the cloister, survive on the

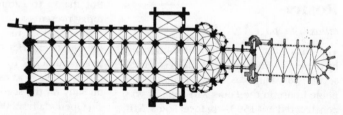

St. Germer-de-Fly (ground plan).

north side of the church. Construction began in the early twelfth century with the narthex, tower, and tribune on the west side. However, the church owes its fame to the choir from the late twelfth century, with five radial chapels and galleries (reduced to a triforium in the thirteenth century, when a system of exterior buttresses was built) that follow the example of the cathedral at Noyon. The first bay in front of the choir, with six-part vaulting, also dates from the twelfth century. The remaining six bays of the nave—the church has no transept —were erected in about 1225. After the heavy bombardments of 1944, the church was very thoroughly restored.

St. Loup-de-Naud

(illus. 85 and 86, page 290)

St. Loup-de-Naud is one of the oldest surviving churches in the Ile de France. It was originally part of a Benedictine priory and was rebuilt in the eleventh century. The choir, parts of the crossing, and the adjacent nave date from this first phase of building. The western bays and the entrance portal were constructed toward the middle of the twelfth century, thanks to a donation from Henri le Libéral, Comte de Champagne. The Porte du Jugement (illus. 85), directly influenced by the Portail Royal at Chartres, is extremely important. Christ is portrayed in the tympanum between the symbols of the Evangelists, and the series of the apostles is shown in the arcades of the lintel. In the archivolts are scenes from the life of St. Loup (or St. Leu, archbishop of Sens, died 623). The saint himself appears on the central pillar amid a sequence of jamb figures (illus. 86) that displays more movement and animation than the more severe figures at Chartres.

St. Martin-aux-Bois

The former priory church of St. Martin-aux-Bois, whose lantern, Henri IV claimed, was the most beautiful in France, goes beyond even Beauvais Cathedral in its dissolution of walls into windows. The choir is a unique conservatory, with seven window walls rising from nearly floor level to the vaulting, an extraordinary 85 feet above. In relation to its height, the church is surprisingly short (101 feet), which has led to the supposition that the existing structure, built in the thirteenth century, represents only a portion of a more extensive building project.

St. Sulpice-de-Favières

This small village in the valley of the Renarde owes its lavish church to St. Sulpice, court chaplain to the Merovingian kings and bishop of Bourges at his death in 647; according to legend, he brought a drowned child back to life at this spot. Relics of the saint are preserved in the Chapelle des Miracles, the remains of a twelfth-century church. A new church, with a nave and side aisles but no transept, was begun in 1260. A fire in the seventeenth century destroyed the vaulting in the first three bays of the nave. The walls of the side aisles are lined with blind arcades, but they do not continue into an ambulatory. The lofty choir, erected in the fourteenth century, is one of the most important examples of the Rayonnant style in the Ile de France. Above low blind arcades at the base of the walls, the glass walls of the richly ornamented windows rise upward in three stories. Fourteenth-century glass panes depicting the Passion and the life of St. Sulpice have survived above the high altar. Choir stools from the beginning of the sixteenth century incorporate humorous carvings on the misericords and backs of the twenty-two seats.

Villarceaux

Built by Jean Courtonne in 1737, Villarceaux is one of the stateliest *maisons de plaisance* in the Ile de France. A quiet elegance is produced by its regular arrangement of bays, its slightly projecting central portal with a triangular pediment, and its flat side façades. In the large park, there are portions of an older Renaissance house.

(Not open to visitors)

Villette

The château of Villette was constructed by an unknown local architect in 1667 for the French ambassador to Venice, Dyel, and its interiors were rebuilt in 1696 according to plans by Jules Hardouin-Mansart. It is an early example of a *maison de plaisance*, with an oval vestibule and an octagonal salon projecting out toward the garden as a three-sided central pavilion. This form, although highly successful in the eighteenth century, was quite uncommon when Villette was built.

At the end of the geometric French park, there is a smaller, 1704 version of the Grande Cascade at Marly. In 1786, the Marquis de Condorcet married into the Grouduy family, which owned Villette, and took up residence in the château. This Enlightenment philosopher carried out his scientific investigations here until, under threat of execution, he took his own life in 1794.

Wideville

Claude de Bullion, the finance minister under Louis XIII, had this château built beginning in 1632. It is one of the most richly ornamented of the generally severe buildings of that period. Its architect is thought to have been either Jacques Lemercier or Louis Le Vau the Elder, the father of the royal architect of Versailles. In layout, the brick and stone structure is reminiscent of Balleroy, a château by François Mansart in Normandy. A loggia, a portal, and dormer windows give the quite regular building and its square pavilions a festive air. Portions of the original interior fittings have survived. At the end of the garden is a grotto from 1636, one of the few that remain from the period in France. Its façade is quite Italianate and Baroque, resembling the somewhat earlier Fontaine Médicis in the Jardin du Luxembourg in Paris. Inside, there is a room with three niches, originally planned to hold urns and statues, all decorated with the small stones and shells (*rocaille*) whose effect as interior decoration in grottoes led to the Rococo style, with its shell-like motifs. The vaulted ceiling contains a poorly preserved fresco by Simon Vouet, *Apollo in the Circle of the Muses and Jupiter with Antiope*. The entrance to the château is closed off by a lovely wrought-iron grille executed by François Marchand.

CHRONOLOGY

Third century B.C.	First settlement of the Parisii on the Ile de la Cité.
A.D. 52	Caesar's conquest of Gaul; the destruction of the Celtic settlement on the Ile de la Cité.
First century A.D.	Emergence of the Gallo-Roman city of Lutetia.
c. 250	Missionary work in the Ile de France by St. Dionysius (St. Denis), the first bishop of Paris, who was martyred on Montmartre.
280	Destruction of Lutetia by Germanic tribes.
360	Julian the Apostate, prefect in Gaul, proclaimed emperor; Lutetia takes the name Paris.
451	St. Genovefa (Ste. Geneviève) saves Paris from Attila's troops.
486	Clovis defeats the Roman army under Syagrius near Soissons and founds the kingdom of Francia.
508	Paris becomes the residence of the Frankish kings.
754	Pope Stephen II anoints Pepin le Bref as king in St. Denis.
888	Eudes, Comte de Paris, elected king of France.
911	The Treaty of St. Clair-sur-Epte ends Norman invasions in the Ile de France.
987	Hugues Capet, Duc de Francia, chosen king of France, in Senlis.
1108–1137	Louis VI le Gros subjugates the vassals to the Crown domains.
1124	Louis VI le Gros takes up the oriflamme at St. Denis for his campaign against the German emperor, Henry V.
1136	Abbot Suger begins construction of the new St. Denis.
1163	Bishop Maurice de Sully begins construction of the new Notre-Dame in Paris.
1180–1223	Philippe Auguste surrounds Paris with a fortified wall that includes the Louvre; he annexes the counties of Valois, Meulan, and Clermont. He is decisively victorious over the English near Bouvines in 1214.
1215	Founding of the University of Paris.
1229	Louis IX (St. Louis) wins the Languedoc in the Treaty of Paris, ending the Albigensian Wars.
1254	Construction of the Sainte-Chapelle begins in Paris.
1260	Paris's first *prévôt* is named.
1307	Philippe IV le Bel orders the arrest and dispossession of the Knights Templar at Maubuisson.
1339–1453	The Hundred Years' War with England.
1358	Revolt of Étienne Marcel in Paris; revolt of the peasants (Jacquerie).
1364–1380	Charles V erects another city wall and the Bastille.
1407	The murder of Louis d'Orléans on orders from the Duc de Bourgogne, Jean sans Peur, leads to

1408–1420	Civil war between the Armagnacs and the Bourgignons.
1413	Revolt of the Paris guilds under Simon Caboche.
1419	Murder of the Duc de Bourgogne, Jean sans Peur, in Montereau.
1429	Siege of Paris by Joan of Arc and Charles VII.
1430	Joan of Arc taken prisoner in Compiègne. Henry VI of England crowned king of France at Notre-Dame.
1441	With the liberation of Pontoise, English rule ends in the Ile de France. Charles VII has been in Paris since 1437.
1465	Battle of Montlhéry between Louis XI and Charles le Hardi, Duc de Bourgogne, who
1472	Besieges Beauvais in vain.
1528	Under François I, Paris once more becomes the royal residence.
1530	François I founds the Collège de France.
1533	Ordonnance de Villers-Cotterêts.
1534	Ignatius of Loyola founds the Jesuit order on Montmartre.
1559	Death of Henri II in a tournament in the Marais.
1572	Catherine de Médicis has the Huguenots slaughtered on St. Bartholomew's Day.
1589	Henri III murdered in St. Cloud.
1593	Henri IV converts to Catholicism; he enters Paris a year later.
1610	Henri IV murdered by François Ravaillac.
1622	Paris becomes an archbishopric.
1635	Cardinal Richelieu founds the Académie Française.
1648–1653	Revolt of the Fronde against Cardinal Mazarin.
1661	Mazarin endows the Collège des Quatre-Nations (Institut de France). Louis XIV orders the arrest of Nicolas Fouquet, and plans the expansion of Versailles.
1667	Colbert founds the Académie des Sciences and the Gobelins factory.
1682	Versailles becomes the seat of government.
1685	Revocation of the Edict of Nantes.
1709	Dissolution of Port-Royal, the center of Jansenism.
1715–1723	Temporary transfer of the court to Paris during the Regency.
1717–1720	Financial speculation of John Law.
1762	Jesuit order forbidden.
1763	France loses its North American colony in Canada. Attempts at reform by Anne Robert Turgot and Jacques Necker.
1789, May 5	Estates General meets in Versailles.
1789, June 17	The Third Estate forms the National Assembly.
1789, July 14	Storming of the Bastille.
1792, September 21	Proclamation of the Republic.
1793, January 21	Louis XVI beheaded.
1793–1794	The Reign of Terror.
1795–1799	The Directory.
1799–1804	Napoleon Bonaparte is First Consul.

1804, December 2	Napoleon crowned emperor.
1814, March 31	Allied occupation of Paris.
1815, June 18	Battle of Waterloo.
1815–1830	Restoration.
1830, July 26	July Monarchy proclaimed.
1832	Cholera epidemic in Paris.
1837	First railway in France, between Paris and St. Germain-en-Laye.
1840	Return of Napoleon's remains to Paris.
1841	Adolphe Thiers's ring of fortifications around Paris begun.
1848, February 22	February Revolution; Second Republic.
1851, December 2	Coup by Louis Napoleon Bonaparte.
1870, September 4	Proclamation of the Third Republic. Paris besieged by the Germans.
1871, March–May	The Commune uprising in Paris.
1905	Separation of church and state.
1914, September	Battle of the Marne.
1918, November 11	Armistice signed in the Forêt de Compiègne ends World War I.
1919, January 18	Peace Conference in Versailles.
1940–1944	Paris occupied by German troops.
1944, August	Liberation of Paris by the Allies.

RULERS OF FRANCE

Merovingians, including

481–511	Clovis, king of the Franks
561–584	Chilperic
595–613	Thierry
622–638	Dagobert

Carolingians

751–768	Pepin le Bref (the Short)
768–814	Charlemagne
814–840	Louis I le Débonnaire (the Pious)
840–877	Charles le Chauve (the Bald)
877–879	Louis II le Bègue (the Stammerer)
879–882	Louis III, and Carloman
882–884	Carloman
884–887	Charles le Gros (the Fat)
888–898	Eudes, Comte de Paris, from

what would become the House of Capet, chosen king of France. After his death, the Carolingians once again took control, but they remained in conflict with the rising Capetian dynasty, to which they finally succumbed in 987.

898–922	Charles le Simple
922–923	Robert I (Capet)
923–936	Raoul (Capet)
936–954	Louis IV d'Outremer
954–986	Lothaire
986–987	Louis V

Capetians

987–996	Hugues Capet

996–1031	Robert II le Pieux (the Pious)
1031–1060	Henri I
1060–1108	Philippe I
1108–1137	Louis VI le Gros
1137–1180	Louis VII
1180–1223	Philippe Auguste
1223–1226	Louis VIII
1226–1270	Louis IX (St. Louis)
1270–1285	Philippe III le Hardi (the Bold)
1285–1314	Philippe IV le Bel (the Fair)
1314–1316	Louis X le Hutin (the Quarreler)
1316	Jean I (died four days old)
1316–1322	Philippe V le Long (the Tall)
1322–1328	Charles IV le Bel

Valois

1328–1350	Philippe VI
1350–1364	Jean II le Bon (the Good)
1364–1380	Charles V le Sage (the Wise)
1380–1422	Charles VI
1422–1461	Charles VII
1461–1483	Louis XI
1483–1498	Charles VIII

Valois-Orléans

1498–1515	Louis XII

Valois-Angoulême

1515–1547	François I
1547–1559	Henri II
1559–1560	François II
1560–1574	Charles IX
1574–1589	Henri III

Bourbons

1589–1610	Henri IV
1610–1643	Louis XIII
1643–1715	Louis XIV, le Roi Soleil
(1715–1723	Regency of Philippe d'Orléans)
1715–1774	Louis XV
1774–1792	Louis XVI

First Republic

1792–1795	The National Convention
1795–1799	The Directory
1799–1804	The Consulate

First Empire

1804–1814	Napoleon

Restoration

Bourbon

1814–1824	Louis XVIII
(1815	Napoleon ["hundred days"])
1824–1830	Charles X

Orléans

1830–1848	Louis-Philippe

Second Republic

1848–1852	Louis Napoleon Bonaparte

Second Empire

1852–1870	Napoleon III

Third Republic

(1871–1940)

Vichy Government

(1940–1944)

Fourth Republic

(1947–1958)

Fifth Republic

(1958–   )

BIBLIOGRAPHY

From the vast literature on Paris, we list only those titles used to develop this text.

Alpatow, Michail W., *Studien zur Geschichte der westeuropäischen Kunst*. Cologne, 1974.

Babelon, Jean-Pierre, *Demeures parisiennes sous Henri IV et Louis XIII*. Paris, 1965.

Beaujeu-Garnier, Jacqueline, *Atlas et géographie de Paris et la région de l'Ile-de-France*. 2 vols., Paris, 1977.

Benevolo, Leonardo, *Geschichte der Architektur des 19. und 20. Jahrhunderts*. 2 vols., Munich, 1978.

Beutler, Christian, *Paris und Versailles* (Reclam's Art Guides, France, Vol. I), 2nd ed. Stuttgart, 1979.

Biver, Marie-Louise, *Le Paris de Napoléon*. Paris, 1963.

Blunt, Anthony, *Art and Architecture in France, 1500–1700* (Pelican History of Art). Harmondsworth, 1970.

—————, *Philibert de l'Orme*. London, 1958.

Borsi, Franco, and Godoli, Enzio, *Paris 1900*. Brussels, 1976.

Bourget, Pierre, and Cattani, Georges, *Jules Hardouin-Mansart*. Paris, 1960.

Braham, Allan, and Smith, Peter, *François Mansart*. 2 vols., London, 1973.

Braunfels, Wolfgang, *Abendländische Stadtbaukunst*. Cologne, 1976.

Champigneulle, Bernard, *Versailles und Fontainebleau*. Munich, 1971.

—————, *Ile-de-France*. Paris, 1967.

—————, *Promenades dans les jardins de Paris, ses bois et ses squares*. Paris, 1965.

Chastel, André, *Paris*. Lucerne, 1976.

Christ, Yvan, *Les metamorphoses de la banlieue parisienne*. Paris, 1969.

Cooper, Rosalys, *Salomon de Brosse*. London, 1972.

Couperie, Pierre, *Paris au fil du temps* (foreword by André Chastel). Paris, 1968.

Delpal, Jacques-Louis, *Paris für Sie*. Bonn, 1975.

Dimier, Louis, *Fontainebleau*. Paris, 1908.

Fichet, François, *La théorie architecturale à l'age classique*. Brussels, n.d.

Fleury, M.; Erlande-Brandenburg, A.; and Babelon, J.-P., *Paris* (photos by Max and Albert Hirmer). Munich, 1974.

Francastel, Pierre (ed.), *L'urbanisme de Paris et l'Europe, 1600–1680*. Paris, 1969.

Gallet, Michel, *Demeures parisiennes l'époque de Louis XVI*. Paris, 1964.

Ganay, Ernest de, *André Le Nostre*. Paris, 1962.

Le Marais (foreword by Pierre Gaxotte). Paris, 1974.

La Cité, l'Ile Saint-Louis, Le Quartier de l'Ancienne Université (foreword by Pierre Gaxotte). Paris, 1972.

Le Faubourg Saint-Germain (foreword by Pierre Gaxotte). Paris, 1966.

Grodecki, Louis, *Architektur der Gotik*. Stuttgart, 1976.

Les Guides Bleus
  Bernard-Folliot, Denise (ed.):
    Paris
    Hauts de Seine
    Seine–Saint-Denis
    Val de Marne (all Paris, 1979)
  Vibert-Guigne, Françoise (ed.), *Ile de France*. Paris, 1976.

Guide Vert (Michelin)
  Environs de Paris. 18th ed., Paris, 1976.
  Paris et sa banlieue. 2nd ed., Paris, 1976.

Hansmann, Wilfried, *Baukunst des Barock*. Cologne, 1978.

Hautecoeur, Louis, *Paris*. I: *Des Origines à 1715*; II: *De 1715 à nos jours*. Paris, 1972.

—————, *Les jardins des Dieux et des Hommes*. Paris, 1959.

Hennig-Schefold, Monica, and Schmidt-Thomsen, Helga, *Transparenz und Masse, Passagen und Hallen aus Eisen und Glas, 1800–1880*. Cologne, 1972.

Hillairet, Jacques, *Dictionnaire historique des rues de Paris*. 2 vols., Paris, 1963.

Hoffbauer, Théodor J. H., *Paris à travers les ages*. 2 vols. (reprint), Paris, 1972.

Kaufmann, Emil, *Architecture in the Age of Reason*. New York, 1968 (1955).

Kjellberg, Pierre, *Le guide des Eglises de Paris*. Paris, 1970.

—————, *Le guide du Marais*. Paris, 1967.

Lameyre, Gérard-Noël, *Haussmann: "Préfet de Paris"*. Paris, 1958.

Marie, Alfred, *Jardins Français, Créés à la Renaissance*. Paris, 1955.

Marie, Alfred and Jeanne, *Versailles–son Histoire*. I: *Naissance de Versailles*, 1968; II: *Mansart à Versailles* (2 vols.). Paris, 1972.

Mollat, Michel (ed.), *Histoire de l'Ile-de-France et de Paris*. Toulouse, 1971.

Morand, Paul, *Paris*. 2nd ed., Lucerne, 1975.

Nouvelle Histoire de Paris:

Boussard, Jacques, *De la fin du siège de 885–886 à la mort de Philippe Auguste*, 1976.

Cazelles, Raymond, *De la fin du règne de Philippe Auguste à la mort de Charles V, 1223–1380*, 1972

Favier, Jean, *Paris au XVe siècle*, 1974

Lavedan, Pierre, *Histoire de l'urbanisme à Paris*, 1975

Reinhard, Marcel, *La Révolution*, 1971

Tulard, Jean, *Le Consulat et l'Empire*, 1970

Pillement, Georges, *Paris poubelle*. Paris, 1974.

——————, *Les environs de Paris disparus*. Paris, 1968.

——————, *Les Hôtels des Boulevards à Charonne*. Paris, 1953.

Poisson, Georges, *Schlösser der Ile-de-France*. Munich, 1968.

Pons, Alain, *2000 ans de Paris*. Paris, 1975.

Coll. Réalités Hachette: *Merveilles des châteaux de l'Ile-de-France* (foreword by Wladimir d'Ormesson). Paris, 1963.

Röver, Anne, *Bienséance. Die ästhetische Situation im Ancien Régime: Pariser Privatarchitektur*. Hildesheim and New York, 1977.

Sacy, Jacques de, *Le quartier des Halles*. Paris, 1969.

Sagave, Pierre-Paul, *1871, Berlin–Paris. Reichshauptstadt und Hauptstadt der Welt*. Frankfurt, 1971.

Sauerländer, Willibald, *Gotische Skulptur in Frankreich, 1140–1270*. Munich, 1970.

Schäfke, Werner, *Frankreichs gotische Kathedralen*. Cologne, 1979.

Schein, Ionel, *Paris construit. Guide de l'architecture contemporain*. Paris, 1970.

Schlink, Wilhelm, *Die Kathedralen Frankreichs*. Munich, 1978.

Simson, Otto von, *Die gotische Kathedrale, Beiträge zu ihrer Entstehung und Bedeutung*. Darmstadt, 1972 (1956).

Speckter, Hans, *Paris, Städtebau von der Renaissance bis zur Neuzeit*. Munich, 1964.

Staehelin, Walter, and Rast, Josef, *Paris*. Olten, 1973.

Stahl, Fritz, *Eine Stadt als Kunstwerk*. Vienna and Munich, 1927; new ed., 1966.

Sutcliffe, Anthony, *The Autumn of Central Paris. The Defeat of Town Planning, 1850–1970*. London, 1970.

Swoboda, Karl M., *Geschichte der bildenden Kunst*. Vol. II: *Die Gotik von 1150 bis 1300*. Vienna and Munich, 1977.

Thibout, Marc, *Eglises Gothiques en France*. Paris, n.d.

Van der Kemp, Gérald, *Versailles*. Stuttgart, 1979.

Wittkop, Gabrielle, and Franz, Justus, *Paris. Prisma einer Stadt. Eine illustrierte Kulturgeschichte*. Zurich, 1978.

ILLUSTRATION CREDITS

Black-and-white photographs

Archives photographiques, Paris   96
Arthaud, Paris   130, 134
Manfred Becker, Bocholt   47, 64
Klaus Bussman   86, 95, 120, 133, 135, 136, 142, 144, 147, 154
Foto Marburg   88
Max and Albert Hirmer, Munich   3, 10, 11, 109, 110
Michael Jeiter, Aachen   102, 106, 114, 115, 124, 128, 129, 138, 139, 150, 151
Werner Neumeister, Munich   4, 103
Léo Pélissier, L'Hay-les-Roses   2, 28, 33, 40, 42, 43, 59, 123
Photo L. Sully Jaulmes, Paris   72, 76–78
H. Roger-Viollet, Paris   6, 8, 12, 14, 15, 17, 19–25, 29–32, 37, 41, 44, 46, 51, 52, 60, 68, 69, 73–75, 79, 80, 83, 85, 90, 91, 97, 104, 105, 108, 112, 116, 117, 119, 121, 126, 132, 137, 141, 143, 146
Jean Roubier, Paris   7, 9, 13, 16, 18, 26, 27, 34, 45, 48, 49, 84, 87, 89, 92–94, 98–101, 107, 111, 113, 118, 122, 125, 127, 131, 140, 145, 148, 149, 152, 153
Peter Stähli-Bossert, Gsteigwiler   39
Werner Stuhler, Hergensweiler   1, 5, 35, 36, 57, 58
Manfred Vollmer, Essen   38, 50, 53–56, 61–63, 65–67, 70, 71, 81, 82

Drawings and Plans

Babelon, Jean Pierre: Demeures parisienne, sous Henri IV et Louis XIII, Paris 1965   48, 179
Blunt, Anthony: Art and Architecture in France, 1500 to 1700, Harmondsworth 1970   202, 205, 390
Bourget, Pierre, and Cattani, Georges: Jules Hardouin Mansart, Paris 1956   399, 410
Braunfels, Wolfgang: Abendländische Stadt-baukunst, Cologne 1976   96, 152
Burckhardt, T.: Chartres   343
Crosby, Sumner Mck: L'abbaye royale de Saint-Denis   282
Dehio, G., and Bezold, G. von: Die kirchliche Baukunst des Abendlandes, Atlas Volumes 2 and 4, Stuttgart 1888 and 1894   106, 107, 110, 111, 129-132, 133t., 136, 285, 306, 308, 309, 310, 311, 312, 313, 314, 316, 317, 318, 338, 339, 342, 344, 444, 448
Du Cerceau, Jean Androuet: Les plus excellents Bastiments de France, Paris 1576, Farnborough 1972   140, 350, 353, 363, 365, 366
Les guides bleus
   Bernard-Folliot, Denise (ed.): Paris   287
   Vilbert-Guigne, Françoise (ed.): Ile de France   356, 408
Hansmann, Wilfried: Baukunst des Barock, Cologne 1978   229
Hautecœur, Louis: Paris. I des Origines à 1715. II de 1715 à nos jours, Paris 1972   141, 149, 245, 246, 248, 260
Henning-Schefold, Monica, and Schmidt-Thomsen, Helga: Transparenz und Masse. Passagen und Hallen aus Eisen und Glas 1800–1880, Cologne 1972   88, 95, 272, 273
Hoffbauer, Théodor J. H.: Paris à travers les ages. 2 vols., Reprint Paris 1972   31, 38, 135, 143, 151, 253, 263
Mariette, Jean: L'architecture française. Paris 1727. Reprint 1929 (Westphalian State Monument Office, Muenster)   63, 147, 153, 158, 160, 189t., 199b., 200, 204, 232t., 233, 234, 235, 236, 237, 238, 240
Marot, Jean: Recueil des Plans, Profils et Elevations des plusiers Palais, Châteaux, Eglises, Sepultures, Grotes et Hostels bâtis dans Paris, 1969   184, 189t.
Michelin-Paris, Karlsruhe, and Clermont-Ferrand 1979   28, 89
Ministère des affaires culturelles: Principes d'analyse scientifique, Architecture: Méthode

447

et Vocabulaire, Paris 1972   199, 386

Perelle, Gabriel: Les Delices de Paris et de ses environs ou Recueil de vues perspectives des plus beaux monumens de Paris c. 1680 (Muenster State University Library)   54, 56, 58, 59, 61, 157, 179b., 181, 183, 190–191, 197, 206, 207, 230, 231, 251, 354, 355, 359, 360, 388, 392, 394–395, 413, 416

Roger-Viollet, H.: Paris   36–37, 40–41, 44, 83, 86, 93, 94, 226, 247, 255, 257

Stadtatlas von Braun, 1575   19

Turgot, Prévôt des Marchands: Perspective Plan of the City of Paris, executed by Louis Bretez, 1734–39   49, 51, 52, 138, 155, 156, 178, 198, 205b., 227, 232

Van der Kemp, G.: Versailles, Stuttgart 1979   401

Wittkop, Gabrielle, and Franz, Justus: Paris, Prisma einer Stadt. Eine illustrierte Kulturgeschichte, Zurich 1978   108–109, 133t., 146, 149b., 180, 187, 253t., 259

PRACTICAL
TRAVEL
SUGGESTIONS

This section of the book offers American, Canadian, and British vacationers a brief overview of all major aspects of traveling in France. In addition to presenting general information about the country, it contains tips about getting to France and getting around in France, about important documents and regulations, and about sources of more detailed information. It also covers local weather, accommodations, entertainment, the addresses and hours of local museums, regional gastronomic specialties, festivals, and so on. Much of this information —addresses and telephone numbers, for example—is notoriously impermanent, so visitors should always try to check local listings upon arrival. Because sudden price changes in France and fluctuations in international exchange rates are inevitable, this guide does not include French prices or their equivalents in dollars or pounds; readers are advised to consult the most up-to-date sources available for such data.

Introduction to France

GETTING TO FRANCE

Air France, Pan Am, TWA, Air Canada, and other airlines provide direct service from the United States and Canada to France. Check with a travel agent for details on schedules, fares, and points of departure and arrival.

People planning to travel to France from the British Isles have many options. Many airlines—British Airways and Air France are only two—connect major cities in both countries. Aer Lingus offers service from Dublin and Cork to Paris and Lourdes.

It is also possible to travel by rail from Britain to France. Most of these services connect with cross-Channel ferries, but through railway carriages between London and Paris also operate overnight. Reservations are advisable, particularly in summer. Contact British Rail or a travel agent for particulars.

Several coach (bus) services offer transportation between major cities throughout Britain and France. Contact a travel agent for details.

Visitors who want to drive to France can use one of many car ferries that connect England and Ireland with France. Reservations on the Sealink services (Dover to Boulogne or Calais, Folkestone to Boulogne or Calais, Newhaven to Dieppe, and Weymouth to Cherbourg) may be made through British Rail (see pages 460–461), but other companies offer car ferries on other routes. The Hovercraft, which crosses the English Channel from Dover to Calais or Boulogne in 30 to 40 minutes, also accommodates cars. There are no customs restrictions on bringing a car into France, assuming one enters as a tourist and for under six months.

GETTING AROUND IN FRANCE

By Air

Air Inter is France's domestic airline, serving thirty major business and holiday centers throughout the country, including Paris (Orly and Charles-de-Gaulle airports), Nice, Marseille, Toulouse, Lyon, Strasbourg, Montpellier, and Nantes. Its central information and reservations number (in Paris) is 1/539-25-25. Information about Air Inter is also available from Air France offices in the United States, Canada, and the United Kingdom. Other domestic airlines include Touraine Air Transport, Air Littoral (serving the South of France, Spain, and Italy), and Compagnie Aérienne du Languedoc. Air France flies key domestic routes as well.

By Rail

The French National Railroads, or SNCF

450

(Société Nationale des Chemins de Fer Français), offers perhaps the best way to see France. SNCF is a dense network of railways connecting major cities and small towns; it has gained an enviable reputation for speed, safety, punctuality, and passenger comfort. The newest star in this system is the TGV (*train à grande vitesse*, which means simply, "high-speed train"), a train that runs between Paris and Lyon at more than 130 miles per hour and cuts travel time to a mere 2 hours—thereby placing relatively distant parts of France within day-trip distance of the capital.

On most long-distance night trains, a traveler can book either a sleeper or a *couchette* berth in either first or second class. For information about routes, reservations, and up-to-date fares, contact SNCF (in France) or French National Railroads (in the United States, the United Kingdom, and Canada). See page 460 for a listing of French National Railroads offices in these countries.

Passengers must validate their rail tickets (except those bought outside France), using the orange stamping machine, before boarding the train. Failure to do so results in an additional fee.

Americans and Canadians can take advantage of three special packages offered by French National Railroads. The Eurailpass entitles the bearer to unlimited first-class rail travel in sixteen Western European countries, including France, for 15 days, 21 days, or 1, 2, or 3 months. The Eurail Youthpass guarantees unlimited second-class rail travel in these same countries for either 1 or 2 months to anyone under 26 years old. The Frances Vacances pass is issued for 7 days, 15 days, or 1 month of first- or second-class travel. This ticket entitles the holder not only to unlimited travel on all SNCF trains (including the TGV) during the period of validity, but also to:

2, 4, or 7 days of unlimited travel on the Paris Métro, RER, and bus system

a free round-trip rail journey to Paris from Charles-de-Gaulle or Orly airport

a free admission to the Centre National d'Art et de Culture Georges-Pompidou (Centre Beaubourg)

a free one-way trip on the privately owned scenic railroad Chemin de Fer de Provence, which runs between Nice and Digne

a 10 percent discount on SNCF bus excursions

a discount on car rentals through the Budget Train + Auto service

All three passes must be purchased at one of the French National Railroads offices in the United States or Canada; see page 460 for a listing of these addresses.

British travelers should consult a travel agent or the local British Rail booking office for comprehensive packages available to them in France.

By Car

France has about 930,000 miles of roads. This extensive network includes the *autoroutes* (motorways or superhighways, with an A prefix), the *routes nationales* (major national roads, with an N prefix), and the *routes départementales* (relatively minor roads, with a D prefix). The entire system is kept in excellent condition.

In France, as in the United States, Canada, and continental Europe, driving is done on the right-hand side of the road. Foreign visitors may drive in France if they have a valid driver's license from their home country (an international license is not required), valid passport or other identity papers, and an international green insurance card. Insurance is compulsory in France for all overland motor vehicles, including those driven by visitors from abroad. On arrival, if a motorist cannot present an international green insurance card, he or she must take out a temporary *assurance frontière* policy at customs. This policy may be issued for 8, 15, 30 days; it cannot be renewed. Visitors staying longer than 30 days must either contact their insurer at home for a green card or take out a temporary policy with a French firm.

Vehicles used in France are required to have safety belts for the driver and the front-seat passenger, an external driving mirror, spare headlight bulbs, and rear warning lights or a phosphorescent warning signal (triangle) in case of breakdown. Yellow headlights are compulsory on French cars, and dazzling headlights are prohibited. The horn may be used only when absolutely necessary; in Paris and certain other cities, its use is expressly forbidden except in case of imminent danger. Children under 10 years old are not allowed to ride in the front seat of a vehicle.

If an emergency car repair is needed, a motorist can call Touring Secours (telephone 1/531-05-05), set up under the auspices of the Touring Club de France. Towing and emergency repairs are free to drivers who have joined Touring Secours. For further information about Touring Secours or driving in France in general, contact the Touring Club de France, 6-8 Rue Firmin-Gillot, 75737 Paris Cedex 15; telephone 1/532-22-15. The Royal Automobile Club of Great Britain (French headquarters at 8 Place Vendôme, Paris, Ier; telephone 1/260-62-12) is a source of additional information.

In case of accident, the drivers of both cars should find a police officer, who will fill out a report, or *constat*, that can be submitted to insurance companies. If the accident is serious, photographs should be taken, if possible. If the accident involves only one's own car, the report may be filled out by an official (*huissier*) in the nearest community. The Bureau Central Français des Sociétés Assurances contre les Accidents d'Automobiles (118 Rue de Tocqueville, 75017 Paris; telephone 1/766-52-64) should also be notified immediately.

Gasoline (petrol) is sold by the liter. An American gallon is equivalent to 3.78 liters; an imperial gallon, 4.54 liters. Distances are measured in kilometers (1 km = about .62 mile; 1 mile = about 1.61 km).

Speed limits are generally 130 kph (80 mph) on toll *autoroutes*, 110 kph (68 mph) on free *autoroutes* and other major roads, 90 kph (56 mph) on lesser roads, and 60 kph (37 mph) in developed zones. The *autoroutes* have parking and rest areas every 6 to 10 miles and emergency telephones every 11¼ miles.

SNCF offers a service, called Motorail, for drivers going toward any of several major cities. Drivers taking advantage of it are entitled to a berth on the same train that their car travels on. Once the destination is reached, retrieving the car can be done quite quickly. Contact French National Railroads (for addresses, see page 460) for more information.

Car Rental. It is quite easy for travelers from abroad to rent a self-drive car in France. The major agencies—Avis, Budget, Citer, Europcar, Hertz, Inter-Rent, and Mattei—have several offices in France. Car-rental arrangements in France can frequently be made through airlines, travel agents, or local car-rental agencies. For further information about firms in France that offer cars for hire, contact a travel agent or CSNCRA (Chambre Syndicale Nationale du Commerce et de la Réparation Automobile), 6 Rue Léonard-de-Vinci, 75016 Paris; telephone 1/502-19-10.

Renters must be a minimum of 21 years old (sometimes 25) and must be able to show that they have held a valid driver's license for at least one year.

For information about hiring a chauffeur-driven car, contact a travel agent or the Chambre Syndicale Nationale des Entreprises de Remise et de Tourisme, 48 Rue de la Bienfaisance, 75008 Paris; telephone 1/562-06-66.

By Coach (Bus)

Long-distance coach services are operated in France by Europabus and other companies. In addition, many local services and sightseeing tours are available; many of these are run by SCETA (Services de Tourisme SNCF-Europabus), 7 Rue Pablo-Neruda, 92532 Levallois-Perret Cedex; telephone 1/270-56-00, ext. 536. Contact SCETA or a travel agent for more details.

By Water

France has a great network of inland waterways—not only famed rivers such as the Seine, the Loire, and the Rhône, but also canals that connect them—and it is possible to rent a boat equipped with living accommodations to explore these byways or to take an organized inland cruise. For further information, you can contact a travel agent or the Syndicat National des Loueurs de Bateaux de Plaisance, Port de la Bourdonnais, 75007 Paris; telephone 1/555-10-49. This organization can also provide information about berthing yachts along France's beautiful Atlantic and Mediterranean coasts and about renting small craft to sail these waters.

By Bicycle

Thousands of miles of bicycle routes throughout France may be explored by energetic travelers. Fixed itineraries are offered by the following organizations:

La Fédération Française de Cyclotourisme
8 Rue Jean-Marie-Jego
75013 Paris
1/580-30-21

Le Bicyclub de France
8 Place de la Porte-Champerret
75017 Paris
1/766-55-92

Loisirs Accueil Loiret
3 Rue de la Bretonnerie
45000 Orléans
38/62-04-88

Loisirs Accueil Loir-et-Cher
11 Place du Château
41000 Blois
54/78-55-50

In addition, the French Government Tourist Offices (see page 459) and local bureaus (*syndicats d'initiative*) provide lists of suggested itineraries. Bicycles may be rented at more than 200 SNCF stations throughout France, and through other outlets as well.

On Foot

France can be crossed on foot on an excellent system of long-distance footpaths and hiking trails. The Fédération Française de la Randonnée Pédestre, Comité National des Sentiers de Grande Randonnée, 8 Avenue Marceau, 75008 Paris, will send out a list of these routes on request.

DOCUMENTS AND REGULATIONS

Passports

Visitors to France from the United States, the United Kingdom, and Canada are required to hold valid passports. No visa is necessary.

Currency

Visitors may bring an unlimited amount of French or foreign currency into France. Visitors who arrive with more than 5,000 francs (or the equivalent sum in other currency) are advised to fill out a special form (declaration of entry of foreign banknotes into France) that customs will provide on request and countersign. Visitors leaving France may not take out more than 5,000 francs (or the equivalent) unless they present this duly certified declaration.

Duty-Free Goods

In addition to personal clothing, jewelry, and effects such as cameras and sports equipment, visitors who are over 17 years old may bring the following goods into France duty-free (see list).

For information, contact the French Government Tourist Office (addresses on page 459) or the French customs office: Bureau IRP, Direction Générale des Douanes, 8 Rue de la Tour-des-Dames, 75436 Paris Cedex 09; telephone 1/280-67-22.

Item	From United Kingdom/ Ireland	From United States/ Canada
Alcoholic beverages:		
Table wines	4 liters (3½ quarts)	2 liters (1¾ quarts)
and either		
Spirits with over 22% alcohol content	1½ liters	1 liter
or		
Spirits with 22% alcohol content or less	3 liters	2 liters
Tobacco:		
Cigarettes	300	400
Cigarillos	150	200
Cigars	75	150
or		
Pipe tobacco	14 ounces (400 grams)	17 ounces (500 grams)
Perfumes and toilet water	2½ ounces (37.5 centiliters)	1¾ ounces (25 centiliters)

Prohibited Goods

Narcotics, goods that constitute copyright infringements, gold (other than personal jewelry), and firearms (other than for hunting or target shooting) are forbidden.

Dogs and Cats

Animals less than 3 months old are not allowed into France. A visitor may bring in up to three animals, only one of which may be a puppy. For each animal that comes from a country that has not recorded a case of rabies for at least three years, a certified veterinafian must complete a certificate of origin and health within five days of the animal's departure from home; the certificate confirms that the animal is in good health, that its country of origin has been free of rabies for at least three years, and that the animal has not left that country since birth or for the six months prior to entering France. Otherwise, owners must show a rabies vaccination certificate for each animal, completed by a veterinarian in the animal's home country, stating that it has been vaccinated more than a month but less than a year before entry into France or that it has been revaccinated within the past year.

Owners of all other animals must apply in advance to the Ministère de l'Agriculture, Bureau de la Règlementation Sanitaire aux Frontières, 44-46 Boulevard de Grenelle, 75732 Paris Cedex 15.

Acquisition of Valuables

Special regulations apply to precious metals, jewelry, artworks, and antiques acquired in France. Visitors who cannot prove that they purchased such items from a standard dealer may, on leaving the country, be required to pay a duty equal to 3 to 4 percent of the item's value.

Staying More Than 3 Months

Visitors who stay in France for more than 3 months must obtain a residence permit from the Service des Étrangers, Prefecture de Police, Place Louis-Lépine, Paris, IV^c; telephone 1/277-11-00 (open daily except Saturday, Sunday, and holidays, 8:30 A.M. to 5:00 P.M.). A visitor who fails to register at this office after 3 months in the country is subject to a heavy fine.

GENERAL INFORMATION

Money

France's unit of currency is the French *franc*, which is divided into 100 *centimes*. Coins exist in the following denominations: 5c, 10c, 20c, ½F (50c), 1F, 2F, 5F, 10F. There are paper notes for denominations of 10F, 20F, 50F, 100F, and 500F.

Major international credit cards—Access, American Express, Diner's Club, MasterCard, Visa—are honored by many establishments throughout France.

Tipping

Station or airport porters. Usually about 5F, depending on the number of bags.

Taxi drivers. 10 to 15 percent of the fare shown on the meter.

Hotel staff. 10F per piece of luggage to the hotel porter; 10F per- day to the chambermaid.

Waiters. In cafés and many restaurants, service is generally included in the bill (*service compris*). If service is not included, tip 15 percent. About 10F should be given to the sommelier.

Coatroom attendants. At least 5F per item; at least 5F for toilet attendants.

Tour guides. About 5F per person in the group.

Public Holidays

By law, France recognizes ten major civil and church holidays, the so-called *jours féries.* These are:

New Year's Day (January 1)

Easter Monday

Ascension Thursday (Sixth Thursday after Easter)

Whit Monday (second Monday after Ascension)

Labor Day (May 1)

Bastille Day (July 14)

Assumption (August 15)

All Saints' Day (November 1)

Armistice Day (November 11)

Christmas (December 25)

On these days, banks and many shops, museums, and restaurants are closed. Check local listings.

Although not a *jour férie,* VE Day (May 8), commemorating the Allied victory in World War II, is also celebrated widely.

Time Zone

France, like most of Western Europe, is 1 hour ahead of Greenwich Mean Time (2 hours ahead in summer). Therefore, for the best part of the year, it is ahead of the following locations by the number of hours indicated:

London, Dublin:	1 hour
Halifax:	5 hours
New York, Montreal, Toronto:	6 hours
Chicago, Houston, Winnipeg:	7 hours
Denver, Calgary:	8 hours
Los Angeles, Vancouver:	9 hours

Banking and Shopping

Banking and business hours vary in different parts of France. In Paris, for example, banks are open Monday through Friday, 9:00 A.M.–4:30 P.M., and they close at 12:00 M. the day before a holiday. In major cities in the South of France, such as Nice and Marseille, many banks are closed between 12:30–1:30 P.M., and in smaller communities, banks are closed 12:00 M.–2:00 P.M.

Store hours also reflect these regional differences. Most Parisian stores and shops are open 9:00 A.M.–6:00 or 7:00 P.M. (many are open Saturday but closed Monday); the fashion boutiques and perfumeries open at 10:00 A.M. and close 12:00 M.–2:00 P.M. In the South of France, department stores and supermarkets do not close for lunch, but smaller shops do—for up to 3 hours (12:00 M.–3:00 P.M.); however, these businesses may open as early as 7:00 or 8:00 A.M. and may close at 7:00 or 8:00 P.M. Food shops remain open on Sunday (during the morning only).

Visitors to France who are at least 15 years old and who stay for less than six months may deduct the value-added tax (VAT) from the price of goods bought in France that are being taken out of the country as personal luggage. The goods must have a certain value to qualify for this deduction. For further information, contact the French Government Tourist Office (addresses on page 459).

The following table lists French clothing sizes and their American and British equivalents. Sizes, of course, may vary slightly among manufacturers, and a prospective buyer should try clothes on whenever possible before buying them.

Women

Dresses,	France	40	42	44	46	48	50	
Suits,	UK	32	34	36	38	40	42	
Overcoats	US	10	12	14	16	18	20	
Blouses,	France	38	40	42	44	46	48	
Sweaters	UK/US	32	34	36	38	40	42	
Shoes	France	35½	36	36½	37	37½	38	39
	UK	3	3½	4	4½	5	5½	6
	US	4	4½	5	5½	6	6½	7½
Stockings	France	1	2	3	4	5		
	UK/US	8½	9	9½	10	10½		

Men

Suits,	France	36	38	40	42	44	46	48
Overcoats	UK/US	35	35	37	38	39	40	42
Sweaters	France	46	48	51	54	56	59	
	UK/US	36	38	40	42	44	46	
Shirts	France	36	37	38	39	40	41	42
	UK/US	14	14½	15	15½	16	16½	17
Shoes	France	41	42	43	44	45	46	
	UK	8	9	10	11	12	13	
	US	8	8½	9½	10	10½	11	
Socks	France	39–40	40–41	41–42	42–43	43–44		
	UK/US	10	10½	11	11½	12		
Hats	France	53	54	55	56	57	58	59
	UK/US	6½	6⅜	6¾	6⅞	7	7⅛	7½

Post Offices

Post offices are usually open Monday through Friday, 8:00 A.M.–7:00 P.M., and Saturday, 8:00 A.M. to noon. However, small branches may close for lunch and may have shorter hours. Stamps may also be bought at tobacconists', hotels, cafés, and news agents and from yellow vending machines. Mailboxes (*bôites aux lettres*) are yellow as well.

Telephones

Except in the Paris area, telephone numbers have six digits and a two-digit prefix that is used only when dialing from outside the region. In and around Paris, telephone numbers have seven digits and a single-digit prefix ("l") for the area.

Public telephones accept 50c, 1F, and 5F coins. The ringing tone is high-pitched and periodic; the busy (engaged) tone is deeper and more rapid.

Overseas calls can be dialed direct from France to the United States, the United Kingdom, and Canada, without operator assistance. The prefix for telephoning the United Kingdom is 19-44; for the United States and Canada, 19-1. A zero at the beginning of the *local* dialing code should be ignored.

Voltage

Most electricity in France is run on a 220-volt current (50 cycles AC), although some remote areas may still run on 110 volts. American and Canadian visitors who travel with electric razors, hair dryers, and so on, should also bring along an adapter. (Outlet prongs are shaped differently in France as well.)

Handicapped Travelers

Facilities designed to accommodate the handicapped are becoming increasingly commonplace in France. For information, contact the French Government Tourist Office.

Hitchhiking

Hitchhiking is prohibited on major highways but permitted otherwise.

Sunbathing

Nudity is permissible on many beaches, and toplessness is virtually the norm on many others.

Police

Throughout most of France, the emergency telephone number to reach the police is "17."

USEFUL ADDRESSES

This section contains listings of addresses that may be helpful to Americans, Britons, and Canadians who are planning a vacation in France or who may need assistance or information while there. Although this listing is as up-to-date as possible, readers are reminded that addresses and telephone numbers change regularly.

French Government Tourist Offices

In the U.S.

610 Fifth Avenue
New York, NY 10020
212/757-1125

645 North Michigan Avenue,
Suite 630
Chicago, IL 60611
312/337-6301

World Trade Center, #103
2050 Stemmons Freeway
PO Box 58610
Dallas, TX 75258
214/742-7011

9401 Wilshire Boulevard
Beverly Hills, CA 90212
213/272-2661

360 Post Street
San Francisco, CA 94108
415/986-4161

In Canada

1840 Sherbrooke Avenue West
Montreal, Que. H3H 1E4
514/931-3855

1 Dundas Street West
Suite 2405, Box 8
Toronto, Ont. M5G 1Z3
416/593-4723

In the United Kingdom

178 Piccadilly
London W1V 0A1
01/493-6594

The London office has special departments dealing with Winter Sports and Youth Travel, Yachting and Canal Cruising, and Conferences. Address any inquiry about these specific areas to the appropriate department.

In Paris

Accueil de France
(Paris Tourist Office)
127 Champs-Elysées
75008 Paris
1/723-61-72
(Open daily 9:00 A.M.–10:00 P.M.)

Embassies and Consulates-General

United Kingdom

Embassy
35 Rue du Faubourg-St-Honoré
75383 Paris
(1) 266-91-42

Consulates-General
15 Cours de Verdun
33081 Bordeaux Cedex
(56) 52-28-35, 52-28-36, 52-48-86, 52-48-87

11 Square Dutilleul
59800 Lille
(20) 52-87-90

24 Rue Childebert
69288 Lyon Cedex I
(78) 37-59-67, 42-46-49

24 Avenue du Prado
13006 Marseille
(91) 53-43-32, 37-66-95

The United Kingdom also maintains consulates at Toulouse, Calais, Boulogne-sur-Mer, Dunkirk, Nice, Perpignan, Cherbourg, Le Havre, Nantes, and St. Malo-Dinard, and a vice-consulate at Ajaccio (Corsica).

United States

Embassy
2 Avenue Gabriel
75008 Paris
(1) 296-12-02, 261-80-75

Consulates-General
4 Rue Esprit-des-Lois
33000 Bordeaux
(56).65-95

72 Rue Général-Sarrail
69006 Lyon
(78) 24-68-49

9 Rue Armeny
13006 Marseille
(91) 54-92-00

15 Avenue d'Alsace
67000 Strasbourg
(88) 35-31-04

The United States also maintains a consulate in Nice.

Canada

Embassy
35 Avenue Montaigne
75008 Paris
1/723-0101

Consulates-General
24 Avenue du Prado
13006 Marseille
91/37-19-37

Croix du Mail
Rue Claude-Bonnier
33080 Bordeaux Cedex
56/96-15-61

10 Place du Temple-Neuf
67007 Strasbourg Cedex
88/32-65-96

French National Railroads

French National Railroads maintains the following offices in the United States, the United Kingdom, and Canada.

In the United States

610 Fifth Avenue
New York, NY 10020
212/582-2110

360 Post Street
San Francisco, CA 94102
415/982-1993

9465 Wilshire Boulevard
Beverly Hills, CA 90212
213/274-6934

11 East Adams Street
Chicago, IL 60603
312/427-8691

2121 Ponce de Leon Boulevard
Coral Gables, FL 33134
305/445-8648

In Canada

1500 Stanley Street, Suite 436
Montreal, Que. H3A 1R3
514/288-8255

409 Granville Street, Suite 452
Vancouver, B.C. V6C 1T2
604/688-6707

In the United Kingdom

179 Piccadilly
London W1 0BA
01/493-9731, 32, 33, 34

Britrail Travel International

Britrail Travel International represents British Rail in the United States and Canada. Travelers in these countries who want to make advance bookings on boat-train services between Britain and France, on through trains from London to Paris, or on Sealink car ferries across the English Channel should contact one of the following offices:

630 Third Avenue
New York, NY 10017
212/599-5400

510 West 6th Street
Los Angeles, CA 90014
213/626-0088

333 North Michigan Avenue
Chicago, IL 60601
312/263-1910

Plaza of the Americas
North Tower, Suite 750
LB356
Dallas, TX 75201
214/748-0860

94 Cumberland Street, Suite 601
Toronto, Ont. M5R 1A3
416/929-3333

409 Granville Street
Vancouver, B.C. V6C 1T2
604/683-6896

Reservations for any of these British Rail
services may also be made at British Rail
booking offices throughout the United
Kingdom.

Sports and Leisure

Travelers who intend to observe or partici-
pate in sports or leisure activities while in
France may obtain information from the following organizations:

Camping

Fédération Française de Camping et de
    Caravaning
78 Rue de Rivoli
75004 Paris
1/272-84-08

Riding

Fédération Equestre Française

164 Rue du Faubourg-St-Honoré
75008 Paris
1/225-11-22

Golf

Fédération Française de Golf
69 Avenue Victor-Hugo
75116 Paris
1/500-62-20

Auto Racing

Automobile Club de France
8 Place de la Concorde
75008 Paris
1/266-43-00

Ice Skating

Fédération Française des Sports de Glace
42 Rue du Louvre
75001 Paris
1/261-51-38

Flying

Aéro-Club de France
6 Rue Galilée
75016 Paris
1/720-93-02

Gliding

Fédération Française de Vol à Voile
29 Rue de Sèvres
75006 Paris
1/544-04-78

Parachuting

Fédération Française de Parachutisme
35 Rue St-Georges
75009 Paris
1/878-45-00

Tennis

La Ligue de Tennis de Paris

74 Rue de Rome
75008 Paris
1/522-22-08

Winter Sports

Association des Maires des Stations
Françaises de Sports d'Hiver
61 Boulevard Haussmann
75008 Paris
1/742-23-32

Basque Pelota

Club de Pelote Basque
8 Rue de la Cavalerie
75015 Paris
1/567-06-34

Mountain Climbing

Club Alpin Français
7 Rue La Boétie
75008 Paris
1/742-36-77

Fishing (permit required)

Conseil Supérieur de la Pêche
10 Rue Péclet
75010 Paris
1/842-10-00

Hunting and Shooting (permit required)

Office National de la Chasse
85-bis Avenue de Wagram
75017 Paris
1/277-81-75

Scuba Diving

Fédération Française d'Etudes et de Sports
   Sous-Marins
24 Quai de Rive-Neuve
13007 Marseille
91/33-99-31

Canoeing

Canoë-Kayak Club de France
47 Quai Ferber
94360 Bry-sur-Marne
1/881-54-26

Sailing

Fédération Française de Yachting à Voile
55 Avenue Kléber
75116 Paris
1/505-68-00

Water Skiing

Fédération Française de Ski Nautique
9 Boulevard Pereire
75017 Paris
1/267-15-66

Surfing

Fédération Française de Surf
Cité Administrative
Avenue Edouard-VII
64200 Biarritz

Wind-surfing

Association Française de Wind-Surf
29 Rue du Général-Delestraint
75016 Paris

Motorboating (license required)

Fédération Française Motonautique
8 Place de la Concorde
75008 Paris
1/073-89-38, 265-34-70

Cave Exploring

Fédération Française de Spéléologie
130 Rue St-Maur
75011 Paris
1/357-56-54

Paris and the
Ile de France

SOME STATISTICS

Paris proper is home to roughly 2.2 million inhabitants, and approximately 9 million live in its greater metropolitan area. Unlike other European capitals, Paris has not incorporated its suburbs. The city boundaries still follow, for the most part, the ring of mid-nineteenth-century fortifications (today's Boulevard Périphérique). The city comprises an area of about 56 square miles (including the Bois de Vincennes and Bois de Boulogne, which lie outside the fortification ring). The suburban communities are independent and belong to the ring of *départements* that make up, together with the *département* of Paris, the Région de l'Ile-de-France. The city is divided into twenty *arrondissements*—each with its own mayor's office, or *mairie*—and eighty *quartiers*.

Paris enjoys a fairly temperate and moderate climate, with less seasonal variation in temperature than central Europe experiences. The average January temperature is 38° F; the average July temperature, 64° F. Summers may be somewhat humid; autumn tends to be the wettest season.

Transportation

Paris has two international airports—Orly, to the south, and Charles-de-Gaulle, near Roissy, to the north. The airport at Le Bourget, to the north of St. Denis, is no longer used for international traffic. Express buses connect the airports directly to the *aérogares* at Porte Maillot and at the Esplanade des Invalides.

Paris is the terminus for France's major railway lines. The city's six main stations—Gare d'Austerlitz, Gare de Lyon, Gare du Nord, Gare de l'Est, Gare Montparnasse, and Gare St-Lazare—handle roughly 760 trains a day and 80 million passengers annually. The Paris region is also covered by a network of suburban railways, with about 340 stations. These operate roughly 5,500 trains daily and transport some 450 million passengers a year.

In recent years, the railway network has been supplemented by the RER (*Réseau express régional*), which connects the center of Paris and the Métro with the surrounding region, especially the various new towns.

Paris has had its underground, the Métro (Métropolitain), since 1900. It numbers 15 lines, roughly 105 miles of track, some 3,500 cars, and 315 stations. It carries about 4 million passengers a day.

Roughly 4,000 city buses travel 316 miles of routes on 56 lines. They carry about 320 million passengers a year. Due to improvement of the buses, the introduction of special bus lanes, and the ever-increasing difficulty of finding parking places, the number of riders has soared in recent years. There are some 135 additional bus lines in the *banlieue*.

Paris has over 14,300 taxis and more than 1 million private automobiles. The Boulevard Périphérique, a freeway that rings the city, and an eight-mile-long expressway along the Seine on the Right Bank help to relieve the traffic.

Tourism

Paris has 1,255 hotels with 116,000 rooms. Of these, 78 are four-star, or luxury, hotels. Some 4.5 million tourists spend the night in a Paris hotel each year. The number of hotel beds in Paris is equal to that in all the rest of France put together.

There are roughly 10,000 restaurants, cafés, and nightclubs in the city, more than 60 theaters, 220 art galleries, 465 cinemas, 50 concert halls, 70 cabarets, and 20 discothèques.

General Information

Everyone who visits Paris should buy one of two weeklies, *Une Semaine de Paris—Pariscope* or *l'Officiel des Spectacles* (new editions appear each Wednesday). These list programs for opera, theater, café theater, *spectacles*, films, concerts, exhibitions, festivals, and markets, as well as addresses of restaurants and cabarets.

A good survey of current art exhibitions is also provided by "Le Monde des Arts" in the Thursday edition (appearing each Wednesday noon) of *Le Monde*. The major art exhibitions generally take place in the Grand Palais (Galeries Nationales du Grand-Palais, Avenue du Général-Eisenhower), the Centre Beaubourg, the Orangerie of the Jardin des Tuileries, or the Pavillon de Flore of the Louvre.

In case of theft, accident, and so on, one should notify the nearest police station or telephone "17." For lost and found articles, inquire at the Bureau des Objets Trouvés, 36 Rue des Morillons, XVe (open daily, except Saturday and Sunday, 8:30 A.M.–5:30 P.M.). If the item is found, its owner will be required to pay 4 percent of its value for services.

If one needs medicine, one should go to a drugstore, called a *pharmacie*. At night and on Sundays, the Commisariat de Police in the area where one is staying will know which nearby drugstores are open and what doctors are on call. If necessary, doctors will call an ambulance. If a doctor cannot be reached, one can call the *ambulances municipales* directly at 378-26-26. For additional information, contact:

American Hospital
63 Boulevard Victor-Hugo
92202 Neuilly
747-53-00

British Hospital
48 Rue de Villiers
92300 Levallois
757-22-58

The city of Paris maintains two information offices:

Office de Tourisme de Paris
  127 Avenue des Champs-Elysées, VIIIe
  723-61-72
Syndicat d'Initiative de Paris, Hôtel de Ville
  29 Rue de Rivoli, IVe
  227-15-40

There are branches of the Office de Tourisme de Paris at the Gare de l'Est, Gare du Nord, and Gare de Lyon and at the departure points for the two major airports, the Aérogare des Invalides and the Aérogare Porte-Maillot. Handier, though, are the detail maps of the city that appear at all major intersections and in and near the Métro stations. They provide information about the important buildings and institutions in the given neighborhood.

The main post office—Hôtel des Postes, 52 Rue du Louvre, Ier—is open twenty-four hours daily. Most post offices are open weekdays from 8:00 A.M. to 7:00 P.M. and Saturday from 8:00 A.M. to noon; they are closed on Sunday. The following branches are exceptions:

71 Avenue des Champs-Elysées, VIIIe
  (open daily, 8:00 A.M.–11:20 P.M.; Sunday, 10:00 A.M.–NOON and 2:00 P.M.–8:00 P.M.)
40 Rue Singer, XVIe
  (open Sunday, 8:00 A.M.–11:00 P.M.)
19 Rue Duc, XVIIIe
  (open Sunday, 8:00 A.M.–11:00 P.M.)
248 Rue des Pyrénées, XXe
  (open Sunday, 8:00 A.M.–11:00 P.M.)
Aérogare des Invalides
  (open daily, 7:00 A.M.–9:00 P.M.)
Orly
  (open daily, 8:00 A.M.–7:00 P.M.; telephone and stamps, day and night)
Roissy
  (open daily, 8:00 A.M.–7:00 P.M.; telephone and stamps, 6:30 A.M.–11:00 P.M.)

Changing money is possible in almost all banks, but rates of exchange and service charges vary greatly. On Saturday, the branch of the Crédit Commercial de France at 103 Avenue des Champs-Elysées, VIIIe, is open; on Sunday, the office of the Crédit Industriel et Commercial in the Gare de Lyon, as well as the banks at the two airports, are open. The *bureaux de change* at the train stations often offer a most unfavorable rate of exchange.

FIRST CONTACT WITH THE CITY

Goethe advised that one acquire one's first impressions of a city from its church towers. If you choose to follow his suggestion, you should first climb the tower of Notre-Dame (entrance on the north side of the left-hand tower; open daily, 10:00 A.M.–5:30 P.M.; in winter, to 4:15 P.M.). But the church towers do not have a monopoly on good views of Paris. The terrace on top of the Samaritaine department store (illus. 80, page 174) is very comfortable, as are the restaurant and open terrace of the Centre Beaubourg (illus. 83, page 176); here, moreover, one can climb above the roofs of Paris in the escalator in front of the façade (open daily, except Tuesday, 10:00 A.M.–10:00 P.M.).

The view from the Arc de Triomphe (illus. 56 and 57, page 127) provides an especially vivid sense of the royal axis as well as a stunning look at the new skyline of La Défense, to the west of the city (open daily, except July 14, 10:00 A.M.–5:30 P.M.).

In fair weather, one can enjoy a grandiose panorama from the three levels of the Tour Eiffel (open daily; the first and second levels, 9:30 A.M.–11:00 P.M., the top level, 10:00 A.M.–10:30 P.M.). No less impressive is the view from the fifty-sixth floor of the Tour Montparnasse (illus. 82, page 175) (open daily, 9:30 A.M.–11:30 P.M.). No less impressive is the view from the fifty-sixth floor of the Tour Montparnasse (illus. 82, page 175) (open daily, 9:30 A.M.–11:30 P.M.).

Visitors to Paris can use the *autocars panoramiques* for an orientation tour of roughly 3 hours. These double-decker buses are equipped with earphones that explain the sights in the major languages. They depart from:

Cityrama, 3 Place des Pyramides, Ier
   (telephone 260-30-14)
Paris-Vision, 214 Rue de Rivoli, Ier
   (telephone 260-30-14)

both of which are near the Louvre. Tours leave at regular intervals during the day and into the evening, when the major landmarks are illuminated. (Notre-Dame, the Arc de Triomphe, the Place de la Concorde, and the Louvre are illuminated daily from about an hour after sunset until midnight.)

In fair weather, a boat ride on the Seine—on either the small *vedettes* or the larger *bateaux-mouches* (with restaurant; capacity up to 1,500 persons)—is an excellent first contact with the city:

Vedettes Tour-Eiffel: Departures every 30 minutes, 10:00 A.M.–6:00 P.M. (November-March), 9:30 A.M.–10:30 P.M. (April-October), from the Port de la Bourdonnais, VIIe (at the Tour Eiffel). Illumination cruises leave every summer night, 7:30–10:30 P.M., and in winter on Saturdays at 9:00 P.M.

Vedettes du Pont-Neuf: Departures at 10:30 A.M., 11:20 A.M., and 12:00 M. and every 30 minutes, 1:30–5:00 P.M., from the Square du Vert-Galant, at the tip of the Ile de la Cité, reached from the Pont Neuf. Between May and October, illumination cruises leave at 9:00, 9:30, and 10:20 P.M.

Les Bateaux-Mouches: Departures every 30 minutes, 10:00 A.M.–12:00 M. and 2:00 –7:00 P.M., from the Port de l'Alma, on the Right Bank next to the Pont de l'Alma. Illumination cruises leave at 8:30 and 10:00 P.M. Lunch is served on the 1:00 P.M. boat, and dinner is served on the 8:30 P.M. boat. These meals are quite expensive, but the setting is remarkable.

These rides take about 1 hour.

Special tours to specific monuments, including entrance into buildings not normally open to the public, are organized by the Caisse Nationale des Monuments Historiques et des Sites, Hôtel de Sully, 62 Rue St-Antoine, IVe. Here, one can request a program of current tours.

GETTING AROUND PARIS

Although this guide suggests a number of walking tours around the historic center of Paris, (pages 473 -489), one should not be deceived by the apparent compactness of the city into embarking on exhausting treks. For those points of interest lying outside the heart of the city, one would do better to use buses, the Métro, or even taxis, which can be flagged down, assuming one has the good fortune to spot an empty one. On the Métro and the RER, one may travel either first class or second class. First class is approximately one and a half times as expensive as second. The various Métro lines are identified by numbers and the names of their termini. The RER lines are identified by letter.

A special tourist ticket is available for a period of two, four, or seven days. It entitles the visitor to unlimited first-class travel on the Métro, the RER, and most of the RATP bus routes. One may buy this ticket on presentation of a valid passport. It is sold at the RATP offices at 53 bis, Quai des Grands-Augustins, VI^c, near the Pont Neuf (open Monday-Friday, 8:30 A.M.–12:00 M., and 1:00–5:00 P.M., Saturday-Sunday, 8:30 A.M.–12:00 M., 2:00–5:00 P.M.), and Place de la Madeleine, VIII^c, next to the flower market (open Monday-Saturday, 7:30 A.M.–6:45 P.M., Sunday, 6:30 A.M.–6:00 P.M.). It is also available at the Gare de l'Est, Gare du Nord, Gare de Lyon, Gare St-Lazare, Gare Montparnasse, and Gare d'Orsay, at the SNCF offices at Charles-de-Gaulle, Orly South, and Orly West, at several Métro and RER stations, and at offices of the Crédit Commercial de France (103 Avenue des Champs-Elysées, VIII^c) and Banque Nationale de Paris (2 Boulevard des Italiens, IX^c).

Visitors who are planning a long stay in Paris and environs may consider a *carte orange*, valid for a calendar month or for a year, that enables the holder to unlimited travel on the Métro, the RER, suburban routes of the SNCF, and suburban RATP bus routes. Otherwise, one ought to buy a *carnet*, a book of ten tickets good for both the Métro and the buses and sold at every ticket counter. Tickets are automatically canceled at every Métro station, and they are valid for all inner-city lines regardless of the

distance traveled or the number of transfers. For the RER, a higher fare is collected for trips outside the city; the amount will be indicated by the machine. It is advisable to hold on to the ticket, for at many stations —including all stations lying outside the valid limit of a normal ticket—the turnstiles open only after a ticket has been inserted. Passengers who ride the buses, Métro, or RER without a ticket are subject to fairly stiff fines.

The Métro generally runs between 5:30 A.M. and 12:30 A.M. During the rush hours, there may be as little as a minute and a half between trains.

Buses run between 7:00 A.M. and 9:30 P.M., and some lines—the 21, 26, 31, 38, 52, 62, 63, 80, 91, 92, 95, and 96—run until 12:30 A.M. Many lines do not operate on Sunday and holidays. Night buses depart every hour, starting at 1:30 A.M., from the Châtelet to the following destinations: Pont de Neuilly, Mairie de Levallois, Mairie de Clichy, Mairie de St-Ouen, Eglise de Pantin, and Mairie des Lilas.

For motorists, the chief problem in Paris is not driving but parking. If you are fortunate enough to find a spot on the street, check to see whether it is in the so-called *zone bleue* (the majority of the central area), where spaces are reserved, or whether there are parking meters on the street. (Often the meters are not placed at each individual space but rather for a whole section of parking.) After paying, place your receipt, with the time indicated, so it is clearly visible behind your windshield.

It is generally better to head for the nearest underground garage rather than to search for a parking space. There are more than 150 such garages beneath the streets and squares, the major department stores, and the Centre Beaubourg. A complete map of underground garages, including their rates, is available at the Syndicat d'Initiative de Paris in the Hôtel de Ville.

You must take care to park so as not to obstruct traffic, for if necessary even foreign cars will be towed off to the police auto depot or locked with a boot that is removed only after payment of a sizable fine. As in every large city, it is inadvisable to leave objects of value lying visible in your car.

Service stations are not as obvious as in other cities; they are often integrated into the ground floor of an apartment block or attached to the larger underground garages. The following stations, listed by *arrondissement*, are open 24 hours:

Ier	BP, 58 Rue du Marché-St-Honoré
IIe	Shell, 82 Rue Réaumur
IIIe	Antar, 42 Rue Beaubourg
IVe	Antar, 4 Quai des Célestins
V^e	Shell, 93 Rue Monge
VIe	BP, Parking St-Germain (next to the Drugstore)
VIIe	Shell, 6–10 Boulevard Raspail
VIIIe	Total, 20 Boulevard Malesherbes
IXe	Esso, Parking Anvers, 41 Boulevard Rochechouart
X^e	Esso, 168 Faubourg-St-Martin
XIe	Elf, 46 Rue Oberkampf
XIIe	Shell, 123 Boulevard Soult
XIIIe	Esso, 22 Boulevard de Port-Royal
XIVe	Shell, 110 Rue d'Alésia
XVe	Elf, 45 Rue St-Charles
XVIe	Mobil, 26 Avenue Paul-Doumer
XVIIe	Antar, 160 Rue Cardinet
XVIIIe	Esso, Avenue de la Porte-St-Ouen
XIXe	Mobil, 39 Avenue Simon-Bolivar
XXe	Mobil, 57 Rue de Bagnolet

Wrecker service is available at:

France-Secours-International, telephone 260-39-39
Service Dépannage (day and night), telephone 236-10-00

S.O.S., telephone 707-99-99
G.A.R.D., telephone 797-23-63

Bicycle riding in Paris is best limited to the Bois de Boulogne. Bicycles may be rented from:

Paris-Vélo
2 Rue du Fer-à-Moulin
75005 Paris
337-59-22

Bicyclub de France
8 Place de la Porte-Champerret
75017 Paris
766-55-92

It is possible to rent bicycles at more than fifty train stations in the Ile de France. Information can be obtained at the Gare du Nord, telephone 878-15-66; Gare de l'Est, telephone 206-84-17; or at the Office de Tourisme de Paris, 127 Avenue des Champs-Elysées, telephone 720-12-80.

Getting from Paris to its Airports

Air France coaches (buses) run from the Aérogare Porte-Maillot to Charles-de-Gaulle (Roissy) every 15 minutes, 5:45 A.M.– 11:00 P.M. (the journey takes 30 minutes) and from the Aérogare des Invalides and Montparnasse to Orly every 12 minutes, 6:00 A.M.–11:00 P.M. (the journey takes 40 minutes). Coaches also connect Charles-de-Gaulle and Orly every 20 minutes, 6:00 A.M.–11:00 P.M.; this journey takes 75 minutes and is free for passengers who are catching a connecting flight (on presentation of a voucher that can be obtained at the connecting flight desk). For further information, contact:
Aéogare Porte-Maillot
2 Place de la Porte-Maillot
75017 Paris
299-20-18/299-21-49

Aérogare des Invalides
2 Rue Esnault-Pelterie
75007 Paris
323-97-10/323-87-79

There is a rail service to Orly from the *gares* d'Orsay, St-Michel, and Austerlitz. It leaves every 15 minutes, 5:30 A.M.–9:00 P.M., and every 30 minutes, 9:00–11:00 P.M. Another rail service connects the Gare du Nord with Charles-de-Gaulle. Trains leave every 15 minutes, 5:30 A.M.–11:00 P.M.

The following RATP buses also go from downtown Paris to the city's airports:

183A.   Port de Choisy–Orly South

215.   Denfert–Rochereau-Orly South and Orly West

350.   Gare de l'Est/Gare de Nord–Le Bourget/Charles-de-Gaulle

351.   Nation–Charles-de-Gaulle

And Héli-France, 4 Avenue de la Porte de Sèvres, 75015 Paris (telephone 557-53-67) operates a helicopter service between Paris and the three airports, and between Charles-de-Gaulle and Orly. For additional information about the airports, contact: Charles-de-Gaulle and Le Bourget (862-12-12), Orly (884-52-52).

SHOPPING: FROM HAUTE COUTURE TO OPEN AIR

Paris is the celebrated home of many of the world's great fashion designers—Christian Dior, Chanel, Givenchy, Yves St-Laurent, and so on. But the city also has countless boutiques that sell more inexpensive clothes by young designers, as well as many specialty shops that sell perfumes, jewelry, leather goods, antiques, and the like. In addition, there are many department stores and low-price chain stores.

The great couturiers are located, for the most part, in the Faubourg St-Honoré, Avenue Montaigne, Rue Cambon, and Rue Royale. Their spring-summer showings run from late January through May; the autumn-winter collections are shown from late July until mid-December. Most of the houses have showings at 11:00 A.M. Though open by invitation only, invitations can be obtained quite easily through the concièrge at a better hotel or directly from the salon.

The jewelers of Paris tend to cluster in the Rue de la Paix and Place Vendôme, and leather shops are found largely in the Faubourg St-Honoré. Many gift shops—particularly those in the Rue de l'Opéra, Rue de Rivoli, and Champs-Elysées—offer significant discounts to visitors from abroad on presentation of their passports; such shops usually post a notice to this effect in their window. Fashion boutiques and specialty shops are generally open Tuesday–Saturday, 10:00 A.M.–12:00 M. noon and 2:00 P.M.–6:30 or 7:00 P.M.

Most Parisian department stores are open Monday-Saturday, 9:00 A.M.–6:30 P.M. (until 9:00 or 10:00 P.M. one or two nights a week); many are closed Monday mornings. The leading ones are:

Au Bon Marché
138 Rue de Sèvres
260-33-45

Franck et Fils
80 Rue de Passy, XVI[c]
647-86-00

Galeries Lafayette
40 Boulevard Haussmann, IX[c]
282-34-56

Galeries Lafayette (Italie)
Centre Galaxie
Place d'Italie, XIII[c]
528-52-87

Au Printemps
64 Boulevard Haussmann, IX[c]
282-50-00

Au Printemps (Nation)
21-25 Cours de Vincennes, XII[c]
371-12-41

Samaritaine Pont-Neuf
19 Rue de la Monnaie, Ier
508-33-33

Aux Trois Quartiers
17 Boulevard de la Madeleine, Ier
260-39-30

The Forum des Halles, 1-7 Rue Pierre Lescot, Ier, on the site of the former produce market, is now the largest pedestrian area in Europe. Its four levels contain shops, restaurants, cinemas, discothéques.

One of the special delights of a trip to Paris is browsing in neighborhood shopping streets and markets, where foodstuffs, vegetables, fruit, meats, and fish of enviable quality and freshness are offered.

The markets (some, but fewer and fewer, are held in nineteenth-century halls, generally on Wednesday and Saturday mornings) are too numerous to list here. Some that take place daily, except Monday, are those in the Rue Buci; in the Rue Mouffetard (color plate, pages 44–45; illus. 67, page 166); in the Place Maubert; in the Rue Cler; in the Carré du Temple; the Marché Lenoir in the Place d'Aligre; and the Marché St-Quentin.

The transfer of the central Halles out of Paris to Rungis has robbed Paris of one of its major attractions, and although it is possible to make the somewhat complicated trip to Rungis, the visit is not what it used to be (tours Thursday, 2:00 P.M.; group tours daily, except Saturday and Sunday, 9:00 A.M.–12:00 M. and 2:00 P.M.–4:00 P.M.; connections from Paris via buses 185 and 285).

The two flower markets—in the Place de la Madeleine and on the Ile de la Cité—boast nineteenth-century stalls and are very picturesque. Every Sunday, beginning at 9:00 A.M., there are bird markets on the Ile de la Cité as well. On Thursday, Saturday, and Sunday, philatelists converge on the stamp market along the Avenue Gabriel, up to the corner of the Avenue de Marigny.

In spite of rising prices and competition from the antique markets in the city, the flea markets have lost none of their appeal. The most famous is the Marché aux Puces de St-Ouen at the Porte de Clignancourt, which offers an inexhaustible selection of everything from expensive furniture to junk and bric-a-brac, often at somewhat higher prices than at dealers' shops in the city (open Saturday, Sunday, and Monday, 7:00 A.M.–7:00 P.M.). The other flea markets are:

Marché aux Puces des Lilas, Avenue de la Porte-des-Lilas (open Sunday, 7:00 A.M.–7:00 P.M.)

Marché aux Puces de Vanves, Rue Georges-Lafenestre (open Saturday and Sunday, 7:00 A.M.–7:00 P.M.)

Marché aux Puces d'Aligre, Place d'Aligre (open every morning)

In contrast to the flea markets, but not necessarily more expensive, are the antique markets: the elegant Village Suisse, between the Avenue de Suffren, the Avenue de la Motte-Picquet, and the Rue Dupleix; and the very convenient Louvre des Antiquaires in the former Louvre department store on the Rue de Rivoli, entrance on the Place du Palais-Royal, with more than 200 dealers. A visit to the Hôtel Drouot, the extremely modern auction house of the Parisian *commissaires priseurs*, between the Rue Drouot, the Rue Rossini, and the Rue Chauchat, can be absorbing.

The Quartier Latin, especially the Rue Jacob, the Rue Bonaparte, and the Rue de Seine, is the traditional center for the antique dealers of Paris. Here, one can also buy old books, engravings, and drawings. Modern-art galleries are also located here, although the area around the Centre Beaubourg is beginning to develop into a haven for these.

RESTAURANTS AND HOTELS

Paris has about 10,000 cafés and restaurants, so we cannot list—let alone recommend —them here. Even though connoisseurs maintain that in recent years the ratio of quality to cost has worsened in Parisian restaurants, the tourist who has not come on a culinary tour may find that the number of establishments where one can eat quickly and cheaply has in fact increased. Self-service bars, museum cafeterias, snack bars—all abhorrent to the gourmet—often serve more interesting fare than do mediocre but expensive restaurants. If one is in a hurry, a dish of *steak frites* in the nearest corner bistro may be a better choice than a meal in one of the imposing restaurants. And remember that one can eat less expensively in the cafés and bistros off the beaten track. The range in price of even a cup of coffee can be considerable, depending on whether one drinks it on a main boulevard or a few yards around the corner.

The Ile de France is one of the great gastronomic regions of France, and one should try to sample some of the area's specialties. These include several creamy soups, or *potages*, such as *potage St-Germain*, made with pureed fresh green peas; *potage Crécy*, which has a carrot base and is named for a village east of Paris; *potage soissonnaise*, a hearty soup flavored with bacon and made thick by the white kidney beans grown in Soissons; and *potage aux primeurs*, a spring vegetable soup that uses leeks, celery, romaine lettuce, and green peas. The region is also known for its pâtés and terrines, which are widely available. A *pâté Pantin*, rectangular in shape, consists of ground pork and strips of veal and ham; a *terrine de gibier* is based on game meat—hare, rabbit, venison, or wild boar.

Typically Parisian entrees include *châteaubriand*, a thick fillet of beef that is grilled; *entrecôte marchand de vin*, a steak in a red wine and shallot sauce; and *entrecôte Bercy*, cooked with a sauce of white wine and shallots. These are often served with souffled or French-fried potatoes (chips); French fries were sold in Paris as early as the sixteenth century. *Gibelotte de lapin*, or rabbit fricassee, chicken *à la ficelle*, cooked over an open fire, and *matelote de l'Oise*, a fish stew, are other local specialties.

The premier cheese of the region is Brie; its production centers in Meaux. Pastries are the favored dessert of Paris and the Ile de France, and some pastries native to the area are *gâteau St-Honoré*, named for the patron saint of pastry cooks, and *gâteau Paris-Brest*, a pâte aux choux filled with a praline- or coffee-flavored cream. *Crème Chantilly* is a rich whipped cream of the region, and *fromage de Fontainebleau* is a local blend of *fromage blanc* and crème fraîche, dusted with sugar.

In addition to French cuisine in all its degrees of quality, a metropolis like Paris naturally offers foreign cuisines, not only for tourists but also for its sizable colonies of foreigners and ethnic groups—Arabs, Indochinese, Jews, Spaniards, Italians, Russians, Poles, and Germans. Accordingly, there are specialty shops of various nationalities in particular quarters.

A separate issue is restaurant décor. Often, even in good places, little attention is given to it—although those large, anonymous, mirrored cafés seem to be as much a part of the city's image as is Notre-Dame or the *flics*. Nonetheless, there are a number of old, enchantingly lovely restaurants—often, sadly, belonging to the higher price category —such as Le Train Bleu in the Gare de Lyon, Julien in the Rue du Faubourg St-Denis, Le Grand Véfour in the Rue Beaujolais, L'Escargot in the Rue Montorgueil, and several old bistros in the Rue St-Denis.

The rustic-looking restaurants in the Quartier Latin, along the Rue Mouffetard, and so on, cater especially to the tourist trade. One would do best to consult one of the standard guidebooks—the Guide Michelin, Kléber, or Gault et Millau—or, if one is to be in Paris for a considerable length of time and wishes to eat economically, like a native, the very handy *Guide de la vie quotidienne: Paris, mode d'emploi* (published by Autrement), which lists restaurants where one can eat inexpensively, the *à la mode* pubs, and countless practical suggestions for daily living in Paris.

For hotels, one should also rely on the pertinent guides, since even a mere listing of accommodations from luxury establishments down to youth hostels is impossible in the confines of this book. Despite the notorious shortage of rooms—especially during the frequent conventions—one can almost always find lodging in one of the small hotels in the Sixth or Seventh Arrondissement. If necessary, consult the Office de Tourisme de Paris, 127 Avenue des Champs-Elysées, VIII^c, telephone 723-61-72, which can be helpful in finding accommodation.

Visitors who arrive at Charles-de-Gaulle Airport can book accommodations at one of more than 300 hotels by using a computerized synoptic board near the airport's information desk. This system displays each hotel's location on a city map and indicates its category, price, availability of rooms, and so on. If the traveler sees a red square when he or she requests information about a hotel, then the hotel is full; a green square denotes available room. The traveler then simply picks up a phone, pushes the "Select" button of the hotel, and reaches the hotel's reservation desk directly to confirm the booking.

Travelers who plan to stay for a month or more and would prefer to rent an apartment can consult their travel agent or write for information to the Fédération Nationale des Agents Immobiliers (FNAIM), 129 Rue du Faubourg-St-Honoré, 75008 Paris; telephone 225-24-26. Young people who hold a valid youth hostel membership card can stay up to a week in one of Paris's simple but inexpensive youth hostels. For further information, contact:

American Youth Hostels, Inc.
132 Spring Street
New York, NY 10012
212/431-0100

Association des Auberges de Jeunesse du
   Canada
1324 Sherbrooke West

Montreal, Quebec
514/842-9048

Youth Hostels Association
14 Southampton Street
London, WC2F 7HY

Fédération Unie des Auberges de Jeunesse
6 Rue Mesril
75116 Paris
261-84-03

ENTERTAINMENT

Paris is France's cultural capital, and all types of entertainment are available, ranging from performances at the Opéra or the Comédie Française, to famed night clubs such as the Moulin Rouge (Place Blanche, XVIII^c) and the Folies-Bergère (32 Rue Richer, IX^c), to jazz clubs, rock clubs, and discothèques. For current listings, check *Pariscope* or *L'Officiel des Spectacles*.

One becomes aware of the importance of film in Paris when one sees the long lines at cinema box offices every day (there are no advance sales). Films are usually shown in their original language with subtitles. One should watch the listings and advertisements for the abbreviations "v.o." (*version originale*) or "v.f." (*version française*).

The Cinémathèque-Musée du Cinéma (in the Palais de Chaillot) and the Cinémathèque Beaubourg (in the Centre Beaubourg) are meccas for all films buffs.

An almost equal range of entertainment is available for children. There are zoos, aquariums, amusement parks, Punch and Judy shows, circuses, and children's theaters. Contact a tourist office for further information.

Parents who wish to hire a baby sitter may do so through one of the following agencies:

American College of Paris
31 Avenue Bosquet
75007 Paris
555-91-73

Baby Sitting
18 Rue Tronchet
75008 Paris
224-18-78, 742-69-02

Gard'Enfants
3 Rue de Duras
75008 Paris
742-30-99

Kid Service
17 Rue Molière
75001 Paris
296-04-16

Medical Students Association
105 Boulevard de l'Hôpital
75013 Paris
586-19-44

STROLLS THROUGH PARIS

The following routes are only suggestions for getting to know the center of Paris. Given the wealth of points of interest, they indicate only the highlights of a given section.

Naturally, they can be combined in any number of ways. The sequence in which they are given follows the chronological development of the city, but because subsequent epochs have left their mark as well, buildings from many periods are included. For finding one's way, a good city map is indispensable; three good ones are Michelin's No. 10 and No. 12, *Plan de Paris*; and No. 11, *Paris Atlas*. The structures that are discussed in the main section of this book are treated only briefly here, at most with an indication of the hours they are open. Churches are generally open between 8:00 A.M. and 6:30 P.M.; inspection of them is not permitted while services are taking place. Wherever possible, connecting streets less burdened with traffic have been chosen, but this could not be done in every case.

Ile de la Cité

The old heart of Paris and of the French monarchy suffered particularly under Haussmann's reorganization of the city. Its medieval residences, its almost twenty churches, and its ancient hospital were all swept away. Today, the Ile de la Cité appears abandoned except for the most important buildings.

The square in front of Notre-Dame, the *Place du Parvis-Notre-Dame*, is the geographical center of France. The national highways that connect Paris with the rest of the country all begin here, and from here all distances are measured—a bronze plaque with the coat of arms of Paris marks the spot. Beneath the square, thanks to the most recent excavations, one can see traces of the Paris of antiquity and of the Middle Ages: remains of a Gallic settlement, portions of the first city wall from the thirteenth century, and the foundations of the old cathedral of St. Étienne.

Freed from automobile traffic (by an underground garage), the square is now open toward the Seine. The monument to Charlemagne with Roland and Oliver dates from 1882. On this side, along the river, stood the old Hôtel-Dieu, where, according to a local saying, there was a sick person, a dying one, and a corpse in every bed. Diet's new Hôtel-Dieu now closes off the north side of the square.

To the right of the cathedral of *Notre-Dame*, there is a small garden on the site of the old archbishop's palace. From here, one can admire the façade of the south transept, which was begun by Jean de Chelles and Pierre de Montreuil, and Jean Ravy's wide flying buttresses, supporting the apse, from about 1320.

On the easternmost tip of the island, there is a memorial to the victims of the deportation designed by Pingusson and dedicated by Charles de Gaulle in 1962. From here, one can look across to the Ile St-Louis, and a footbridge leads to it. A detour is possible at this point.

To the north of Notre-Dame, there are remnants of old buildings in the Rue Chanoinesse, the Rue Chantres, the Rue des Ursins, and the Rue de la Colombe. These once belonged in part to the canons of Notre-Dame. It was here that the canon Fulbert lived with his niece Héloïse, who was seduced by the young theology teacher Abélard—the beginning of one of the most dramatic love stories of the Middle Ages.

The Quai de la Corse leads to the Marché aux Fleurs between the Hôtel-Dieu, the Préfecture de Police to the south, and the Tribunal de Commerce to the west. The Rue de Lutèce connects the market with the extensive complex of the *Palais de Justice* with its elegant *Cour de Mai, Sainte-Chapelle* (open daily, 10:00 A.M.–5:00 P.M.), and *Conciergerie* (entrance from the Quai de l'Horloge; open daily, except Tuesday and

July 14, 10:00 A.M.–5:30 P.M.).

The Palais de Justice was rebuilt by Joseph-Louis Duc and Daumet beginning in 1871, after it had been torched by the Commune. Especially in the more famous rooms, the Salle des Pas-Perdus and the Chambre Dorée, they attempted to re-create the open historic originals (open daily, except Sunday and holidays, 9:00 A.M.–6:00 P.M.).

Proceed along the Quai de l'Horloge to the *Place Dauphine*, which is still one of the most charming squares in Paris despite the many changes it has undergone. At the point of the square is the *Pont Neuf*, the oldest bridge in Paris. At its center is a monument to Henri IV, to whose memory the small garden below the bridge, the Square du Vert-Galant, is dedicated. From here there is a lovely view of the Seine, the Louvre, the Hôtel des Monnaies, and the Institut de France.

Left Bank

Quartier Latin

An exodus of professors and students to the Left Bank from the Cathedral School of Notre-Dame established the academic tradition of the Quartier Latin. In spite of its broad, straight streets (Boulevard St-Germain, Rue des Écoles, Rue Lagrange, Boulevard St-Michel), this old district has reclaimed a great deal of its medieval character through restoration in the past few years. In the nineteenth century, whole sections had degenerated into virtual slums.

Begin at the Square René-Viviani, next to the church of *St. Julien-le-Pauvre*, from which one can look across to Notre-Dame. The oldest tree in Paris stands in this square, a false acacia planted by the naturalist Jean Robin in 1683. Proceed along the Rue de la Bûcherie and Rue Frère-Sauton, both lined with seventeenth- and eighteenth-century buildings, to the Place Maubert, where Albertus Magnus taught in the thirteenth century. The Rue Maître-Albert commemorates this saint; it has been restored in recent years.

A bit farther east stood the Bernardine convent, the church and collegiate house of the Cistercians in Paris. Its three-aisle refectory is preserved in the Rue de Poissy and is today a part of the fire-department barracks.

Nearby is the church of *St. Nicolas-du-Chardonnet*, built between 1656 and 1709. In it are the tombs of the painter Charles Le Brun and his mother, as well as those of Antoine Coysevox, Jean-Baptiste Tuby, and Jean Collignon. The church is richly furnished with paintings and tombs. It made headlines not long ago because of the sit-in staged here by adherents of the traditionalist Archbishop Lefèvre in 1977.

Return by way of the Rue Lagrange, which has a number of medieval buildings and remnants of the Chapelle St-Blaise (in the restaurant at No. 48). This street crosses the Rue du Fouarre; tradition has it that here, in the Middle Ages, the students sat on bales of straw while their professors lectured.

Proceed along the Rue St-Julien and the western portion of the Rue de la Bûcherie —here, facing the Seine, stood the Petit Châtelet and an annex of the Hôtel-Dieu until 1782—to the Rue de la Huchette. This street boasts several picturesque old buildings, but it is close to the tourist crunch of the Boulevard St-Michel. Turn down the astonishingly narrow Rue du Chat-qui-Pêche, from the sixteenth century, for a good idea of what the medieval streets of Paris must have looked like.

Now take the Rue Xavier-Privas and the Rue St-Séverin to the church of *St. Séverin*.

South of the church are its charnel houses on the Rue des Prêtres-St-Séverin, which leads to the Rue Boutebrie (*detour:* across Boulevard St-Germain to the *Thermes de Cluny* and the *Hôtel de Cluny*) and the Rue de la Parcheminerie, the street of scribes, book dealers, and parchment sellers in the Middle Ages. Via the Rue St-Jacques, one arrives in the Rue de la Harpe, once the main street of the quarter, with lovely seventeenth- and eighteenth-century mansions. Today it is a pedestrian area, as is the major part of the quarter from here to the Place St-Michel.

The Rue de la Huchette extends across the Place St-Michel, with its fountain by Gabriel Davioud, and the Place St-André-des-Arts—on the site of a Gothic church of the same name—to the Rue St-André-des-Arts, the old street leading to the monastery of St. Germain-des-Prés. In this street and the alleyways leading from it, a wealth of old structures have survived with lovely wrought-iron gates, elegant stone façades, and picturesque courtyards. Of these alleyways, the following are worth looking at: the Rue des Poitevins, with the remains of the *hôtel* of the abbots of Fécamp at No. 5; the Rue Suger; the Rue Gît-le-Cœur, with the Hôtel de Luynes at Nos. 5–9; the Rue de l'Hirondelle, which has buildings of the former Collège d'Autin; and the Rue Séguier. The name of the Rue des Grands-Augustins recalls the important monastery whose grounds once reached to the Seine and through whose gardens Henri IV had the Rue Dauphine laid out as an extension of the Pont Neuf.

The intersection of the Rue Dauphine and the Rue St-André-des-Arts, the Carrefour de Buci, forms one boundary of the Quartier Latin. Near here was the Porte de Buci, the gate to the village of St. Germain (at the corner of the Rue Mazarine there is a quite beautiful block of flats from the time of Louis XVI). The Rue de l'Ancienne-Comédie follows the course of Philippe Auguste's wall. The Comédie Française, founded in 1680, was located at No. 14 until 1770. Opposite is the famous Café Procope, which was a meeting place for the literary and political world as early as the seventeenth century. The Encyclopedists frequented it, as did Voltaire, the revolutionaries Danton, Marat, and Robespierre, the Romantics Alfred de Musset and George Sand, and later Paul Verlaine. No. 23 opens onto the Cour de Commerce-St-André, whose buildings were erected in 1776 after a medieval moat was filled in. In No. 9 lived Dr. Joseph-Ignace Guillotin, who here perfected his "philanthropic beheading machine" by experimenting with lambs. In the small Rue du Jardinet is the entrance to the Cour de Rohan, with remains of the fortress and *hôtel* of the archbishops of Rouen.

Cross the Boulevard St-Germain to the *École de Médecine*. The property along the Rue de l'École-de-Médecine belonged to the Franciscan monastery of the Cordeliers, whose refectory survives at No. 15. At No. 5 is the old Amphithéâtre de St-Côme, originally the lecture hall of the École de Médecine, with its tall cupola dating from 1691. The Rue Monsieur-le-Prince runs atop the moat from Philippe Auguste's wall, which serves as a foundation for a row of houses. Auguste Comte lived at No. 10; Blaise Pascal, at No. 54. By way of the Rue de Vaugirard one comes to the square in front of the *Sorbonne*. The chapel is normally accessible only when an exhibition is on; to see the grand amphitheater and main staircase, one should apply at the office.

Now take the Rue Victor-Cousin to the Rue Soufflot, which was laid out when the Panthéon was built. This street leads to the Place du Panthéon with its *Faculté de Droit,* built by Jacques-Germain Soufflot in 1771, on the north side, and its complement, Jacob Hittorf's *mairie* for the Fifth Arrondissement, built between 1844 and 1846. To the north of the *Panthéon* (open daily, except Tuesday, 10:00 A.M.– 5:30 P.M.; tours of the crypt every half-hour) is the *Bibliothèque Ste-Geneviève*, built between 1844 and 1850 by Henri Labrouste. In the adjacent Rue Valette, at No. 4, is the entrance to the *Collège de Ste-Barbe,* from 1460, one of the few surviving medieval collegiate structures. At No. 2 is the Tour de Calvin, where the Protestant reformer lived in 1531 and 1532 while studying at the Collège Montaigu (where the library now stands). Erasmus of Rotterdam, Ignatius of Loyola, and Rabelais had studied at this college before him.

Behind the Panthéon is the *Lycée Henri IV,* which encompasses several buildings from the abbey of Ste. Geneviève: the Tour de Clovis, the thirteenth-century kitchens and refectory, the eighteenth-century library, and the cloister from 1746. The monastery's church was razed when the Rue Clovis was cut through; on the north side of this street, the church of *St. Étienne-du-Mont* closes off the square. From the church, the Rue de la Montagne-Ste-Geneviève leads down to the Place Maubert, one of the oldest and most picturesque streets in Paris, which has preserved—as have a number of other streets on the north side of the hill, such as the Rue Laplace and the Rue Lanneau —a large percentage of its ancient buildings.

On the east, the street is bounded by the grounds of the former École Polytechnique, an elite scientific academy founded in 1794. This school took over the properties of two famous colleges, the Collège de Navarre and the Collège de Boncourt, in 1805. Since 1977, it has occupied new facilities in Massy-Palaiseau.

The Rue Lanneau leads across the Rue Jean-de-Beauvais (where, beyond the Rue des Écoles, there is the small chapel of the Collège de Dormans-Beauvais, built by Robert Du Temple in 1375) to the *Collège de France*. This institution was founded in 1530 by François I. As a "republic of scholars," it is independent of the University and subject only to the government. A number of France's most important scholars, from both the sciences and the humanities, are numbered among its members. The Collège took on its present-day appearance with the construction of Jean-François Chalgrin's distinguished wing on the Place Marcelin-Berthelot in 1778. One should apply to the concierge to view the interior.

St. Germain-des-Prés

Although the Quartier Latin continues to be largely dominated even today by the institutes of the University, colleges, and schools, much of its medieval architecture has unfortunately been replaced by unattractive nineteenth-century buildings. The area around St. Germain-des-Prés, however, has managed to preserve its character as a residential section for intellectuals. It still has numerous bookshops and publishing houses, galleries for traditional and modern art, antique shops, rare-book dealers, and famous cafés and restaurants—among the latter, Aux Deux Magots, Café de Flore, Lipp, and Vagenende. The home of Existentialism in the early postwar years, the quarter still thrives today because of its proximity to the institutions of learning, some of which have settled here—for example, the Institut de Sciences Politiques and the Faculté de Médecine. Its southern part, the area around the Odéon and the Palais du Luxembourg, blends imperceptibly into the Quartier Latin.

Our starting point is the square in front

of the abbey church of *St. Germain-des-Prés*. To the north of the church tower, there is a small plot containing architectural fragments from the former Lady Chapel by Pierre de Montreuil and the abbey's cloister. In the center of the space is Pablo Picasso's memorial to Guillaume Apollinaire, placed here in 1959. The Rue de l'Abbaye leads across the former abbey grounds to the *Palais Abbatial*, which has been recently restored and is one of the most important buildings from the late sixteenth century in Paris. On the site of the formal courtyard in front of this palace is the intimate Place de Fürstenberg, with its uniform architecture. Eugène Delacroix had his studio and his residence at No. 6, which is now a museum. The white buildings, the old lanterns, and the airy catalpa trees give the square its distinctive atmosphere. At one time the abbots' stables stood on the right and left of it. The street and the square are named for the bishop of Strasbourg, Franz Egon von Fürstenberg, who assisted France in capturing that city and ended his days in Paris as a cardinal and abbot of St. Germain-des-Prés. The narrow Rue Cardinale is also named after him. This street, like the nearby Rue de l'Echaudé and Rue Bourbon-le-Château, preserves a number of picturesque old buildings.

Proceed via the Rue de Buci, the old main street of the quarter, to the Rue Mazarine, a street full of art dealers and rare-book shops. Molière set up his theater in No. 12 in 1643. Nearer the Seine, the Rue Mazarine and the Rue Guénégaud border the site of two of Paris's most important buildings: the *Hôtel des Monnaies*, with its Musée de la Monnaie, and the *Collège des Quatre-Nations*; the Bibliothèque Mazarine, with the cardinal's book collection and the room's original furnishings, is open daily, except Tuesday and Sunday, 10:00 A.M.–6:00 P.M.).

Between the two palaces on the Quai de Conti is the small *Hôtel de Guénégaud* by François Mansart from 1659. To the same architect is attributed the *Hôtel de Chimay* a bit farther along, at Nos. 15–17 Quai Malaquais. Erected in about 1640, this is now part of the *École des Beaux-Arts*, the national art academy, which occupies a number of buildings and courtyards between the Quai Malaquais and the Rue Bonaparte. These are the grounds of the former Pré-aux-Clercs, where Marguerite de Valois founded an Augustinian convent in 1608. The convent's cloister and chapel (with the oldest cupola in Paris) have survived within this extensive complex. From the school's courtyard on the Rue Bonaparte, one has a view of the front of the chapel, against which the three-story central façade from the château at Anet was placed in the nineteenth century. During the Revolutionary period, Alexandre Lenoir here set up his Musée des Monuments Français; in so doing, he saved priceless works of art from secularized churches—and, most notably, the tombs from St. Denis—from destruction.

The Rue de Seine and Rue Bonaparte, along with their cross streets the Rue des Beaux-Arts, Rue Visconti, and Rue Jacob, have preserved a wealth of old apartment houses and *hôtels,* some of them with picturesque inner courtyards. In spite of the heavy traffic along these streets, which connect the Boulevard St-Germain with the Seine, they remain fascinating because of their first-class antique shops, bookshops, and specialty shops for artists. In the Rue Jacob, whose western end was sadly disfigured by the structure built to house the Faculté de Médecine in the 1930s, there are a few quite distinguished middle-range hotels. From the point where it intersects with the Rue des Saints-Pères, the Rue Jacob continues westward as the Rue de l'Université with no essential change of character.

Here begins the Faubourg St-Germain.

From the Rue Jacob one passes via the Rue St-Benoît into the center of St. Germain-des-Prés, home of the famous Aux Deux Magots and Flore cafés, the Brasserie Lipp, and the bookshop La Hune. The Boulevard St-Germain is flanked by modern-art galleries, bookshops, and pleasant bistros; the American-style drugstore at the corner of the Rue de Rennes caused a considerable sensation in the 1960s. The south side of the boulevard consists, between Nos. 155 and 175, of old buildings that once stood in the Rue Taranne; the rest of that street disappeared in Haussmann's reorganization. Following either Haussmann's Rue de Rennes, at the end of which one can see the Tour Montparnasse, or the old, picturesque Rue du Dragon, named for an elegant eighteenth-century block of flats that was decorated with a dragon and sadly torn down before World War II, one arrives, via the Rue du Four, at the Rue du Vieux-Colombier. These last two streets have been associated with the abbey of St. Germain-des-Prés since the Middle Ages. On the lane that extended southwestward from the Rue de Buci (today the Rue du Four and Rue du Cherche-Midi) was the oven where the inhabitants of St. Germain had their bread baked. On the Rue du Vieux-Colombier, the abbey had its dovecote, a privilege that was restricted to the nobility and religious houses until the Revolution. This street was one of the intellectual centers of Paris in the seventeenth century.

This part of the quarter is stamped by its many nineteenth-century buildings and its fashion boutiques. A number of older streets here have been preserved, such as the Rue Bernard-Palissy and the Rue des Canettes, in which small restaurants and bars have been established. The Rue du Vieux-Colombier leads to the Place St-Sulpice. Here one can admire Louis Visconti's *Fontaine des Quatre-Évêques*, from 1844, and the church of *St. Sulpice* with its façade by Giovanni Niccolò Servandoni, who also designed the square. Near St. Sulpice, there are numerous shops selling clerical articles, *pompes-funèbres*, and Catholic literature. Proceed along the Rue St-Sulpice to the Rue Garancière, passing below the wall of the Lady Chapel next to the church choir. Here one finds the lovely *Hôtel de Sourdéac* at No. 8, the small *Hôtel de Nivernais* at No. 11, and an unobtrusive extension of the Senate at the end of the street. In the Rue de Vaugirard, one comes upon the Petit-Luxembourg, the residence of the president of the Senate, and to the left of it the *Palais du Luxembourg*, seat of the Senate itself.

Detour: Jardin du Luxembourg, Avenue de l'Observatoire, then left across the Boulevard St-Michel and along the Rue de Val-de-Grâce to the church of *Val-de-Grâce* and the adjacent hospital in the former convent buildings. Then take the Rue St-Jacques to *Port-Royal* and the Avenue de l'Observatoire to the *Observatoire*.

From the Palais du Luxembourg, pass the *Odéon* and the beautiful semicircular square on which it stands; then return to St. Germain-des-Prés via either the Rue de l'Odéon or the Rue de Tournon.

Faubourg St-Germain

Despite all the changes it has undergone, the aristocratic Faubourg St-Germain continues to project an image of eighteenth-century nobility. Although most of its mansions have been converted into ministries or embassies, it continues to be the preferred residential area for the old bourgeoisie and noble families of France, a discreetly elegant section that eludes the prying gaze of the tourist. Until only recently, the archbishop of Paris also lived here (Rue Barbet-de-Jouy, where the prefect of the Région de l'Ile-de-France also resides), and it is full of ecclesiastical establishments, seminaries, and convents—though not even one of the important churches of Paris.

Given the extraordinarily rich store of old and interesting residential architecture, it is not an easy task to suggest a walking tour that includes everything of importance. The best plan is to use the most important streets, the Rue du Bac, once the main commercial street of the quarter, and Haussmann's Boulevard St-Germain and Boulevard Raspail, both of which cut across the old network of streets, as points of departure for detours into the intersecting streets.

A good orientation tour might begin at the intersection of the Boulevard Raspail and the Rue de Sèvres, at the Square Boucicaut. Here stands the oldest Parisian department store, *Bon Marché,* built in 1876 by Gustave Eiffel and Louis-Charles Boileau. An addition in the Art Déco style was built by Boileau's son, who also designed the large Hotel Lutétia, at this same intersection, with its rich neo-Rococo decorations from about 1900.

The Rue de Sèvres has developed into one of the most important fashion centers of Paris during the last two decades. It has a wealth of ready-to-wear boutiques, especially along the section between the Boulevard Raspail and Carrefour de la Croix-Rouge. The small Rue Récamier commemorates the cultured woman who lived here, in the former convent of Abbaye-aux-Bois, from 1819 to 1849 and who received all the great personalities of the time in her salon, among them, almost daily, Chateaubriand.

Take the Rue des Saints-Pères to the Rue de Grenelle. At No. 15 is the *Hôtel de Bérulle,* an early work by Alexandre Bron-gniart from 1776. Then turn right into the Rue St-Guillaume, where the Institut des Sciences Politiques is housed in various eighteenth-century *hôtels.* In the courtyard of No. 31 is the famous *Maison du Docteur-Dalsace,* a functionalist construction of glass brick and iron by Pierre Chareau and Bijvoet from 1931.

Turn right across the Boulevard St-Germain and proceed to the Rue des Saints-Pères on the left. At the corner of the boulevard is the former Chapelle St-Pierre by Robert de Cotte. Its façade dates from the Revolution and was designed by Clavareau. Next to it is the disproportionately massive *Faculté de Médecine,* built by Jean Walter and Madeline from 1937 to 1953, with reliefs by Paul Landowski. Opposite, at No. 28, is the *Hôtel de Fleury,* built by Jacques-Denis Antoine, the architect of the Hôtel des Monnaies, in 1768. Since 1845, it has housed the civil-engineering school, École des Ponts et Chaussées.

At the intersection with the Rue des Saints-Pères, the Rue Jacob becomes the Rue de l'Université, which boasts some lovely eighteenth-century buildings. No. 13 is the former Venetian embassy; it was restored in 1978 and now houses the elite school for administrative officials, the École Nationale d'Administration. No. 15 is the *Hôtel d'Aligre,* headquarters of the respected journal *Revue des Deux Mondes.* No. 17 is the *Hôtel Bochart-de-Saron* from 1639, now the Gallimard publishing house. No. 24 is the *Hôtel de Senneterre,* with a peristyle by Giovanni Niccolò Servandoni from 1728. Detour to the left to 46 Rue du Bac, the *Hôtel de Jacques-Samuel-Bernard,* built by Germain Boffrand in 1742, and to the church of *St. Thomas-d'Aquin,* the chapel of the former Dominican novitiate, which was begun by Pierre Bullet in 1682 and furnished with a classical façade in 1740.

Return to the Rue de l'Université and notice one of the loveliest *hôtels* of the *faubourg,* the *Hôtel Pozzo di Borgo,* No. 51, begun by Lassurance in 1707. Continue through the Rue de Portiers to the Rue de Lille, where the Musée du XIXe Siècle will eventually occupy the former Gare d'Orsay and display works of art from the Romantic period to the Art Nouveau movement. Turning left past the *Hôtel du Président-Duret,* No. 67, from 1706, one reaches the *Hôtel de Salm,* the headquarters of the Légion d'Honneur since 1806. At No. 78 is Germain Boffrand's *Hôtel de Beauharnais,* now the embassy of West Germany. It boasts an Egyptian-style portico and some of the most splendid interior decorations from the Empire. Viewing hours are posted at the entrance. Next door—at No. 80, also by Boffrand—is a 1744 mansion that houses the Ministry of Commerce and Trade.

Cross the Boulevard St-Germain to the *Palais-Bourbon,* the seat of the National Assembly. Its sober, templelike façade facing the Seine was erected on orders from Napoleon by Bernard Poyet in 1803—a deliberate counterpart to the Madeleine across the river and beyond the Place de la Concorde. On its south side is a colonnaded *cour d'honneur* from the reign of Louis-Philippe, which manages to reinterpret Lassurance's old Palais-Bourbon in terms of Parisian classicism. In front of this courtyard is one of the most elegant squares in Paris, in the Louis XVI style, the Place du Palais-Bourbon. Slightly west of it stands the *Hôtel de Lassay,* built in 1722 by Jean Aubert and now housing the offices of the president of the National Assembly. Beyond this is the rather uninteresting Foreign Ministry, erected after plans by Lacornée in 1845 on the Quai d'Orsay—a name synonymous with French diplomacy.

From the Place du Palais-Bourbon, take the Rue de Bourgogne and then turn left into the Rue St-Dominique, whose north side is occupied by the Ministry of Defense, in the buildings of the former convent of the Daughters of St. Joseph (Nos. 8–12) and the two *hôtels* (Nos. 14 and 16) built by Aubry in 1714. It was here that Charles de Gaulle set up his provisional government in 1944. On the south side of the street, at No. 35, is the *Hôtel de Broglie* from 1724, modernized during the Empire. Standing on the Square Samuel-Rousseau is the neo-Gothic church of *Ste. Clotilde,* begun in 1846 after plans by Franz Christian Gau. Camille Saint-Saëns was organist here from 1858 to 1891.

At No. 1, where the Rue St-Dominique runs into the Boulevard St-Germain, is the very interesting *Hôtel Amelot-de-Gournay.* It was built by Germain Boffrand between 1695 and 1710 and incorporates a splendid oval courtyard. Cross the Boulevard St-Germain, turning right past the Ministry for the Environment. This occupies the *Hôtel de Roquelaure* at No. 246, a work by Lassurance from 1722, and the *Hôtel de Lesdiguières* at No. 248, from 1740. This brings one to the Boulevard Raspail, on the right, from which one turns right again into the Rue de Grenelle. With the Rue de Varenne, this is one of the most important streets of *hôtels* in the *faubourg.*

In front of the buildings at Nos. 57–59 is the *Fontaine des Quatre-Saisons,* constructed by Edme Bouchardon from 1739 to 1746 and one of the earliest examples of the return to antiquity in Paris. Its effect is limited by the lack of distance afforded the viewer in this narrow street. At No. 73 is Antoine-François Legrand's *Hotel de Gallifet* from 1775, an important example of early classicism. Beyond the intersection with the Rue du Bac, at No. 79, is the *Grand Hôtel d'Estrées,* built in 1713 for the Duchesse d'Estrées by Robert de Cotte. Since the end of the nineteenth century, this has housed the Russian embassy. Next to it is the *Petit Hôtel d'Estrées,* from 1709. At No. 83 is one of the oldest buildings of the quarter, the *Hôtel de Bonneval* from 1672, next to which, at No. 85, is the *Hôtel d'Avaray,* constructed by Jean-Baptiste Leroux in 1718 and now the residence of the Dutch ambassador.

The *Hôtel de Bauffremont,* at No. 87, boasts rich façades dating from 1721 to 1736. Across the street, at No. 102, stands the *Hôtel de Maillebois* by Pierre Delisle-Mansart, where Saint-Simon lived until 1755. No. 106 is the former Bernardine convent by Pentémont, with its (now Protestant) chapel by Pierre Contant d'Ivry from 1747 to 1756. The convent buildings extend along the Rue de Bellechasse and now house various departments of the Ministry of Defense. No. 101 is the *Hôtel de Charolais,* by Lassurance, from 1700 to 1714. At No. 110, the corner of the Rue de Bellechasse, is one of the masterpieces of the Louis XVI style, Mathurin Cherpitel's *Hôtel de Roche-chouart,* from 1778. Today it houses part of the Ministry of Education. Passing the *Hôtel de Villars,* at No. 116, a work by Germain Boffrand from 1709, one comes to the important *Hôtel du Châtelet,* No. 127. This was built in 1770 by Cherpitel; today it houses a section of the Ministry of Labor.

At the end of the street is the *Hôtel de Chanac,* now the Swiss embassy, designed by Alexis Delamair in 1750. Head south down the Boulevard des Invalides to the Rue de Varenne. At this corner, the grounds of the *Hôtel Biron* begin. These comprise the main structure, courtyard, and garden portion of the Musée Rodin. At the intersection of the Rue de Varenne and the Rue Barbet-de-Jouy is the *Hôtel de Broglie,* originally constructed by Germain Boffrand in 1735 and reworked in 1785 by Leboursier.

Next, one passes the ugly modern building of the Ministry of Agriculture and the *Petit* and *Grand Hôtels de Castries,* Nos. 74 and 72, built in 1760 and 1700, respectively, before coming to the *Hôtel de Matignon,* No. 57, the residence of the prime minister. This mansion boasts one of the largest private gardens in Paris. The Italian embassy occupies the *Hôtel de Boisgelin,* at No. 47, built by Henri Parent in 1787. Its cultural section is located across the street in the Hôtel de Gallifet.

Turning right along the Rue du Bac—on the corner, at No. 85, are remnants of the former convent des Récollets—one passes the *Hôtel de Ste-Aldegonde,* No. 102, and the *Hôtel de La Feuillade,* No. 101, both from the early eighteenth century. At Nos. 118–120, is the *Hôtel de Clermont-Tonnerre,* with lovely Rococo decorations. Chateaubriand lived here from 1838 to 1848. At No. 128 is the Séminaire des Missions Étrangères, with its pilgrims' chapel in the courtyard. Next to it, across the Rue de Babylone, is the convent of the Sisters of the Order of St. Vincent, its severe buildings surrounding the former Hôtel de la Vallière. Turn left into the Rue de Babylone back to the Square Boucicaut.

Invalides, École Militaire, and Tour Eiffel

The huge Hôtel des Invalides and the École Militaire dominate the western portion of the Seventh Arrondissement. The major world's fairs of the nineteenth century were held here between the Esplanade des Invalides and the Champ-de-Mars. Today, this area is covered with modern buildings and parks. The residential buildings along the broad avenues and the Champ-de-Mars are quite elegant. A relatively popular old quarter is the Quartier du Gros-Caillou, in the bend of the Seine between the Avenue de

La Bourdonnais and the Boulevard de Latour-Maubourg.

Begin the tour at the Esplanade des Invalides. This was laid out, starting in 1704, after plans by Robert de Cotte. It stretches between the broad north front of the Hôtel des Invalides and the Seine. Since 1978, when an underground garage was built beneath it, the Esplanade des Invalides has been restored to its original state, with its grand perspective across the *Pont Alexandre III* to the *Grand Palais* and the *Petit Palais* and on to the Champs-Elysées.

Work your way through the *Hôtel des Invalides* (open daily, 7:00 A.M.–7:00 P.M.; St. Louis-des-Invalides, 10:00 A.M.–5:00 P.M., except Tuesday and Sunday morning; Napoleon's tomb in the Dôme des Invalides, Sunday, Tuesday, and Thursday, 10:00 A.M.– 5:00 P.M., Saturday, to 6:00 P.M. [an admission ticket is required]; Musée de l'Armée).

In front of the Dôme des Invalides is the semicircular Place Vauban; five avenues radiate from it. The lovely French garden on the right, between the Avenue de Tourville and the Boulevard de Latour-Maubourg, was restored in 1980. Take the Avenue de Lowendal to the Place de Fontenoy, where various modern ministries and the *Maison de l'UNESCO* (tours daily, 10:00 A.M.–12:00 M. and 3:00 P.M.–5:00 P.M.) are situated.

Behind an elegant gate on the west side of the square lies the forecourt of the *École Militaire* (to see the interior, one must write to the Général Commandant d'Armes de l'École Militaire, 1 Place Joffre; the chapel is open for services on Sunday, 9:00 A.M.– 12:00 M.).

Proceed along the Avenue de Suffren to the corner of the Avenue de la Motte-Picquet. Here is the Village Suisse, which contains dozens of antique shops. A right turn brings one to the main façade of the military academy facing the Champ-de-Mars; then walk through this park to the *Tour Eiffel*.

Take the Avenue de La Bourdonnais to the Avenue Rapp, where there are a number of interesting Art Nouveau buildings by Jules Lavirotte. At No. 29 is the house that he built for the ceramicist Alexandre Bigot, with whom he constructed the Céramic-Hôtel in the Avenue de Wagram. At the end of the Square Rapp is a somewhat earlier building, from 1899, comparable to the Lycée Italien in the Rue Sédilot, which can be reached via the Rue St-Dominique.

In the Rue St-Dominique, near No. 129, there is a small, symmetrical square graced by Bralle's Fontaine de Mars from 1806. Proceed past the church of *St. Pierre-du-Gros-Caillou,* designed by Étienne Godde in 1822, back to the Esplanade des Invalides.

Right Bank

Quartier des Halles

This is one of the oldest quarters in the city, surrounding what used to be the "belly of Paris." But even long before the transfer of the Halles outside the city, the area had undergone fundamental changes.

Start the tour at the Place du Louvre. On one side is the east front of the palace, with Claude Perrault's colonnades. At André Malraux's suggestion, the unfinished moat, intended to run in front of this façade in the seventeenth century, was excavated beginning in 1964. Opposite is the church of *St. Germain l'Auxerrois*. Its quite beautiful Renaissance portal on the north side of the apse is visible only from the courtyard of the elementary school in the Rue de l'Arbre-Sec.

Go left down the Rue de Rivoli to the *Oratoire*. In front of its choir, there is a statue of Admiral Coligny, the French Protestant leader who was the first victim of the St.

Bartholomew's Day massacre. Walk down the Rue de l'Oratoire and turn left into the Rue St-Honoré, which is much less snobbish at this eastern end than it is farther west. It is one of the oldest streets in Paris; merchants began settling here in narrow, high-gabled houses in the thirteenth century.

Turn right into the Rue Jean-Jacques-Rousseau, where there are a number of old buildings as well as the entrance to the *Passage Véro-Dodat*. Constructed in 1826, this was once one of the most luxurious *passages* in Paris. Even now, its faded charm and its remarkable shops make it well worth a visit.

Across the Rue du Louvre is the round *Bourse de Commerce*. It stands on the site of the old Halle aux Bleds and of Catherine de Médicis's even earlier Hôtel de Soissons. The tall, fluted column on the south side of the round building is supposed to have been used as an observatory by Catherine's astrologer Ruggieri.

Take the Rue Sauval back to the Rue St-Honoré. To the left, at the intersection of the Rue de l'Arbre-Sec, is the *Fontaine de la Croix-du-Trahoir* by Jacques-Germain Soufflot, from 1776. Another left turn puts one in the Rue Baltard, which leads across the site of the former Halles. The pavilions of Les Halles used to obscure the view of the south side of *St. Eustache*. Take the Rue du Jour along the façade of St. Eustache. Here, at No. 4, is the former *hôtel* of the abbots of Royaumont. Then go to the right, down the Rue Montmartre, off which there is a cul-de-sac leading to the north portal of the church. Across from it, at No. 16, is the entrance to the *Passage de la Reine-de-Hongrie*, through which one proceeds to the Rue de Montorgueil. This is one of the busiest streets of the quarter. It boasts not only the lovely façade of the building at No. 15, created by Martin Goupy in 1729, but

also the venerable restaurant L'Escargot, with its gigantic ornamental snail and Belle Epoque décor.

Now turn into the Rue Mauconseil, which has been of great importance in the history of Parisian theater. It was here that the first theater in Paris was established in 1548, the Théâtre de l'Hôtel de Bourgogne. It was located on the grounds of the palace of the dukes of Burgundy, of which the Tour de Jean-sans-Peur—at No. 20 in the nearby Rue Étienne-Marcel—is a remnant.

The Rue Française takes you to the Rue Tiquetonne, which has old, restored buildings. Parallel to it, between the Rue Dussoubs and the Rue St-Denis, runs the *Passage du Grand-Cerf*; its glass roof dates from 1824.

The Rue St-Denis is one of the old main streets of the city. Through it, the kings used to enter the city and funeral processions would wind toward St. Denis. To a great extent, it has preserved its old architectural substance, although the shops of its wealthy merchants have long since given way to sex shops, porn theaters, and the like.

Turn right as you emerge from the Passage du Grand-Cerf and proceed to the church of *St. Leu–St. Gilles*. The alleys and cross streets along this route are quite picturesque, and in recent years, as the area has been renovated, they have become increasingly filled with chic clothing stores, boutiques, and galleries. Proceed to the *Fontaine des Innocents* in the center of the newly laid-out square bounded on the south by the uniform façade—392 feet long—of one of the largest old apartment blocks in Paris, built in 1669. This extends along the Rue de la Ferronnerie, where, in front of the building at No. 11, Henri IV was murdered by François Ravaillac in 1610.

On the west side, the square opens onto the site of the old Halles, containing the

Forum des Halles, the Pavillon des Arts, which holds temporary exhibitions, the underground RER station, and, to the north, the vast concrete structure containing the railroad's air-conditioning system, for which a curtain façade is planned.

Return to the Rue St-Denis, following it past the Rue des Lombards, named for the first moneychangers in Paris, to the Quartier Ste-Opportune. This is a section of narrow, twisting lanes through which Haussmann cut the Rue des Halles in the nineteenth century. Its name commemorates the parish, now no longer in existence, that was the largest landowner on the Right Bank in the Middle Ages.

Take the Rue des Lavandières-Ste-Opportune, then the Rue des Orfèvres, to the Rue St-Germain-l'Auxerrois, which leads to the great department store Samaritaine along the Seine quay. A café terrace on the roof of Samaritaine provides a splendid view of the center of the city. Return to the Place du Louvre.

Quartier de l'Hôtel-de-Ville and Centre Beaubourg

The Halles quarter continues beyond the Boulevard de Sébastopol into the area of the new Centre Beaubourg, which a decade ago was among the problem areas of Paris, with slums that seemed impossible to raze. With the creation of the Centre Beaubourg, however, its character has changed completely. Restoration and renovation have caused the district to become one of the most expensive residential areas in Paris. Most of the old craftsmen have moved elsewhere, and in their place art galleries, bookshops, and fashionable boutiques have opened.

Begin at the Place du Châtelet, where, until the Revolution, the fortress of the Grand Châtelet guarded the Pont au Change.

Two theaters by Gabriel Davioud from 1862 flank the square. Across the Avenue Victoria is the Square St-Jacques, with the Late Gothic tower of the church of St. Jacques-la-Boucherie, torn down in 1802.

Take the Rue St-Martin, recently designated as a pedestrian zone, to the new cultural center. This street, following the course of the Roman *cardo,* is one of the oldest streets in Paris, and leads past the church of *St. Merri* to the square in front of the *Centre National d'Art et de Culture Georges-Pompidou.* In recent years, this so-called Piazza Beaubourg has become one of the city's main attractions, thanks to its constantly changing offerings of jugglers, acrobats, mimes, and so on. The west side of the street bordering the "Piazza" has been painstakingly restored in recent years; the buildings on the north side of the square were removed to make way for the residential complex known as the Quartier de l'Horloge-St-Martin, a dense agglomeration of luxury-class apartments.

Parallel to the Rue St-Martin is the old Rue Quincampoix, which we approach via the Rue des Lombards; here, the Scottish financier John Law carried out his speculations from his bank at No. 65. Return to the Rue St-Martin by way of the narrow Rue de Venise. Go north on the Rue St-Martin as far as the Rue de Montmorency, where, at No. 51, the Gothic house of Nicolas Flamel from 1407 still stands, though considerably changed, or on to the church of *St. Nicolas-des-Champs* and the adjacent former abbey of *St. Martin-des-Champs.*

Return via the Rue Beaubourg, which achieved grim notoriety under its former name, Rue Transnonain, because of the massacre that took place under Louis-Philippe, the Citizen King. Turning left into the Rue Michel-le-Comte, one comes upon the *Hôtel d'Hallwyll,* at No. 26. This is an early work by Claude-Nicolas Ledoux from 1765, built for the finance minister Jacques Necker; his daughter, later Mme. de Staël, was supposedly born here. Take the Rue du Temple to the right as far as the Rue Ste-Croix-de-la-Bretonnerie, passing through the square of the same name to the church and cloister of the Billettes on the Rue des Archives. This was a Carmelite house and boasts the only surviving medieval cloister in Paris. Its Baroque church dates from 1756 and is now Protestant.

Take the Rue des Archives to the *Hôtel de Ville* on the Place de Grève (tours of the Hôtel de Ville take place on Monday at 10:30 A.M., starting from the Syndicat d'Initiative de Paris, 29 Rue de Rivoli).

The Marais

The Marais contains the most important ensemble of seventeenth-century private residential architecture in France. Beginning with Henri IV, it was the section favored by the nobility, which built its mansions between the Rue du Temple and the Bastille. Spectacular restoration campaigns carried out since the 1960s have returned much of its splendor but at the same time destroyed its unique social structure. The Marais Festival—held annually from mid-June to mid-July in the churches, *hôtels*, and gardens of the quarter and consisting of concerts, plays, operas, and folklore exhibits —has greatly contributed to the area's new popularity and has helped to save some of its neighborhood fabric. From May 1 to October 15, the most important buildings are illuminated every evening from 9:30 P.M. to 11:30 P.M.; the rest of the year, these buildings are illuminated on Saturday, Sunday, and holidays from 9:00 P.M. to 12:00 P.M.

Information about the area and its restoration can be obtained from the Centre Culturel du Marais, 28 Rue des Francs-Bourgeois, and the Association pour la Sauvegarde et la Mise en Valeur du Paris Historique, 44–46 Rue François-Miron.

Begin the tour at the Place St-Gervais, in front of Salomon de Brosse's façade of the church of *St. Gervais–St. Protais*. Along the Rue François-Miron, on the north side of the church, are the elegant, uniform buildings of the former Pourtour-St-Gervais, rental housing from 1732 belonging to the church. These surround the old charnel houses (entrance at No. 2), and it was their careful restoration that began the renovation of the entire quarter. Nos. 2–4 contained the home of the Couperin family, organists at St. Gervais–St. Protais. The elm trees worked into the second-floor railings are the symbol of the parish; in the Middle Ages, legal judgments were proclaimed beneath the elm in front of the church.

A right turn into the Rue des Barres leads to lovely half-timbered buildings and a view of the top of the choir of St. Gervais–St. Protais. Take the Rue du Grenier-sur-l'Eau to the *Mémorial du Martyr Juif Inconnu*, a monument to the persecuted Jews of Paris, erected in 1956 by Goldberg, Arretche, and Persitz. Across from it, in the Rue Geoffroy-l'Asnier, is the *Hôtel de Châlons-Luxembourg*, erected between 1600 and 1615 by Henry IV's ambassador to England, Antoine Le Fèvre de La Broderie.

Turn left into the Rue François-Miron once again. At Nos. 11 and 13 are two characteristic half-timbered buildings from the reign of Louis XI. Across from them, at No. 42, is the *Hôtel de la Barre-de-Carron* from 1772 by Pierre de Vigny. The adjacent seventeenth-century buildings stand above the cellars of the Paris residence of the monks of Ourscamps, built in the twelfth century. At No. 68 is the unusual *Hôtel de Beauvais*, whose wings extend to the Rue de Jouy. The south side of this street is dominated by the *Hôtel d'Aumont*. Stretching across an underground garage, the garden of this mansion opens onto the Quai de l'Hôtel-de-Ville and its Cité Internationale des Arts, a studio building for foreign art students that opened in 1965.

To the east are the grounds of the *Hôtel de Sens* with their restored French garden. The structures surrounding the *hôtel* were built in a first postwar reconstruction campaign.

From the Rue des Jardins-St-Paul, one can view the remains of Philippe Auguste's city wall and the church of *St. Paul–St. Louis*. The *Lycée Charlemagne*, across the street from the church, incorporates portions of the old Jesuit hall, and the school's library was once Père Lachaise's apartment. Leading from the Rue St-Antoine, in front of the façade of the church, is the Rue de Sévigné. Here, on the left, in the courtyard of the fire department, are the remnants of François Mansart's *Hôtel Bouthillier de Chavigny*.

Follow the Rue St-Antoine eastward to the *Hôtel de Sully*. The street entering opposite it is the Rue de l'Hôtel-St-Paul, where the medieval residence of kings, the Hôtel St-Paul, used to stand. Its gardens once extended to the Rue Charles V, which still has some lovely seventeenth-century façades. At 12 Rue Charles V is the *Hôtel d'Aubray*, which was built at the beginning of the seventeenth century by Balthazar de Gobelin, from the famous family of dyers and weavers, who was president of the accounting office. Return to the Rue St-Antoine and continue past the *Hôtel de Mayenne* to François Mansart's *Temple de la Visitation Ste-Marie*.

Proceed to the Place de la Bastille, the site of the old fortress. In the center is the *Colonne de Juillet,* topped by Augustin Dumont's statue of the Spirit of Liberty, commemorating the victims of the fighting in July 1830.

Follow the Boulevard Beaumarchais past the home of Jules Hardouin-Mansart, whose garden side is visible from the boulevard. Then take the Rue du Pas-de-la-Mule to the *Place des Vosges*, the center of the Marais and the site of the former royal palace, the Hôtel des Tournelles. Not all of the façades of the thirty-eight houses surrounding the square have been restored, but a number of bistros and shops have returned to the arcades. In the southeast corner, at No. 6, is the Musée Victor-Hugo.

The Rue des Francs-Bourgeois leads to the *Hôtel Carnavalet,* with its vast collection relating to the city's history and relics of Parisian architecture standing about in its courtyards. Proceed to the *Hôtel Lamoignon* at the intersection of the Rue des Francs-Bourgeois and the Rue Pavée.

Detour: At 10 Rue Pavée is Hector Guimard's *Synagogue* from 1913; the Rue des Rosiers is the Jewish center of the Fourth Arrondissement.

From the Hôtel Lamoignon, follow the Rue Payenne past the *Hôtel de Marle* at No. 11, now a Swedish cultural center, and the *Hôtel du Lude* at No. 13 to the Rue du Parc-Royal. Here, there is a whole row of Louis XIII houses including, at No. 10, Louis Le Vau's *Hôtel de Vigny* from 1628. To the left, at 1 Rue de la Perle is the residence of the architect Libéral Bruant. Go down the Rue de Thorigny to the *Hôtel Salé,* which will house a Picasso museum.

On the opposite side of this street, there are some lovely Louis XVI houses. Behind these, some gigantic apartment houses have been built over the past few years; their façades are surprisingly well adapted to the existing structures. Return down the Rue de la Perle—due to widening in the late nineteenth century, only its south side is old—to the Rue Vieille-du-Temple. A left turn brings one to the *Hôtel de Rohan*.

At the corner of the Rue des Francs-Bourgeois is the Gothic *Hôtel Hérouet* (heavily restored) from about 1510. A bit farther along, at No. 47, is the *Hôtel Amelot de Bisseuil*, or Hôtel des Ambassadeurs de Hollande.

Return to the Rue des Blancs-Manteaux and the church of *Notre-Dame-des-Blancs-Manteaux*; a passageway to the right of its choir leads to the Rue des Francs-Bourgeois. Farther to the left down the Rue des Francs-Bourgeois is the *Hôtel de Soubise*, the most splendid of the Marais palaces and seat of the French Archives Nationales.

Turn right down the Rue des Archives to François Mansart's *Hôtel de Guénégaud*, which has housed the Musée de la Chasse since its restoration. Across from it, at the intersection of the Rue des Haudriettes, there is a lovely fountain, with reliefs of Naiads, by Pierre-Philippe Mignot from 1765. The Rue des Haudriettes has been restored to a great extent, and its old buildings have been transformed into luxury apartments.

Take the Rue du Temple to the left. At No. 79 is the *Hôtel de Montmor* from 1623, and a bit farther, at No. 71, the *Hôtel de St-Aignan*. The latter was begun in 1640 by Pierre Le Muet for the finance minister Claude Mesmes. Across the street is the Passage Ste-Avoie, through which one returns, via the Rue Rambuteau, to the Rue des Archives. At No. 40 are remnants of the home of Jacques Cœur, Charles VII's financier, from the beginning of the fifteenth century. Return past the church of the Billettes to the Place St-Gervais.

Quartier du Palais-Royal and the Louvre

Start the tour at the Place du Louvre in front of the colonnades. Enter through the central portal into the *Cour Carrée* with its façades by Pierre Lescot, Jacques Lemercier, and their successors. Take the north portal (right) into the Rue de Rivoli. Across this street is the former Louvre department store, now, among other things, a center for antiques. Turn left to the Place du Palais-Royal.

In the former palace of Cardinal Richelieu are the Council of State, the Constitutional Council, and the National Office for Cultural Affairs. Adjoining it on the west is the *Théâtre Français*, which has portraits of famous playwrights and actors in the vestibule, including Jean-Antoine Houdon's seated figure of Voltaire from 1781.

The Place du Palais-Royal extends to the west into the Place Colette and Place Malraux; the latter is adorned with lovely nineteenth-century fountains. Here begins the grand Avenue de l'Opéra, one of Paris's main thoroughfares and the favored address for international tourist agencies and airlines.

Take the passageway between the theater and the Palais-Royal into the *cour d'honneur*. Next to the east wing of the palace, the Aile de Valois, is the so-called Galerie des Proues with its ship trophies, the only surviving portion of the original palace of Cardinal Richelieu, who was also the admiral of the French fleet. Walk through the gardens of the Palais-Royal and note the lovely façades by Victor Louis, then through the passage at the north side of the garden, the Galerie Beaujolais, where Colette lived, at No. 9, and where, in the northwest corner, the noble, Empire-style restaurant Le Grand Véfour is still in business. This passage brings you to the Rue des Petits-Champs, which leads, to the right, into the *Place des Victoires*. From this square, one can look down the Rue Catinat to the main entrance of the Banque de France.

North of the square and slightly hidden is the Place des Petits-Pères, which includes the church of *Notre-Dame-des-Victoires*. Return by way of the Rue des Petits-Pères to the Rue des Petits-Champs. On the right, at the corner of the Rue Vivienne, is the *Hôtel Tubeuf*, now part of the Bibliothèque Nationale. From the Rue Vivienne, one can admire the Galerie Mansart and other additions to the library. The main entrance, with Robert de Cotte's forecourt, is on the Rue de Richelieu.

Farther along the Rue des Petits-Champs, at No. 45, is the house of Jean-Baptiste Lully, built by Daniel Gittard in 1671. In the cross streets—the Rue Chabanais, Rue Ste-Anne, Rue des Moulins, and so on—much of the late-seventeenth- and eighteenth-century architecture has been preserved.

Cross the Avenue de l'Opéra (or detour to the *Opéra* itself) into the Rue Danielle-Casanova as far as the Rue de la Paix, then take a left into Jules Hardouin-Mansart's *Place Vendôme*. In its center is the *Colonne Vendôme*, or Colonne d'Austerlitz. Patterned after Trajan's Column in Rome, its reliefs glorify the exploits of the French army between 1805 and 1807. The Place Vendôme, the connecting Rue de la Paix, Rue de Castiglione, and western end of the Rue St-Honoré (and its extension, the Rue du Faubourg-St-Honoré) comprise one of the main areas for luxury shops, jewelers, perfumers, boutiques, and purveyors of high fashion.

The Rue de Castiglione leads to the Rue St-Honoré. Turn right, passing the church of *Notre-Dame-de-l'Assomption* and the accounting office before reaching the Rue Royale. Turn right here for the *Madeleine*. On the Place de la Madeleine are some of the most famous fine-food emporiums in Paris, including Fauchon and Hédiard.

Take the Rue Royale to the *Place de la Concorde*, from which you can look all the way up the Avenue des Champs-Elysées to the *Arc de Triomphe* and the skyscrapers of *La Défense*.

Return to the Louvre through the *Jardin des Tuileries*. On the right is the Orangerie, with Claude Monet's *Nymphéas*; on the left, the Jeu de Paume, which contains the Louvre's Impressionist collection. Since the time of André Malraux, a number of the chief works by Aristide Maillol have been placed between the end pavilions of the Louvre. Near the Pavillon de Marsan, on the north, the Rue de Rivoli widens into the nearly square Place des Pyramides, framing Emmanuel Frémiet's gilt equestrian statue of Joan of Arc. The Rue des Pyramides leads to the church of *St. Roch*. Return on the Rue St-Honoré to the Louvre.

Alternative: From the Place de la Concorde, pass the horses from Marly into the *Champs-Elysées*. At their eastern end, these are parklike, a continuation of the Jardin des Tuileries, with only scattered nineteenth-century buildings, the restaurant Ledoyen, and the Espace-Cardin. Paralleling the Champs-Elysées to the north is the Avenue Gabriel, bordered by the gardens of the American and British embassies. Farther along, where the Avenue de Marigny runs into the Avenue Gabriel, is the *Palais de l'Elysée*, whose entrance is in the Rue du Faubourg-St-Honoré. The palace was built by Armand-Claude Mollet in 1718 for the Comte d'Evreux, but it was repeatedly renovated for its various inhabitants, who included Mme. de Pompadour, her brother the Marquis de Marigny, the Duchesse de Bourbon, and Murat. Since 1873, it has been the residence of the president of the French Republic. At the intersection of the Avenue des Champs-Elysées and the Avenue de Marigny, you can appreciate the grand perspective as far as the Hôtel des Invalides, past the Grand Palais and Petit Palais and across the Pont Alexandre III.

Another portion of the Champs-Elysées begins at the Rond-Point des Champs-Elysées. This section is characterized by tall nineteenth- and twentieth-century buildings, luxury shops, restaurants, cinemas, automobile showrooms, banks, insurance agencies, and travel bureaus. Its broad sidewalks and *contre-allées*, its rows of trees and streetlights from which flags flutter whenever there is a state visit, its grandiose perspec-tives down to the Louvre and up to the Arc de Triomphe, and its endless stream of humanity make the Avenue des Champs-Elysées one of the most famous streets in the world. It has been the scene of national mourning and national triumph, the victory parades of 1919 and 1944, and the annual celebration on July 14. It is 232 feet wide and almost 2 miles long, gently rising to the heights of Chaillot and Jean-François Chalgrin's brilliant triumphal arch. Altogether, it forms one of the most compelling urban ensembles in Europe.

MUSEUMS IN PARIS

Paris has as many museums and as large and as comprehensive collections as any city in the world. You should not be intimidated by this array, nor should you feel obliged to see as much as possible; nothing, for example, is more exhausting (or pointless) than trying to see the entire Louvre in one visit. However, an aimless stroll through the Louvre can be extremely pleasant indeed. It is best to visit museums that represent your own areas of interest rather than to force yourself to include the tourist "musts."

This section lists, in alphabetical order, the most important museums of Paris and the Ile de France and describes their specialties. Given our space limitations, it is impossible to be completely comprehensive or to provide detailed inventories of specific collections.

Note: Because the Louvre is so vast, it has not been included in the alphabetical sequence; rather, its collections appear at the end of the listing of Paris museums.

Musée de l'Affiche

18 Rue de Paradis, X^c
Métro: Gare de l'Est, Château d'Eau
Open daily, except Tuesday and July 14, NOON.–6:00 P.M.

Charming poster museum in a former salesroom of the Choisy pottery firm from the turn of the century.

Musée de l'Armée

Esplanade des Invalides, VII^c
Métro: Invalides, Latour-Maubourg
Open daily, 10:00 A.M.–5:00 P.M. in winter, 10:00 A.M.–6:00 P.M. in summer; Napoleon's tomb visible until 7:00 P.M. in July and August. Closed January 1, May 1, November 1, December 25.

This museum incorporates collections from the Arsenal (started in 1685), from noble families—such as those of the dukes of Zweibrücken, d'Aumale, and de Bouillon—that were confiscated during the Revolution, and Napoleon III's great collection from Pierrefonds. Weapons, suits of armor, maps, and plans; military-history mementos from the Middle Ages to the present.

Musée d'Art Moderne de la Ville de Paris

11 Avenue du Président-Wilson, XVIe
Métro: Iéna, Alma-Marceau
Open daily, except Monday and civic and church holidays, 10:00 A.M.–5:30 P.M., Wednesday, 10:00 A.M.– 8:30 P.M.

Located in the eastern part of the Palais de Tokyo, from the 1937 world's fair, this museum houses, in addition to its permanent collection, various spaces used for changing exhibitions of contemporary art and the ARC (Animation, Recherche, Confrontation), a studio for experimental art.

The permanent collection includes important classics of modern art: Fauvism (Matisse, Vlaminck, Rouault); Cubism (Picasso, Braque, Gris, Villon, Gleizes, Metzinger, Léger, Picabia, Delaunay); Surrealism (Arp, Lam, Masson); the School of Paris (Soutine, Modigliani, Chagall, Wols); and postwar art.

Musée National des Arts Africains et Océaniens

293 Avenue Daumesnil, XIIe
Métro: Porte Dorée
Open daily, except Tuesday, 9:45 A.M.– NOON. and 1:30 P.M.–5:15 P.M.

The buildings were constructed for the Colonial Exposition of 1931. The museum displays fine art from Africa and Oceania; folk art is not given primary emphasis (ethnographic displays are in the Musée de l' Homme). In addition to the permanent collections, the museum includes an aquarium and a terrarium.

Musée des Arts Décoratifs

107–109 Rue de Rivoli, Ier
Métro: Palais-Royal, Tuileries
Open daily, except Tuesday, 2:00 P.M.–5:00 P.M.,Wednesday, 2:00 P.M.–10:00 P.M., Saturday and Sunday, 11:00 A.M.–6:00 P.M.; library open daily, except Sunday, 10:00 A.M.–5:30 P.M., Monday, 2:00 P.M.–5:30 P.M.

Note: As a result of extensive ongoing modernization work, portions of the collection are temporarily inaccessible.

This important museum of applied art, including a library and a documentation center, belongs to a private society, the Union Centrale des Arts Décoratifs. It is rather poorly housed in the north wing of the Louvre, along the Rue de Rivoli between the Pavillon de Marsan and the Finance Ministry. In the mezzanine rooms to the right of the entrance there are frequent exhibitions dealing with modern cultural history. The collection comprises over 50,000 items of handicraft, sculpture, and painting from the Middle Ages to Art Nouveau (including the School of Nancy and Hector Guimard) and Art Déco. A book and gift shop, which offers reproductions of items in the collection, was opened recently.

Musée National des Arts et Traditions Populaires

6 Route du Mahatma-Gandhi (Bois de Boulogne), XVIe
Métro: Les Sablons
Open daily, except Tuesday, 10:00 A.M.– 5:15 P.M.

A center for the study and presentation of French folklore arranged according to the most modern principles. In the Galerie Culturelle (opened in 1975), folklore objects are organized by their context—

historical, local, religious, for example. In the Galerie d'Etudes, the items are grouped according to type. There is an extensive Iconothèque, including over 45,000 posters, popular prints, playing cards, and so on. Pictorial archive, music-history collection, and library.

Maison de Balzac

47 Rue Raynouard, XVIᶜ
Métro: Passy, Muette
Open daily, except Monday and July 14, 10:00 A.M.–5:40 P.M.

Honoré de Balzac's only surviving residence in Paris. It was here that he produced his late works from 1840 to 1847. Rich documentation relating to the life and work of the author; in the library, a unique collection of first editions, the majority of them from the Imperial Library at Zarskoje Selo.

Musée Carnavalet

23 Rue de Sévigné, IIIᶜ
Métro: St-Paul, Chemin-Vert
Open daily, except Monday and civic and church holidays, 10:00 A.M.–5:40 P.M. (several rooms closed, 12:30 P.M.–2:00 P.M.)

This museum of the history of Paris is located in one of the most important *hôtels* of the Marais. In spite of nineteenth-century additions, it is still much too small for its extensive collections. An annex is planned in the adjacent Hôtel Le Peletier de St-Fargeau.

As an introduction to the history of old Paris, it is indispensable, though it presupposes considerable factual knowledge. A series of rooms displays decorations from demolished Parisian *hôtels*: Room 23, the Cabinet de L'Hôtel de Colbert; Rooms 24 and 25, the Grand Cabinet et Grand Chambre de l'Hôtel de La Rivière. The staircase from the Hôtel de Luynes, the Café Militaire (Room 6), and Claude-Nicolas Ledoux's Salon de Compagnie from the Hôtel d'Uzès (Room 6) provide, together with the Bouvier collection, a splendid picture of the domestic life of the Parisian upper class in the seventeenth and eighteenth centuries. In Rooms 65 through 75, there are exhibits depicting the history of the Revolution and the Empire.

Centre National d'Art et de Culture Georges-Pompidou

Rue St-Martin, IVᶜ
Métro: Hôtel de Ville, Rambuteau; *RER*: Châtelet–Les Halles
Open daily, except Tuesday, Noon–10:00 P.M., Saturday and Sunday, 10:00 A.M.–10:00 P.M.

The Beaubourg does not function so much as a museum as an "animation center," and it actually does present something of the restless vitality of a department store, not necessarily to the taste of every art lover. It incorporates the Centre de Création Industrielle (C.C.I.), which presents—in addition to its permanent displays on the history of modern design—changing exhibitions on design, architecture, and modern lifestyles; a library, the Bibliothèque Publique d'Information (B.P.I.); the Institut de Recherches et de Coordination Acoustique/Musique (I.R.C.A./M.), a studio for contemporary music; a Cinémathèque; a print collection; and a number of audio-visual information centers. Changing exhibitions of contemporary art and experimental presentations take place in the raised southern portion of the ground floor.

The entire fourth floor and a part of the third are reserved for the presentation of the collections of the Musée National d'Art

Moderne, which span the art of the twentieth century from the Fauves to Joseph Beuys. Among its highlights are:

Fauvism (Derain, Vlaminck, Marquet, Matisse, Picasso, Braque)

Expressionism (the German movements Die Brücke and Der blaue Reiter)

Cubism (one of the most important collections of Cubist paintings by Braque, Picasso, Gris, Léger)

Russian Constructivism (Malevich, Goncharova, Larionov)

Orphism (Robert and Sonia Delaunay, Kupka, Picabia)

Kandinsky (complete survey of his work)

Chagall, Soutine, Utrillo

Surrealism (Arp, Miró, Magritte, Ernst, Calder, Gonzales, Dalí)

Constructivism (Vantongerlo, Hélion, Moholy-Nagy, Mondrian, Van Doesburg, Pevsner, Gabo)

School of Paris (De Staël, Hartung, Poliakoff, Soulages)

American painting from Abstract Expressionism to Pop Art (Francis, Pollock, Rothko, Reinhardt, Johns, Warhol, Oldenburg, Dine)

Kinetic Art and Op Art (Vasarely, Morellet, Soto)

Nouveau Réalisme (Klein, Arman, Raysse)

The major retrospectives from the Musée National d'Art Moderne are shown on the fifth level.

At the north edge of the forecourt, the studio of Constantin Brancusi has been reproduced, providing insight into the work of this important sculptor of the twentieth century.

Musée de Cluny

24 Rue du Sommezard, V^c
Métro: St-Michel, Odéon

Open daily, except Tuesday and civil and church holidays, 9:45 A.M.–12:30 P.M. and 2:00 P.M.–5:30 P.M.

This is the most important collection of medieval art in Paris. Although a fitting setting, the Late Gothic *hôtel* that houses it is anything but spacious. It was built in 1485 by Jacques d'Amboise on the site of the city residence of the abbots of Cluny and in the surviving chambers of the Roman baths. Since 1977, a major portion of its Renaissance art collection has been displayed in the château of Ecouen. The collection consists primarily of applied art, but it also includes sculpture and tapestries from the early Middle Ages through the sixteenth century. Among its treasures are the votive crowns of the West Gothic kings from the seventh century (Room 13); the stone heads of the kings of Judah from the Galerie des Rois of the façade of Notre-Dame, discovered in 1977; and the great tapestry sequence *The Lady with the Unicorn*.

Musée Eugène-Delacroix

6 Place de Fürstenberg, VIe
Métro: St-Germain-des-Prés
Open daily, except Tuesday, 9:45 A.M.– 5:15 P.M.

The studio and home, in the former stables of the palace of the abbot of St. Germain-des-Prés, of the man whom Baudelaire called the last of the Renaissance artists and the first of the moderns. Includes paintings and drawings by the artist.

Musée Guimet

6 Place d'Iéna, XVIe
Métro: Iéna
Open daily, except Tuesday and civil and church holidays, 9:45 A.M.–NOON and 1:30 P.M.–5:15 P.M.

Built around a core collection that belonged to Lyon industrialist Emile Guimet, and since 1945 the Département des Arts Asiatiques des Musées Nationaux, the Musée Guimet is one of the world's most important repositories for the art of China, Japan, India, and Indochina. It is also a research institute for the several cultures of these countries.

Highlights of the collection are:

Ground floor: art of the Khmer (the most important collection outside Cambodia), Champa (old central Vietnam), Java, Thailand, Laos, the Himalayas, Tibet

Second floor: art of China from the Yang-Chao culture to the nineteenth century, old Vietnam, India, Afghanistan, the excavations at Begrâm

Third floor: art of Japan, Korea, central Asia, Chinese pottery, Chinese porcelain

Musée Gustave-Moreau

14 Rue de La Rochefoucauld, IXe
Métro: Trinité
Open daily, except Monday, Tuesday, and holidays, 10:00 A.M.–12:45 P.M. and 2:00 P.M.–5:45 P.M.

Moreau was the chief representative of Symbolist painting in France. The house in which he lived and worked was given to the state after his death in 1898; since 1902, his work has been on display here. The collection includes over 1,000 paintings and oil sketches, more than 7,000 drawings, and 23 cartoons, including those for his major works such as the *Apparition* (1874), *Salomé* (1874), and *Jupiter et Sémélé* (1890). Moreau's work had a considerable influence on the Fauves, the Surrealists, and the School of Paris.

Musée de l'Histoire de France (Archives Nationales)

60 Rue des Francs-Bourgeois, IIIe
Métro: Rambuteau, Hôtel de Ville
Open daily, except Tuesday and civic and church holidays, 2:00 P.M.–5:00 P.M.

On the second floor of the Hôtel de Soubise, the Archives Nationales present a number of documents relating to the history of France. These span from the time of the Merovingians to the present, and the selection is changed regularly. Larger special exhibits on particular themes are also mounted from time to time in the nearby Hôtel de Rohan, which also belongs to the Archives.

The museum is well worth visiting if only for the largely intact decoration of the apartments of the Princesse de Soubise, created between 1732 and 1740 under Germain Boffrand and with the collaboration of Charles Natoire, François Boucher, Carle van Loo, Jean Restout, Pierre-Charles Trémolières, Jean-Baptiste Lemoyne the Younger, and Lambert-Sigisbert Adam. The Salle d'Assemblée, Chambre de Parade, Salon Oval, and Chambre à Coucher comprise one of the best interior ensembles in the Louis XV style.

Surviving from the old Hôtel de Clisson (Hôtel de Guise) are the Salle de Garde and the Chapelle de Guise, which was originally decorated with frescoes by Niccolò dell' Abate. The apartment of the Prince de Soubise, from 1735 to 1739, on the ground floor, was recently painstakingly restored. To see it, you must apply in advance.

Muséum National d'Histoire Naturelle

57 Rue Cuvier, V^e
Métro: Monge, Jussieu, Gare d'Austerlitz, Censier-Daubenton
Open daily, except Tuesday and civil and

church holidays, 1:00 P.M.–5:00 P.M., Sunday, 10:30 A.M.–5:00 P.M. (admission tickets are good only for the mineralogy, geology, comparative anatomy, and paleontology galleries).

This museum was founded as the Jardin Royal des Plantes Médicinales in 1626, and as the Jardin du Roi, under the direction of Buffon from 1739 to 1788, it became one of the centers of natural-history research in Europe. The Convention renamed it the Muséum National d'Histoire Naturelle in 1793, provided it with ten teaching chairs, and expanded it to include the king's zoo from Versailles. Today, the museum is still primarily a research and teaching institute, but various galleries display its priceless collections in the fields of comparative anatomy, paleontology, paleobotany, mineralogy, and geology to the public. The Trésor du Muséum, with over 1,000 gems and art objects in precious stone, in part from the royal collections, is also part of this museum, as is the Jardin des Plantes (Botanical Gardens), at whose southwest corner Buffon's house still stands. It comprises the Jardin d'Hiver, the Jardin Alpin, an aquarium, a vivarium, and the small, old-fashioned zoo that inspired Rilke to write several of his poems ("The Flamingos," "The Panther").

Also belonging to the museum are the Zoological Gardens on the western edge of the Bois de Vincennes and the Musée de l'Homme in the Palais de Chaillot.

Musée de l'Homme

Palais de Chaillot, West Wing
Place du Trocadéro, XVIe
Métro: Trocadéro
Open daily, except Tuesday and holidays, 10:00 A.M.–5:00 P.M.

A museum for folklore and a research center for prehistory, anthropology, and ethnology. In addition to the permanent collection, it regularly holds major temporary exhibitions. It includes a large library, photo library, and documentation center.

The collection includes:

Second floor: Central and South Africa and Madagascar, North Africa and the Levant, Europe (except France)

Third floor: Arctic regions, Asia, Oceania and Australia, North and South America

The Department of Ethnomusicology encompasses a musical-instrument collection, a Phonothèque, and the Service d'Edition de Disques, which has issued recordings of traditional folk music since 1977.

Musée Jacquemart-André

158 Boulevard Haussmann, VIIIe
Métro: St-Philippe-du-Roule
Open daily, except Monday and Tuesday, 1:30 P.M.–5:30 P.M.

One of the most priceless nineteenth-century Parisian art collections, housed in a Second Empire *hôtel* that was begun in 1860 by Henri Parent for Edouard André. André's wife, the painter Nélie Jacquemart, bequeathed the collection, the house, and her fortune to the Institut de France in 1912.

Highlights of the collection include:

Italian Renaissance, with works by Mantegna, Uccello, Carpaccio, Donatello, Botticelli

Seventeenth-century Dutch painting, including Rembrandt, Hals, Ruysdael

Eighteenth-century European art, with priceless furniture and tapestries; paintings by Chardin, Roslîn, Quentin de la Tour, Fragonard, Boucher, Tiepolo, Guardi; sculptures by Slodtz, Lemoyne, Coysevox, Houdon, Clodion, Bernini

Musée du Jeu de Paume

Place de la Concorde, Ier
Métro: Concorde
Open daily, except Tuesday, 9:45 A.M.–
5:15 P.M.

French cultural policy was late and timid in its recognition of Impressionism. Nevertheless, Paris possesses, thanks to the donation of private collections, the most complete survey of this movement, which was France's most important contribution to nineteenth-century art and heralded the beginning of the modern era.

The Jeu de Paume was built by Napoleon III as a tennis court for his son. It is, as a counterpart to the Orangerie, at the end of the Jardin des Tuileries. Since 1947, it has housed part of the Impressionism collection of the Louvre. Here, and in the Musée Marmottan, the visitor to Paris not only can become familiar with a number of late-nineteenth-century masterpieces but also can form an impression of an Ile de France that no longer exists; many of these works were created there—in Pontoise, Argenteuil, Auvers, and along the Seine. Most of the galleries of this museum are dedicated to the founders of Impressionism, and one can follow its development from its beginnings at Honfleur, where Monet and Sisley carried out their first *plein-air* studies, together with Boudin and Jongkind, through the formation of a fraternity of painters in Paris that included Manet, Pissarro, Bazille, and Cézanne. Here are Manet's *Déjeuner sur l'Herbe*, the scandal of the 1863 Salon and something like the group's manifesto; the works that Pissarro and Cézanne created in Pontoise, beginning in 1871; and those of Monet, Renoir, Sisley, and Degas from Argenteuil. One can see the dissolution of the group after 1880 and the work of its successors: the Pointillists Seurat and Signac;

Toulouse-Lautrec, whose painting is a continuation of Degas's; Rousseau, "Le Douanier," and the two loners Gauguin and Van Gogh, the precursors of Fauvism. Virtually no important aspect of the movement is unrepresented.

One ought to follow a visit to the Jeu de Paume with a detour to the Orangerie on the opposite side of the terrace of the Jardin des Tuileries. There, in two long rooms on the ground floor, is the sequence of *Nymphéas* painted by Monet in Giverny between 1890 and 1921 (open daily, except Tuesday, 10:00 A.M.–5:00 P.M., Saturday, 10:00 A.M.–8:00 P.M.).

Musée de la Marine

Palais de Chaillot, West Wing
Place du Trocadéro, XVIe
Métro: Trocadéro
Open daily, except Tuesday and holidays, 10:00 A.M.–6:00 P.M.

This naval museum owes its extraordinary collection of ship models to Colbert's insistence that the achievements of the major shipyards of France be captured in *maquettes*—a tradition that has continued into the twentieth century. Also on display are naval mementos, busts of famous men associated with navigation, the series of paintings of major French harbors commissioned from Claude-Joseph Vernet by Mme. de Pompadour's brother, the Marquis de Marigny, in 1752, and the models of the arsenal of naval weapons up to the atomic submarine *Le Redoutable.*

Musée Marmottan

2 Rue Louis-Boilly, XVIe
Métro: Muette
Open daily, except Monday, 10:00 A.M.–6:00 P.M.

This is the most important Impressionist collection in Paris after the Jeu de Paume's. It has been on display since 1971 in the underground exhibition rooms of a nineteenth-century *hôtel* at the edge of the Jardin du Ranelagh. Here, the industrialists Jules and Paul Marmottan assembled very valuable collections of art of the Netherlands from the fifteenth and sixteenth centuries and of the French Empire. In 1932, the estate was bequeathed to the Institut de France. The Impressionist collection comprises bequests from Donop de Monchy in 1950 and from Michel Monet, the youngest son of the painter. It includes the painting that gave the movement its name: *Impression, Soleil levant*, and studies, some of them virtually abstract, for Monet's series of paintings of water lilies. Also on display are works by Monet's friends Renoir, Sisley, Pissarro, Boudin, and Signac from the painter's personal collection. When Michel Monet made this bequest, he also gave the Institut the house at Giverny, near Vernon, where his father lived from 1883 to 1926. This property has been restored, and the famous garden that Monet designed has been replanted. It has been open to the public since 1980.

Musée de la Monnaie

11 Quai de Conti, V^e
Métro: Pont-Neuf
Open daily, except Saturday, Sunday, and holidays, 11:00 A.M.–5:00 P.M.

A visit to the collections of the Mint—including medallions, coins, dies, tools, and documents on minting history—simultaneously affords one a view of the most important rooms of Jacques-Denis Antoine's Hôtel de la Monnaie, one of the masterpieces of the Louis XVI style in Paris.

Musée des Monuments Français

Palais de Chaillot, East Wing
Place du Trocadéro, VIIIe
Métro: Trocadéro
Open daily, except Tuesday, 9:45 A.M.–12:30 P.M. and 2:00 P.M.–5:00 P.M.

Originally the Musée de Sculpture Comparée, opened in 1882, this collection owes its existence to Eugène Viollet-le-Duc. He envisioned it as an "imaginary museum" of French monumental sculpture that would present the most important examples of sculpture from the Merovingians to the nineteenth century in full-size casts. By collecting these in a single location, such a museum could provide art-history students with a chance to make comparative studies of them. It is also of incalculable value because it contains numerous originals in unrestored condition. Since 1945, its collection has been augmented by copies of the most important medieval French frescoes.

Musée Nissim de Camondo

63 Rue de Monceau, VIIIe
Métro: Villiers
Open daily, except Monday, Tuesday, and holidays, 10:00 A.M.–12:00 M. and 2:00 P.M.–5:00 P.M.

An extremely fine collection of applied art—furniture, tapestries, glass, porcelain—as well as paintings and sculptures from the eighteenth century. It is displayed in a *hôtel* in the Second Empire style at the edge of the Parc Monceau, bequeathed to the Union Centrale des Arts Décoratifs by Moïse de Camondo, whose family was murdered at Auschwitz.

Musée du Palais de Tokyo

13 Avenue du Président-Wilson, XVIe

Métro: Alma-Marceau, Iéna
Open daily, except Tuesday and July 14,
9:45 A.M.–5:15 P.M.

This neoclassical exhibition palace from
1937 has served as the home of the Musée
National d'Art Moderne since 1947. Even
after the Centre Beaubourg was opened in
1977, portions of the collection have remained here, especially artists' bequests—
for example, those of Brauner, Braque, Lau-
rens, Chagall, Rouault, Delaunay, Dunoyer
de Segonzac, and Uhde.

In addition, the right wing of the Palais
de Tokyo—the left wing is occupied by the
Musée d'Art Moderne de la Ville de Paris—
houses the Musée d'Art et Essai, where the
Louvre mounts temporary exhibitions from
its storerooms, and the Musée d'Art Post-
impressionnisme, where paintings created
primarily between 1886 (the last Impressionist exhibition) and 1905 (the first show
by the Fauves) are displayed. The represented schools are Pointillism, with works
by Seurat, Signac, Van Gogh, and Pissarro;
the School of Pont-Aven, represented by
Gauguin, Bernard, Sérusier, and Van Ryssel-
berghe; the Nabis, with pictures by Denis,
Sérusier, Bernard, Vuillard, Bonnard, Vallotton, and Maillot; the Symbolists, represented
by Lévy-Dhurmer, Redon, and Mazek; and
the Naturalists, including Meunier, Edelfelt,
Salmson, and Liebermann.

*Petit Palais (Musée des Beaux-Arts de la
Ville de Paris)*

Avenue Winston-Churchill, VIIIᵉ
Métro: Champs-Elysées–Clémenceau
Open daily, except Monday, 10:00 A.M.–
5:30 P.M.

In addition to its changing exhibits, the Petit
Palais presents works of art that were bequeathed to the city from private sources.

Its highlights are: Greek, Roman, and Egyptian antiquities; medieval art; Renaissance
art; seventeenth-century Dutch painting;
seventeenth- and eighteenth-century French
painting and applied art; nineteenth-century
French painting from Géricault and Delacroix to the Belle Epoque and the Symbolists. It also boasts a large collection of
Carpeaux's patterns.

Musée Rodin

77 Rue de Varenne, VIIᵉ
Métro: Varenne
Open daily, except Tuesday, 10:00 A.M.–
5:00 P.M.

Auguste Rodin lived in Jean Aubert's Hôtel
Biron, at the edge of the Faubourg St-
Germain, from 1908 until his death in 1917.
His works and his collections were left to
the state, which here set up the Musée
Rodin. This museum presents a nearly complete survey of the work of this important
sculptor. Included in its collection are his
most significant projects, the major works
in bronze (*The Burghers of Calais, The
Gates of Hell, The Thinker, Balzac*), the
works in marble (*The Hand of God, The
Kiss, Cathédrale*), and the preparatory
studies for them.

A great number of the artist's patterns,
sketches, and works in clay are exhibited
in a branch of the museum at Rodin's former
atelier in Meudon. The sculptor's personal
collection includes, in addition to pieces
from antiquity, several major paintings by
Van Gogh, Monet, and Renoir.

A visit to the museum also provides a rare
opportunity to admire a private *hôtel* from
the early eighteenth century. The disposition of rooms is typical, and portions of the
wall décor are original.

Musée de Sculpture en Plein Air

Quai St-Bernard, V^e
Métro: Sully-Morland, Gare d'Austerlitz

The first open-air museum for modern sculpture in Paris, still under construction and also being developed as a park. It includes works by Schoeffer, César, Di Teana, Étienne-Martin, Stahly, and others, as well as temporary exhibitions by young sculptors.

Musée National des Techniques

292 Rue St-Martin, IIIe
Métro: Réaumur-Sébastopol, Strasbourg—St-Denis, Arts-et-Métiers
Open daily, except Monday and holidays, 1:00—5:15 P.M., Sunday, 10:00 A.M.—5:15 P.M.

This is the oldest technological museum in the world. It is housed picturesquely but inadequately in the former priory of St. Martin-des-Champs. There are airplanes in the church nave, and bicycles and steam engines in the choir. It is awaiting its reincarnation in the roomy slaughteryards of La Villette, where—together with the Palais de la Découverte and the Musée des Travaux Publics, it will comprise the huge Musée des Sciences et Techniques.

Until this occurs, the most important items in the collection are shown in temporary exhibits, including a priceless collection of clocks and automata. Only a tiny percentage of its holdings may be seen in its present buildings, which it shares with the Conservatoire National des Arts et Métiers.

Of considerable art-historical interest is the reading room of the museum's library, which was the refectory of the former monastery.

Musée Victor-Hugo

6 Place des Vosges, IVe
Métro: Chemin-Vert, Bastille, St-Paul

Open daily, except Monday, 10:00 A.M.—5:40 P.M.

Victor Hugo lived in the Hôtel de Lavardin (Hôtel de Rohan-Guéménée) from 1832 to 1848. Here, he wrote a number of his major novels and received his famous contemporaries Honoré de Balzac, Prosper Mérimée, Alfred de Vigny, Alexandre Dumas, Alphonse de Lamartine, and others.

Acquired by the city of Paris and set up as a museum in 1902, the house preserves, in addition to Hugo's apartments on the third floor and an invaluable collection of mementos, roughly 300 of the novelist's drawings (exhibited on the second floor), which show him as a Romantic precursor of the Symbolists. An educational display on the fourth floor provides an introduction to the artist's life and works.

Musée Zadkine

100-*bis* Rue d'Assas, VIe
Métro: Vavin, Notre-Dame-des-Champs, Port-Royal
Open daily, except Monday and holidays.

The residence and studio of the Russian-French sculptor Ossip Zadkine, who worked here from 1928 until his death in 1967. It provides a virtually complete survey of his cubistically oriented work.

Musée du Louvre

Palais du Louvre, Ier
Métro: Palais-Royal, Louvre
Open daily, except Tuesday and holidays, 9:45 A.M.—6:30 P.M. in the main galleries, otherwise, 9:45 A.M.—5:00 P.M.

Even before the National Assembly legislated that a museum be established in the Louvre in May 1791, the old royal residence contained a hoard of art. François I had already laid the foundations of the royal art collection, and Henri IV specified that the ground floor of the Grande Galerie was to serve as housing and studio space for artists working for the Crown; it was Napoleon, more than 200 years later, who finally banished the artists from the Louvre. The Académie Royale de Peinture et de Sculpture was headquartered here, and between 1737 and 1848, the official art exhibitions, the Salons, were held in the Salon Carré.

Renovation of the palace for use as a museum began under Napoleon. The project was resumed in 1932, the Pavillon de Flore was acquired in 1961, and the Grande Galerie was modernized in the 1970s; the job is still not complete. Only the wings of the Cour Carrée and the south wing along the Seine were given to the museum; the north wing, along the Rue de Rivoli, is provisionally occupied by the Ministry of Finance and the Musée des Arts Décoratifs.

The following portions of the national collection are housed in the Louvre:

Greek and Roman antiquities
Oriental antiquities
Egyptian antiquities
European painting
European sculpture
Applied arts
Prints

The prehistory and ancient history collections are located in the château of St. Germain-en-Laye; the Asiatic art collection in the Musée Guimet; folk art in the Musée des Arts et Traditions Populaires; modern art in the Jeu de Paume and the Orangerie (Impressionists), the Palais de Tokyo (Post-Impressionists and various bequests), and the Centre National d'Art et de Culture Georges-Pompidou.

The main entrance at the Porte Denon leads into the Salle de Manège, where the ticket counters, museum shops, information desk, foreign-exchange office, and rest rooms are located. A small cafeteria is located next to the Escalier Mollien on the second floor of the Aile Mollien, which branches off from the Grande Galerie.

With its more than 400,000 objects, the Louvre is one of the richest museums in the world. It is by no means easy to find one's way in such a confusing abundance. Instead of even a summary overview of its holdings, we have therefore attempted to provide a kind of orientation guide to the major departments.

GREEK AND ROMAN ANTIQUITIES

From the main entrance, one passes through the Galerie des Sarcophages to the Escalier Daru, the main staircase of the museum. Standing on its middle landing is the *Winged Victory of Samothrace*, virtually a symbol for the entire collection. On the ground floor to the right of the staircase lies the Cour du Sphinx, with its mosaic of the seasons and, on its east side, the old façade of the Petite Galerie by Louis Le Vau. Around it are grouped a fresco room, a mosaic room, the Augustus room, and a room of Roman reliefs. The collection continues into the southwest corner of the old palace, on both the ground floor and the floor above, between the Pavillon de l'Horloge and the Passage des Arts. On the ground floor, to the left, is the Salle des Cariatides, the oldest room in the palace, built by Pierre Lescot; it contains Jean Goujon's gallery supported by caryatids. Beneath it is the doorway to the Escalier Henri II (an entrance to the Department of Oriental Antiquities). The room preserves Greek sculpture from the fourth century B.C.—the works of Lysippus, Praxiteles, and Scopas in antique copies, many of them of excellent quality. Included from the royal collection at Versailles is *Diana as Huntress*, which dominates the room, as well as Hellenistic sculptures from the third to first centuries B.C.

The double suite of rooms in the south wing of the Cour Carrée, to which one returns from the Salle des Cariatides, lies between the Passage des Arts and the corner pavilion. These ten galleries trace the development of Greek sculpture from the seventh century B.C. (*Lady of Auxerre* in the last room of the right-hand suite) up to Hellenism. Highlights are the *Hera of Samos* (sixth century B.C.), the *Horseman* from the Rampin Collection (mid-sixth century B.C.), copies of works by Phidias and Polyclitus, fragments from the Parthenon (a portion of the Parthenon frieze and a metope), fragments from the Temple of Zeus at Olympia, the so-called *Barberini Supplicant*, the *Aphrodite of Cnidos*, the *Venus de Milo*, and the *Borghese Gladiator*.

Returning up the Escalier Daru past the *Winged Victory*, one reaches the second floor. The Rotonde d'Apollon leads to the rooms of the southwest part of the old Louvre. These include the Salle des Bijoux (*Treasure of Boscoreale*), the Salle Etrusque (*Cerveteri Sarcophagus*), and the Salle des Bronzes (*Apollo of Piombino*, *Athlete of Benevento*, *Ephebe of Agde*) in Lescot's wing, and a further suite in the south wing reached by way of the Salle des Sept Cheminées (Italian painting of the seventeenth century). In this suite of nine galleries, which run along the outside of the wing and are known collectively as the Galerie Campana, is one of the world's foremost collections of Greek vases, statuettes, and applied art.

EGYPTIAN ANTIQUITIES

The Department of Egyptian Antiquities occupies the southeast portion of the ground floor of the old Louvre between the Passage des Arts and the Guichets de St-Germain-l'Auxerrois, and, on the second floor, the inner suite of rooms in the south wing. From outside, one enters at the south wing of the Cour Carrée, the Guichets des Arts. From inside, it is bes reached by the connecting stair in the room behind the *Venus de Milo*. Entrance from the Department of Oriental Antiquities in the Passage St-Germain is not recommended, for one then runs counter to the chronological arrangement of the collection.

The Department of Egyptian Antiquities has been in existence since 1826. Its first curator was Jean-François Champollion, the man who succeeded in deciphering hieroglyphs.

The collection begins in the crypt beneath the Passage des Arts with a large sphinx of pink granite from the Middle Kingdom and the so-called *Mastaba*, a tomb chapel from the Old Kingdom with exquisite reliefs on its inside walls. Next come relics and columns, sarcophagi, and sculptures from the Old Kingdom, including the statue of the *Seated Scribe*.

The rooms surrounding the staircase in the corner pavilion contain the art of the Middle Kingdom (wooden statue of the chancellor Nakhti, the *Offering Bearer*, a colossal statue of Sethi II), while in the large hall of the east wing, the Galerie Henri IV, there are sarcophagi and statues from the New Kingdom—among them, the real highlights of the collection (the god Amon as protector of Tutankhamen, the sarcophagus of Ramses II, the goddess Hathor handing the magic collar to Sethi I, the goddess Sekhmet).

The *Osiris Crypt* beneath the Passage St-Germain ends this portion of the collection. It is followed by the rooms of Coptic art through which one passes, still on the ground floor, to return to the point where the tour began.

Taking the staircase to the second floor, past the statue of the bull Apis from the Serapeum at Memphis and the bust of Amenhopis IV, one comes upon the suite known as the Musée Charles V. Here, again in chronological order, are displays of Egyptian handicrafts and tomb finds, including some very important jewelry.

ORIENTAL ANTIQUITIES

Opened as an Assyrian museum in 1847, the Department of Oriental Antiquities admirably presents the ancient culture of the Near East. It occupies the ground floor of the entire north half of the old Louvre around the Cour Carrée. One enters it behind the Salle des Cariatides, in the Crypte de Sully beneath the Pavillon de l'Horloge. The collection is in twenty-four galleries grouped according to regions and epochs: Sumer and Akkad (the Tello find), Mari and Larsa, Babylon (*Code of Hammurabi*), Susa and Iran (bull capital from the palace of Darius), Persia, Parthia, Phoenicia, Syria, Cyprus, and Assyria (reliefs of winged bulls and the giant Gilgamesh).

OBJETS D'ART

Comprising objects from the royal Garde-Meubles, the treasuries of various churches tied to the Crown (the Sainte-Chapelle, the abbey of St. Denis), as well as what survived of the crown jewels after wars and the Revolution, the Department of Objets d'Art contains the third major applied-art collection in Paris, following those of the Musée Cluny and the Musée des Arts Décoratifs.

It is displayed in the Galerie d'Apollon and on the second story of the east, north,
and west wings of the old Louvre up to the Pavillon de l'Horloge. One enters the Galerie d'Apollon from the Rotonde d'Apollon, at the top of the Escalier Daru. Splendid wrought-iron gates from the château of Maisons-Laffitte, from around 1650, guard the entrance to the gallery.

This gallery, an elongated hall 31 feet wide, 36 feet high, and 200 feet long, occupies the entire upper floor of Henri IV's Petite Galerie. Rebuilt by Charles Le Brun after the fire in 1661 and lavishly decorated, it now contains what remains of the crown jewels and other valuables (a Carolingian statuette of a horseman, St. Louis's reliquary crown, crystal and diamonds of the crown, the treasure of the "Ordre de St-Esprit" from about 1580, two Byzantine panels from the twelfth century from the Sainte-Chapelle, the eagle vase of Abbot Suger, and coronation insignia).

To enter the forty-one galleries of the collection, one first passes through the upper floor of the Department of Egyptian Antiquities. In the first three rooms of the east wing, behind the colonnades, are portions of the wall paneling and ceilings of the royal chambers from the time of Henri II and Henri IV, reassembled by Louis Le Vau in 1654 for Louis XIV. The actual collection begins chronologically in the fourth room with applied art from the High Middle Ages. It includes a rich array of ivory (*Harbaville Triptych*, a coronation of the Virgin, and a Madonna from the Sainte-Chapelle), reliquaries, Limousin enamels, tapestries (*The Hunts of Maximilian*), bronzes and goldsmithing, ceramics and faïences (by Palissy and from Italy and Spain), and furnishings from the Renaissance to the Empire (Boulle, Cressent, Riesener, Napoleon's throne from St. Cloud, the cradle of the king of Rome).

Since 1931, the sculpture collection has been housed in the ground floor of the Grande Galerie, between the Porte de la Trémoille and the Pavillon de Flore. Expansion into the pavilion itself was made possible in 1969. The outside entrance at the Porte de la Trémoille, where the chronological arrangement of the display begins, is often closed. Other entrances are from the Pavillon de Flore and from the main entrance at the Porte Denon, then through the Galerie Médicis.

The collection permits a virtually complete survey of the development of French sculpture from the Romanesque period to the nineteenth century. It also encompasses important German Gothic as well as Italian Renaissance and Baroque works.

Romanesque: Capitals from Moutiers-St-Jean; *Madonna and Child* (Auvergne, second half of the twelfth century)

Gothic: *Vierge de La Celle* (Ile de France, fourteenth century); statues of Childebert (from the portal of the refectory at St. Germain-des-Prés), Charles V, and Jeanne de Bourbon (fourteenth century); jamb figures of King Solomon and the Queen of Sheba from the cathedral at Corbeil (end of the twelfth century); head of St. Peter from the Lazarus tomb in Autun; rood screen from the cathedral of Bourges (mid-thirteenth century); tomb of Philippe Pot, from Cîteaux (fifteenth century); the *Virgin of Isenheim* (c. 1480); a *Madonna of the Annunciation* by Riemenschneider; Italian sculpture of the thirteenth century—Ravenna, through Pisano, da Settignano, della Robbia, delle Quercia, to da Fiesole

Renaissance: Colombe, Pilon, Goujon's *Diana of Anet,* Cellini's *La Nymphe de Fontainebleau*

Mannerism and Baroque: de Vries, Bernini, Anguier, Puget (statues for the garden at Versailles), Lemoyne, Coysevox (statues for Marly), Coustou, Falconet, Bouchardon, Adam, Pigalle, Houdon

The Pavillon de Flore contains, in addition to Michelangelo's *Slaves* in the basement, galleries devoted to the Empire and to sculpture of the nineteenth century (Canova, Rude, Barye, Carpeaux, Rodin).

After having been long neglected, the eighteenth- and nineteenth-century galleries were modernized and reorganized during the 1970s. They now house some of the Louvre's most well-planned displays.

PAINTING

In the public consciousness, the Louvre is often identified exclusively with its Department of Painting, which, with more than 10,000 paintings, is among the largest in the world. Its most important holdings go back to the royal collections founded by François I when he acquired works by Raphael, Titian, and Leonardo. These were augmented by Henri IV. But it was primarily Louis XIV who set about a systematic expansion by buying whole collections, such as those of Cardinal Mazarin, from which major portions of the drawing collection also come.

The collection was first opened to the public from 1750 to 1759 at the Palais du Luxembourg under Louis XV. Declared the Museé.de la République during the Revolution, and hugely expanded by the addition of works confiscated from the nobility, the Louvre collection reached its high point under Napoleon, thanks to his plundering of Europe.

Although most of these pieces had to be returned after the collapse of the Empire, the Louvre still owes significant holdings (especially of the early Italians) to Napoleon's conquests. Through bequests and a systematic acquisition policy, the Louvre filled noticeable gaps in the collection in the nineteenth and twentieth centuries.

Ever since the time of Henri IV, the collection has centered around the Grande Galerie. A reorganization of pictures according to country and in chronological order has been under way since 1968. This work has not yet been completed, which makes it more difficult to find one's way through the collection.

Basically, the holdings may be divided as follows:

French Schools
This is the only section that can be viewed in a single, logical circuit. It begins near the landing of the Escalier Daru, where the *Winged Victory* is located, with the Salle Duchâtel (two rooms, in which Botticelli's frescoes from the Villa Lemmi are mounted, intervene). The sequence begins with paintings from the fourteenth century. It continues through the Salon Carré, the eastern part of the Grande Galerie, with paintings of the fifteenth through eighteenth centuries. It then turns to the right into the Aile Mollien, returning to the Escalier Daru by way of the rooms that run parallel to the Grande Galerie. On the third floor of the south and west wings of the Cour Carrée, there are paintings from the eighteenth and nineteenth centuries for which there was no room in the main sequence.

Highlights include:

Old French painting, including the portrait of Jean II le Bon from about 1360 (the oldest known portrait north of the Alps)

The altar-cloth of Narbonne, ink on silk, donated by Charles V to the cathedral at Narbonne

Beaumetz, *Calvaire aux Chartreux* (end of the fourteenth century)

Malouel (?), *Pietà* (c. 1400)

Bellechose, *Communion and Martyrdom of St. Dionysius* (c. 1400)

The Retable de Thouzon from Villeneuve-les-Avignon

Quarton (?), *Pietà* from Avignon (end of the fifteenth century)

Fouquet, portraits of Charles VII

Juvénal des Ursins (mid-fifteenth century)

School of Fontainebleau [in the Salon Carré]

Clouet, portrait of François I

Poussin, *Echo et Narcisse, L'Enlèvement des Sabines, Bergers d'Arcadie, Self-Portrait*

La Tour, *St. Joseph Charpentier, Adoration of the Shepherds, Maria Magdalena*

Le Nain, *La Charette, Repas de Paysans*

Baugin, *Still Life*

Le Lorrain, *Port de Mer au Soleil Couchant*

Champaigne, *Portrait d'Homme, Ex-voto*

Le Brun, *Le Chancelier Séguier*

Rigaud, *Double Portrait of the Artist's Mother*

Watteau, *Pèlerinage à l'Ile de Cythère, Gilles, Portrait d'un Gentilhomme*

Fragonard, *Portrait de Diderot*

Robert, *Le Pont du Gard*

David, *Le Serment des Horaces, Le Sacre de Napoléon à Notre-Dame, Madame Récamier*

Prud'hon, *Portrait de Joséphine à la Malmaison*

Ingres, *La Grande Odalisque, La Grande Baigneuse*

Géricault, *Radeau de la Méduse*

Delacroix, *La Liberté Guidant le Peuple*

Courbet, *L'Enterrement à Ornans, L'Atelier*

Italian Schools
The section begins in the second half of the

Grande Galerie with paintings of the thirteenth to fifteenth centuries. It continues in the Salle des États with the sixteenth century and resumes at the end of the Grande Galerie, after the Galerie Médicis. Seventeenth- and eighteenth-century works are shown in the Aile de Flore. Particularly large works from the seventeenth century hang in the Salle des Sept Cheminées in the southwest corner of the Cour Carrée.

Highlights in the Grande Galerie include:

Cimabue, *Madonna with Angels*
Giotto, *St. Francis of Assisi*
Martini, *The Bearing of the Cross*
Monaco, *Crucifixion, Scenes from the Lives of St. John and St. James*
Veneziano, *Madonna and Child*
Pisanello, *Princess from the House of Este*
Fra Angelico, *Coronation of the Virgin*
della Francesca, *Portrait of Sigismund Malatesta*
Uccello, *Battle of San Romano*
Botticelli, *Virgin with the Infant Jesus and John, Allegories* [in the Salles Percier et Fontaine]
Mantegna, *St. Sebastian, Crucifixion, Madonna della Vittoria*
Messini, *Il Condottiere*
Bellini, *The Suffering of Christ*
Carpaccio, *Sermon of St. Stephen*

Highlights in the Salle des États include:

Titian, *Man with the Glove, Rustic Concert, Venus of Pardo, The Crowning with Thorns, Portrait of a Man*
Veronese, *Wedding at Cana*
Tintoretto, *Self-Portrait, Paradise*
Raphael, *Virgin with Jesus and John (La Belle Jardinière), St. George and St. Michael, Portrait of B. Castiglione*
da Vinci, *The Annunciation, The Madonna of the Rocks, Mona Lisa, Bacchus (St. John), Virgin and Infant Jesus with St. Anne*

Highlights in the Salle des Sept Cheminées include:

Caravaggio, *Death of the Virgin*
Reni, *Deianira and the Centaur Nessus, David*

Highlights in the Aile de Flore include:

Caravaggio, *Portrait of Alof de Vignacourt, The Fortune-Teller*
Reni, *Ecce Homo, St. Sebastian*
Magnasco, *St. Jerome*
Guardi, *The Doge on the Bucentaurus,* series of views of Venetian festivals
Tiepolo, *Last Supper*

Dutch, German, and Flemish Schools
The works of the early Dutch masters hang in the cabinets on the Seine side of the Galerie Médicis; the sixteenth- and seventeenth-century works are on view on the courtyard side. The long hall in front of the Galerie Médicis displays Flemish art of the seventeenth century. The corridor connecting the Grande Galerie with the Escalier Daru houses Dutch painting from the seventeenth century.

Highlights in the cabinets (closed, 12:00 M.–2:00 P.M.):

Painting of the Netherlands
van Eyck, *Madonna with Chancellor Rolin*
van der Weyden, *Annunciation, Jean Braque Triptych*
Memling, *Portrait of a Woman, Resurrection and Ascension*
Massys, *The Money-Changer and His Wife*
Moro, *Cardinal Granvells's Dwarf*

German Painting
Dürer, *Self-Portrait*
Holbein, *Erasmus, Anne of Cleves, Nicolas Kratzer*
Cranach, *Elector Johann Friedrich of Saxony, Venus*

Flemish Painting

Rubens, *The Life of Marie de Medici,* nineteen large canvases from the Palais du Luxembourg; also, outside the Galerie Médicis, *The Three Fates, The Triumph of Truth, Adoration of the Shepherds, Helene Fourment, The Raising of the Cross*

Breughel, *The Battle of Arbela*

Jordaens, *The Four Evangelists, The King Drinks!*

van Dyck, *Portrait of Charles I of England*

Highlights in the cabinets and in the Salle des Sept Mètres include:

Dutch Painting

Hals, *The Gypsy, Portrait of René Descartes*

Rembrandt, *The Angel Raphael Leaving Tobias, The Pilgrims of Emmaus, Bathsheba, Self-Portrait with Easel, St. Matthew, The Slaughtered Bull, Castle in a Storm*

Vermeer, *The Lace-Maker*

de Hooch, *The Card Players, Interior of a Dutch House*

Terborch, *The Concert*

Spanish Schools

Highlights in the Pavillon de Flore (second floor) include:

El Greco, *Christ on the Cross, King with Page*

Velázquez, *Portrait of Queen Maria Anna of Austria*

Murillo, *The Young Beggar*

Goya, *Lady with a Fan, Portrait of the Marquise de Santa Cruz, Self-Portrait, Portrait of the Marquise de Solona* (in the Beistegui Collection)

MUSEUMS IN THE ILE DE FRANCE

Beauvais

Musée Départemental des Beaux-Arts

Ancien Palais Episcopal
Open daily, except Tuesday, 10:00 A.M.–12:00 M. and 2:00 P.M.–6:00 P.M.

Excellently reorganized in recent years, the Beauvais museum displays the art and cultural history of the region since the Middle Ages, important examples of French painting (including Caron and Couture), and important works from about 1900: frescoes by Denis; ceramics by Delaherche, who worked in Beauvais; furniture by Serrurier-Bovy; vases by Gallé; and so on. It also has a collection of paintings of the moderns since Cubism.

Chantilly

Musée Condé

Château de Chantilly
Open daily, except Tuesday, 9:30 A.M.–12:30 P.M., 2:00–5:00 P.M.; the park is open at the same times.

The extensive art collection that was bequeathed to the Institut de France on the death of the Duc d'Aumale in 1897—one of the most priceless private collections assembled in the nineteenth century—is still displayed essentially in the manner in which it was arranged by the former owner. For the modern viewer, it is a dizzying hodge-podge of paintings, sculpture, applied art, and curiosities from diverse epochs and schools.

The collection is world famous for its holdings from the fifteenth and sixteenth centuries: the *Très Riches Heures du Duc de Berry*, painted by the Limbourg brothers between 1400 and 1415 (facsimiles on display); the forty leaves from the book of hours of Estienne Chevalier, executed in about 1455 by Fouquet; Raphael's *Madonna of the House of Orléans* and *Three Graces*; Leonardo's sketch for *La Gioconda (Mona Lisa)*; Cosimo's portrait of Simonetta Vespucci; the most important series of drawings and paintings from sixteenth-century French portraiture by Jean and François Clouet, Lyon, and their schools; and the Galerie de Peinture, with works by Poussin, Reni, Nattier, Lancret, Gérard, Gros, and Delacroix.

In the Petit Château, the old furnishings created for the Duc de Bourbon in the eighteenth century have been largely preserved, with paneling of the very highest quality, the Salon des Singes, attributed to Christophe Huet, and the library. Included in the manuscript collection in the latter is the psalter of Queen Ingeborg, the breviary of Jeanne d'Evreux, and the *Très Riches Heures du Duc de Berry*. The chapel preserves valuable works of the French Renaissance from the château of Ecouen: the altar by Goujon and Bullant; stained-glass panels from 1544; and inlaid paneling from 1548. In the back is the mausoleum of Henri II, Prince de Condé and father of the Grand Condé, by Jacques Sarrazin in the seventeenth century.

The Grandes Ecuries, near the château, are now open to the public as a museum of the horse. It is open daily except Monday, 10:30 A.M.–6:30 P.M. Demonstrations with horses are given at 11:45, 3:15, and 5:15.

Malmaison

Musée National du Château de Malmaison

Avenue du Château-de-Malmaison
RER: La Défense, then *bus* 158A
Open daily, except Tuesday, 10:00 A.M.–12:00 M. and 1:30 P.M.–4:30 P.M.

In 1799, Joséphine de Beauharnais bought a simple, early-seventeenth-century country house here and commissioned the architects Charles Percier and Pierre Fontaine to expand and furnish it. During the Consulate, between 1800 and 1803, it was Napoleon Bonaparte's real home. Bourienne, his secretary, claimed, "Next to the battlefield it was the only place where he was truly himself." After he became emperor, Napoleon favored the old royal residences: the Tuileries, St. Cloud, and Fontainebleau. When the couple separated in 1809, Joséphine moved back to Malmaison, where she died in 1814. Nearly a year later, Napoleon took leave of his family here before departing for St. Helena.

After a checkered history, Malmaison was given to the state by the banker Daniel Osiris in 1904. Although most of the original furnishings were dispersed during the nineteenth century, the museum that was established here sought, through restoration and reconstruction, to reproduce the half-private, half-official atmosphere of the house. In addition, by incorporating furnishings from the other imperial residences—silver and porcelain owned by Napoleon, sculptures, and paintings—it has become one of the most brilliant ensembles from the Empire in France.

The official rooms on the ground floor include:

The Vestibule d'Honneur, in a sober Ionic style

The Salle de Billard, with furniture by Jacob-Desmalter

The Salon Doré, with paintings by Gérard and Girodet, furnishings from St. Cloud, and an elegant piano

The Salon de Musique, with pictures from Joséphine's collection (most of which was bought by Czar Alexander)

The Salle à Manger, with the Henry Auguste vermeil service given by the city of Paris to Napoleon on his coronation

The Salle du Conseil, restored according to Percier's plans

The library, in its original state, with furnishings from the Tuileries

On the second floor are Napoleon and Joséphine's private chambers. The Appartements du Premier Consul are:

Salon, with a portrait of the Bonaparte family

Salon de l'Empereur, with Napoleon's furniture from the Tuileries

Exhibition rooms containing David's famous painting *Bonaparte on the Pass of the Grand St. Bernhard* (1801); the Table d'Austerlitz, with portraits of Napoleon and his marshals; the Sèvres service belonging to the emperor; the robes and vermeil pitcher and bowl from the coronation ceremony

The Appartements de Joséphine are:

Grande Chambre de l'Impératrice, in the form of an oval tent

Chambre à Coucher Ordinaire, with furniture from St. Cloud

Cabinet de Toilette, with dressing table by Félix Remond

Boudoir

On the north side of the *cour d'honneur* is the Pavillon des Voitures, containing coaches and carriages that belonged to the emperor, including the one taken from him by Gebhard Blücher at Waterloo.

The large park laid out by Joséphine has been largely broken up, but thanks to a gift from the American Edward Tuck it was possible to reclaim the Domaine Bois-Préau, whose château was restored in 1855. Here, additional mementos of Napoleon and his family from the period of the Empire are displayed (some five minutes away; same hours as Malmaison).

Port-Royal-des-Champs

Musée National des Granges de Port-Royal

Open daily, except Monday, Tuesday, and holidays, 10:00 A.M.–11:30 A.M. and 2:00 P.M.–5:00 P.M.

This museum documents the history of Jansenism in France, for it was the cloister of Port-Royal-des-Champs that was the movement's center. The nunnery of Notre-Dame-de-Porrois (the name Port-Royal was the result of a scribe's error) was founded in 1204 and was subject to the Cistercian order. But it was completely secularized in the fifteenth century. In 1602, the eleven-year-old Jacqueline Arnauld, the daughter of an advocate in the Parisian Parlement, was appointed abbess. Six years later, after a serious illness, she determined to reform the life of the cloister in accordance with the rules of St. Bernard. She reintroduced seclusion, continual prayer, meditation, and physical labor. The strict religiosity of the reformed cloister attracted attention in Paris and won a large number of converts.

By 1625, the cloister had become too small, and it appears that the marshy surroundings were too unhealthy for the young ladies. Thus, they moved to the Faubourg St-Jacques in Paris.

The new abbey of Port-Royal attracted a significant portion of the Parisian intelligentsia, especially from the nobility and the bourgeoisie. In 1636, the abbot of St-Cyran, a student of the Dutch theologian Jansenius, became rector of the cloister. (Jansenius opposed the Jesuit thesis that a person can achieve salvation by his or her own will and good works. Instead, he emphasized that salvation depended on the grace of God, thereby approaching the Protestant view.) Blended with the moral rigor of Port-Royal, which was in part a reaction against the luxury of the court, Jansenism rapidly divided Parisian society in two. The Jesuits, supported by the king, succeeded in having the movement declared heretical by the theologians of the Sorbonne.

Nevertheless, the Jansenist dispute continued to rage until the close of the reign of Louis XIV. In 1709, the last remaining nuns at Port-Royal-des-Champs were driven away by musketeers, and the cloister, which was threatening to become a place of pilgrimage for the movement, was razed.

The *granges* that were constructed by the teaching brothers in 1652 for their school have survived and now house the museum. Also preserved is the seventeenth-century farm with its house of the Solitaires, used when a portion of the women's community moved back to their original cloister.

In the nearby church at Magny-les-Hameaux, there are a number of grave slabs from Port-Royal as well as its altar, a baptismal font, and a holy-water font.

St. Denis

Musée d'Art et d'Histoire de la Ville de Saint-Denis
22-*bis* Rue Gabriel-Péri

Métro: St-Denis, Porte de Paris
Open daily, except Tuesday, 10:00 A.M.– 5:30 P.M., Sunday, 2:00 P.M.–6:30 P.M.

A rich documentation of the historical role of St. Denis, housed in the former Carmelite cloister. The cloister's chapel was donated by Mme. Louise, a daughter of Louis XV who entered the order in 1770. It was designed by Richard Mique, the last of the king's architects. The municipal museum of St. Denis owns an extensive collection on the history of the Commune rebellion of 1871.

St. Germain-en-Laye

Musée des Antiquités Nationales

Château de Saint-Germain-en-Laye
RER: St-Germain-en-Laye
Open daily, except Tuesday and holidays, 9:45 A.M.–12:00 M. and 1:30 P.M.–5:15 P.M.

When he ordered restoration of this palace in 1862, Napoleon III also commanded that a Gallo-Roman museum be established here. It was dedicated in 1867. The museum's collections cover the history of the territory of modern France from the Paleolithic to the Merovingian era.

The thorough restoration of the palace under Napoleon III compromised the appearance of the building's architecture considerably. Greater care was taken with the Sainte-Chapelle, built roughly ten years earlier than the Sainte-Chapelle in Paris, between 1230 and 1238. Attributed to the architect Pierre de Montreuil, it is one of the most important examples from the beginning of the Rayonnant style in the Ile de France. Some scholars have held that the heads that ornament the keystones are the earliest portraits of St. Louis and his family.

Musée Départemental du Prieuré

Rue Maurice-Denis
RER: St-Germain-en-Laye
Open daily, except Monday, Tuesday, and
holidays, 10:30 A.M.–5:30 P.M.

This was the home and studio of painter
Maurice Denis from 1914 to 1943. It contains an important collection of Symbolist
painting, with a number of the chief works
by Denis as well as paintings by Bonnard,
Vuillard, Mucha, Vallotton, and others.

Sceaux

Musée de l'Ile de France

Château de Sceaux
RER: Parc de Sceaux
Open daily, except Tuesday. Monday and
Friday, 2:00 P.M.–5:00 P.M. Wednesday, Thurs-
day, Saturday, and Sunday, 10:00 A.M.–12:00
M. and 2:00 P.M.–5:30 P.M. .

This important museum is housed in the
château built in 1856 by the Duc de Trevise
on the site of Colbert's structure. The collection is organized primarily according to
the geography and administration of the
region, concentrating largely on the history
of the various princely seats. It contains excellent materials illustrating the no longer
existing châteaux of Sceaux, St. Cloud,
Meudon, Neuilly, Marly, Choisy, Méreville,
Pierrefonds, and Chantilly. It also includes
priceless stoneware and porcelain produced
in the Ile de France and more than 1 million drawings, engravings, photographs, and
so on, on the region.

Sèvres

Musée National de Céramique

Place de la Manufacture-Nationale
Métro: Pont de Sèvres
Open daily, except Tuesday, 9:30 A.M.–
12:00 M. and 1:30 P.M.–5:15 P.M.

In 1738, the state porcelain factory at Vincennes was established—the first factory
in France. In 1756, it was moved to Sèvres,
and from 1759, it belonged exclusively to
the king. Since 1824, a museum has been
attached to it. This museum documents the
history of the factory itself but also holds
ceramics, faïence, and porcelain from all
countries and periods—one of the most important collections of its type in the world.
Regular thematic exhibitions supplement
the permanent displays. (It is possible to
tour the factory with a guide on the first
and third Thursdays of each month from
4:00 P.M. to 5:00 P.M.)

SOME TIPS FOR TRAVELING IN THE ILE DE FRANCE

It is difficult to recommend an ideal time of
year to visit this region. The large parks at
Versailles, Fontainebleau, Sceaux, Marly,
and so on, are most beautiful in the autumn.
But even in the summer, when all the Parisians are on holiday, one is relatively alone
in the Ile de France except in the major
tourist attractions.

If possible, you ought to avoid Versailles, Chartres, and Chantilly on weekends, unless you wish to attend the *jours des grandes eaux* at Versailles or buy your children an ice cream with *crème Chantilly* in a festival atmosphere.

The Ile de France is fortunate that the average Parisian would never dream of going for a stroll in the Forêt de St-Germain. At most he might drive his family to the Forêt de Fontainebleau for a picnic —for which reason it would be better to save this for a weekday.

But all of these spots can be magically beautiful from Monday to Friday.

Aside from the centers of international tourism such as Versailles, Fontainebleau, and Chartres, the Ile de France is relatively undeveloped. Every small town has adequate hotels and restaurants, but one ought to be prepared to discover, for example, that the published hours for the various museums may be treated somewhat loosely.

Because Paris lies in the very center of the Ile de France, there is no other convenient point of departure for the entire region; those who do not wish to work their way out of Paris each morning to discover the region are out of luck to some degree. However, on a longer visit, one may choose several bases—one for the north, such as Pierrefonds or Senlis; another for the southeast, possibly Provins, Fontainebleau, or Moret-sur-Loing; and yet another for the southwest, such as Maintenon, Chartres, or Montfort-l'Amaury. If one selects a base along the Seine to the west as well, in La Roche-Guyon or Vétheuil, side trips into Normandy would be possible.

HIKES AND BICYCLE TOURS

The Ile de France is admirably suited for hiking and cycling. In the southern part of the region, a number of bicycle routes are clearly marked—from Dourdan to Dreux, for example.

Seven of the major national hiking trails are located in the Ile de France or run through it:

GR (Grande Randonnée) 1—Sentier de l'Ile de France: 363 miles around Paris. Start: Pont de St-Cloud

GR2—Sentier de la Seine: Yvelines, Val d'Oise, Eure, Melun, Pont-sur-Yonne, Sens

GR22—Paris–Pont St-Michel: from Orgerus to Anet and Dreux

GR13—Ile de France–Burgundy: from Fontainebleau to Château-Laudon through the Loing Valley

GR11—Grande Sentier de l'Ile de France. Start: the park at Sceaux

GR111—Sentier du sud de l'Essonne: cuts through the Ile de France

GR12—Paris–Brussels: through the forests of Chantilly, Halatte, and Compiègne

Hiking maps are available in most bookshops, or from *Topo-guides*, published by the Comité National des Sentiers de Grande Randonnée, 92 Rue de Clignancourt, Paris, XVIIIe, telephone 255-86-73. The Michelin maps No. 97 (*Paris Region*) and Nos. 55, 56, 60, and 61 are recommended for hikers and drivers alike.

AUTOMOBILE ROUTES IN THE ILE DE FRANCE

Driving into the Ile de France from Paris, it is recommended to cross the *banlieue* as rapidly as possible, preferably via one of the expressways. Otherwise, one can lose a great deal of time in this urbanized area. The larger towns in the Ile de France may all be reached by public transportation as well. During the peak season, from spring until late fall, one must of course expect sizable traffic jams on the highways on weekends.

The Paris transport agency RATP organizes bus excursions to the most important points of interest in the Ile de France during the season. Information may be had at the Bureau des Excursions, Marché aux Fleurs, Place de la Madeleine, VIIIe, or at the Bureau Central de Renseignement, 53 bis Quai des Grands-Augustins, VIe.

The SNCF offers round-trip bus tours to Versailles; the forests of Fontainebleau, Compiègne, and Chantilly; Chartres; and the Chevreuse Valley, leaving either from Paris or from the local train stations. Information and reservations:

Office de Tourisme de Paris, 16 Boulevard des Capucines, IXe
Office de Tourisme de Paris, Avenue des Champs-Elysées, VIIIe

The following section suggests various tours for those with their own cars. Equal attention is given to areas of scenic charm and points of historical interest. In each case, the starting point may be either Paris or the town named first in the tour. Once outside the *banlieue*, it is advisable not to take the major national highways, for they tend to run straight across the flat, high plateaus, through endless and somewhat monotonous fields of grain and vegetables. Instead, it is more interesting to take the smaller *département* roads through the forests or along the charming valleys.

Through the Forests of the Valois

From *Compiègne* via the D332 to the Romanesque church of *Morienval*, then the D32 via Elincourt to *Vez*, from whose castle the country was ruled in the Middle Ages. Past the ruins of the abbey of *Lieu-Restauré* and on to *Villers-Cotterêts*, via the D80 and D17 to *Longpont*, through the Forêt de Retz to the Rond de la Reine, and the D973 to the castle of *Pierrefonds*. From there, take the D85 to *St. Jean-aux-Bois,* where there is a thirteenth-century church, then the D14 through the Forêt de Compiègne back to Paris.

From the Noyonnais to the Laonnais

From *Noyon*, head toward Compiègne. At the edge of town, turn right toward Pont l'Évêque-Sempigny, where the D165 will take you to *Ourscamps*. Return to Sempigny and take the D145 through the Forêt de Carlepont. Turn left when you reach the D130, then take the D934 to *Blérancourt*. Continue to *Coucy-le-Château*, with its romantic castle ruins, then the D13 to Septvaux in the Forêt de St-Gobain. Follow the D14 to *Prémontré*. There, turn left onto the

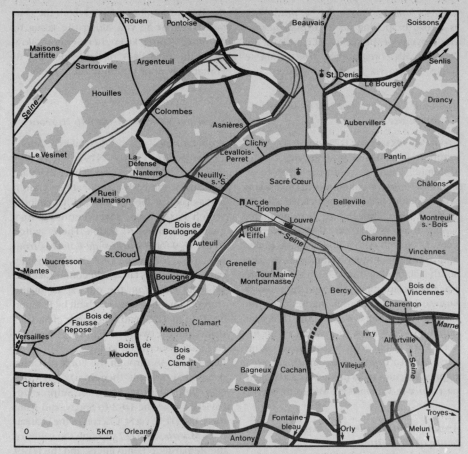

The Boulevard Périphérique around Paris and the most important exit roads and freeways in the Paris region.

D552 as far as Cessières, and then take the D7 to Laon.

Castles and Palaces in the Brie Français

From *Meaux*, take either the D405 and D938 or follow the valley of the Ourq to *La Ferté-Milon*; continue along the Ourq to Oulchy-le-Château, then take the D1 to Grand-Rozoy. Follow the D2 to *Fère-en-Tardenois*, where there is an old market hall and where one can detour via the D967 to the ruined *Fère Castle*, which boasts remains of a gallery by Jean Bullant. The D967 then takes you to *Château-Thierry*, after which the D969 and D402 follow the Marne to La Ferté, above which stands the abbey and crypt of *Jouarre*. Follow the N3 until there is a road branching off to *Montceaux*, to the remains of the palace of Catherine de Médicis with a broad view across the Marne Valley. Return via Trilport to Meaux.

Medieval Churches and Towns in the Brie Champenoise

From *Provins* take the D71 to *Voulton*, then return via the D403 past Provins to Ste. Colombe. There, get onto the D106 to *St. Loup-de-Naud* and continue on it (unless you wish to detour to *Lizines*, which has a lovely Early Gothic church) to *Donnemarie*, where there is a remarkable thirteenth-century church with a Romanesque tower and a twelfth-century tympanum on the south side. Follow the D75 to the ruins of the Cistercian abbey of *Preuilly*, today a farmyard. Return to Donnemarie, taking the D76 past Meigneux to *Rampillon*. Then take either the N19 back to Provins or go toward Paris as far as Mormant, there taking the D215 to *Champeaux*, *Blandy*, with impressive ruins of its medieval castle, then past *Vaux-le-Vicomte* via Melun to Paris.

Around Fontainebleau: Towns and Châteaux of the Gâtinais

Starting from *Fontainebleau*, take the N7 as far as the Gorges d'Apremont, then to *Barbizon*. Now take the D64 to the intersection with the D11, turning right on it to *Fleury-en-Bière*. Take the D410 to *Courances* and continue to *Milly-la-Forêt* with its open market hall from 1479, remains of a feudal castle, and Chapelle St-Blaise-des-Simples with frescoes by Jean Cocteau, who is buried here (the bust of the artist is by Arno Breker). Follow the D16 to *Larchant*, which has the picturesque ruins of the church of St. Mathurin, then continue on

the D16 to *Nemours*, from which the D40 and D104 bring you along the Loing to *Moret-sur-Loing*. From there, either follow along the right bank of the Seine back to Fontainebleau or continue on to Melun.

From the Northern Beauce to Hurepoix

From *Étampes* (possibly first taking a detour to *Farcheville* via the N191 and D837), take the D17 past *Morigny*, where there are remains of the Early Gothic abbey church and a classical abbot's palace, Chamarande, which has a large seventeenth-century château complex, to Torfou. There, switch to the D99 for *St. Sulpice-de-Favières*, from which you follow the D82 along the valley of the Renarde as far as Villeconin. Take the D148 to *Dourdan*, the old capital of the Hurepoix whose castle was built by Philippe Auguste in 1222 and its church of St. Germain from the twelfth and thirteenth centuries and modernized in the fifteenth. Now take the D838 through the Forêt de Dourdan past St. Arnoult, then the D27 to *Rambouillet*. *Variant*: From St. Sulpice-de-Favières, take the D82 to Souzy, and from there the D132 via St. Chéron to the château of *Le Marais*, the D27 through the valley of the Rémarde to Longvilliers, and the D149 and D61 to the N306 at the château of La Celleles-Bordes. There, you can either proceed to Rambouillet or turn into the valley of the Chevreuse to see the château of *Dampierre* and the museum of the abbey at *Port-Royal-des-Champs*. From there, you can reach Paris directly by the N10 or follow a large curve past Les Vaux-de-Cernay via the D24 and the N191 to the château of Les Mesnuls, thence through *Montfort-l'Amaury* via the N12 to *Pontchartrain* and on to Paris. From Rambouillet to Montfort-l'Amaury, the D936 is best.

Through the Valley of the Seine to the Châteaux of the Vexin Français

From *St. Germain-en-Laye*, take the N190 to Poissy, then the D22 and D922 to Meulan and the D913 to Vétheuil. Proceed along the Seine to *La Roche-Guyon*.

Variant: Take the N13 from St. Germain-en-Laye and then the freeway straight to *Mantes*, the N13 past the château of *Rosny* to Bonnières, and the D100 to La Roche-Guyon.

Now take the D37 and D142 to *Villarceaux*. The château can be seen from the D171. The D86 will now take you through Omerville to the Renaissance château of *Ambleville*, with its richly decorated façade facing the restored gardens. Take the D135 through St. Gervais to *Alincourt*, a picturesque castle complex from the fifteenth century. Now the N14 via Magny-en-Vexin until the turnoff to *Guiry*, with its classical château from the seventeenth century, then through the valley of the Aubette to *Vigny*, the family seat of the writer Alfred de Vigny. Its château was built in the manner of the Loire châteaux for Cardinal Georges d'Amboise, Louis XII's minister, but romantically enlarged in the nineteenth century. Follow the N14 past *Cergy-Pontoise*, there taking the N184 and N308 to *Maisons-Laffitte* and back along the Seine to St. Germain-en-Laye.

The Heartland of the Ile de France: Senlis and Pays de France

Take the N16 from Paris via *St. Denis* to *Écouen*. Passing the château of *Champlâtreux*, continue to *Luzarches*. Now take the D922 to Viarmes. There, get onto the D909 to the former Cistercian abbey of *Royaumont*. Via the D118 and N16 to *Chantilly* (*detour*: via the D44 to *St. Leu-d'Esserent*). Take the D924 to *Senlis* (*detour*: the D932 and D26 through the Forêt d'Halatte to the château of *Raray*).

From Senlis, take the D330 to the Abbaye de la Victoire and the abbey of *Chaalis* and go on to *Ermenonville*, whose park preserves the memory of Rousseau. Via the D922 to St. Witz, then take the freeway to Paris.

CALENDAR OF FESTIVALS AND MAJOR EVENTS IN PARIS AND THE ILE DE FRANCE

January	Horse racing, Vincennes
March	Festival International du Son, Paris
Late March	Wine and Cheeses Fair, Coulommiers
Palm Sunday	Horse racing, Auteuil
April–May	Printemps Musical (Musical Spring), Paris
May	National Music Festival, Provins

May–June	Versailles Festival (drama, concerts, opera)
May–July	Ile de France Festival, Part I (concerts in parks and châteaux)
May–September	Spectacular fountain displays in the gardens at Versailles, 4:00 P.M., first, third, and fourth Sundays of each month
Late May	Jazz Festival, Fontainebleau
Early June	International Air Show, Le Bourget Airport (odd-numbered years)
June	White Wine Festival, Nogent-sur-Marne
June	Lightermen's Pilgrimage, Conflans-Ste-Honorine
Beginning last Sunday in June	La Grande Semaine—a week of horse racing at Auteuil, Longchamp, St. Cloud, and other courses in the area
Late June–July	Tour de France (bicycle race)
June–July	Festival du Marais, Paris (plays, concerts)
June–September	Son et lumière, every Saturday, Moret-sur-Loing
June, August, September	After-dark historical pageant, Saturdays and Sundays, Meaux
July 14	Bastille Day (processions, dancing, fireworks)
July–September	Summer Festival, Paris
Summer	Chamber Music Festival, the Orangerie, Sceaux
September–December	Ile de France Festival, Part II (concerts in museums and churches)
Early October	Motor Show, Parc des Exhibitions, Paris (even-numbered years)
October	International Film Festival
October–November	International Dance Festival
October–November	Autumn Festival
Late October–early November	Jazz Festival

Consult *Pariscope, L'Officiel des Spectacles*, or a tourist office for particulars.

NOTES

NOTES

NOTES

NOTES

Indexes

Index of People

Paris

Entries and numbers in boldface indicate the main points of interest and main discussions of the place cited. References to illustrations are noted in parentheses: color plates by page number; black-and-white plates by plate number.

The Ile de France

Entries and numbers in boldface indicate the main points of interest and main discussions of the place cited. References to illustrations are noted in parentheses: color plates by page number; black-and-white plates by plate number.

The Publisher has made every effort
to verify that the information in this book
is accurate and up to date.
Readers are invited
to write with more recent information.

The text was set in ITC Garamond by U.S. Lithograph Inc.
New York.
The book was printed and bound by Novograph, S.A.
Madrid.